ROMAN RELIGION AND THE CULT OF DIANA AT ARICIA

The sanctuary dedicated to Diana at Aricia flourished from the Bronze Age to the second century C.E. From its archaic beginnings in the wooded crater beside the lake known as the "mirror of Diana," it grew into a grand Hellenistic-style complex that attracted crowds of pilgrims and the sick. Diana was also believed to confer power on leaders. This book examines the history of Diana's cult and healing sanctuary, which remained a significant and wealthy religious center for more than a thousand years. It sheds new light on Diana herself, on the use of rational as well as ritual healing in the sanctuary, on the subtle distinctions between Latin religious sensibility and the more austere Roman practice, and on the interpenetration of cult and politics in Latin and Roman history.

C. M. C. Green is professor of classics at the University of Iowa. A scholar of Roman religion, she has contributed to the *American Journal of Philology, Arion, Classical Antiquity, Classical Philology, Latomus,* and *Phoenix.*

ROMAN RELIGION
AND THE CULT OF DIANA
AT ARICIA

C. M. C. GREEN
University of Iowa

CAMBRIDGE
UNIVERSITY PRESS

CAMBRIDGE UNIVERSITY PRESS
Cambridge, New York, Melbourne, Madrid, Cape Town, Singapore, São Paulo

Cambridge University Press
32 Avenue of the Americas, New York, NY 10013-2473, USA

www.cambridge.org
Information on this title: www.cambridge.org/9780521851589

First published 2007

Printed in the United States of America

A catalog record for this publication is available from the British Library.

Library of Congress Cataloging in Publication Data
Green, C. M. C. (Carin M.C.), 1948–
Roman religion and the cult of Diana at Aricia / C.M.C. Green.
p. cm.
Includes bibliographical references and index.
ISBN-13: 978-0-521-85158-9 (hardback)
ISBN-10: 0-521-85158-0 (hardback)
1. Diana (Roman deity) 2. Rome—Religion. I. Title.
BL820.D5G74 2007
292.2′114–dc22 2006001218

ISBN-13 978-0-521-85158-9 (hardback)
ISBN-10 0-521-85158-0 (hardback)

For Peter

Glad to have sat under
thunder and rain with you . . .

Louis MacNeice, "Sunlight on the Garden"

CONTENTS

vii

LIST OF MAPS AND FIGURES

PREFACE

This book had its beginnings in the stacks of the library of the American Academy at Rome in 1992, where late on a warm summer afternoon I was working on Lucan and came across an old school text of book 1. There, in one of those spare but informative footnotes so characteristic of the genre, was an explanation of 1.446 with reference to Diana the huntress and the *rex nemorensis*. I had long ago read the abridged version of Frazer's *Golden Bough*, as well as parts of the full text, and I was, at that very moment, not more than a dozen or so miles from the sanctuary. At the time I was mulling over the idea that Lucan, in imitation of the Greek tragedians, was using ritual to shape his narrative. Here, it seemed to me, I had unearthed a small but important test case. I began the pursuit of a glimmer of an idea, arising from the initial supposition that the ritual of the hunting goddess' priest lay behind the image of Lucan's enraged Caesar pursuing the aging and failing Pompey from Brundisium to Pharsalus: Caesar the young hunter on the heels of his weakening prey, the vigorous challenger closing in on the ailing priest-king.

In the next year, as I began my first effort to analyze Lucan's use of the ghastly priest, the "slayer/who shall himself be slain," I ran into one of those academic walls that had stopped better and more experienced scholars. If I had not had a leave shortly after that, it probably would have stopped me as well. According to the best authorities on Roman religion and culture, I learned, Diana was not a hunting goddess; the Romans did not hunt; there was no hunting ritual until it was brought in from Greece. Diana represented a rather tenuous native Roman tradition that could be glimpsed vanishing under the wholesale

importation of Greek religion around the third century B.C.E. The
effect of this importation was to render a nymphlike women's deity
into a huntress, who was thus given a face, graced with a myth, and
provided with a complex religious tradition under which she was then
worshipped, although none of it actually belonged to her.[1] The ghastly
priest, always acknowledged as belonging undeniably to Diana, was left
as one of those cultural oddities that persuade scholars that the Romans
were wise to adopt Greek ideas as soon as possible.

This made no sense to me, in either cultural or religious terms,
and, perhaps foolishly, I was determined to work out how it was that
a culture that did not hunt (and, according to the same authorities,
despised hunting) would change a successful local women's goddess
into a huntress. I could see the nymphlike Diana in the role of, say,
Syracuse's Arethusa, that is, as the beautiful symbol of a vital city. Why
then was a successful nymph made over into a huntress? I wondered.
Or, if she had not been successful as a watergoddess, it seemed important to ask why it was that she then became successful in a form that
had no meaning for the people who were worshipping her. What
I hoped to say about Lucan's reference to Diana's cult depended on
some understanding of what the Romans around him thought about
it. As I worked on, I discovered – again to my surprise – that very few
scholars of Roman literature had any idea that the Romans did not
hunt and were surprised to learn it. When I consulted anthropologists,
I found – after they stopped chuckling – that I had neither diminished
my discipline's reputation for fustiness nor gotten much help for my
trouble. An archaic culture that did not hunt, I was told, simply had no
parallel and no model. Yet historians of Roman culture and religion
took it as read that Diana, in her *Ur* form, was not a huntress and
thus were firmly committed to Wissowa's exposition of the cult, with
Diana as a women's goddess, in his seminal 1912 study, *Religion und
Kultus der Römer.*

Religion und Kultus remains a central text for the study of Roman
religion and will not be replaced any time soon. It is essential that I state
at the outset the enormous debt that I, like all other scholars of Roman

[1] A summary of Wissowa's discussion of Diana 1912, 247–50, and Orth's article in *RE* on
hunting (cf. Green 1996a).

religion, owe to this great polymath, whose like we will not see again. Wissowa's stature is such that Bernard of Chartres' famous apothegm comes to mind: we are dwarves standing on the shoulders of giants. It is useful, though, to remember the conclusion of the maxim: we stand on the shoulders of giants to see better and farther than they.[2] Wissowa is a giant of classical scholarship and I am looking toward the horizon from my perch on his right shoulder, trying not to fall off. The range and the depth of his knowledge of the ancient world, of ancient literature and culture, are matched only by the astonishing orderliness and clarity of his exposition. Only those things that have been discovered since he wrote will not be found in his work: everything else is there.

That is, however, a limitation of increasing importance. In the last century, and particularly during the last thirty years, archaeology has produced a radically different picture of early Rome and Latium from that available to an early-twentieth-century scholar. Because Wissowa is justly authoritative and will continue to be so, it is imperative that we should be prepared to rethink his arguments in the light of new evidence of material culture and in response to new theoretical analyses of Roman culture, history, and religion.

On the other hand, there is Frazer and the *Golden Bough*. It is now almost a reflex to disparage Frazer's work. Recently there have appeared a few brave souls prepared to argue that this disparagement has been both unfair and unscholarly (cf. Ackerman, 2–3; Dyson, 18–19). In Frazer we once more meet the extraordinary range and command of the evidence that are characteristic of the great nineteenth-century scholars, but Frazer applied his mastery of the material in a quite different way. He was distinctly original (always an unsettling quality in a classical scholar), developing the field of anthropology as he wrote and encouraging the first generation of field anthropologists in their work. But even as he was still writing the last volume of the *Golden Bough*, the unfavorable academic view of him was hardening (Ackerman, 1–2, 266–70). Frazer became "a kind of evil spirit, whose influence must be kept away by constant ritual utterances: in fact by what is sometimes

---

[2] Robert K. Merton, *On the Shoulders of Giants: A Shandean Postscript: The Post-Italianate Edition*, Chicago 1993, holds a jester's mirror to the image of academic solemnity and reveals much more than the extended genealogy of this favored quotation.

called apotropaic magic" (Griffin 1998, 44). Nevertheless, like Wissowa, Frazer had a command of ancient literature and culture that we can only envy. Here is another giant of scholarship, and I am again keeping my precarious foothold on his left shoulder. As will be clear, especially in Chapters 7–9, I am no more persuaded by Frazer's interpretations of the cult than I was by Wissowa's; yet this does not in any way vitiate Frazer's great virtues, which, it seems to me, were these: he thought the Latin writers might know more about their religion than we do, and he had an overriding sense that religion – even Roman religion – had its own internal logic, and that trying to understand that logic was a necessary part of the study of ancient religion as a cultural phenomenon.

Between them, Frazer and Wissowa brought the study of Diana to a halt, Frazer because he inspired too many doubts, Wissowa because he inspired none. Diana was severed from the principal function recognized by those who worshipped her. The pieces of her cult that were left – the *rex*, Virbius/Hippolytus, Orestes, Egeria – were rendered down into a clutch of stray religious footnotes. The idea that the Romans had no real religion, just bits of cult practice and job lots of deities borrowed from here and there, was thus validated, and the strangeness of it all was regarded as "normal" for Roman religion. The notion that the Romans did not hunt was a projection onto the Romans of mid-nineteenth-century social prejudice and the result of misdefinition. "Hunting" was taken as referring not to the general pursuit of animals with the intent of capturing them but rather to the aristocratic pursuit of specific animals on the back of a horse. Furthermore, because the Romans had expelled their kings and established a republic, they were not aristocrats, and because they pursued animals on foot, they did not "hunt" (Johannes, 49, 52, and especially 61; Green 1996a, 223–30). The prejudice of the argument was easy to establish; to demonstrate that the conclusion was false was more difficult. I was pitched, willy-nilly, into a field I then knew little about, that of Roman and Latin archaeology (Green 1996a, 228–35).

It was a harbinger of what was to come. In completing this work I have been forced to give (to borrow Ackerman's phrase, 3) more hostages to fortune than is comfortable. That the Romans hunted (as did the Latins) I finally demonstrated – at least to my own satisfaction – and the justification for doubting that Diana was a hunting goddess seemed to be removed. Despite that, it was going to prove a great deal more difficult than I ever imagined to reestablish her as the goddess the Latin writers actually described: a moon goddess, a huntress, a goddess of kings and leaders. Archaeology, art history, anthropology, ancient medicine, law, and Roman religion itself are only the most important disciplines into whose territory I, a stranger and exile from my native field of Roman literature, was compelled to travel. Can Strife, I ask myself, be far away?

As I taught myself as much as I could in each of these areas (and knowing it would never be enough), I found, to the immeasurable benefit of this work, that scholars in every one of the fields could be amazingly generous with their time and help and wonderfully encouraging of what must sometimes have seemed annoying if mild lunacy on my part. Specialists will no doubt quickly recognize where my argument is insufficient, unnuanced, unfamiliar with certain material, or unaware of new trends. It is my hope that any failings of mine will stimulate them to consider the study of Diana themselves and to respond by developing what I have only been able to begin; to fill out what I have been able only to sketch. The study of Roman religion is an intensely interdisciplinary field, and it cannot advance without the work of experts in all these areas of scholarship. I have only been able to point the way, and even that only with their welcome assistance.

Although I originally intended to write a general study of Diana as an Italic goddess and to include her cults on the Aventine and at Tifata, this work ended by being necessarily focused on Diana Nemorensis, the goddess of the grove sanctuary just outside Aricia. The other Dianas have not been neglected entirely, particularly Diana Aventinensis (Chapter 5), but the preponderance of archaeological and artifactual material comes from the sanctuary in the crater, and a substantial portion of our literary references, and certainly those that have most to tell us about cult and religion, belong to Diana Nemorensis. Linguistic evidence indicates that Diana was a very old Italic goddess, and historical evidence shows that she had a cult there certainly as far back as the sixth century B.C.E. The *rex nemorensis*, everyone agrees, indicates the cult is in fact far older than that. The archaeological evidence, although not as generous as one would have liked, certainly in no way contradicts these conclusions, and they are generally accepted. And then there is the site. This presents every characteristic of sacred space in Etrusco-Italic cultures. It soon became apparent to me that it was essential to begin with the place and the cult that could tell us the most about Diana, and that meant the sanctuary of Aricia.

Here a word must be said about terminology. The ancient Greek and Latin writers were not any more interested than Thoreau in the consistency that is the hobgoblin of little minds. The sanctuary is often called "Arician," although generally *nemus*, "the grove" (to give it its most familiar translation) was enough to identify it. There is a question among scholars as to what *nemus* originally meant, and then as to what it meant in the later centuries of the sanctuary's existence. Diana herself is Aricina or Nemorensis, but more often she is distinguished from other Dianas (when this is important) by some reference again to the *nemus*, or to one of the several figures – Virbius/Hippolytus, Egeria, Orestes, or the *rex* – that belonged to this cult and to no other. To be more rigorous or less inclusive than the ancients seemed to me to offer no advantage. My subject is Diana Nemorensis, and I have made every effort to identify the other Dianas – Aventinensis, Tifatina – clearly when they enter the discussion.

I generally use "grove" as a translation of *nemus*, not because "grove" (which, to me, means a cultivated area of trees) is more correct than, say "forest" or "wood," but because through use it has become the English word that most readily calls up the idea of a sacred, wooded place particularly associated with Diana. In relation to the sanctuary, Latin authors used *nemus* evocatively, rather than descriptively. "Grove," it seems to me, does the same in English.

Like the Romans, also, I sometimes use "Aricia" as a shorthand for the sanctuary that the Aricians controlled. I have found that I do this most often when the discussion has become distanced from the sanctuary (usually because it has become centered on Rome), and this was a way of reestablishing the location of the sanctuary on my mental map. Technically, it is incorrect – the sanctuary was outside the Arician *pomerium* – but it avoids unnecessary periphrasis. I ask my readers' indulgence. Again, when other Diana sanctuaries enter the discussion, they are clearly identified.

Then there is the question of "Roman religion." Here I show myself inconsistent even in inconsistency. The cult of Diana Nemorensis belonged to Aricia, a Latin community just over the crater's edge on the west. Originally, I thought, as most seem to, that I was studying what can, for convenience's sake, be called "Roman religion." Rome was Latin and Aricia was Latin, and eventually Aricians became Roman citizens. Insisting on a separate "Latin" terminology would be a quibble, it seemed – at the time. I have by now come emphatically to the opposite conclusion, and indeed regard the casual lumping of Latin cults together with Roman as if they were indistinguishable as one of the more significant ways we have misled ourselves in our attempts to understand what Roman religion *is*. The Latin cities were not just little Romes; Rome was not what any Latin city would have become if it could. They had and maintained their own particular identities, especially through religion. I came to this conclusion slowly. The argument for it is built chapter by chapter. The discussion of the sixth-century competition between Rome and Aricia over Diana required me to make a distinction very early, however, and I therefore identify Diana Nemorensis as a Latin deity, and a representative of Latin religion, throughout. When I speak of Roman religion, I mean the religious practices specific to the city of Rome. My primary focus is on the development of the cult in the Republican and Augustan period. As I make clear, a very particular relationship to Augustus inadvertently fixed the character of the cult in its late Republican form. Although it continued to flourish for two centuries after Augustus, and Diana's popularity increased in that time, changes in the essential character and organization of the cult of Diana at Aricia no longer occurred. As a result, although imperial religion to some extent makes the entire Mediterranean part of "Roman" religion, this does not really impinge on the cult of Diana Nemorensis.

All translations are my own, throughout, unless otherwise noted.

This book, like Gaul, is divided into three parts. The first part, comprising six chapters, is about Diana herself and treats the evidence of her sanctuary and her representation in art and literature. I review the archaeological evidence for the sanctuary in Chapters 1–3 and place it in the cultural and historical context of Latium, the Latin cities, Rome of the kings and Republic, and the empire. Chapter 4 discusses how Diana of Aricia was seen, presenting the linguistic evidence for her identity as a moon goddess and the evidence of her statues and votives – which show her primarily as a huntress – from the earliest period through the empire. Because the sixth-century rivalry between Rome and Aricia over Diana constitutes critical evidence for what the Latins saw in her as a goddess before the archaeological evidence can become really helpful, Chapter 5 is devoted entirely to the examination of that historical rivalry. I then turn in Chapter 6 to a discussion of the ways in which Latin writers described Diana, first addressing the (supposed) problem of how to reconcile the moon goddess with the hunting goddess and then using the evidence for her other aspects – Trivia, Hecate, (Juno) Lucina, – as well as her epithets – Victrix, Opifer – to construct a complete portrait of this goddess.

The second part focuses on the priest and subordinate *numina* personal to this cult and examines the religious qualities they represented. Chapter 7 is devoted to explicating the ritual of the *rex nemorensis* and his significance vis-à-vis Diana. Orestes and the functions performed by fugitives and slaves in the cult are examined in Chapter 8. Virbius and Egeria are the subject of Chapter 9; they are the elusive, hidden *numina*, closely linked to Diana Nemorensis, but both with external *comparanda* that were widely accepted – there was a famous Egeria at Rome, and Virbius was identified with Hippolytus.

The third part seeks to establish Diana's relationship with her worshippers. Healing was practiced in the sanctuary, and Diana's healing function offers the best insight into the ways in which the cult interacted with individuals. It also demonstrates how the cult responded to developments in the external world on behalf of the people it served. In Chapter 10, I show that techniques used in the cult included rationalist, empirical medicine, and I examine how this accords with ancient ideas of religious healing. Chapter 11 focuses on the use of the *maniae* – pastry figures of deformed people – in healing, in circumstances in which rationalist medicine would not work. It also traces the connections between the *maniae*, humoral theories of rationalist medicine, and the cosmogonies of the south Italian philosopher-mystics, which lay behind so much medical thought.

Finally, I turn in Chapter 12 to a question that sanctuary healing particularly raises but which should be asked much more often about ancient cults in general. People came to the sanctuary, made vows, and asked for help. They asked, and hoped, to be healed. Setting aside the possibility that miracles were, or were thought to be, a regular occurrence there, I consider what it was that such petitioners found in the worship of Diana that brought them back, that persuaded so many of them to make dedications, offerings, and sacrifices that this became and remained one of the richest sanctuaries in Italy (App. *B.C.* 5.24). What did they expect from Diana, and how did she deliver it? How Diana fulfilled her suppliants' expectations leads to a review of the cult and an opportunity to look at the differences in the development and practice of religion between Aricia and Rome. Both came out of a common cultural and religious background, but the way they developed in fact reveals that the Aricians and Romans made distinct and independent choices, and points to a differing religious sensibility that each cultivated. In the end, it leads us to a more nuanced understanding of the nature of religion in Rome and Latium in the historical period.

Because the practice of ritual was the way in which the cult was experienced as a religious institution, I have regarded it as important to consider the nature of ritual in the cult and, where there is any evidence, to suggest or outline what it might have involved. Chapter 7 is particularly devoted to the ritual by which the *rex nemorensis* achieved his position. My arguments for considering Vergil an extremely reliable guide to that ritual are found in Chapters 2 and 7, but I must emphasize that, although the evidence is good, my reconstruction remains an informed speculation. The outline of a possible ritual using the *maniae*, the pastry figures of deformed people, in Chapter 11 is also speculative, although it, too, is based on good evidence, the ancient testimony for what the *maniae* were, and on the extensive work done by scholars in the anthropology of medicine on religious healing in premodern and modern societies. In dealing with ancient religion we must continually direct our course between the Scylla of projection and overinterpretation and the Charybdis of excluding the people and their expectations from our study. Diana and the sacred grove did not exist as entities independent of the people who came there and who came because they acknowledged it as a sacred place and wished to approach Diana as the goddess of that place. There is an old children's hand game with a rhyme, "here's the church and here's the steeple; open the doors and see all the people." Unless we use every available scrap of evidence to understand the people whom the sanctuary served, we cannot begin to understand the religion practiced there. Informed speculation will always risk error, but it is no less an error to forget the living human beings whose religious experience made the sanctuary what it was.

A few years after I returned from Rome and was well into my pursuit of Diana the huntress, I mentioned to a colleague that I was proposing to teach a course on Roman religion. "I didn't know they had any," he said, not entirely in jest. If I have made that position, even as the basis for a joke, a little less tenable, if now it is possible to see a little better the nature and character of Roman and Latin religion, I will be satisfied.

ACKNOWLEDGMENTS

In a work that has extended more than a decade, and into areas of scholarship at which I am a tyro, I have incurred numerous debts. I have been the recipient of much scholarly kindness; many people occupied with a multitude of projects of their own have taken time to read parts of this book at various stages; scholars who began as perfect strangers have answered queries with amazing generosity and have become friends in the process; and colleagues and friends alike have endured many hours of my sometimes obsessive concerns regarding Diana. It has been an experience that has taught me how fortunate I am to be in a profession so marked by high scholarly standards and warm personal concern. It is my pleasure here to express my gratitude to the people and institutions that have made this work possible.

First to be mentioned must be Beatrice Rehl, whose brisk and unflagging confidence has been such an important catalyst for the book from its earliest days. I am truly fortunate to have had her as my editor.

The University of Iowa Arts and Humanities Initiative funded my first trip to Nemi and the Dean's Scholarship, awarded to me by Dean Linda Maxson, funded further travel to examine that site and others, to visit museums in Rome, London and most particularly Nottingham where the Savile collection is kept at the Brewhouse Museum. This generous assistance from the university made everything else possible.

The greatest debt of all of those who study Diana is to the archaeologists who have worked to bring the sanctuary at Nemi to scholarly light. Professor Giuseppina Ghini with characteristic generosity welcomed me to the museum at Nemi, took time from a very busy day (complete with reception for visiting dignitaries) to answer my questions and talk with me about the site, and then graciously gave me every facility to tour her excavation of the sanctuary. Her work is central to any discussion of Diana of Aricia, and my gratitude to her for all she has done is enormous. Pia Guldager Bilde, who is excavating the villa near the sanctuary, responded to my inquiries very generously and gave me a much clearer understanding of the evidence from the villa. Great thanks are also due to Ann Inscker in Nottingham, who took me around the Brewhouse Yard and showed me every piece from the Savile collection of artifacts from Nemi. It was a tremendously exciting morning when I finally saw the votives and was able to look on Fundilia Rufa's herm. Irene Romano introduced me to the other excavations in the sanctuary, and has been helpful in so many ways, particularly sharing her knowledge of the University of Pennsylvania Museum collection of sculptures from Nemi.

I gratefully thank Dr. Stefanos Geroulanos, professor of the history of medicine at the University of Ioannina and director of the Onassis Cardiac Surgery Center in Athens. In personal communication and by sharing his work in publication, he has kindly spent much time explaining to me how the healers in the sanctuaries would study patients and diagnose them and has offered many suggestions for thinking about healing in a religious context.

Many other scholars and friends have shared their knowledge with me. I owe particular thanks to Constance Berman, my mentor since I arrived at the University of Iowa, who has taught me much about academic giants and dwarves, and has also helped me with her insights into the practical and spiritual organization of women's religious institutions. She also provided a steady supply of French and Italian mysteries to keep me sane as I worked. I am grateful to Diana Cates for deepening my insight into the vital connection between religion and healing; to Mary Depew for insightful conversations on ancient religion; to Ingrid Edlund Berry for her guidance on Etruscan and Latin sanctuaries; to Elaine Fantham for encouragement, support over many years, and for helping me to read Lucan more knowledgeably; to Rebecca Huskey for her help in thinking about what ancient religion meant; to Samuel Huskey for an ongoing conversation on Roman religion and the ways in which Latin writers used it; to Lesley Dean

Jones for her expertise on ancient medicine; to Rosemary Moore for her expertise in Roman military religion; to Richard DePuma, a fount of knowledge relating to Roman and Etruscan religion, art, and archaeology; to Susan Treggiari for help on slaves and slavery and for her support and advice at a crucial point.

I could not have had a more congenial colleague in the study of Diana than Lora Holland, who has so kindly shared her wide knowledge of Diana with me over the years. Her work on Diana Aventinensis will undoubtedly contribute greatly to our knowledge of this goddess. Julia Dyson is another scholar who has shared her knowledge unstintingly with me, and it has been a comfort to know there is someone out there whose ear I can always bend on the subject of the *rex nemorensis*. Sinclair Bell, most knowledgeable of art historians, was always able to provide exactly the insight, direction, or crucial reference that I needed when I had the evidence but did not know what to do with it. His kindness and sardonic humor equally lightened my task and lifted my spirits as I trekked through the unfamiliar paths of art and archaeology.

Thomas Habinek and David Konstan both read the book in draft form. Their wise comments and perceptive support for this work made far more difference to me as I wrote than either can imagine. Jane Wilson Joyce started it all by introducing me to Lucan all those years ago. Her work on Statius has advanced *pedetemptim* with my work on this book and our conversations have gone wide and deep on both subjects for many years now (more than either of us want to recall). The price of such friends is above rubies.

Two who were my professors and have become my friends, John Miller and Elizabeth Meyer, have been constant in their support since I first arrived at the University of Virginia. One of the first conversations I ever had with John, on the steps of Jenny Strauss Clay's porch, was on the October Horse. If life were a novel, it would count as foreshadowing. I have learned much from him about Roman religion, and have benefited from his many kindnesses to me. When I sent Elizabeth some early chapters of this book, she spent hours poring over them even as she was finishing the proofs of her own book and nursing a detached retina. There can be no greater favor from a scholar than to expend possibly endangered eyesight over another's manuscript. I am enormously grateful to her, and this book is the better for her bracing yet sympathetic comments.

My senior colleagues here at the University of Iowa Classics department, Helena Dettmer and John Finamore, have offered me unstinting support and encouragement over the years it has taken to complete this book. My debt to them is great.

The University of Iowa has an extraordinarily rich collection in classics. We possess all but a small number of the books and journals I needed, extending even to the Italian excavation reports from the nineteenth century. Chris Africa, the classics bibliographer, has been resourceful and innovative in managing to uphold, and even to raise, the standard of the collection in times of tight budgets. Amy Paulus and the staff of Interlibrary Loan Services have lived up to their justifiably high reputation by finding and delivering everything I have requested with speed and courtesy. Kathryn Penick and the staff in Circulation have also been paradigms of courtesy and helpfulness. These are the people who make research possible, and it is a pleasure to thank them here. The deepest gratitude of a harried author goes to Barbara Hird, my indexer, for her superb professionalism, speed, and calm. Likewise, my thanks go to Pamela Skinner for her lynx-eyed editing of the ancient citations.

I was extremely fortunate to have as an undergraduate research assistant Rory Cline, who was ably succeeded by Katie Ekvall. They found books, photocopied articles, made lists, and verified references for me with exemplary speed and precision. I am grateful to them both.

Any virtue in this work can with certainty be traced back to the assistance of these many people; the errors constitute my most secure claim to originality. For all mistakes, I am entirely responsible.

Finally, my greatest debt is to my husband, Peter. Without his loving confidence, this book could never have been written; without our hours of conversation and debate, my ideas could never have taken shape; without his wise and unstinting love and support, I could never have survived the trials of authorship. The dedication of this book to him is a small offering in our lifelong exchange of love, conversation, work, and happiness.

ABBREVIATIONS

Standard abbreviations (from *LSJ* or the *OLD*, sometimes expanded) are used for ancient authors and works cited in the notes. Journal titles are written out in full in the bibliography.

ANRW   *Aufstieg und Niedergang der römischen Welt*, H. Temporini and W. Haase, eds. (1972–), Berlin and New York.

BMC   *Coins of the Roman Republic in the British Museum*, London, 1910.

CAH²   *The Cambridge Ancient History*, 2nd ed., various editors, Cambridge, 1961–.

CIL   *Corpus Inscriptionum Latinarum*, various editors, Berlin, 1863–.

KRS²   *The Presocratic Philosophers*, 2nd ed., G. S. Kirk, J. E. Raven, and M. Schofield, eds., Cambridge, 1983.

IGRR   *Inscriptiones graecae ad res romanas pertinentes*, 3 vols., R. Cagnat et al., eds., Paris, 1906–27.

ILLRP   *Inscriptiones latinae liberae rei publicae*, A. Degrassi, ed., 2 vols., Florence, 1963–5.

ILS   *Inscriptiones latinae selectae*, H. Dessau, ed., 3 vols., Berlin, 1892–1916.

LSJ   *A Greek-English Lexicon*, H. G. Liddell et al., eds., Oxford, 1996.

LTUR   *Lexicon Topographicum Urbis Romae*, 5 vols., E. M. Steinby, ed., Rome, 1992.

Neue Pauly   *Der Neue Pauly: Enzyklopädie der Antike*, H. Cancik and H. Schneider, eds., Stuttgart, 1996–.

OCD   *Oxford Classical Dictionary*, 3rd ed., S. Hornblower and A. Spawforth, eds., Oxford, 1996.

OLD   *Oxford Latin Dictionary*, P. G. W. Glare et al., eds., Oxford, 1982.

RE   *Real-Encyclopädie der classischen Altertumswissenschaft*, A. F. von Pauly et al., eds., Stuttgart, 1894–1963.

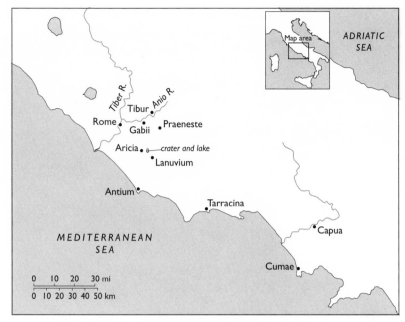

1. Map of Latium.

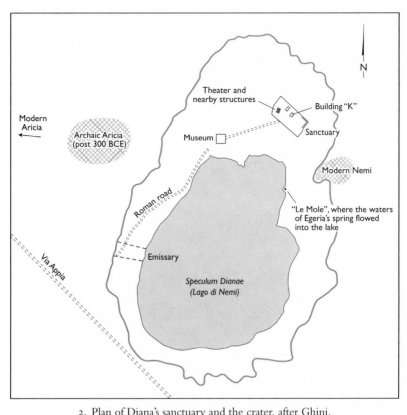

2. Plan of Diana's sanctuary and the crater, after Ghini.

PART I

GROVE AND GODDESS

THE SANCTUARY OF DIANA AT ARICIA
TO THE AUGUSTAN AGE

THE APPROACH

Aricia and its sanctuary of Diana are about eleven miles from Rome along the Via Appia. Although there were a few kilometers between the city walls and the sanctuary, the cult belonged to the city. Taking the Via Appia south from Rome, one approaches Aricia up a long incline to the point where the sanctuary road turns off (map 1). In Martial's day (2.19) the route was almost impassable for the beggars taking advantage of the long slope that slowed down vehicles. Aricia itself had a fine, fortified position, originally near the ridge of the crater of an extinct volcano looking west across the Latian plain all the way to Antium, later slightly further down the slope on the Via Appia (Strabo 5.3.12).[1] Today the view is just as commanding, although modern Anzio can sometimes be obscured by smog. The road to the right will take one to Lanuvium; that to the left still leads to the sanctuary.

Aricia is now a rather elegant Roman suburb. Driving south towards Lanuvium on the Via Appia, one passes through to the far side of Aricia, staying on the road to the left, dodging children and shoppers and other cars at a minor roundabout, then turning off onto a narrower road nearly invisible among apartment buildings. From here the road curves, cresting the crater's ridge, and one finds oneself in a world of incredible remoteness and, indeed, sacredness,[2] even while the noise

---

[1] See Lilli 2002 for the archaeology of archaic (52–62) and Republican (62–66) Aricia.
[2] For an analysis of the characteristics of sacred space, see Eliade (1959).

of schoolchildren playing has not yet died away.[3] The sanctuary is set in the crater of a small, extinct volcano, above a lake that appears almost perfectly round, although a cartographer would show it as slightly irregular and oblong (map 2).[4] Within the crater the woods are thick and green, birdsong fills the air, and the perfect blue of the lake reflects the sky and the crater's sloping sides. The old Roman road has, it is true, been asphalted, but it still slopes gently down from the crest to skirt the lake, moving away toward the sanctuary at a point where the lake leaves a blunt triangle of level land. To pass over the ridge into the crater is a very real experience of crossing a boundary into what is still effectively sacred space (fig. 1).

Neolithic man was here (Lenzi 2000, 157). Human activity in the crater began to increase from the middle Bronze Age, as bronze axe heads attest (Giardino 1985, 9–11; Lenzi 2000, 157–8). From the late Bronze Age through the early Iron Age the hunters and farmers inhabiting the Latin countryside seemed to prefer the more accessible and prosperous settlements along the river and land routes in the plain, and the Alban Hills were comparatively less inhabited (Smith 1996, 52). Yet there is evidence of eighth-century burials in the cemetery of Aricia (Gierow 1964, 354–6), and from then on the town grew in size, along with the other Alban communities. The Alban Hills were thickly wooded, and wild animals flourished there. Animal bones and fragments of an antler have been found just outside Aricia in the context of human habitation rather than burial and are datable to the eighth and seventh centuries (Gierow 1964, 358). The hills would have been a paradise for hunters, whether aristocrats in pursuit of boar or simple men looking to supplement a meager diet. Such hunters, coming over the ridge into the crater, would have had an awe-inspiring scene before them.[5]

---

[3] "The threshold is the limit, the boundary, the frontier that distinguishes and opposes two worlds – and at the same time the paradoxical place where those worlds communicate, where passage from the profane to the sacred world becomes possible" (Eliade 1959, 25).

[4] Cf. the detailed isometric "pianta generale del territorio nemorense" (fig. 44) in Lenzi. Lenzi is now the indispensable source for the topography of the sanctuary. There were actually two craters collapsed into one that the lake has filled (Lenzi, 155).

[5] Cf. Edlund 1987, 35–8 on the origin of sacred places, 42–93 on extra-urban and rural sanctuaries in Etruria and Magna Graecia, and especially 87 on the Lucus Feroniae.

The crater is steep and the lake 30 meters deep (Guldager Bilde 1997a, 166), with only a narrow shoreline. On the northeast side is the one bit of level land beside the lake, roughly triangular in shape. Here the sanctuary was eventually located, beside the lake, itself a kind of *templum*, a sacred space marked out by nature.[6] Just to the east, beneath the sheerest rise of stone, a great spring poured from the crater wall and into the lake (Rosa 1856, 7; Frazer 1.17, n. 4). Its stream was substantial enough to turn mill wheels in the Middle Ages, from which the place Le Mole ("the millstones") took its name. The crater is large enough to define a world of its own but not so large that it invites fragmentation of its interior space; and in this very contained space, the triangular flatland forms a single orienting point (figure 2). Behind this orienting point, the peak of the Alban Mount, the focus of Latin communal worship at the shrine of Jupiter Latiaris, rises above the crater walls.

"Man becomes aware of the sacred because it manifests itself, shows itself, as something wholly different from the profane" (Eliade 1959, 11). This crater is the natural place for a hunting cult. It is the universe writ small, uniting the three cosmic levels – the earth, the canopy of the heavens,[7] and, through depths of the lake and the caves at its shore, the underworld.[8] It was then, as now, a place of stunning beauty and peace, sacred and remote. In the twenty-first century, the sacredness of the place is marked by the contrast between the turbulent urban landscape outside the crater and the serene nature within. That same contrast would surely have been evident, although not so intensely, two millennia before, when one moved away from the rumbling, noisy

---

[6] G. Colonna, "La Dea Etrusca CEL e i santuari del Trasimeno." *Rivista Storica dell'Antichità* 6–7 (1976–1977), 45–62; see also Holland 1961, 6 n. 10 and 19 n. 42, on the religious importance of "living water."

[7] Cf. Varro, *LL* 5.17: sic caelum et pars eius, summum ubi stellae, et id quod Pacuvius cum demonstrat dicit – "hoc vide circum supraque quod complexu continet terram." (Thus *caelum*, "sky" is both a part of itself, the top where the stars are, and that which is meant by Pacuvius, when he indicates it thus – "See you that /Which round and over holds earth in its embrace"). Text and translation are those of Warmington (1979), who assigns it to Pacuvius' *Chryses* (fr. 107–8), the story of Orestes pursued by Thoas, whom he will eventually kill. See also fr. 115, a direct translation of Euripides' *Chrysippus* fr. 836 N, on Earth the mother who gives birth to the body and aer/aether as the entity that gives breath.

[8] Following Eliade (1959) 36–42.

traffic of a commercial city and principal staging post on the heavily traveled Via Appia. But the Bronze Age hunter no doubt saw it in its truest form, not needing the contrast with hectic urbanism to recognize "the sanctity of a lake and the setting in nature" (Edlund, 56).[9]

It is a small lake, spring fed, no more than 1.8 kilometers at its widest and 34.5 meters deep once the *emissarium* was built to maintain its level.[10] As there was no natural above-ground outlet, the lake level would have changed according to seasonal rain or drought although over time such changes would be moderated by the underground outflows (Lenzi 2000, 155). The summer's lush lakeside meadows would have been turned to marsh during the rainiest winter months, and in years of high rainfall the triangular piece of lowland would have been flooded. This triangle, broad across the curve of the lake and narrowing into the crater walls, is where the terrace for the lower sanctuary was eventually built. It resembled the stubby handle embracing the bottom of an Etruscan bronze mirror. On a calm day the lake reflects the sky and the shoreline with shimmering perfection. The Romans, much more attuned to the visual impact of the setting than we can be, called the lake the *speculum Dianae*, the "mirror of Diana."[11]

The crater has its own microclimate. Violent thunderstorms, earthquakes, and thick fogs are all more frequent there than they are in the plains of Latium beyond (Guldager Bilde 1997, 166). Trees – today chestnuts but in antiquity also beech and oak – as well as scrub and the larger woody bushes grew thick on the crater slopes: the area was densely populated with wildlife. Trees and bushes would have found the level ground inhospitable, however, intermittently sodden as it would have been before the *emissarium* was built. Meadow grass, on the other hand, would have grown well there. So the lake and the springs provided water for wild animals, the meadow offered grass for

---

[9] Cf. Edlund's discussion of the sacred nature of lakes in Italy (1987, 55) and on Monte Falterona and Lago degli Idoi in particular (56–8): "The site in all of Etruria which provides the most profound sense of the link between the sanctity of a lake and the setting in nature" (56).

[10] Zahle 1997, 169; the depth was measured in 1928 when the lake was drained to raise the great imperial ships. Since then the water level has dropped as a result of the dense population outside the crater, which uses the water that previously would have flowed into the lake.

[11] Servius *ad Aen.* 7.515; *CIL* XIV 2772.

grazing, and the woodlands refuge for animals and a source of forage year-round for animals and for man himself. Today the town of Nemi, a medieval foundation on the highest and steepest point of the crater rim right above the ancient meadow and sanctuary, is famous for the tiny wild strawberries that are celebrated with a festival at the end of May, and the old meadow, now rich agricultural land, is ribbed with lines of greenhouses protecting flowers grown for the Roman market. It is a haven for wildlife.[12] In that, it has not changed so very much from the time when the first Bronze Age hunter arrived. He saw the crater, its distinctive and separate nature, and its abundant wildlife as an inevitable focus for his religious experience of the hunting goddess.

THE SITE

What we know about the sanctuary as an expression of religious ideas, as a place shaped by human design for religious (and other) purposes, must come first from archaeological investigation. Until the excavations undertaken by Professor Giuseppina Ghini in the 1990s inaugurated a new era, the site of Aricia's sanctuary had been beset by misfortune – centuries of scavenging, followed by another century of poorly documented or unfinished excavations. It is not certain how much of the original sanctuary survived once it was closed. About the end of the second or the beginning of the third century C.E., a landslide destroyed part of the structure (Guldager Bilde 1997, 167). The sanctuary may have been closed down after this misfortune, or its closing may have been a response to increasing opposition on the part of Christian authorities. No coins after the reign of Antoninus Pius have been discovered (Guldager Bilde 1997, 167), and the fourth-century grammarian, Servius, indicates that Diana's priest, the *rex nemorensis*, had been transferred to Sparta (*ad Aen.* 2.116), although he does not say when this happened. By late antiquity, the sanctuary was certainly deserted and in ruins. Through the Middle Ages and the Renaissance nothing specific is known. No doubt the structures were used as a quarry for building materials. In the seventeenth century two Marchesi

---

[12] See figure 2. It was still maintained as a hunting preserve by the Chigi family in the eighteenth century, as attested by Lucidi (1791, 71) in his history of Aricia.

Frangipani explored the sanctuary and found various votive statuettes. In the eighteenth century digging was done for the Spanish Cardinal Despuig, whose collection from the sanctuary and surrounding areas ended up in Majorca a century later (Hübner 1862, 292–311). Cardinal Despuig's collection is distinguished by the fact that the provenience of the artifacts was preserved, but otherwise the finds uncovered by these treasure-hunting expeditions all went unnoted into private collections.

Then, in 1885, a serious, scientific (for the time) excavation was undertaken by Lord Savile (*Not. Scav.* 1895, 424–31) under license from Count Orsini, who had bought the castle at Nemi in 1870. When Savile wanted to resume excavations in the following year, Orsini imposed intolerable conditions on him and forced him to fill in the previous year's work. Savile had divided the "finds" of the previous year with Orsini. By the standards of the time, which valued imperial over Republican artifacts and objets d'art over archaeologically and historically significant material, Orsini acquired the lion's share of the finds. The bright side is that, as a result, the Republican artifacts were preserved in a single collection by Lord Savile. He turned it over to the Nottingham Castle Museum, and it is now kept in Nottingham at the Brewhouse Yard Museum.[13]

After the break with Savile, Orsini commissioned Roman art dealers to "excavate." They did so in 1886–8 and 1895 (*Not. Scav.* 1887, 1888, and 1895; cf. Rossbach 1885 and 1890; Helbig 1885; Rohden 1886), and the finds were sold. Although unknowable numbers of artifacts disappeared into private collections, some beautiful pieces were acquired by museums. The most significant collections are at the Ny Carlsberg Glyptotek in Copenhagen and the University Museum in Philadelphia.[14]

At the beginning of the twentieth century the castle of Nemi became the property of the Ruspoli family. A new excavation was undertaken, published by L. Morpurgo (*Not. Scav.* 1903), who did not know where the pieces from the excavations of 1886 or after had gone

---

[13] Blagg (1983, 19–24) surveys the history of excavations for the Nottingham Museum, Crescenzi (1977) the history of the identification and excavation of the site.

[14] Surveys covering the history of excavations and collections are Guldager Bilde 1997a, 171–2 (Glyptotek), and Guldager Bilde and Moltesen 2000, 7–18 (Philadelphia).

(316, n. 2) with the exception of some items acquired by the Museum of Fine Arts in Boston. Orsini apparently had not sold everything he claimed for himself from Savile's excavation. These remaining pieces eventually made their way to the Museo Nazionale and are now in the Terme Museum, together with the finds from all of the twentieth-century excavations.

From 1924 to 1928 excavations were undertaken under the auspices of the state by Edoardo Gatti. Gatti was unable to finish uncovering the buildings (particularly the theater) and died before he could write up the report. L. Morpurgo (*Not. Scav.* 1931) nobly tackled the diffi-cult task of publishing a dig she had not supervised (and that had been covered up when the work was completed), so that many questions raised by the partial excavation inevitably remained unanswered. Fur-thermore, Gatti's excavations in the sanctuary were overshadowed by the discoveries of the imperial ships at the bottom of the lake. These magnificent "floating palaces" were raised (1927–32) and housed in a museum built for them beside the lake. The ships were destroyed in a fire on May 31, 1944 (Ghini 1992, 3–7), possibly the result of arson by retreating German troops. New excavations, admirably conducted and swiftly published, were begun in 1989 by Ghini (Ghini 1997, 2000).

This complex and unfortunate history has always complicated the study of Diana. The treasure hunts were for artifacts that were sep-arated from the site without any record, either of where they were found or of where they went. Savile cared about the site itself, as did Gatti, but neither had the opportunity to complete his excavation. Their sketches and maps (such as they were) lacked precise measure-ments. Thus we have no reliable record of the size of the buildings nor any precise indication of where the reburied remains were situated in relationship to each other or to the structures that are now visible. Ghini's current excavations are focused on the colonnade and niches at the back of the sanctuary.

Allowing for these considerable uncertainties, what have been dis-covered are the remains of a late-Republican sanctuary, rebuilt in stages during the first two centuries of the imperial period. The broad outlines of this sanctuary, as Gatti and Savile found it, are as follows (map 2): There was a well-paved Roman road leading over the rim of the crater on its southwest side, and proceeding down the slope to the sanctuary on the northeast quarter of the lake. This part of the sanctuary was defined by a large rectangular terrace of the late Republican period, set beside the lake and bordered on two sides by a colonnade. Behind the colonnade there were high arched niches set into the slope. These niches were constructed in the early imperial period, and some held statues of the emperors. A small rectangular building once identified as the Republican temple stood on the terrace, underneath a medieval farmhouse. There was a small theater and an attached building complex with a bath. The ships found sunk in the lake and raised during the excavations of the late 1920s may or may not be directly relevant to the sanctuary.

The lakeside face of the terrace, the niches, and parts of the colonnade are visible today, and the quondam supposed temple lies under the farmhouse among the greenhouses. The theater and the other buildings have been covered over. The separate parts of the sanctuary and the artifacts found there are discussed in detail later. Unavoidably, the excavations conducted to date have for the most part raised questions that can only be answered by new and more exhaustive scientific excavations. There is still much to be done, and it is hoped that Professor Ghini's work will be adequately funded in the next decade, so that she may reestablish the evidence already brought to light and add to it – especially by revealing whatever may be left of the temple.

FROM THE ARCHAIC AGE TO CA. 300 B.C.E.

Sacred space is defined by use. Buildings represent only one way to define the places where men and women come to worship a god. There were worshippers in the crater meadows long before there were buildings to receive them. This is not only appropriate for a goddess whose domain is the wild; the absence of buildings must also define a certain religious quality of the goddess which had to be preserved when the sanctuary *did* acquire structures.

The sanctuary was functioning as a place of established worship in the archaic period. Miniature pots – unmistakably votive offerings of the archaic period, and characteristic of similar sanctuary offerings elsewhere in Latium – have been found near the terrace (Gierow 1966, 39–40), and a bronze fibula dates from the late eighth or early seventh century (Blagg 1983, no. 713, p. 56). A remnant from an even earlier period than this, a cultural rather than a physical remnant, was the ritual of the priest-king, the *rex nemorensis*, the king of the wood. This priest is unique to the cult of Arician Diana in the historical period. (Among the Latins there may have been other similar priesthoods that had faded away by the time notice was taken of such figures.) The *rex* was the fugitive slave who, by breaking off a bough of a sacred tree in the sanctuary, earned the right to meet the reigning priest in mortal combat. The victor of the combat became the new priest-king (Servius *ad Aen.* 6.136).[15] It is a truth of the wild that one being must die so that another may live, and the ritual of the man who kills his predecessor and then himself becomes priest-king doubtless had its origins among the hunter ancestors of the Latin communities. Its survival at Aricia may be due in part to the continued excellent hunting in the Alban Hills; but it must also reflect the interpretive adaptability of the priesthood as managed by the Arician elders in control of the sanctuary.

The ritual of the *rex nemorensis* enacts an eternal anxiety of the early hunter-warrior: when does the hunted become the hunter, and what is the meaning of the death of the one hunted? Such anxieties, and the curious authority of the priest who represents them, are well-known to anthropologists who study hunter-gatherer cultures. The *rex* exhibits the characteristics of the central protagonist of hunter-gatherer mythology, who regularly becomes problematical when societies become politically organized and troubled by the ethical and legal implications of his behavior. The actions of such a protagonist, Guenther says (1999, 426–7), "are in line with his own fluid and flawed nature . . . [T]he striking prominence of this quasi-divine figure in its classic 'archaic' form within the mythological world of hunter-gatherers contrasts with the figure's relative insignificance in the myths and beliefs of state-organized societies."[16] As we will see, the

---

[15] A detailed discussion of the *rex nemorensis* and the numerous references to this figure in Latin and Greek literature can be found in Chapter 7.

[16] Guenther, as an anthropologist, is more comfortable with the terms "trickster" and "shaman" than most classicists will be; however, for a recent and wide-ranging application of the trickster paradigm to Roman culture, see R. Stewart, "Who's Tricked: Models of Slave Behavior in Plautus' *Pseudolus*," in *Role Models: Identity and Assimilation in the Roman World*, ed. S. Bell and I. L. Hansen (Ann Arbor 2006).

rex nemorensis, and similar priesthoods, may indeed have existed at the same time as Latin state-organized societies were coming into being, but it is clear that his "flawed nature" – symbolized by his fugitive status and the necessary murder of his predecessor, matters that have disturbed both the ancients and so many modern scholars as well – made him a figure whose ultimate containment in the sanctuary at Aricia best served everyone's interests. Once confined to that context, the priesthood continued through the age of the Antonines. Problematic though it is, the *rex nemorensis'* perpetually renewed vitality as a religious symbol cannot be doubted.

At the end of the sixth century the sanctuary emerged into the light of political-military history and is revealed as a place of considerable importance to a number of allied Latin cities. A fragment from the elder Cato's *Annales* demonstrates (Cato fr. 58 Peter; see Chapter 5 for the text and translation) that a dedication of the grove in the Arician woods was once made by the Dictator Latinus, a certain Egerius Baebius from Tusculum. The dedication was made communally by Tusculum, Aricia, Lanuvium, Laurentum, Cora, Tibur, Pometia, and Rutulian Ardea.

The date of the events to which this passage refers has been deduced from context, and, it is argued, should be placed within a decade before or after 500 B.C.E.[17] A consecration of this sort would not have necessarily implied a temple, so Cato may have been recording no more than the consecration of a sod altar in the clearing by the named allied Latin cities. It is now generally agreed, however, that this cannot mark the original dedication of the sanctuary itself (Cornell 1989, 273; restated 1995, 297–8). It must therefore represent a special occasion regarding the alliance of the named cities. This fragment holds much of great importance both for the nature of the cult and for Latin history and is discussed at length in the context of Latin history of the sixth

---

[17] Gordon (1934, 1) dates the events in the passage to around 500 B.C.E. This date is generally accepted and reaffirmed by Cornell. Pairault's argument (1969, 440–1) for the fourth century is not sustainable, based as it is on his view of Diana as fundamentally a Greek goddess, whose Greekness could not have been acquired before that date. I would certainly agree that this passage reflects the historical fact of the importance of the sanctuary to the alliance of Latin cities. I am not so certain it can be taken as testimony to a known historical event. See the discussion in Chapter 5.

and fifth centuries in Chapter 5. There are, however, at least two firm conclusions we can draw from it. First, in the archaic age this sanctuary of Diana held a significant position of religious power that extended beyond Aricia itself to the Latin people in general. Second, *in nemore Aricino* indicates that the site was not understood to be a communal sanctuary, then or ever, but was recognized as being in the control of Aricia. Whatever the significance of these two facts taken together, the hunting goddess' sanctuary first appears on the historical stage as a religious site for the negotiation of political and military power. As we shall see, this is no accident. The hunting cult was particularly suited to such purposes, and the sanctuary's ability to mediate and interpret power was one of its most important, and most sought-after, functions throughout its existence.

The alliance recorded by Cato did not, as far as we can tell, include Rome. In Rome, however, Servius Tullius had founded the Aventine cult to Diana as a bid to make this the center of worship for all the Latin cities (Livy 1.45; DH *AR* 4.25.3–4.26.5). For a while, then – perhaps half a century at the end of the sixth and beginning of the fifth centuries – the cult of Diana, both in Rome and in Aricia, was preeminent in forging Latin alliances. This is rightly taken as an indication of the conflict between Rome and Aricia (at the head of the Latin alliance), these being, at the time, the two most powerful political forces in Latium. During this period, Diana was the symbol and the guarantor of leadership among the Latins (Livy 1.45).

The first resolution of that conflict, the *Foedus Cassianum*, a treaty signed by the Latin League in 493 (Livy 2.33.9; DH *AR* 6.95), created a formal Roman hegemony in Latium. For the time being, the Latins had yielded to Rome's superior might, but they would return to the struggle periodically over the next century and a half.

Aricia's preeminence among the Latins, both before and after the *Foedus Cassianum*, was due, in part, to her geographic position. It was not just that she overlooked the plain. The most important land connection between Latium and Campania had to pass through Arician territory, just below the city, because the Pomptine marshes in the plain itself made the higher ground along the slopes of the crater the best route for the movement of travel and trade even before the building of the Via Appia. Aricia's military and political alliance with Cumae in the sixth and fifth centuries (Livy 2.14.5–7; DH *AR* 5.36; 7.6) is a small but visible part of her extensive influence among the Latins and their trading and political partners in southern Italy from the later part of the regal period onward.

It might have been thought that the Arician people, spurred on by their rivalry with Rome and the need to rally the Latin allies, would have turned with ever-increasing frequency to their sanctuary of Diana, the goddess who bestowed leadership among the Latins. Yet only a few votive pieces, bronze brooches and figurines, ranging in date from the eighth to the sixth centuries have been found in the sanctuary (Blagg 1986, 211). It is generally supposed that this absence of material remains can be explained by the fact that at this time there was no more than a sod altar in the sanctuary. This may have been the case, for there is no evidence of a temple or permanent sanctuary to Diana on the Aventine during this period either. An alternative possibility is that there *was* a late archaic temple, but that it was built on the slope of the crater, an area that has never been excavated (Coarelli 1987, 187–8; Ghini 2000, 61). There is a beautiful archaic bronze head that may have belonged to a fifth-century cult statue of Diana,[18] in which case, so elegant a cult statue would have surely required some permanent shrine for it to stand in, on, or before.[19]

THE TRANSFORMATION OF THE SANCTUARY

The end of the Latin revolt in 338 signaled the historical moment when the Latin cities became part of Rome forever. For reasons we

---

[18] Riis has argued that an archaic bronze head, once in the collection of Cardinal Despuig, was from a fifth-century cult statue that appears as a triple statue on the coin of P. Accoleius Lariscolus (cf. also Blagg 1986, 212; Coarelli 1987,169; Pairault 1969, 458–62; cf. Gradel (2000, 202–3) for the reasonable doubts concerning the identification). See Paribeni (1961) for a discussion of a marble head that appears to be a copy of this statue, and the full discussion in Chapter 4.

[19] It is often supposed that a cult statue – not this one, but the triple Diana reproduced on the coin of P. Accoleius 43 B.C.E. (discussed in Chapter 4) – was set out in the open (Blagg 1986, 211–14; Coarelli 1987, 167–70). This seems to me unlikely. Anthropomorphism and buildings go together, and in most cases one would suppose that any building would precede the introduction of an anthropomorphic cult statue. Diana may well have been represented by a sacred tree, but that is quite different.

do not know, Aricia was one of five cities (the others were Lanuvium, Nomentum, Pedum, and Tusculum) incorporated into the Roman state and granted full Roman citizenship. One result was that Rome was now able to build the Via Appia on this land route to Campania. Appius Claudius, the force behind the building of the Appian Way in 312 (Richardson 1992, 414), made perhaps the greatest single contribution to the success of Diana's sanctuary in its entire history. Aricia was the first way station for those traveling south from Rome and the last for those coming north to the great city (Horace, *Sat.* 5.1–2). Offerings and dedications could flow from pilgrims who now had easier access and readier accommodations for longer stays.

In political terms, the loss of Arician autonomy must have affected the leading families, who were also the administrators responsible for running the sanctuary (Bodei Giglioni 1977, 45–6). Even if they now gained the opportunity to serve in magistracies at Rome, they had been moved from the center to the periphery of political and civic influence. The religious dimensions of this loss of autonomy are difficult to determine, especially in regard to the sanctuary. Diana's failure to protect her people's independence ought have led to doubts of her power and anxiety as to her possible vulnerability, the divine correlation to the political marginalization of her leading families. What we might expect from the Arician sanctuary is, however, as so often, *not* what we get.

Within decades of their surrender to Rome, around 300 B.C.E., the Aricians built a grand new temple, possibly the first sacred building in the sanctuary (Morpurgo 1903, 344; Blagg 1986, 213–14). It had a gilded roof. Antefixes, acroteria, and other architectural elements have been found, but not the foundations of the building.[20] Ghini, the current excavator, has found a wall of mortar conglomerate in a trench dug in the upper terrace, and thinks (rightly I am sure) that

---

[20] Vitruvius (4.8.4) briefly describes the temple of Diana in the grove, but he mentions particularly columns added *ad umeros pronai*, "at the shoulders (or sides) of the pronaos." There is nothing found so far that might fit Vitruvius' description (Morpurgo 1903, 311–12; Blagg 1985, 35; see also Castagnoli on the various proportions of the "Italic" temple).

this is an indication of the location of the temple[21] on the slope above the sanctuary terrace. If this eventually proves to be the case, traces of an archaic temple or shrine may eventually be discovered on an upper terrace as well. This temple, in either case, was no small, tentative effort. It was a monumental structure,[22] crowned with gilt-bronze revetment plaques, frieze and roof-tiles, and elegant sculptures.[23] If this was the first structure ever raised in the sanctuary, it represents a truly astonishing and dramatic shift in religious ideas. Set on the slope amidst the trees, Diana's magnificent new temple must have appeared to be raising its golden roof out of the forest.[24]

> Iam subeunt Triuiae lucos atque aurea tecta.
> Verg. *Aen.* 6.13[25]

Now they [Aeneas and Anchises] *passed into Diana's grove and the gold-roofed temple.*[26]

The religious significance of the temple can only be understood when it is seen in relationship to the treaty signed in 338. Aricia and the Latins had been irrevocably defeated. Aricia, to be sure, gained full Roman citizenship. But what did that mean in terms of religion?

---

[21] Ghini 1997, 182, Coarelli 1987, 171–3, and Guldager Bilde 1997c, 183–4, for a discussion of late Republican temple complexes, which are built on sites with commanding positions and artificial terraces, thus turning the landscape itself into part of the architecture.

[22] Känel discusses the architectural terra-cottas of this temple (184–7), among them a terra-cotta figure of Diana that he calls a "masterpiece" (185).

[23] Morpurgo 1903, 318–19; Della Seta 1918, 223 (no. 6733, 6744); Andrén 1940, 383; Blagg 1986, 215.

[24] Terra-cotta antefixes, revetments, pedimental sculpture, and bronze plaques are the only evidence so far. No structural remains have been found; Blagg 1983, 25–6.

[25] The text of the *Aeneid* is that of Mynors throughout.

[26] Aeneas, of course, has landed in Cumae, but there was an ancient and close connection between Cumae and Aricia (Livy 2.14.5–7; DH *AR* 5.36 and 7.6) that no doubt had long continued (see Chapter 5). Vergil is creating a world of magical realism for book 6; he cannot be held to geographic specificity. Nevertheless, the gold roof, the epithet "Trivia," and the ritual of the golden bough (no doubt foreshadowed imagistically by the extraordinary gold of the roof) all point to Aricia. As Aricia was Augustus' mother's home, Vergil is, as Servius says, paying a compliment to the princeps. Cumae may have had a similar gold-roofed temple (Pairault suggests a cult of Diana at Cumae on the basis of this passage 1969, 448), but it would not have been in a *nemus*, as the temple of Diana at Aricia certainly was.

Gold-roofed temples in particular were unacceptable in Rome, and more than a hundred years would pass before the first gold ceiling was acceptable even on the Capitol.[27] This had nothing to do with an inability to pay for such luxuries. If Aricia could afford a gold roof for her temple, so could Rome. Thus, when we consider Aricia's relationship to Rome, we must look carefully at this gilded temple of Diana. It displays such striking contrast to the Roman temples of the period that we must recognize the existence of clear cultural differences between the Romans and their former Latin enemies, at least at the élite level. It was the élite that commissioned and paid for (or, at Rome, refused to allow) a gold roof. These differences continued to find expression independently of the experience of shared citizenship. The contrast reveals much about the supple strength of Roman political authority as well. The Latins did not necessarily share Rome's austere view of religion, and Rome was not concerned to make her new citizens conform to her own religious *mos maiorum*.

At Rome, the bias toward religious austerity clearly remained in the ascendant into the third century.[28] At the same time, the Aricians, although they had submitted to Rome, were anything but submissive in their self-presentation to the world. There the leading families decided to transfer the advancement of their city (and themselves) to a different level, moving from the political to the more generally religious, centered on the sanctuary to Diana. The changes they made in the sanctuary with the introduction of this magnificent temple indicate a determination to alter the way the sanctuary was used by worshippers, to widen the reach of the cult, and to draw an increasing number of pilgrims. This gilded temple to Diana was a triumphant assertion of Aricia's importance and the goddess' wealth.

It is salutary and informative to compare to this Athens' response to her defeat by Demetrios Poliorketes in 291/0. The Athenians commissioned a paean to Demetrios (Athen. 6.253b–f) in which he was

---

[27] Blagg 1986, 215. Catulus was criticized for having the brass ceiling tiles of the Capitol gilded; Pliny *NH* 33.57.

[28] Only thirteen temples were dedicated or built in Rome from 302 to 264 (Richardson 1992, 446–7), although these were four decades of accelerating Roman imperial expansion and increasing wealth, all leading to the crisis of the First Punic War.

hymned as a present god, and therefore worthy to be prayed to, unlike the other gods who were far away. It was, in fact, a relatively mild act of flattery, since in 306 they had installed Demetrios, his mistresses, and his boys in Athena's temple, the Parthenon, according to Plutarch (*Dem.* 23 and 26).[29] The Aricians, on the other hand, make it evident that military defeat, or political annexation, did not necessarily entail loss of faith in one's patron deity, nor did it necessarily create doubts about the validity of traditional city-state religion, nor did it foster skepticism about the value of the acts of worship.

This extraordinary gold-roofed temple was conceived and built by the Arician social élite. They were radically changing the sanctuary, and therefore the worship of the goddess, and at the same time the ordinary suppliant of Diana was also finding a new way to express religious devotion. Votive terra-cottas begin to appear in the sanctuary about this time (Blagg 1986, 214–15; Blagg 1993, 107), as they do elsewhere throughout central Italy. Some are figurines of the goddess as huntress, in an imitation of the Artemis iconography; others are ex-votos of body parts or animals or indeterminate heads. Those that appear at Aricia come from the same molds that produced figurines found at Segni, Rome, and Lanuvium. The production of such terra-cotta votives was clearly a small industry serving this new and expanding religious practice. So Aricia was not unique. Her temple and the transformation of her sanctuary must be seen as part of a larger religious impulse in

---

[29] Green 1990, 55–6, and more extensively, 2003. "During the fourth and third centuries B.C., then, we observe...the erosion of faith, not only in traditional city-state values, but also, and more importantly, in the civic deities who had shown themselves so seemingly indifferent to their worshippers' welfare" (Green 2003, 270). Mikalson (1998, 101) observes that "we may suspect that the later honors to Demetrios, promoted by a small group of powerful partisans, were in fact ratified by many Athenians who were unwilling but afraid. The honors given to Demetrios became a travesty, in part because of Demetrios' immoderate reaction to them, in part because of his supporters' encouragement. The next government and the next Antigonid, Antigonos Gonatas, would react quite differently, and ruler cult would soon fade in importance in the religion of Hellenistic Athens." Even if Athens' response to Demetrios was the exception, rather than the rule, political advantage had trumped piety without causing significant public outrage. This in itself would have contributed to the erosion of faith in traditional deities like Athena, even if ruler cult itself faded. The building of Diana's gold-roofed temple in Aricia so soon after defeat by the Romans, and in contradiction to Roman custom of the time, thus illustrates the Aricians' response to defeat, as well as the Romans' response to victory.

the Latin world. Instead of retreating under the shadow of Roman domination, the Latin cities were now affirming the reality of their religious power to a wider and more varied audience.[30] There were bronze dedications as well, a third-century ladle handle inscribed to Diana (Blagg 1983, no. 637, p. 56), a mirror handle (Blagg 1983, no. 647, p. 56), and a multitude of bronze figurines of Diana of various Republican dates (Blagg 1983, p. 56). The temple in Diana's sanctuary can thus be seen as the product of a reinvigorated religious confidence, which, through the temple, was intended to make its presence felt in the world of Italy and beyond (Blagg 1986, 215).

THE WEALTH AND FINANCES OF THE SANCTUARY

Obviously the Aricians who built the temple were wealthy, and their sanctuary had to have shared in that wealth. The religious and financial confidence at Aricia was in part connected to developments quite independent of political changes in Italy. The fourth century was the period in which both Hippocratic and Asclepian medicine, as well as the Asclepian sanctuaries at Cos and Epidauros, transformed the practices of healing in the Mediterranean. Apollo was a hunting god, and the early medical theorists Alcmaeon, Pythagoras, and Empedocles, as well as the Eleatics, all in southern Italy, were associated with Apollo. This is hardly surprising, as hunting cults were rich in the lore of plants and animals and in the knowledge of how to heal wounds as well as to inflict them.[31] Though the Asclepieia became the most powerful and widespread religious healing centers, they were hardly unique. The anatomical terra-cottas appearing among the votives at Aricia, Segni, Rome, and Lanuvium[32] were associated with new healing practices in Italy, part of the same intellectual developments that affected Cos and Epidaurus. Most of the anatomical ex-votos appearing at Diana's

---

[30] "This [the new kinds of votive offering] suggests a new self-awareness, a mental and spiritual equivalent to the opening up of the territory with new roads and new cities, a new mobility of people and ideas"; Blagg 1986, 215.

[31] See Chapter 10.

[32] These were not confined to Aricia. The expansion of healing sanctuaries in central Italy after 400 B.C.E. is well documented (Edlund 1985, 28; 1987, 131–2). For the healing at Aricia, see Chapters 10–12.

sanctuary at this point are genderless heads, hands, and feet, but some, including one of a woman's exposed intestines and others of the uterus, are female.[33] Though dating from a later period, medical instruments were also found in the sanctuary (Morpurgo 1931, 247). Much of its increasing reputation and wealth must surely have been connected with healing.[34]

That wealth had to be managed. It is a safe assumption that the sanctuary accepted tithes, income from property and other sources, and eventually also acted as a bank, as many temples and sanctuaries did.[35] New work on how temples functioned as financial institutions suggests ways in which the Arician elders could have used their sanctuary's income to the greater glory of the goddess.[36] Aricia, like Delphi, had an international clientele, so the foreign currency the sanctuary collected might have been used for preferential loans to favored families, in support of their international business deals. By the end of the second century B.C.E., money changing was a significant business at Aricia, which reflected both the sanctuary's popularity and the traffic on the

[33] The change in anatomical ex-votos (particularly those representing internal organs), as regards both their form and their prevalence and use, is probably related to the increase in formalized anatomical knowledge emanating first from the Hippocratic schools (which did not do human dissection) and then from Alexandria, where Herophilus of Chalcedon in the early third century was given special permission to dissect human bodies (von Staden 1989, 139–53). Even when divine aid is sought, the knowledge and theories of the doctors will affect petitioners' views of their illnesses. See Chapter 11 on the necessity for healing theories.

[34] Although marginally more ex-votos can be identified with women or women's bodies, the presence of male ex-votos and gender-nonspecific votives means there is no substantive evidence to suggest that the healing was oriented toward women or women's "problems" (cf. Blagg 1986, 214; Hänninen 2000, 49); See Chapter 10 for the votives and Chapter 6 for Diana Lucina.

[35] Cf. Bodei Giglioni 1997, 49–54, on offerings as a sources of temple wealth, and 54–8 on sanctuaries' practice of holding deposits.

[36] *Nummularii*, money changers who eventually became bankers, appear in an inscription at the sanctuary of Fortuna at Praeneste from the end of the second century (*ILLRP* 106a; Andreau 1999, 31, n. 8). This would have been about the *floruit* of Octavian's Arician great-grandfather (*proavus*). Certainly Octavian's enemies thought they could accuse him of being a *nummularius* (Suet. *Div. Aug.* 4). See J. Sosin, "Accounting and Endowments," *Tyche* 16 (2001): 161–75; "A Missing Woman: Hellenistic Leases from Thespiae Revisited," *Greek Roman and Byzantine Studies* 41 (2000): 47–58; and "Alexanders and Stephanephoroi at Delphi," *Classical Philology* 99 (2004): 191–208. All three are essential for understanding Hellenistic charitable endowments and temple investing. See Andreau 1999, 30–49, for an outline of banking in the Roman world.

Via Appia.[37] Because Aricia was very concerned with grain (by the first century the sanctuary had its own granaries), it is also possible that preferential loans were made to Arician grain merchants, some among them no doubt also elders of Diana's cult, to guarantee a stable price and adequate supplies of grain in the sanctuary.

From the charges made against Octavian's Arician ancestor (Suet. *Div. Aug.* 4), we know that by the late second century B.C.E., *unguentaria* – not perfume shops, in all likelihood, but the ancient equivalent of pharmacies, which dispensed ointments, bath preparations, and other medicaments[38] – and bakeries were a highly profitable feature of the sanctuary and in the city of Aricia as well, serving not only the pilgrims who came to seek help from Diana but also various other visitors, not all of whom were there for purely religious reasons. The businesses made money for the sanctuary and for those who ran them.

Their customers were the petitioners, suppliants, and worshippers who sought help from the goddess. Having received it, they left their offerings. That, too, created wealth. They came from every social class and from many places. A spearhead was dedicated by the nurse of the Papirian family (*Diana merito/noutrix Paperia*, "For Diana, with good cause, the nurse of the Paperian family [gave this]" *CIL* 1^2 45 = *ILL* 3235). She would have been a slave. From Ariminum in the mid- or late Republic came a city representative, C. Manlios Acidinos, to make a dedication recorded on a small bronze sheet on behalf of his people (*CIL* XIV 4269 = *ILL* 6128). Working men and artists also worshiped Diana. At the end of the second century B.C.E., the collegium of flute and tibia players dedicated a statue, the base of which has only recently come to light (Granino Cercere, 37–8 and fig. 2). Another statue was set up by C. Aurelius Cotta (*CIL* XIV 4268), praetor at Rome in 202 (Livy 30.26.11; 27.9).[39] Magistrates seemed to favor this sanctuary. A certain M. Livius, son of Marcus Livius, praetor (probably at Aricia or

---

[37] Cassius of Parma attacked the young Octavian, saying that he was the descendant (or grandson, *nepos* of a money changer with "dirty hands" (*manibus decoloratis*, Suet. *Div. Aug.* 4.2). In the ancient world, as later, individuals who handled money – and whose hands were discolored by contact with the coins – were a despised a class.

[38] See Chapters 10 and 11 for the discussion of sanctuary medicine at Aricia.

[39] So Granino Cercere (2000, 36) dates it; Pairault (1969, 441. n.2) assigns it to C. Aurelius Cotta, cos. 75 B.C.E.

Rome), left a dedication, the tufa base of which was rediscovered in the garden of the Palazzo Ruspoli at Nemi (CIL *XIV* 4268, Granino Cercere, 36). The spelling *praitor* and the letter formations point to a date at the end of the third or beginning of the second century B.C.E.

And then there was C. Terentius Lucanus, *monetalis* in 135–4 B.C.E. He had staged a funeral show with thirty pairs of gladiators for three consecutive days in the forum at Rome in honor of his grandfather who had adopted him. According to Pliny, he was the first person to have a picture made of a gladiatorial show, and he placed it in the grove of Diana (*NH* 35.52).[40] Terentius or his grandfather may have had a particular connection that determined the dedication in the sanctuary at Aricia, of course, but the ritual of the *rex* had a meaning that enriched and illuminated the tradition of gladiatorial combat as a funeral rite. In turn, the performance of the funeral gladiatorial combat at Rome and elsewhere highlighted the significance of the ritual. The openness to religious conversation with other rituals, other cults, other meanings of ritual acts seems to have been characteristic of the sanctuary in all eras.

There is a splendid archaizing bas-relief,[41] now at Copenhagen, showing the murder of a king by a young man, a scene generally identified as the murder of Aegisthus by Orestes.[42] The bas-relief was found in the Valle d'Ariccia, outside the sanctuary. This work of art was both a record and an exploration of the nature of the *rex*. In terms of its cultural meaning, it is unimportant whether it was a copy made of an

---

[40] Wiedemann (1992, 15) thinks that Terentius might have put the painting in the sanctuary of Diana on the Aventine, but this is not really possible. "Nemus Dianae" meant the grove at Aricia to Pliny's readers.

[41] *LIMC* I "Aigisthos" n. 50, 178. Poulsen's description (1951, no. 30, pp. 47–8) is by far the clearest and most informative. It is uncertain whether this is an original or a copy, although it is certainly archaizing; also uncertain are the names to be applied to the figures. The significance of this relief for the sanctuary is in the clear outline it presents of the archaic murder of a "great man." The outline's impressive adaptability is demonstrated by the variant identifications (all associated with murders in the house of Atreus). There is no compelling need to limit the identification to Aegisthus, or to the *rex*. It is an image of what both the myth and the ritual represent, and the names can be supplied as appropriate to time and circumstance. The figures of Orestes and Iphigenia are discussed later in Chapter 8.

[42] For example, by Pairault 1969, 450; Haffner 1967; also *I Dianas Hellige Lund* 1997, 132, and Ascani 1997, 178; *LIMC* "Aigisthos" 50.

actual cult relief or an archaizing original made for a private individual; nor does it matter whether it originally came from the sanctuary or merely reflected the sanctuary's proximity. Dedications, whether works of art or ancient *bondieuserie*, were set up in the sanctuary and given a more specific meaning by the rituals there. The dedicators, as well as subsequent visitors who observed their offerings, learned about the rituals, saw the ways in which the rituals could be understood, and took that knowledge away with them to the world outside the sanctuary.

THE SANCTUARY THROUGH THE LATE REPUBLIC

In the archaic age, unadorned Nature had been all the community of Arician and Latin worshippers needed as sacred space for Diana. Once the gold-roofed temple had been built, and had brought renewed wealth and importance to the sanctuary of the middle to late Republic (App. *B.C.* 5.24), popularity began to have its costs. Nature on her own could no longer handle the flood of pilgrims, curiosity seekers, and the sick in need of help. At some time during the second and first centuries B.C.E., those who controlled the sanctuary were forced to find new ways to contextualize the goddess' rituals. Diana's sacred space required reorganization.

So in the late Republic we find another dramatic change introduced into the sanctuary, the massive construction of a terraced precinct surrounded on three sides by arcaded revetment walls and open toward the lake.[43] This new precinct had a total area of about 44,000 square

---

[43] It was once thought that an outlet for the lake was bored through the crater wall to control the water level at the time when the first temple was built, but this is no longer considered probable; Morpurgo 1903, 344; Lenzi 2000, 157. As Zahle notes (1997, 169), there is no objective way to date the *emissarium*. As a structure, it could have been built at any time between the fourth century B.C.E. and the first century C.E. Because the construction projects at the end of the fourth century imply successful use of that land, it has made sense to some to date the *emissarium* to the same period (cf. Coarelli 1987, 167). Guldager Bilde, however, is certain the *emissarium* is late Republican (personal communication). Whatever its date, or the purpose of its construction, the *emissarium* did in fact control the lake level and prevented the flooding of the road and the lower sanctuary.

meters.[44] A portico was built, running parallel with the walls most of the way, with an open corridor between. Its style is unmistakably that of the Hellenistic religious architecture appearing in sanctuaries across central Italy at that time. Within the terrace another rectangular structure, called building K (and originally identified as a temple), was also built, perhaps at this time,[45] as well as a small theater (Morpurgo 1931, 237–51), baths (*CIL* XIV 4190), a pool (Morpurgo 1903, 311–12), and a granary (*CIL* XIV 4190). The granaries must have been among those Marius captured at Aricia in 87 when he was trying to stop all grain supplies from reaching Rome (App. *B.C.* 1.69). The sanctuary had become almost a small city in itself now, something far from the wildness in which the huntress Diana had once been worshipped.

In pure nature we must expect close ties between the divine and his or her chosen place of epiphany and worship. But when man enters into nature, the forms change and become subjected to the rules established by man. From then on, man has two ways in which to proceed. One is to conceive of nature as the physical expression of the human mind. . . . Nature is as wild as man's emotions will permit . . . [the other is when] man incorporates nature into his sphere of daily activities, agriculture, husbandry, and trade.

Edlund 1987, 35

The Aricians were compelled to find a way to demonstrate that nature was something that could be re-created through human activity rather than destroyed by it.

The whole complex is considered as an organised construction project, where temples, porticoes, monumental stairs and other forms of access are planned together as an architectural whole. The complex will thus bear the stamp of a trained mind in that the architect uses sophisticated modules or geometric figures to structure the relationship between the buildings and their individual components. The whole design is held together by such governing architectural principles as axiality, symmetry and frontality. Architecture is moreover

---

[44] Morpurgo 1928; Gordon 1934, 5; Blagg 1985, 35–6; Blagg 1986, 216. For the clearest and most recent report with photographs, reconstructions, and (most important) plans, see Ghini, 2000.

[45] This is a most problematic structure. If it were a temple (which is quite uncertain), it is unlikely to have been the principal temple to Diana; Morpurgo 1903, 307–11.

the means whereby the religious experience of the visitor is guided; it is also what manipulates the feelings of the pious.

Guldager Bilde 1997c, 181–2

Their goddess was Diana Nemorensis, Diana of the woodland. Where, in all this Hellenistic architecture, was her wild wood, her forest? Necessarily, the emphasis in the sanctuary must shift to *symbolic* wildness and landscaped naturalism. Servius Auctus makes a famous distinction between *lucus, nemus,* and *silva,* defining *nemus* as *vero composita multitudo arborum* ("a multitude of trees indeed artfully disposed," *ad Aen.* 1.310[46]). Whether Servius was speaking only of Diana's *nemus* or, more generally, the woodland had to become a landscaped forest. Thus, the *nemus* stood in contrast to *silva,* which was *diffusa et inculta,* "scattered and untended." Regardless of whether Servius is to be believed on linguistic grounds, the *nemus* of Diana was compelled to become that very paradox he described, a cultivated wildness. Along with the grove of trees, we should also remember the mazelike hedgerows mentioned by Ovid (*Fast.* 3.267–8). High green hedges along the paths can still be found near the site of the sanctuary, and to walk among them is a salutary reminder of just how effective such symbolic natural features are at creating that separation from the ordinary and the sense of being lost in nature.

In this way Diana's sanctuary, although formalized and Hellenized, could still engage a large crowd of people in a religious experience which, despite its formal arrangement, was able to manifest a necessary wildness. Such symbolic representations shaped cultural definitions of wildness and were shaped by them in turn. As we shall see, beyond the artful tending of the grove, the sanctuary had begun to symbolize

---

[46] Malaspina 2000, 146–7, argues that Servius Auctus *ad Aen.* 1.310, in defining a *nemus* as "a multitude of trees indeed carefully disposed," must be wrong and that *nemus,* on the contrary, must mean specifically the forests of Latium. Malaspina's argument depends on the ancients exhibiting a modern philological consistency. The point to notice is that the line in the *Aeneid* that inspires Servius' comment describes as a *nemus* the place in which Venus appears to Aeneas in the guise of a huntress, and clearly that is the appropriate place for a huntress-goddess to manifest herself. For the many ways in which both Venus and Dido appear as Diana figures, see Dyson 2001, 148–67.

wildness with an increasing emphasis on wildness as barbarism. The greatest and most enduring symbol of wildness in the sanctuary was then, and always, the *rex nemorensis*.

THE END OF THE REPUBLIC AND THE POLITICIZATION OF THE SANCTUARY

By the end of the Republic, Diana was worshipped in a notably wealthy, Hellenistic-style sanctuary. It attracted many people and (this is most important) satisfied them to the degree that they made the offerings on which the sanctuary's wealth ultimately rested.[47] Preservation in time of trouble — war or natural disasters — was a particular reason for dedications. The Abbaitae and Epictetes, two peoples in central Anatolia, on the border of Mysia and Phrygia, made a bilingual dedication, in Latin and Greek (*CIL* XIV 2218; Coarelli 1987, 179; Granino Cercere 2000, 38), of a statue of C. Salluuius Naso, one of Lucullus' legates, in gratitude for his protection during the Mithradatic war. Gaius Voconius C.f. and Lucius [probably] Licinius L.f. together made a dedication at the sanctuary (now lost, *CIL* XIV 2222, Coarelli 1987, 178–9). The Voconii were Arician noblemen (Cic. *Phil.* 3.6. 16), and this Voconius commanded Lucullus' fleet that had nearly been destroyed in a terrible storm (Plut. *Luc.* 13.2–3); Licinius was another of Lucullus' legates.

At the same time as these greater events were taking place, ordinary people who traveled south from Rome on the Via Appia stopped at Aricia in lodgings (Horace on his way to Brundisium stayed at Aricia in a *hospitium modicum*, *Sat.* 5.1–2). Those with money began to buy or build their own villas in the region.[48] Aricia and the area around the sanctuary had become an immensely popular retreat from the city, with villas springing up everywhere (Ovid, *AA* 1.259; Lenzi 2000, 157), on the outer and inner slopes of the crater, on the rim, and surely on the promontory overlooking the sanctuary where the medieval and modern town of Nemi was settled. Among those who appreciated the

[47] The Capitoline temple, and those at Antium, Lanuvium, and Nemi, were in Appian's day (second century C.E.) still the wealthiest sanctuaries (App. *B.C.* 5.24).

[48] For Roman villas in the Alban Hills, see Chiarucci 2000.

beauty of the hills and lake was Julius Caesar, whose sister had married an Arician, M. Atius Balbus. The Atii were a wealthy family, and some of their wealth derived from the manufactury that supplied the tiles for all this new building in the sanctuary (Guldager Bilde 1997, 168–9). While Caesar was in Gaul, he commissioned a villa to be built at Nemi. When he saw this splendid new villa, however, "because the whole had not met his expectations, he wholly destroyed it"[49] (*quia non tota ad animum ei responderat totam diruisse*[50]).

As the villa was under construction that spring and summer of 50 B.C.E.,[51] Caesar could not have returned to Rome to see it before the morning he crossed the Rubicon in 49. His first view of it, then, and the razing of it to the ground, occurred sometime after Pharsalia. What had happened to change his mind so dramatically about a villa at Nemi?[52] If the villa had simply displeased him, he could have sold it. He did not. He removed every trace of it, and thus of his potential presence there. The explanation for this ruthless and complete destruction is not far to seek. Diana's precinct, for all that it was thick with buildings and crowded with people, preserved and celebrated wildness in one way that presented enormous difficulties for the new dictator-for-life, the victor over Pompey. The ritual of the *rex nemorensis*, the king who

---

[49] Suet. *Div. Jul.* 46; it was paid for with money lent by Pompey to Atticus who then lent it to Caesar, much to Pompey's irritation, Cic. *ad Att.* 6.1.25 (Shackleton Bailey 115). Pia Guldager Bilde is now excavating a villa in the crater about which she says the following: "There is hardly any doubt about the villa being torn down to socle level sometime between ca. 50 BC and the late Augustan period" (personal communication). I am pleased to have this opportunity to thank Dr. Guldager Bilde for her generosity in answering my inquiries and to express my pleasure that she is continuing this important excavation. She goes on to indicate the possibility that the entire Suetonius story was a fabrication, perhaps reflecting Augustus' later destruction of the villa. As should be evident, I am not persuaded that Caesar was indifferent to the implications of the close connection with the *rex nemorensis*. The identification of the villa as Caesar's, if it can be sustained, will be as important as the dating. Much more will be known about these and other questions when the results of this ongoing excavation are published.

[50] This is so elegantly phrased, so beautifully balanced, so clear and simple on the surface, yet so nuanced, and ultimately opaque when read carefully, that it is reasonable to identify it as a direct quotation from Caesar himself. The architectural meaning of *respondeo* "to be aligned with" (*OLD s.v. respondeo* 12c) *ad animum ei responderat* is particularly worthy of note, but the deliberate violence of *diruisse* must not be overlooked.

[51] Cicero's letter is dated to 20 February of that year.

[52] Although Romans are not often exact about specifying place, it does seem likely that he was building his villa as near the sanctuary as possible.

killed his predecessor in mortal combat – and who would in turn be killed by his successor – was still there, the central symbol of the power of wildness, and the wildness of power, in the now otherwise very civilized sanctuary.

We cannot know where the *rex* lived in the sanctuary or what functions he performed beyond the terrible ritual by which he was initiated to his priesthood.[53] The more hidden he was, the more he became the sacred "wild man" of Aricia and the more he was able to attract the hopes and fears about the power of a king in popular imagination. Yet the ritual somehow had made him so emphatically a part of the meaning of the cult that Caesar, the fugitive and challenger who had fought Pompey, the ruling (if not reigning) Roman, to the death, could not have a villa overlooking the sanctuary and hope that his enemies would fail to use the symbolism of this other *rex* against him. So the villa was destroyed, and on the Ides of March the victorious challenger was indeed himself challenged – to the death. The point would not be lost on his heir, Octavian, who had not only an Arician villa but also an Arician mother.

The strange barbarism of the *rex*, who was always present but seems to have led a fairly secretive existence in the *nemus*, was heightened by the well-to-do suburban context of the sanctuary in the late Republic. According to Ovid, one aspect of the sanctuary's fascination was the sharp contrast between the inherent wildness of what the sanctuary celebrated and the now civilized surroundings of the sanctuary itself. With so many Roman villas around it, it was not just civilized; it was "suburban."

> Ecce suburbanae templum nemorale Dianae
> Partaque per gladios regna nocente manu:
>
> *AA*, 259–60

Behold the woodland temple of Suburban Diana, and the kingdom obtained through swords by a hurtful hand.

The hiddenness of the *rex nemorensis* is suggested by Ovid's careful metonomy; only his hand, hurtful but also guilty, appears in the text.

---

[53] See Chapter 7 for discussion of the ritual and its meaning.

The hand is the king; the woods are his kingdom. The *rex* himself is not mentioned. It is as though he could not be seen, as though he were a wild animal, sighted here and there through the trees, perhaps by the gleam of a sword. Caesar understood the implications of the *rex*, the more dangerous because he was hidden and could not be confronted directly. After his defeat of Pompey had given the title *rex* new and terrible significance for Rome, Caesar destroyed (so he hoped, no doubt) every connection that might be made between himself and that ghastly priest. As he tried, and failed, to create a monarchy out of the tatters of the Republic, he had every reason to respond to those who greeted him: "he was 'Caesar,' not 'King'" (*Caesarem se, non regem esse* Suet. *Div. Jul.* 59.2).

Cicero was quite another kind of man. None of Caesar's subtlety or poetic intuition troubled him. Two months after Julius Caesar's murder, Brutus suggested (the sarcasm and mockery are unmistakable) a meeting at Nemi between L. Caesar (a distant cousin of the dictator) and Cicero. Rather embarrassed, L. Caesar passed the message along with an apologetic addendum inviting Cicero to name an alternative meeting place and making it clear it was all Brutus' idea. Cicero reports all this to Atticus, surprised, but receptive to the idea that the great conspirator has him in mind.

ecce autem de traverso L. Caesar ut veniam ad se rogat in Nemus aut scribam quo se venire velim; Bruto enim placere se a me conveniri. o rem odiosam et inexplicabilem!

Ad Att. 15.4 = Shackleton Bailey, 382[54]

And now unexpectedly L. Caesar asks me to visit him in the Grove or to write and name my own meeting place – he says Brutus thinks I ought to meet him. A damnable situation, and no way out of it.

Yet even Cicero, touchingly eager to believe that others shared his high seriousness and estimation of his own importance, responds with *o rem odiosam et inexplicabilem!* Two Latin phrases are revealing: *de traverso,*

---

[54] The text of Cicero's letters to Atticus is that of Shackleton Bailey throughout, the translation my own. Brutus' naming Nemi as the meeting place for Cicero and L. Caesar surely sprang from the assassin's scorn for the man who wanted the assassination but could never have contemplated carrying it out. L. Caesar and Cicero were both quite safe at Nemi.

a phrase that means "from the side" or "from an unexpected quarter," and *inexplicabilem* – an adjective that describes places "from which one cannot find a way out, labyrinthine."[55] They reflect, if on the wrong emotional register, the connection with Diana's sanctuary, with the mysterious and complex approaches of her "paths," and the ambushes that occur there. *Rem odiosam* also hints at the shadow of the *rex*, and the murder of Caesar thus invoked by Brutus' choice of place. The meeting in itself has nothing to inspire the reaction *rem odiosam*, and indeed, Cicero's indecision (*puto me ergo iturum et inde Romam, nisi quid mutaro*; "So I suppose I shall go, and from there on to Rome unless I change my mind") on the matter, from the context of the other letters at the same time, has more to do with his friends' repeated and emphatic warnings to stay away from Rome[56] than any distaste for the proposed meeting.[57] His response would be witty had he not been deaf to the black humor of Brutus' original suggestion. The allusions provided by the sanctuary perform for him at a purely literary level, as ornament for a discussion of politics as usual. To take the allusion on a religious level would be superstition, and Cicero is truly free of that vice. To him, Diana's grove was a place, no more, no less. In this he proves that he was more of a philosopher and less of a poet than Caesar.

In the next year, 43 B.C.E., the moneyer P. Accoleius Lariscolus, an Arician, was responsible for the minting of a denarius that celebrates the triple Diana of the sanctuary on the reverse, with a bust of Diana on the obverse.[58] The bust may be a copy of an archaic cult statue. The triple Diana on the reverse wears a chiton with an unusual, and unmistakably archaic, drape across the front. It surely reproduces an important statue group at Aricia. The original may have been a genuine

---

[55] *OLD s.v. inexplicabilis* 1b.
[56] Cf. *ad Att.* 15.3 (Shackleton Bailey, 380); *ad Att.* 15.7 (Shackleton Bailey, 383), with Varro's warning; *ad Att.* 15.8 (Shackleton Bailey 385), the threatened attacks on Cicero's house at Tusculum.
[57] Cicero is a rationalist, and he is clearly using the allusion as a good writer would, without responding to it in any way personally or politically.
[58] The definitive work on this coin is that of Alföldi, 1960. For a full discussion, see Chapter 4.

archaic work, or a later, archaizing creation. The goddess on the left is holding a bow, the goddess on the right a poppy, and the goddess in the center has a mantel over her shoulder. In the prototype each of the two figures on the left places her right hand on the hip of the one next to her. Inferior die cutters, unable to cope with the detail, simply raised the three goddesses' arms at the elbow, scissor fashion. The three are joined by a bar at neck level, and behind them rises a grove of cypress trees, always a symbol of death and the underworld.

The coin cannot tell us for certain what the cult image looked like, nor can it confirm or refute the existence of an archaic statue. In this uncertainty, we should not, however, overlook what the coin *does* tell us. The archaic bust on the obverse *claimed* antiquity, whether it was a legitimate survivor from the archaic period or not. The triple Diana shows how the old characteristics of natural wildness were being recast in a more threatening image of social wildness, of barbarism. Strabo (5.3.12): "They say that the sacred image of the Arician goddess is a copy of the one from Tauropolos. And in fact, a somewhat barbarian and Scythian element predominates in the temple customs." The elders of the sanctuary – perhaps beginning in the third century, when the gold-roofed temple was built – actively cultivated visual and mythological connections with barbarism, with the Scythians, so much so that – as Strabo indicates – she was familiarly known as "Scythian Diana," and that this epithet referred to her nature particularly in her sanctuary at Aricia (Ovid, *Met.* 14.331; Lucan, *BC* 1.446; 3.86; 7.776). This Scythian nature had to have been illustrated by some image, the purported to be "from Tauropolos," as Strabo said. The more we suppose that the triple Diana was an archaizing creation of the late Republic, the more we must acknowledge that the association with barbarism was an intentional construct of the sanctuary leaders. In the high noon of late Republican religious organization, with its complex of buildings and pilgrims and profitable finance, the aspects of Diana's cult made known to the world on a Roman denarius are those stressing the archaic tradition, the wildness, and the barbarism of the goddess.

Yet Scythian Diana was also Ovid's "Suburban" Diana (*AA* 1.259). The striking contradictions between a real or imagined barbarism and the complex civilization of a Hellenistic-style sanctuary, all flanked by tiers of expensive Roman villas, served Diana's religious purposes. The message of these contradictions must not be overlooked, and particularly we cannot ignore the sophisticated manipulation of cultural as well as religious icons in the sanctuary that this indicates. A year after Caesar's death, Accoleius chose to advance Aricia's patron goddess, in all her archaic and barbaric glory, on a Roman denarius. We can conclude that there were many in his audience who were intensely aware of the sanctuary's cult, including the ritual of the *rex* and its potential meanings, and understood this increasing religious identification with barbarism. Equally, there were many in Accoleius' audience who, although aware, remained unimpressed, and there would also have been some who took no notice at all. Nevertheless, despite Cicero's rather touching obliviousness to the issues at stake, Caesar's assassination had already guaranteed that the rituals of the sanctuary, and particularly those of Diana's *rex nemorensis*, would now be irrevocably elevated to the level of an ambiguous and dangerous religious commentary on autocratic power.

What Caesar, Cicero, and P. Accoleius Lariscolus give us is a brief glimpse of how the sanctuary was received at this critical point in Roman history. The priest and his ritual were well known, and the sanctuary's "wildness" and "barbarism" were clearly part of that received image. The stronger our belief that the triple statue group was a later imaginative substitution for a nonexistent archaic statue, the more we must acknowledge the degree to which the image of barbarism was a strategic choice made by the sanctuary elders. Cicero, Caesar, and Accoleius certainly all grasped the rudiments of this theology of divine barbarism, worked out through an understood religious symbolism (no longer the reality) of the forest, the priest-king, and the cosmology of the hunting goddess. Such a reading and reinterpretation of the goddess and her rituals cannot have been a recent development.

So the building of the temple around 300 B.C.E. had marked not only the beginning of a shift in the nature of the sanctuary and the ways in which that nature was given religious meaning but it also symbolized the extraordinary adaptability of the cult and its ability to respond to needs and crises of the time without becoming detached from its essential nature.[59] By means of continued building the elders had made their sanctuary even more significant on the stage of Roman history. In the aftermath of Caesar's murder, the sanctuary once again offered an all-too-obvious gloss on the nature of regal power. This politically and ideologically dangerous religious inheritance was something with which Caesar's heir – Octavian, the son of an Arician mother – would inevitably have to come to terms.

[59] Cf. North 1989, 176, on this strength of Latin religion.

2

THE SANCTUARY IN THE AUGUSTAN AGE

OCTAVIAN'S "ARICIAN MOTHER"

At some point during the last days of the Republic or the very beginning of the Augustan period, a certain M. Servilius Quartus caused an
ala, a room set into the north portico of the sanctuary (room A [Savile],
room 5 [Guldager Bilde], also known as the Fundilia Room), to be
ornamented for Diana. It was an elegant dedication. The room was
floored with a black-and-white mosaic and had an inscription naming
Servilius as the donor of what was placed there (*CIL* XIV 4183).[1] As
there is no patronymic, Servilius was probably a wealthy *libertus*, a freed
slave. He was certainly rich, and he was also important, for his *ala* was
no out-of-the-way corner and the decoration must have been impressive. His dedication elevated Servilius the *libertus* into the company of
senatorial families such as the Voconii and Aurelii Cottae and eques-
trian élite such as the Atii. This showy presence of rich freedmen like
Servilius in the sanctuary was going to become a part of the vitriolic
political attacks on Caesar's successor, Octavian.

Octavian was heir to Caesar's name and all that meant in terms
of influence with powerful armies in the field and powerful men in
Rome. Because of the name, he was also heir to Caesar's enemies.
To this formidable opposition he rather quickly added the enmity of
Antony, who had every interest in weakening Octavian's claim to be a
worthy heir to the dictator. In Cicero's *Philippics* we catch an oblique

---

[1] The clearest description and summary of the finds in this room is Guldager Bilde 2000,
98–102. For a good reproduction of the original sketch of Servilius's mosaic inscription
and a discussion of the dating, see Bombardi 2000, 121–4.

glimpse of the way in which Antony used Octavian's Arician ancestry to accomplish this end. These attacks in turn tell us something about the reputation of the sanctuary as the city's defining institution.

Ignobilitatem obicit C. Caesaris filio, cuius etiam natura pater, si vita suppeditasset, consul factus esset. "Aricina mater." Trallianam aut Ephesiam putes dicere.... Quamquam huius sanctissimae feminae atque optimae pater, M. Atius Balbus, in primis honestus, praetorius fuit... qui autem evenit, ut tibi Iulia natus ignobilis videatur, cum tu eodem materno genere soleas gloriari? Quae porro amentia est eum dicere aliquid de uxorum ignobilitate, cuius pater Numitoriam Fregellanam, proditoris filiam, habuerit uxorem, ipse ex libertini filia susceperit liberos?

Phil. 3.6. 15–17

He [Antony] taunts the son of Gaius Caesar with his low birth, a man whose natural father, had he lived, would have been made consul. "His mother is an Arician." You would think he was saying she was from Ephesus or Tralles.... And yet, this most devout and excellent woman's father, M. Atius Balbus, a particularly honorable man, was an ex-praetor.... how does it come about that one born from a Julia seems to you low-born, when you are accustomed to boast about the same maternal ancestry? Besides, what madness is it that a man remarks on the low birth of wives, when his father married Numitoria of Fregellae, the daughter of a traitor, and he himself has acknowledged his children by the daughter of a freedman?

Aricina mater. That was the phrase Antony had used to wound, and it implied low birth – that is, not just the middle-class obscurity of a municipal family but something more like the obscurity of *liberti*, men and women such as M. Servilius Quartus, whose past was the impenetrable blankness of slavery. Cicero's refutation is carefully constructed. Antony's attack, he says, was absurdly like calling Atia a foreigner (*Trallianam aut Ephesiam*[2]). Next he praises Atia's virtue and notes the high standing[3] and the official distinctions of her father, M. Atius Balbus – he had been praetor and would have been consul (as

---

[2] These towns may not have been chosen at random. The Atii owned tile works that supplied the sanctuary and no doubt also produced much pottery there. Tralles was particularly well known for its pottery (Pliny *NH* 35.161). Ephesus, of course, was famous for its temple to Artemis.

[3] As Wiseman (1965), 334, observes, the fact that Cicero does not name any ancestors who achieved public office indicates that Suet. (*Div. Aug.* 4.1) must have been wrong to suppose that M. Atius Balbus had senatorial ancestors. If there had been any such, Cicero would have mentioned them at this point.

Caesar's nephew, his election could not have been in doubt). Cicero then goes on the attack. Antony claimed descent from the Julian clan. The implication is that it was the Julian clan that Antony was reviling, and Atia's claim to Julian ancestry, unlike Antony's, was impeccable. In any case, Cicero ends nastily, Antony was in no position to cast aspersions when his own father had married a "traitor's daughter" (*proditoris filiam* – this is all that is known about her), and he himself had acknowledged children by a freedman's daughter.

Cicero's attack is largely made on a *tu quoque* basis: pot is calling kettle black. That is helpful to us, for it gives a more specific sense of the social implications contained in *Aricina mater*. If Cicero emphasized Octavian's Julian connections, then Antony's original attack had obviously been shaped in a competitive spirit, to show who was more truly "Julian." If Cicero reminded people of Antony's stepmother Numitoria, "daughter of a traitor," then Antony will likewise have dredged up long-standing Atian family connections with "a traitor," a reference that certainly recalls their conservative alliances with Pompey (Suet. *Div. Aug.* 4.1). If Cicero's final counterattack (and therefore the one that he wishes to remain most vivid in people's minds) is that Antony had acknowledged children by the daughter of a freedman, then Antony must have charged either directly or indirectly that Atia was a freedman's daughter.

Where Cicero is oblique, Suetonius is explicit (*Div. Aug.* 4.2). Antony, he says, disparaged the *maternam Augusti originem*, the maternal ancestry of Augustus, by throwing in Octavian's teeth a great-grandfather of African birth who kept, first, a dispensary of herbal remedies, and then a bakery, at Aricia. This supposed African ancestry, no doubt, is what drove Cicero to mock the implication that as an Arician, Atia was a woman of "foreign" stock. Suetonius goes on to cite another attack along similar lines made by Cassius of Parma, a contemporary and open opponent of Octavian. As Cassius repeated the charge of "ancestor with a bakery" (Suet. *Div. Aug.* 4.2), it obviously had great appeal, even if not great truth. As Cassius' attack shows, however, the more serious charge at the time was that Octavian's ancestor was a *nummularius*, a money changer. *Nummularii* were in general slaves who assayed coins, although it is possible that at this early period the term may sometimes have been applied to the bankers who owned such slaves.[4] Cassius' rather complicated attack[5] plays on the importance of the businesses of grain dealing, baking, and money changing at Aricia. The attack is made more hostile by the implications of slave or freedman status attached to each occupation.[6]

Was Atius a freedman like Servilius, or a freedman's son? Would the patrician family of C. Julius Caesar have allowed their daughter to marry so far beneath her? It would not have been impossible. If we are to believe Cicero, Antony himself had made such a marriage. In the 90s and 80s, Caesar and his family had been in need of money; from time immemorial aristocratic females have made declassé alliances to recoup the family fortunes.[7] It is far more likely, however, that the Atii were Arician businessmen with international connections – and in the process of making these connections they may well have married non-Italians, or even the odd ex-slave. The family finances would have been based on a wide range of businesses, particularly those associated with the sanctuary, among which were the tile manufactury, grain imports, various shops, and banking interests.

Nevertheless, what Antony's *Aricina mater* hinted at was not a family of businessmen so much as former servile status, something that a scrap of evidence in Macrobius makes absolutely clear.

Octavius, qui natu nobilis videbatur, Ciceroni recitanti ait: *non audio quae dicis.* ille respondit: *certe solebas bene foratas habere aures.* Hoc eo dictum quia Octavius Libys oriundo dicebatur, quibus mos est aurem forare.

Macrob. *Sat.* 7.3.7[8]

---

[4] The evidence for the late Republic and Augustan period is not clear, but *nummularii* seem to have been slaves who were responsible for assaying coins (Andreau 19–20), which clearly constitutes the grounds for Cassius' slander.

[5] Discussed in detail Chapter 11.

[6] Nerulo, this ancestor's place of origin, probably lay west of Thurii/Sybaris and on the road that connected Sybaris with the western coast of Italy (*Barrington*, 46, C2). The ancestor must be the source of the young Gaius Octavius' cognomen *Thurinus* (Suet. *Div. Aug.* 7.1). According to Suetonius Antony said, further, that Octavian's great-grandfather was a freedman and a rope maker from the area around Thurii, and that his grandfather was a money changer (*Div. Aug.* 2.3). Suetonius suggests that the cognomen came from the Thurian ancestor, or as an alternative, that Thurii was where Augustus' father had won a dispute over some runaway slaves just after his son was born. Note how unfortunately this connects the family, once again, with slaves.

[7] Cf. Gruen, 118–19, on Caesar's policy of surrounding himself with wealthy Italian magnates and marrying off his sisters to equestrians.

[8] The text of Macrobius is that of Willis throughout.

Thus Octavius, who seemed to be of noble birth, said to Cicero, as the latter was reading aloud: "I can't hear what you are saying," to which the other replied: "Yet you certainly used to have nicely pierced ears" – the point of the gibe being that Octavius was said to be of Libyan extraction, and it is a custom of the Libyans to pierce their ears.

Macrobius will have found this scene in some source contemporary with Cicero – possibly in a letter, now lost, either from Cicero himself or from one of his *familiares*. The source was favorable to the orator, whose dignity is offended and who produces a clever riposte on the spur of the moment; it was hostile to Octavian, who is portrayed as a teenager with an attitude. The essence of Cicero's gibe, however, is what concerns us. Pierced ears may or may not have been a Libyan (i.e., North African) custom, but in Rome it was generally acknowledged as a characteristic of slaves from Africa or the east.[9] That is the point of Cicero's snub to the arrogant youth – his Arician/African connection implied a servile ancestor. Even almost five centuries later, this earned Octavian a deprecating *natu nobilis videbatur* ("he *seemed* to be of noble birth") from Macrobius, who in this way left it open to the reader to suppose otherwise.[10]

Of course, coming from a Latin town did not, in the ordinary way of things, imply that one was of slave extraction. This was something peculiar to Aricia and specifically connected with the sanctuary. As we have seen, the kind of barbarism suggested by "Scythian Diana" had come to be connected with the ideas of "uncivilized foreigner" or even "slave" as a way of maintaining the essential wildness of the sanctuary in contrast to its ever more urbanized physical presence. Foreignness and the association with slavery would have been reinforced by certain

[9] Note the speech of the *libertinus* born on the Euphrates in Juv. 1.103–9. Cf. Leclant (253 and n. 69) on the possibility that there was an enclave of Egyptians at Aricia.

[10] Of course, the entire exchange may have been a fabrication. Still, the instantaneous response and the biting wit and play on words are characteristic of an orator who is practiced in responding to political heckling from the crowd – and who *enjoys* it. Coming from Cicero, it is utterly convincing. Such political conditions ended with the Republic. Whether fabrication or fact, however, it accurately represents the nature of the problem Octavian faced in having an Arician mother. Note that the slave connection is African, and thus associated with grain, rather than the Thurian rope-making paternal ancester of Cassius' attacks.

factors that were simply incidental to the management of religious affairs. Leclant (253 and n. 69) has argued that there was an enclave of Egyptians at Aricia, and the granaries in the sanctuary suggest that the Aricians had substantial interests in African grain imports, which would explain such an enclave. A highly visible (because wealthy) group of African businessmen resident there would easily have led to the charges that Octavian had an "African" ancestor. As we shall see, the making of images in bread or cake was an important part of the treatment at the sanctuary. The granaries supplied the bakeries. The existence of *unguentaria*, dispensaries of medicaments, in and near a healing sanctuary does not need explanation.[11] Nor does the existence of money changers, who would have been needed by the sanctuary in their dealings with the grain suppliers, as a convenience for pilgrims, and for the general management of financial resources, often international in nature.

Bakeries, *unguentaria*, and money changing also imply the presence of educated slaves, who would normally run such businesses. Most cities with important healing sanctuaries will have had similar institutions, all operated by slaves, and streets or areas of town known to be inhabited by certain groups of foreigners. Certainly they all had resident rich *liberti*. Diana's sanctuary seems to have particularly encouraged ex-slaves to find some kind of self-identification in its rituals, however, and to have honored their contributions openly. The *rex nemorensis* in the sanctuary was the decisive factor in shaping Aricia's reputation as the place where ex-slaves lived. As a symbol, he was a reminder of the equation between slavery, wildness, and barbarism. Yet the barbarism of civil war, the barbaric deaths of Pompey and Caesar, as well as those of the conspirators, and the continuing conflict between Antony and Octavian, all *could* be seen in the context of Aricia's most famous priest, he who slew the previous priest-king and who would in turn be slain by his successor. Aricia: the name alone and in itself carried an enormous weight of meaning. It is not in the least surprising that Octavian's enemies chose to exploit his Arician family connections to the fullest.

---

[11] Many small unguent bottles, mostly of glass (and also called *unguentaria*) have been found in the sanctuary (Tatton-Brown 1983, 68–9).

APOLLO AND DIANA, ROME AND ARICIA

Although Cicero had been among those who were willing to make Aricia a problem for Octavian, he had also pointed out the way to manage it. Octavian could not, and should not, avoid the maternal Arician connection, but should use it rather to his advantage. This should not, ideally, include borrowing money on the strength of it, as Octavian had already done to finance his army after Philippi (App. *B.C.* 5.24).[12] Such a loan only drew attention to his potentially disgraceful financial connections with the sanctuary. Octavian required something more appropriate to his image as the descendant of a semidivine uncle.

Diana was Apollo's sister. Arician Diana already had – borrowed from Greek Artemis – a resident mythical brother-sister pair in Iphigenia and Orestes (Strabo 5.3.12; Ovid *Met.* 15.488–90; Serv. *ad Aen.* 1.116 and 11.226; Hyginus 61; see Chapter 8). At Rome, Octavian's family could benefit from such a mythical brother-sister relationship as well. Ghedini (1988) has pointed out that a vase in St. Petersburg shows Octavian as Apollo, Octavia as Diana, and Livia as Aphrodite (with a little Cupid hunting butterflies), and she argues it should be understood that Octavia/Diana is blessing the union of Octavian and Livia. Octavian's identification with Apollo allowed him to claim Diana as his sister, and Latona, as his mother.[13] *Aricina mater* indeed!

As Apollo was to Diana, so Rome was to Aricia, and so Octavian was to his sister and mother. In Vergil's line, *casta faue Lucina: tuus iam regnat Apollo* ("Chaste Lucina, be gracious: your Apollo now reigns," *Ecl.* 4.10), Lucina, according to Servius (*ad Ec.* 4.10), is referring to Octavia. Lucina *could* be either Diana or Juno but as Apollo is "hers" (*tuus . . . Apollo*), the compliment must at one level be meant to equate Augustus' sister Octavia with Diana as sister to Apollo. Certainly Octavian's identification with Apollo and all that was Apolline has many other sources and many other purposes beyond escaping the calumny surrounding Atia's Arician background. Nevertheless,

---

[12] There was a famine at Rome at the time (App. *B.C.* 5.18), and that also may have moved Octavian to go to Aricia to get help from their granaries as well as their treasure chests.

[13] Cf. Zanker's analysis (1990, 63–5, and fig. 50) of the elegant relief (ca. 30 B.C.E.) of Apollo with his sister, Diana, and mother, Latona, at a sacrifice.

40

the more he presented himself as Apollo, the more he gained interpretive authority over the religious symbolism of Diana's sanctuary,
even as he escaped being defined by it.

Diana was already a Roman goddess associated with supreme hegemony (Livy 1.45). Accordingly, Octavian had celebrated his victories
over Sextus Pompeius and Antony at Actium by issuing gold aurei
with a bust of Diana on the obverse.[14] Augustus' daughter Julia was
the model for the portrait of Diana on a denarius of 13 B.C.E., a date
that corresponded with her return from a journey to the east where
she was honored as the new Artemis.[15] Wherever Apollo/Augustus
was, his family members – sister Octavia, wife Livia, daughter Julia –
could also be, his lovely imperial satellites. The symbolic range of this
divine family was remarkable. Diana coins had been a part of Roman
numismatic iconography for a long time and would long continue
to be so.[16] Octavian, with his connection to Arician Diana, simply
adopted this established symbol for his own needs.

OCTAVIAN AND THE BONES OF ORESTES

However, this appropriation of Diana is best confirmed by one magnificent and innovative action that Octavian took, probably soon after
Actium, which altered the entire relationship between Rome and
Aricia and between the *rex nemorensis* and the Caesars. The alleged
bones of Orestes, long preserved at Aricia, were transferred to Rome
and prominently displayed in an urn before the temple of Saturn, near
the temple of Concord (Hyg. *Fab.* 261; Servius *ad Aen.* 2.116; 7.188;
there is a frieze of the Claudian era that shows Diana and Apollo
on either side of the urn, in front of these two temples[17]). Although

---

[14] Jentoft-Nilsen 1985, 23, no. 13. He had also celebrated the victory over Sextus Pompeius
with a Diana *aureus* (*LIMC* 1, "Artemis/Diana" no. 171, discussion, p. 822).

[15] *LIMC* 1, "Artemis/Diana," Diana fig. 172; discussion 822; *BMC* 104; cf. Jentoft Nilsen
1985, 23 no. 14, and discussion 92–4; Mikocki 1995, 31. The Kos inscription: *IGRR*
IV 1095, cf. Jentoft-Nilsen 92–4. For Livia as Diana, Mikocki 21; as Hecate, Mikocki
22–3. The tradition was kept up: for Agrippina the Younger as Diana, Mikoci 40.

[16] *LIMC* 1; "Artemis/Diana," Diana, no. 151–271; Jentoft-Nilsen 1985, 17–64. The dates
of the latest Diana coins in Jentoft-Nilsen's catalogue are at the very end of the third
century C.E., that is, just before Christianity and Constantine.

[17] *LIMC* 1; "Artemis/Diana" no. 276, discussion, 830.

Servius does not indicate the date at which the move was made nor who caused it to be done, the responsibility for moving them was surely Octavian's (Hölscher 1991; Champlin 2004, 308–11). The *terminus ante quem* must be the Augustan era, as Hyginus certainly knows of the event. The *terminus post quem* is slightly more difficult to define, yet the tradition that Orestes and Iphigenia had *come* to Aricia was a prerequisite for the removal of bones that were supposedly his.

Radke (166) suggested that the bones were moved in the regal period, an imitation of the removal of Orestes' bones (as reported by Hdt. 1.67–8) from Tegea to Sparta in the mid–sixth century B.C.E., which would mean that the earliest knowledge of the Orestes myth at Aricia had to predate the sixth century.[18] Even granted that the appropriation of the Orestes myth had already begun at Aricia in the regal period, it is still impossible to suppose that Aricia allowed the bones to be removed then. Herodotus has much to tell us about the power struggles implicit in such actions at the time. As he indicates, the Spartans needed a rather elaborate ruse to get Orestes' bones from the Tegeans, and they succeeded only because the Tegeans did not know these bones *were* those of Orestes. Rome and Aricia were in competition in this period, if not at war. The Aricians would not have given up the bones, unless they were compelled to do so, and the Romans were not then in a position to make them. Aricia remained independent of Rome until the mid–fifth century and was only nominally subject to her until well into the fourth, so the same objections still meet the alternative of the fifth century proposed by Coarelli (1987, 169) and Pairault (445).

In fact, however early we postulate Orestes' arrival at Aricia, it is hard to argue that the sanctuary could have established a widely known claim to the bones before the fourth century, when Euripides' plays were becoming so hugely popular in Italy. From the fourth century to the end of the Republic, there is no apparent or even suspect reason to justify Rome's desire for, or Aricia's release of, those bones. The continued vibrancy of the Orestes connection in Aricia itself argues

---

[18] Coarelli (1987, 169) suggests that the connection with Cumae may explain how Orestes came to Aricia. Certainly the Arician ties to Magna Graecia through Cumae must have facilitated the movement of this Greek myth to the Latin sanctuary.

that throughout the Republic, Orestes belonged to the goddess at Aricia. Ovid calls her "Orestean Diana" (*Met.* 15.489).

When Aricia finally handed over her hero's sacred remains, she must have had a good reason to do so. At Rome the bones of Orestes joined a few other sacred objects that were "seven pledges of Roman *imperium*" (Servius *ad Aen.* 7.188). Besides the remains of Orestes, these pledges were whatever lies behind the corrupted text of †*aius matris deum* (perhaps "the sacred stone of the Mother of the Gods"); the *quadriga fictilis Veientanorum* (a terra-cotta four-horse chariot from Veii, presumably that placed on the roof of the temple of Jupiter Optimus Maximus[19]); the *sceptrum Priami* (Priam's scepter); the *velum Ilionae* (Ilione's cloth,[20] Hyg. *Fab.* 109); the *palladium* (the sacred image of Athena taken from Troy and kept in the temple of Vesta); and the *ancilia* (the shields of Mars). Each of these objects was in itself an omen confirming Rome's greatness, her hegemony in the world, at a time of crisis. The *palladium*, the cloth of Ilione, and the scepter of Priam were all supposedly brought to Rome by Aeneas and mark both the heritage and the foundation of Rome; a shield (of which eleven copies were made) was sent down by Jupiter himself, and Numa founded the priesthood of the Salii for the care of these when he became king (Livy 1.20.4); the *quadriga* would have been brought to Rome after the wars with Veii (at the same time as Juno Regina was brought to Rome, Livy 22.3–6); the †*aius* of the Mother of the Gods marked the end of the Hannibalic wars (Livy 29.11). Each object came from another place – Troy, the heavens, Veii, Pergamon. It follows that the

[19] Pliny, *NH* 28.16, says that the *quadriga fictilis* grew as it was fired in the furnace and that this was regarded as an omen: the city possessing it would be the most powerful of all (Festus 342 L). It was said to have been made by Vulca, who was brought from Veii to make both it and the statue of Jupiter (*NH* 35.157), but the implication of Festus' interpretation, as of Servius' *Veientanorum*, is that the *quadriga* was fired at Veii, and recovered by Rome after Veii fell.

[20] Ilione, the eldest daughter of Priam, was part of the Trojan myth, but a rather late part. Pacuvius' tragedy on Ilione was famous (Cic. *Acad.* 2.88; Tusc.1.44; Hor. *Sat.* 2.3. 61– 4). She gave the scepter of Priam to Aeneas (Verg. *Aen.* 1.653–4; Serv. *ad Aen.* 1.653) and protected Polydorus from Polymestor, a Thracian king, who was bribed by the Achaeans to kill this surviving son of Priam. Because of Ilione's protection, he killed their son instead of Polydorus. Ilione and Polydorus then put out Polymestor's eyes and killed him (Hyg. *Fab.* 109). Vergil, though, in *Aen.* 3, holds that Polydorus was killed by Polymestor in Thrace.

remains of Orestes, coming from Aricia, must likewise have marked the resolution of another great crisis in Roman history.

The move was ordered by Octavian, as part of his conscious adoption of Orestes as a mythic hero on whom to model himself and his actions (Hölscher 1991; Champlin 2004, 308–11). In the period right after Actium, L. Munatius Plancus had a temple of Saturn built,[21] as a testament to the success of his new alliance with Octavian. Plancus had changed sides, abandoning Antony at a critical moment. It was to his temple that the remains of Orestes were brought. Octavian needed to resolve the agonies of the civil war, the demands for revenge, the urgent need for peace.

> Orestes was the mythical prototype of revenge, as Octavian had made revenge the principal motif of his political ascent; Orestes had avenged his father Agamemnon who had been murdered, as Octavian had avenged his father Julius Caesar; Orestes had thereby become the antagonist of Klytaimnestra, wife of Agamemnon, as Octavian had been the antagonist of Kleopatra, who had lived with Caesar in marriage-like relations; Orestes, moreover, had thereby become the antagonist of Aigisthos, the lover of Klytaimnestra, as Octavian was the antagonist of Antonius, the lover of Kleopatra; Orestes had to fight for the rightful heritage of his father against the pretended claims of this couple, as Octavian had to fight for the political succession of Julius Caesar; Orestes had accomplished his revenge by order of Apollo, as Octavian had fought under the protection of this god; Orestes finally had shed the blood of relatives and had to be absolved; in the same sense the victory of Octavian over fellow-citizens was a pollution which needed purification.
>
> Hölscher 1991, 164

Orestes was also believed to have come, with his sister Iphigenia, to Aricia (yet another foreigner in the enclave). He was a resident of

---

[21] This temple, originally a dedication from the early years of the Republic, was rebuilt by Plancus, consul in 42 (Suet. *Div. Aug.* 29.5; *CIL* VI. 1316 = *ILS* 41; *CIL* X.6087 = *ILS* 886). Plancus had served under Julius Caesar and allied himself with the second triumvirate; he then threw his lot in with Fulvia and Antony until just before Actium, when he came over to Octavian. The meaning of Plancus' dedication is difficult to assess (see Versnel 1993, 164–89, for possible lines of inquiry), but the reason for Octavian's transfer of the bones of Orestes to the temple of Saturn is quite clear from Vergil's description of Saturn in the *Aeneid*: primus ab aetherio uenit Saturnus Olympo/arma Iouis fugiens et regnis exsul ademptis ("Saturn first came from high Olympus fleeing the arms of Jupiter and an exile once his kingdom was stolen," *Aen.* 8.319–20). Having come to Rome, he inaugurated the "golden age" (8.321–7).

the sanctuary, a sacred second cousin, as it were, of Octavian himself. If the Aricians were ever going to hand over the bones of their hero, it would be at this time and to this man. The whole empire and its new leader had great need of the kind of religious atonement, reconciliation, and regeneration that had long been invested by the sanctuary in Orestes (see Chapter 8). This was the time (after Actium), the place (the new temple of Saturn), and the reason (the civil war) to bring such a new and potent image of reconciliation to Rome. Octavian was the Roman with Arician ancestry who could do it. It would seem that he encouraged even the visual and cultic identification between himself and Orestes, for at Argos Pausanias (2.17.3) saw a statue of Augustus that was said to be, in fact, Orestes.[22] If the scion of one of their most important families, heir to Caesar and victor over Antony, wanted the bones of Orestes in support of his efforts toward reconciliation, the Aricians were hardly likely to refuse.

But what bones were the Aricians actually giving to Octavian and Rome? Tradition had Orestes coming to Aricia and there founding the priesthood of the *rex nemorensis*. The ritual described in the following passage was enacted in celebration of Orestes' experiences.

Orestes post occisum regem Thoantem in regione Taurica cum sorore Iphigenia, ut supra (2.116) diximus, fugit et Dianae simulacrum inde sublatum haud longe ab Aricia collocavit. in huius templo post mutatum ritum sacrificiorum fuit arbor quaedam, de qua infringi ramum non licebat. dabatur autem fugitivis potestas, ut si quis exinde ramum potuisset auferre, monomachia cum fugitivo templi sacerdote dimicaret: nam fugitivus illic erat sacerdos ad priscae imaginem fugae. dimicandi autem dabatur facultas quasi ad pristini sacrificii reparationem. nunc ergo istum inde sumpsit colorem.

Servius ad Aen. 6.136

Orestes, after the killing of King Thoas in the Tauric land[23] *fled with his sister (as we stated above [2.116]), and the image of Diana that he brought from there he set up*

---

[22] ἀνδριάντες τε ἐστήκασι πρὸ τῆς ἐσόδου καὶ γυναικῶν, αἳ γεγόνασιν ἱέρειαι τῆς Ἥρας, καὶ ἡρώων ἄλλων τε καὶ Ὀρέστου· τὸν γὰρ ἐπίγραμμα ἔχοντα, ὡς εἴη βασιλεὺς Αὔγουστος, Ὀρέστην εἶναι λέγουσιν (Paus. 2.17.3).

[23] The etiology is dependent on the story of Orestes and Thoas made famous by Euripides' *Iphigenia in Tauris*, although the tradition at Aricia held that Orestes had *killed* the king (Servius *ad Aen.* 2.116) to steal the sacred statue. Euripides does not have Thoas killed.

not far from Aricia. In her precinct, after the sacrificial ritual was changed,[24] there was a certain tree, to break off a branch from which was not permitted. On the other hand, the right was given to any fugitive who contrived to remove a branch thence to contend in single combat with the fugitive priest of the temple, for the priest there was [also] a fugitive, to symbolize the ancient flight. And indeed, this opportunity of fighting was given as though in renewal of the original sacrifice: so at this point that is from where he [i.e., Vergil] got his material.[25]

It seems most economical, therefore, to suppose that the remains of some deceased *rex nemorensis* were moved to Rome. In this ritual established (it was believed) by Orestes, the *rex* was killed by his successor. Each *rex* must normally have been buried in the sanctuary where he had reigned and died. If *Aeneid* 6 offers even a distant reflection of this ritual, as Servius indicates, then the pyre for the dead priest-king was set up before a tomb in woodland belonging to the sanctuary, just as Misenus' pyre was set up in the forest. That tomb was also understood to be (as tombs generally were) an entrance to the underworld. Each ritually murdered *rex* would have been buried there in turn.

After the new *rex nemorensis* had killed his predecessor and celebrated his funeral, there had to be a burial; this burial, in all probability, required the new *rex nemorensis* to descend into the burial chamber for his own initiation and underworld dream-vision, taking with him in an urn the bones and ashes of his predecessor. The burial chamber will thus have had an extensive collection of such urns, going well back to the early Iron Age in Latium. These would have been known to the *rex* himself, to the priests of the sanctuary responsible for the ritual, and perhaps to others. One particular urn, either by traditional identification, or because it seemed to be the oldest, the most magnificent, or the most "barbaric," would have been generally accepted as the one containing the bones and ashes of Orestes, the first *rex nemorensis*.

This was the urn, with its contents, that Octavian, as I believe, had transferred to Rome and placed before the temple of Saturn near

---

[24] That is, changed from the human sacrifice practiced in Diana/Artemis' name in the Tauric Chersonese.

[25] See Appendix for the text of the entire passage of Servius, a translation, and a discussion of the significant points in the translation.

the temple of Concord. Like Orestes, Saturn was an exile (banished from heaven by Jupiter), and, like Romulus, he was taken up to heaven (Verg. *Aen.* 8.319–29; Ovid *Fasti* 1.233–9, Macrob. *Sat.* 1.7). Some regarded Saturn not as an Olympian but as an underworld deity (Plut. *QR* 34), and thus one who could properly accept a sacred burial in his sacred space. Most important, he was a god-king who introduced agriculture to Latium (then mythically called Saturnia), and through agriculture he suppressed the barbaric savagery of the aborigines and introduced a golden age (Verg. *Aen.* 8.319–29; Varro *LL* 5.42; Macrob. *Sat.* 1.7; Festus 430, 432 L).[26] Even so, there was a barbaric aspect to him, for Saturn was identified with Kronos and thus acquired the myths that made him the attacker of his father and the enemy of his own children (Ovid *Fast.* 4.197–206; Macrob. *Sat.* 1.8.6–10) before he brought civilization to Latium. Octavian would be the person to unite the two exiles and kings, Orestes as *rex nemorensis* at Aricia and Saturn in Rome, to inaugurate his own golden age. The temple of Saturn thus encapsulated, in its essence, both what Orestes had been – an exile, a man of violence and revenge – and the reconciliation and peace he promised. Concord, as a neighbor, defined the ideal aimed at by the religious act of honoring Orestes.

Having successfully appropriated Orestes, Augustus was able to turn to the even more sympathetic Hippolytus (another important element in the complex symbolism of the Arician sanctuary; see Chapter 9) as a further extension of his image. Hippolytus was equated with Virbius (Ovid *Met.* 15.543–4) or was his son (Verg. *Aen.* 7.761–2). Virbius' mother was (according to Vergil) Aricia (*Aen.* 7.762). Conveniently, Apollo was the father of Asclepius, and it was Asclepius who had saved Hippolytus.[27] The image and cult of Diana came to be accepted as a divine paradigm for empire and the imperial family.

---

[26] The meaning of this dedication for Plancus, apart from the transfer of Orestes' remains, is difficult to assess; cf. Versnel 1993, 164–89.

[27] Ghedini (1987) has argued that the death of Drusus in 9 B.C.E. was commemorated by an image of Livia as Diana mourning Hippolytus on a vase in St. Maurice d'Augaune. Whether this tableau had been suggested by Augustus and Livia or was created as the artist's meditation on the death of Drusus, it can only be seen as a reverent gesture employing symbols that were significant to the imperial family.

Cicero's remarks on the holes in Octavian's ears might never have been made.

THE SANCTUARY IN AUGUSTAN LITERATURE

When Octavian moved the remains of Orestes to Rome, the sanctuary of Diana at Aricia acquired a new significance in the living fabric of Roman religion, Roman religious architecture, and Roman civic landscape. Orestes' living priest-descendant, the *rex nemorensis*, continued to serve the goddess in the wooded sanctuary, and Diana continued to be worshipped in long-established rituals involving Orestes, Iphigenia, Hippolytus, and Egeria. Augustan writers, it is hardly surprising, found this material rich with possibilities – and dangers. The many allusions to the cult in Augustan literature must be read with the consciousness that every writer was well aware of the princeps' personal interest in Diana and thus had to grapple with both the inherited and the contemporary political meaning of the cult. The advantage for us is that each reference had to be handled with the utmost delicacy and deliberation. It is highly unlikely that anything written in the Augustan period about Diana or the *rex* is without political as well as religious meaning. It is even more unlikely that anyone would have misrepresented the known facts of the cult or interpreted Diana's nature or rituals in a way that did not meet with the approval, implicit or explicit, of Augustus. What the Augustans have to tell us about the *rex*, then, and about the whole cult, must be taken very seriously as evidence for the contemporary practices and religious context of the sacred figures in the sanctuary of Diana at Aricia.

Vergil, particularly the *Aeneid*, and Ovid (passim) are the principal authors who must be studied for what they have to say about the sanctuary and its priest. Their concerns are appropriate to the high literary genres in which they wrote, and it is they who give us the greatest insights into the mythic complex at the sanctuary as grounded in Orestes, Iphigenia, Hippolytus/Virbius, Egeria, and the *rex* himself. That is, they offer us a view of the way in which sophisticated artists could use, for their own ends, the contemporary theological-cum-philosophical interpretations embedded in the figures, mythic and real, that populated the sanctuary. We come to them in a moment.

GRATTIUS AND THE SACRIFICE

Another author just as serious, but not quite so accomplished (and thus generally overlooked), actually describes the performance of a ritual – people *using* the sanctuary. It is thanks to Ovid's bitterness in exile that we know anything at all about Grattius (*Ex Pont.* 4.16.34). He and his poem on hunting, *Cynegetica*, appear in a list Ovid makes of poets who were contemporaries. They were poetasters to a man, Ovid says, while *he* was read (*Ex Pont.* 4.16.45–6). The way in which Ovid adds Grattius to this unexalted group (*aptaque venanti Grattius arma daret,* "Grattius would offer weapons suited to the hunter"; *Pont.* 4.16.34) also suggests that he was a one-poem poet. He made Ovid's list because he had what Ovid did not: residence in Rome and freedom from the hostility of the princeps (*Pont.* 4.16.49–52).

Grattius wrote about Diana. The title of his poem, *Cynegetica*, "On Hunting," is misleading, for its subject is primarily the raising of hounds, their training, and the treatment of their illnesses. When it breaks off after 541 lines, it seems that he intended to do the same for horses. *Cynegetica* is a remarkable mixture of hymn and didactic. In the hymnic sections in particular (1–23, 95–126, 427–66, 477–96) Grattius describes the practice of the cult of Diana at Aricia,[28] and introduces the philosophical-theological ideas implicit in the cult. His poetic skills may be run-of-the-mill, but his language is nuanced and his thought finely attuned to the political and religious currents of the high-Augustan period. To take one example – also informative for the way in which hunting was used as a symbol – Grattius hymns Diana in his proem as the divinity who gave man the protection of *artes* against the *bellum ferinum* (*Cyn.* 1–15). *Artes* here are, of course, the techniques of hunting, but they also embrace special skills, ingenuity, art (in its modern sense), systematic bodies of knowledge, cultural pursuits, and the rules, training, and principles that lead to or come from any of

---

[28] Although Grattius does not name Aricia specifically, it cannot now be doubted that he is speaking of that cult. If he had any cult in mind other than that which was so identified with Augustus and his family, he would have said so (and it is hard to imagine why a member of the imperial circle would even think of writing about another Diana while Augustus lived). Formicola (193) and Verdière (412–13), the two modern authorities on Grattius, assume, without discussion, that Grattius is speaking of Aricia.

these (*OLD s.v. ars* 1–10). Here we have the protection against the *bellum ferinum* – war against beasts: hunting, of course, but "bestial war" too, in all its manifestations. This accords well with Augustus' own religious portrayal of Diana and is just what he intended to celebrate with the Diana *aurei* issued after the defeat of Antony at Actium and Sextus Pompeius in Sicily. Diana has given man the means to hunt, and through that, she has given humans the means to achieve peace.

The proem closes with two lines of layered meaning:

> Contra mille feras et non sine carmine iussus,
> Carmine et arma dabo et venandi persequar artes.
>
> *Cyn.* 22–3

Ordered out against a thousand wild beasts, though not without a song, with a song will I both furnish weapons and pursue the arts of the chase.

As the reader of the *Cynegetica* will discover, the "thousand wild beasts" are not wild animals but errors to be avoided or problems overcome in the preparation of nets and traps or in the choosing or raising of dogs. In particular they are the "thousands of diseases" (*mille . . . pestes*, 479) that afflict the dogs. So the wild beasts – and hunting itself – are firmly allegorized, although they are never just allegory. A few lines later (493–6) Grattius makes it clear that the worshippers of the goddess praised her for arming them against affliction in general. How are they armed? With a poem, a song, a ritual chant, a prayer, an incantation.[29] Included among these must be, of course, Grattius' own *carmen*, his poem. So poetry must be numbered among the weapons given by Diana to her followers.

Toward understanding the sanctuary, however, Grattius' greatest gift to us is the description, near the end of the surviving text, of the conclusion to an important civic remnant of an initiation ritual held in the sanctuary. As Burkert (1985, 260–1) observed, such rituals in city cultures were "reduced to ceremonies that accompany the course of an otherwise normal life." It is no longer an initiation per se, but

---

[29] Grattius surely has Horace in mind. *Namque me silva lupus in Sabina, / dum meam canto Lalagen et ultra / terminum curis vagor expeditis, / fugit inermem* ("For a wolf flees from me unarmed in the Sabine forest as I sing of my Lalage and wander past the boundaries, all my cares resolved"; *Odes* 1.22.9–12).

a performance by the young for the benefit of the city. Here, at last, we catch a glimpse of people inhabiting the sanctuary and using it for religious purposes.

> Idcirco aeriis molimur compita lucis
> spicatasque faces sacrum ad nemorale Dianae
> sistimus et solito catuli velantur honore,
> ipsaque per flores medio in discrimine luci
> stravere arma sacris et pace vacantia festa.
> tum cadus et viridi fumantia liba feretro
> praeveniunt teneraque extrudens cornua fronte
> haedus et ad ramos etiamnum haerentia poma,
> lustralis de more sacri, quo tota iuventus
> lustraturque deae proque anno reddit honorem.
> ergo impetrato respondet multa favore
> ad partes, qua poscis opem; seu vincere silvas
> seu tibi fatorum labes exire minasque
> cura prior, tua magna fides tutelaque Virgo.
>
> Grattius *Cyn.* 483–96[30]

Therefore we set up shrines in the soaring forest where the path divides, and fix the tufted torches at the edge of Diana's sacred clearing, and the young hounds are wreathed with the customary decorations, and among the flowers at the turning point in the middle of the forest the youths spread those weapons discarded for the sacred rites and the festal peace. Then first there come the urns and the steaming cakes on the greenwood bier, and the goat with velvet-soft horns budding on his forehead, and the fruit still clinging to the branches, all in the fashion of a lustral rite, where all the young are purified and render honor to the goddess for the year. Accordingly, once her favor has been sought, she responds generously in those areas where you seek her aid; whether your greater concern is to conquer the forests or to evade the marks and threats of fate, the Virgin is your great security and protector.

Each action as Grattius describes it tells us about those who perform the ceremony, and the meaning assigned to what they do. First are the preparations: "we" set up the shrines and lay out the torches. "We" probably also are the ones who wreathe the young hounds. So the preparations for the ritual are performed by the group to which the poet claims to belong, who are either the priests or the elders of the community. There is a procession led (*praeuenio*, 489) by the sacrificial

---

[30] The text is that of Formicola. For the life of Grattius, see Formicola, 20–2.

beast. The entire procession is for the purpose of sacrifice, that of initiates who must yield their old selves before they can gain admittance
to the adult community. The ritual sacrifice involves mingled symbols
of youth and ripeness (the young goat whose horns are just sprouting, the ripe fruit still clinging to the branches, the greenness of the
greenwood bier) and death (the urns and the cakes on biers[31]).

This procession makes its way toward the *discrimen*, the decisive
moment, the meeting-point of paths in the forest. This sacred objective is, in every sense, the point of decision. When the initiates reach
it, they lay down their weapons and make a dedication of them. Then,
together with the *iuuentus* (the young men of military age already initiated, *OLD s.v. iuuentus* 1) whom they now join, they will complete the
sacrifice and all give thanks to the goddess for the blessings of the year.

Thus *fumantia*, a present participle, "smoking," represents the
moment of sacrifice at the heart of the ritual, and with green wood
(no doubt hard to burn, signifying perhaps the difficulty of making
the sacrifice[32]), there would be a great deal of smoke. The participants
must "die" as children and be reborn as adults. The ashes of the sacrifice are placed in the funerary urn. Initiation is not just about the
lives of the young men taking on adult responsibilities but about the
continuing life and success of the community as a whole. The young
goat represents the success of the herds, and the fruit the success of
the crops, underlining the idea that the initiate's gift of his childhood to the goddess is a parallel sacrifice for the well-being of the
community.[33]

---

[31] *Cadus* can be a wine jar, but it is also a funerary urn (*OLD cadus* 2). The primary citation
for *cadus* as a funerary urn is a passage from Vergil, *Aen.* 6.228, which echoes the funeral
of the *rex nemorensis* (see Chapter 7). In the same passage (*Aen.* 6. 222) Vergil uses *feretro*,
a bier (*OLD feretrum*). This is unlikely to have been an accident. See Chapter 3 for the
stone funerary urns found in the sanctuary. The *liba*, which are ritual cakes (*OLD libum*),
being carried on a bier suggest that they are like the *maniae*, the pastry human figures
used in other rituals at this sanctuary (Festus 115, 128, 129 L).

[32] See Chapter 7, on the use of green wood in the ritual of the *rex nemorensis*.

[33] The parallel but opposite ritual is that of the Sacred Spring, in which the year's youth and
produce are excluded from the community and surrendered wholly to the gods (Livy
22.10, 33.44.1, 34.44; DH *AR* 1.16). Dumézil 1970, 208, points out that the band of
young men thus sent out in a Sacred Spring carried their animal identities with them.
The animals became eponymous for the new communities (e.g., *hirpus* [wolf] Hirpini;
picus [woodpecker] Picentes). See also Heurgon 1957.

One interesting point is the verb, *velantur*, "to wreathe." It has as its subject *catuli*, the young hunting hounds. Certainly it is possible that these young dogs are there as part of the symbolism of newness and youth. Yet normally dogs belong to specific masters and attend them; they are not participants on their own. (It is clear that the dogs are not *hostia*, sacrificial animals.) A natural reading of lines 485–7 would easily lead one to assume the same subject for *velantur* ("they are wreathed") and *stravere* ("they lay spread [their weapons]"). Editors are unwilling to have young dogs laying their weapons at the turning point and understand Grattius to mean that the subject of *velantur* is the *catuli*, the dogs, and a subject must be supplied for *stravere*. Because the initiates are the principal human actors in the ceremony, it is puzzling, if not impossible, that Grattius failed to give them an identifying noun. However, it is typical of hunting rituals for the humans to take on animal characteristics – just as the Athenian girls at Brauron perform as "little bears."[34] Diana is particularly identified with hunting dogs,[35] and it is certainly possible that the initiates in Diana's rites were in some way identified as young hunting hounds.

There is one last group that Grattius brings to the *discrimen* of the ritual: "you," the reader of the poem. You *too* may ask the goddess for help. The archaic ideal of the city has been redefined. The initiation has strengthened and confirmed the ritual community in its relation to the goddess, and this community has now been extended to include the literary public. The Virgin, Diana, is the security and the guardian of a community whose boundaries are the greater community predicated by the *orbis terrarum* of the Roman Empire.

Augustus could hardly have been less than gratified, for his program of religious reform was to restore the "old" Roman religion while at the same time transforming it into a religious ideology that could embrace the empire. Yet internationalization must not be seen as something new, something specifically "Augustan" at Aricia. The sanctuary had become wealthy in the first place by attracting strangers and pilgrims and by performing its rites for their benefit. When it adopted

[34] Cf. Sourvinou-Inwood 1988.
[35] For example, Blagg 1983e, p. 48 and no. N 125 (second century B.C.E.); *LIMC* Artemis/Diana, Diana 248 (late Republic, early empire), 255 (early empire).

Orestes, the quintessential exile, the cult had long since defined itself as a refuge for those who had been materially or culturally dispossessed in any part of the world. Grattius merely records a natural extension of a practice established long before Octavian was born. The *Cynegetica* was yet another form of the conscious self-presentation to the world beyond Aricia that so clearly distinguishes Diana's sanctuary there.

3

THE SANCTUARY IN THE EMPIRE

THE CENTURY AFTER AUGUSTUS

After Octavian had created a useful and unthreatening role for Diana's cult to play in the religious culture of the principate, and it had become a kind of touchstone of divinely authorized imperial power for the Augustan writers, the sanctuary settled back into its hardworking existence as a cult center for pilgrims and the sick. All kinds of people still came, as the dedications make clear. At some point toward the end of Augustus' lifetime or early in the reign of Tiberius, Servilius Quartus' elaborate *ala* in the portico was renovated to display portrait statues of Fundilia and her *libertus* C. Fundilius Doctus; a portrait herm of the *rhetor* Q. Hostius Q.f. Capito; the portrait herms of two *libertae*, Staia Quinta and Licinia Chrysarion; and the statue of L. Aninius Rufus L.f., a quaestor or quattuorvir, dedicated by his wife, Prima. All the sculptures seem to date from about the same period. As with so much else about this fascinating room, we do not know why these private portrait statues and herms were set up together here.[1] What the collection does tell us is that ex-slaves, as well as magistrates and their wives, continued to make visually impressive statements of their devotion to the goddess. The absence of Augustales,[2] however, is perhaps even

---

[1] Fundilius statue, Poulsen no. 77–8; Fundilia statue Poulsen no. 537; Fundilia herm Blagg 1983b, no. 827; Hostius Capito, Poulsen no. 641, pp. 447–8; Staia Quinta, Poulsen no. 639, p. 446; Aninius, Poulsen no. 640, p. 447; discussion and photographs from Ny Carlsberg Glyptotek exhibition, Moltesen 2000.

[2] There may be one exception: *CIL* XIV 2176 is a funerary epitaph of a *biselliarius* (Gordon 1934, 20). A *bisellium* was a double seat of honor awarded mostly to Augustales, so it is possible this man was a priest of Augustus.

more interesting than the presence of *liberti*. The Augustales were men who belonged to the religious and social organization established by Augustus to give freedmen rank and position in provincial cities.

About the time of Tiberius also, a certain Chio,[3] a *libertus*, possibly connected to the milieu of the imperial family freedmen, made a very substantial dedication to Diana of four marble amphorae and four griffin cauldrons. These were found in one of the rooms to the east of Servilius' *ala* (room F [Savile], room 9 [Guldager Bilde]). They may have been moved there after some disaster, possibly an earthquake or landslide, damaged the sanctuary, perhaps in the second century. Guldager Bilde (1997e) has argued cogently that these magnificent pieces were part of a funerary structure, perhaps a heroön, a tomb to Hippolytus/Virbius, just as there were tombs of Hippolytus at Troezen (Paus. 2.32.1) and Athens (Paus. 1.22.1). She identifies this heroön with the round structure uncovered by Savile behind the "temple" on the terrace.

Pausanias confirms that it is likely that such a monument would have existed in the second century. He saw at Epidauros (2.27.4) an "old" stone tablet in the Peribolus[4] that was a commemoration of a dedication of twenty horses by Hippolytus. This inscription included the Arician version of the myth in which the hero, once restored to life, went to live in the woods at Nemi. This is a quite extraordinary dedication and is discussed in Chapter 9. It bears witness to a close relationship between Epidaurus and Aricia, between Asclepius and Diana as healers. Given the iconography and the practical connections between Epidauros and Aricia, the bust can be all but certainly identified as Asclepius. So the eight Chio vases were part of a dedication, probably to Virbius/Hippolytus or just possibly to Asclepius. Both Asclepius and Virbius/Hippolytus were brought back from the dead, and apparently shared a significant iconography. At Troezen, where both were worshipped, a certain statue was said by some to

---

[3] Not "Chius," so it must be the Latinized form of a Greek placename adjective Χίων, the Chiote. There is a Julio-Claudian *libertus*, Chius, and there may have been some relationship (Guldager Bilde 1997e, 67). The Greek name and the absence of a patronymic or other distinction indicate that he was a *libertus*.

[4] See Chapter 9 for the discussion of this passage of Pausanias. The Peribolus was a round enclosure.

be Asclepius, and by others, Hippolytus (Paus. 2.32.3; Guldager Bilde 1995, 213).

Another of the rooms along the north portico held an acrolithic marble bust of a bearded idealized male figure, a hero or deity.[5] Iconographically, it is most likely to have represented Asclepius (Guldager Bilde 1995, 209–12). This means that other deities were accorded visible honors within the sanctuary structures, and that reciprocity with other cults was not unusual. The presence of a head of Hercules in the theater (Morpurgo 1931, 245) is suggestive; figurines of Minerva, Venus, Apollo, Mercury, and Bacchus have also been found (Blagg 1993, 106 and n. 30). An inscription dated to the first century C.E. lists various items, the number and costliness of which makes them very distinctive. These items had been given to shrines of Isis and Bubastis which are thought to have been located nearby in Aricia (*CIL* XIV 2215, Gordon 1934, 15; Bombardi 1994, 37–8). A small head of Isis (or perhaps of an Isiac priestess) was found in the theater (Morpurgo 1931, no. 127, 282–3; Bombardi 2000, 125), prompting Bombardi (1994, 40) to suggest that the Navigium Isidis, the great festival of Isis in March, was celebrated at the lake in front of the sanctuary. An ivory figure of a woman's head wearing an Isis-diadem is also recorded (this figure has disappeared; Bombardi 2000, 125). The worship of Isis in or near the sanctuary is certainly possible. Diana and Isis had many connections – both were queens of heaven, both had lovers whom they brought back to life after death. It may be, for instance that a particular impetus to the acceptance of Isis by Diana was the fact that the sanctuary attracted or hired actors who were also associated with the temple of Isis at Pompeii (Bombardi 1994–5, 45–7; 2000, 122–3).

The presence of these actors (figure 3) is testimony to the now invisible daily, practical, human associations of Diana's cult. The sanctuary was a working institution and there must have been a significant group of people devoted to its operation from the second century on, involving, besides the priests and the temple workers, members of the Arician élite and a number of slaves and freedmen. They clearly knew, and were known by, the corresponding officials in similar sacred institutions

---

[5] The bust was found in room B [Savile], room 4 [Guldager Bilde]. Cf. Guldager Bilde 2000, 97–8.

in Italy and the Mediterranean. It was natural that they should be interested in each other, and evidence showing the effects of such associations need not surprise us.

Augustus' successors did not neglect the sanctuary after his death. Their interest, as the dedications associated with them make clear, was in the ability of Diana's priest to contextualize and interpret the nature of kingly – or imperial – succession. In room 1 was a group of imperial portrait statues: Tiberius, Drusus, and Germanicus.[6] This sculpture group defines Tiberius' hoped-for succession. It suggests that the cool, rationalistic Tiberius either invested genuine trust in the goddess' concern for the imperial family, or (more likely) that he saw it was advantageous to maintain a visible presence for the family in the sanctuary. Whether he or others caused the statues to be set up, the statue group was put there with his approval.

When Tiberius' hopes had been thwarted and Caligula inherited the throne instead, he, too, brought his concerns about the succession to Nemi. He decided that the current *rex nemorensis* had reigned long enough. He therefore sent in a picked challenger and forced the ritual to be performed at his command (Suet. *Cal.* 35.3). By ordering the ritual to be held, Caligula proved to himself he was in control of it; by getting rid of the incumbent and replacing him with his own man, he could believe he (rather than the goddess, or, more to the point, any ambitious would-be emperor) also controlled the priest who represented kings.[7] The great pleasure ships that were lifted from the mud of the lake in the 1920s were very possibly built for Caligula as well,[8] although what their relationship to the sanctuary may have been

---

[6] Room G [Savile], room 1 [Guldager Bilde].

[7] Here I primarily follow Bernardi 1953.

[8] It is also likely that he was responsible in some way for King Darius' dedication to the sanctuary. The name *Darius rex* was found on pieces of lead plumbing for the baths behind the theater and the nymphaeum (Morpurgo 1931, 252–4; 280; Leone 29). Darius was a boy, a hostage of the Parthian king's family, whom Caligula liked to have attend him (Suet. *Cal.* 14, 19; Cass. Dio 59.17.1–11; Darius may have come to Rome while Tiberius was still alive, see Karras-Klapproth, 32–3 and 50–1). It is possible, as Leone has argued (2000, 30–1), that Caligula was amused by having the boy claim "kingship" in the territory of the *rex nemorensis*. The possibility, also scouted by Leone (29–30), that *Darius rex* was one of the *reges nemorenses* is improbable to the point of impossibility. The priest was a fugitive, hidden in the forest. He did not commission building projects for the sanctuary.

is not known. It has often been supposed, however (without any proof being possible), that they were built so the emperor could watch the combat of his chosen challenger and the old *rex* from an extravagant floating palace.[9]

Caligula's successor Claudius likewise turned to the sanctuary when the question of his successor became a crisis. Being about to marry his niece Agrippina, he ordered public rituals of purification for incest (Tac. *Ann.*12.8.2). Seeking purification from Diana for an incestuous marriage has many implications, particularly in terms of a possible *hieros gamos* in the sanctuary (Green 1998).[10] Claudius received his purification, and there is an inscription (*ILS* 220) of a prayer for the welfare of the imperial family that must have been dedicated immediately after the wedding. According to the inscription, Claudius and Agrippina are married, but Britannicus still takes precedence over Nero, a situation that did not last for more than a few days.[11]

Nero later took great pleasure in exploiting Orestes as the mythical paradigm that justified his killing of his mother (Champlin 2003, 310–14), but this is his only known (and very remote) connection with the sanctuary after the dedication to Claudius. Whether this is the result of a *damnatio memoriae* of the emperor or happenstance, we cannot say. Certainly there was no diminution of imperial interest in the sanctuary. An inscription of 71 C.E. (*CIL* XIV 2216) to Vespasian and his sons Titus and Domitian was in all likelihood part of a dedicatory sculpture group like that of Tiberius, Drusus, and Germanicus, to which a statue of Domitian, reworked to portray Nerva, belonged (Guldager Bilde and Moltesen 1997, 208). Vespasian, too, received (and therefore had approved) a dedication by the senate and the people of Aricia

---

[9] Ghini 1992 has the most complete report on the original finds and those that survived the fire of 31 May–1 June 1944; for a brief but coherent review, see Zahle 1997, 169–71. The lead pipes date the ships to Caligula's reign and indicate that there was running water on them – not the least of the luxuries of these extraordinary constructions.

[10] There is also a ritual marriage we can glimpse behind the actions of Caligula, who had incestuous relationships with his sisters (Suet. *Cal.* 24.1; 36.1) and claimed his mother was the result of an incestuous union between Julia and Augustus (*Cal.* 24). He treated his sister Drusilla as his lawful wife who was deified after her death (*Cal.* 24.1 and 24.2). For the implications of this and the connection to the ritual of the *rex nemorensis*, see Bernardi 1953, and Green 1998, 784–7. See also the discussion in Chapter 10.

[11] Granino Cecere (2000, 40–1) discusses these dedications to the emperors.

(*CIL* XIV 4191). Trajan was made Dictator Aricinus (*CIL* XIV 2213; *ILS* 3243), perhaps a minor honor for an emperor who spent little time in Rome or its environs, but probably the result of the Aricians' recognition that this was a warrior emperor who would understand the significance of the position.

STATIUS AND THE IDES OF AUGUST

Octavian had made Diana and her cult part of the religious identity of the imperial family and of imperial Rome. For that reason alone, it seems clear, the central festival of Diana at Aricia on 13 August became a widely celebrated holiday in Italy, an unusual distinction for a provincial cult. On the Ides of August all Italy honored Diana of the woodlands.[12]

> Tempus erat, caeli cum torrentissimus axis
> Incumbit terris ictusque Hyperione multo
> Acer anhelantis incendit Sirius agros.
> Iamque dies aderat, profugis cum regibus aptum
> Fumat Aricinum Triviae nemus et face multa
> Conscius Hippolyti splendet lacus; ipsa coronat
> Emeritos Diana canes et spicula terget
> Et tutas sinit ire feras, omnisque pudicis
> Itala terra focis Hecateidas excolit idus.
> Statius *Silv.* 3.1.52–60[13]

It is the season when the most scorching region of the heavens takes over the land and the keen dog-star Sirius, so often struck by Hyperion's sun, burns the gasping fields. Now is the day when Trivia's Arician grove, convenient for fugitive kings, grows smoky, and the lake, having guilty knowledge of Hippolytus, glitters with the reflection of a

---

[12] Rome celebrated Aventine Diana on the same day. For what this means concerning the two separate cult foundations, see Chapter 5. From Statius' evidence, and that of other authors of the late first and early second century, it is clear that the general celebration was identified (rightly or wrongly) with Arician Diana.

[13] Text is that of Mozley. Momigliano (1962) argued that the festival on the Ides was originally Roman, not Arician. His argument has not found acceptance, for it ignores Statius' emphasis on the very specific landscape of the lake and the association of Hecate and Hippolytus, which unmistakably identify this as an Arician festival that has become an Italian feastday. See Chapter 5.

multitude of torches; Diana herself garlands the deserving hunting dogs and polishes the arrowheads and allows the wild animals to go in safety, and at virtuous hearths all Italy celebrates the Hecatean Ides.

Statius makes it clear that this is the festival of Diana Nemorensis (not Aventinensis) and an occasion quite distinct from that described by Grattius. Grattius' initiation is held in the late spring or early summer, when fruit is still clinging to the branches (*ad ramos etiamnum haerentia poma, Cyn.* 490). The middle of August, on the other hand, is the height of summer, too late for most fruit trees to still be bearing fruit in the climate of central Italy, and certainly an unkind month for the tender young of the human, the animal or the plant world – as Statius' "gasping fields" (*anhelantis . . . agros, Silv.* 3.1.54) demonstrate.[14] Grattius portrays the young who strengthen the community under Diana's protection, whereas Statius celebrates the goddess herself in all her complexity.

Statius moves through the three cosmic levels: from the vault of the sky to the grove, and thence to the lake and Hecate of the underworld, the symbols at the heart of the cult and grounded in the nature of the place.[15] The dog-star in the sky provides an etymological link connecting the heavens to the garlanded hounds in the procession. The hounds are here on the Ides of August because they are companions of the goddess; as well as being her fellow-hunters they symbolize her guardianship of those in her care. The fact that the hunting dogs are garlanded and the hunting spears are being polished is a way of emphasizing that no hunting was allowed in these festival days. The wild animals could go about in safety. Diana's protection is extended to all.

The idea of refuge is pervasive in Statius' lines. The cool of the wooded hills and the lakeside would naturally have offered an ideal

[14] Verdière 413; Formicola *ad loc.* 483. One function of Statius' passage on Diana is to set the date (*diem Triviae*, "Trivia's day," 3.1.68) for the meeting between Statius and Pollius. Throughout Statius emphasizes the heat and the desire to escape from it in shade near the water (e.g., 61–75).

[15] The identification of Diana with Hecate (a Greek name) has been made unnecessarily complicated. Diana the huntress was identified with the moon, as Apollo was with the sun. As the moon grows dark once a month, it is inevitable that a moon-goddess will have some part of her identity located in the underworld. Hecate is simply the convenient Greek name for that part of her identity (see Chapter 4).

retreat from the August heat in the plain.[16] A refuge is for those who are fleeing, and fugitives are extremely important to Diana in all their shapes and forms. The *rex nemorensis*, the runaway par excellence, had always symbolized the nature of Diana's sanctuary as a refuge,[17] but so did Hippolytus, the refugee from death, and Orestes, the refugee from murder, pollution, and madness. The *rex*, Orestes and Hippolytus are the religious images, the cultic representations for the meaning of exile, flight, escape, protection. Crossing the crater's rim, moving into the sacred space of the sanctuary, bearing a torch in the procession to the shrine, was to flee the *thanatos*-laden world and to take refuge in the eternal world of the sacred, cool, shady, and nurturing.

The festival probably lasted three days. Although it would be a conventional amount of time for a major festival, it is particularly appropriate for Diana Trivia. Statius refers to her on the Ides as Hecate (*Silv*.3.1.60) and closely associates her with Hippolytus. St. Hippolytus, a supposed third-century Christian martyr, had his festival date on 13 August, that is, the Ides of August; and the Virgin Mary was taken bodily into heaven on the 15th, the feast of the Assumption. Given the Christian Church's habit of appropriating what it could not eradicate, it is possible that the great festival of Diana began with her descent to the underworld on the Ides, 13 August, perhaps in search of Virbius/Hippolytus. The third and last day of the festival would then celebrate Diana's ascension, as the queen of heaven, the full moon, the Virgin, as Grattius calls her (*Virgo*, 496), on 15 August. Frazer (1.14) suggested that Diana's ascension would have been the origin of the Christian Assumption of the Virgin. Certainly during the early centuries C.E. the Christian Church and the sanctuary of Diana were in competition over the meaning of some essential phenomena – the descent to the underworld and return of the youthful male god; human sacrifice; the mother and her beloved son-priest; the queen of heaven – and it is not improbable that Christians would want to replace the popular and widely known festival of Diana with Christian festivals that redirected worshippers' attention to the Church. Isis (to whom Diana

---

[16] The Alban Hills are still a retreat from the heat of Rome, a truth to which popes and princes as well as ordinary Romans have long testified.

[17] Note that the thunderstorm on this day forces Statius and his companions to take refuge in a shrine to Hercules (80–5).

was often assimilated) and Demeter were likewise celebrating similar religious concepts during the imperial period.

FROM TRAJAN TO THE THIRD CENTURY

By now the sanctuary had become extensively Hellenized. As we can tell from even the small proportion of inscriptions and dedications that have been excavated and edited, the terrace at least was crowded with statues and steles and shrines, all somehow crammed in among the portico, the baths, the theater, and the granaries. It would have been crowded with people, too. Where there was wealth, there had to be people: making dedications; buying medications, food, and ex-votos; borrowing money and repaying it. One indication of the wealth flowing into Diana's coffers is the substantial rebuilding project undertaken through the assistance of Volusia Cornelia, a woman of the senatorial class. Volusia should be the daughter of Q. Volusius Saturninus, consul in 56.[18]

> volvsia q. f. cornelia theatrvm
> vetvstate corrvptvm restitvit et excolivit[19]

Volusia Cornelia, daughter of Quintus, restored and decorated the theater damaged by age.

If the theater was in disrepair by the late first century, then the original theater must have been built during the expansion of the sanctuary in the second and first centuries B.C.E. (Morpurgo 1931, 292–9). This restoration cannot have been an inexpensive undertaking and senatorial families were still clearly taking a substantial interest in the cult.

The theater reminds us again how little we know of the way in which the space and structures in the sanctuary were actually used. It was apparently connected, at an angle, to a structure with a hypocaust, more or less parallel to a set of baths aligned with the western end of the terrace.[20] These structures also probably both date from the great

---

[18] Cf. Granino Cecere (39).

[19] Morpurgo 1931, 292; now in the Museo Nazionale Romano, inv. 112218 (Granino Cecere, 43 n. 37).

[20] On the baths and the hydraulic system, see Morpurgo 1931, 297–8; Nielsen, 188 (with figs. 25 and 44).

building projects of the late Republic, as another inscription (*CIL* XIV 419) commemorating a similar restoration of the "old baths" suggests. The theater immediately adjoins the sanctuary terrace. That and the many sculptures of divine figures, particularly two that could be Diana (Morpurgo 1931, 261–3), and the characteristic triangular antefixes with the head of Diana (Morpurgo 1931, 294, no. 136) indicate that this was a place for sanctuary ritual (Morpurgo 1931, 302). Yet it is not aligned with the nearby terrace and portico (Morpurgo 1931, 240). The theater's axis indicates a different orientation. There is another oddity. In the ordinary way of things a theater's cavea would be dug into the side of an available slope, taking advantage of the natural support. This theater's cavea was freestanding, and the audience in Diana's theater *faced* the slope. It is as though the audience was being directed to look not only at the *scaena* but also over it, at a particular part of the slope of the crater behind it. It is thus possible that the sight line of the theater directed the audience to look at a significant structure or landmark on the slope behind.

There was a wall around the theater and at the entrance was a pool. On one side was a nymphaeum, and on the other, probably, a fountain. In the cavea itself, there were special rows of seats on a raised marble level around the orchestra. In the orchestra itself was a marble pool. The stage front had marble-lined niches that may have contained fountains, and the *scaenae frons* presented the conventional three doors for entrance and exit. In a room to the right of the *scaena* there seems to have been some kind of dump.[21] Unfortunately, the room was not completely excavated, the original floor was never brought to light, and neither the function of the room nor the reason for the collection of refuse is known (Morpurgo 1931, 247).

A deep pit, located directly in front of the central entrance on stage, was connected to an entrance to the actors' rooms at the back (Morpurgo 1931, 296; Nielsen 1997, 188). Some part of the ritual, or some play, may have required the actors to rise from, or disappear into, this pit. The room adjoined the actors' room behind the *scaena*, which

---

[21] A variety of objects was found there: lamps, vases, glass bottles, bronze utensils, pliers, surgical instruments, keys, locks, glass paste fragments, bone fragments.

had a mosaic floor and frescoes. The frescoes are fascinating and show costumes, boots, armor, a bough, and a scroll of what might be the text of some ritual that was performed (Morpurgo 1931, 302). This partial text has the words *manium/manes*[22] written on it repeatedly, as though part of an acting script. The *manes* were the spirits of the dead and must have been an important part of the script of some performance here. Were these performances exclusively ritual, or were translations of Greek plays (Euripides especially) and the Latin plays of Ennius, Pacuvius, and the rest also performed? We cannot be certain,[23] but the conventional three doors for entrance to the stage do suggest normal theatrical usage. Similar small theaters have been found at Arpinum (Castagnoli 1966, 23) and Ostia (Meiggs 1973, 163–4), and other theaterlike structures of the late Republican period have been excavated at the sanctuaries of Juno at Gabii, Fortuna at Praeneste, and Hercules at Tibur (Nielsen 1997, 189). The pools in and around the theater at Nemi, however, seem to be unique, and must be there for ritual purposes (Nielsen 1997, 189).

And what audience did this theater serve? Certainly not the Aricians as a citizen body at the festival. It was far too small – less than 26 meters in diameter.[24] The entire structure could almost fit into the orchestra

---

[22] Morpurgo 1931, 302. See Chapter 11 for a discussion of these words in the context of ritual healing.

[23] Among the plays of Naevius there was an *Iphigenia*; Pacuvius portrayed Orestes and Pylades pursued by Thoas in his *Chryses*, and the murder of Aegisthus in *Thraldorestes*; Accius has an *Aegisthus* and an *Agamemnonidae*; Ennius an *Iphigenia*. None of these plays need have been written for the sanctuary; perhaps they were never performed there. Nevertheless, by appropriating Orestes, the cult was implicitly glossed every time these plays were performed. Equally, whenever Orestes and Iphigenia were presented in the cult, the plays were called to mind.

[24] On the theater: Morpurgo 1931, 240–51; Nielsen 1997, 188. (Morpurgo says the theater was 28 meters in diameter; Nielsen gives 25.5–30 east-west and 42–3 north-south.) Morpurgo suggested that the theater was used for the staging of the combat between the *rex nemorensis* and his challenger (1931, 302). This has not been widely accepted, and it cannot be right. The combat could only have occurred once or maybe twice in a generation – rituals this serious are only undertaken under the compulsion of divine direction (see Chapter 7). More important, however, is that actors are clearly provided for in a building that is made for performances. The real ritual of the *rex* existed long before the theater, and therefore the theater cannot have been essential to it. The ritual could have been dramatized even so.

of the theater at Epidauros. The audience had to be a select group, who were perhaps suppliants (as I think most likely), or initiates, or particular priests, magistrates, and elders from the city.

The function of the building that stands between the theater and the baths to the east, and the relationship between them and building K further to the east on the terrace, remains unknown. The baths certainly must have had ritual significance. In the Roman versions of the Orestes tragedy, Orestes was pursued by Thoas during a rough sea voyage that led him to exile (cf. Pacuvius frr. 79–90 Warmington). The baths may have been used in ritual imitation of the sufferings of the figures associated with the cult, for ritual purification, or both. They were in all likelihood also associated with ritual healing. Springs of magnesia-bearing water have been discovered near the lake, and the baths may have been supplied with this mineral water (Nielsen 1997, 188); the mere act of bathing to get clean would in itself have had health benefits for many.

Those who came to the sanctuary would often have had need of such simple comforts. Slaves and the poor still made up a recognizable portion of Diana's suppliants. For Persius (6.55–60) Aricia was a place where a man without a family acquired ancestors and heirs; another allusion indicated that in Nero's day, Aricia was still important to the freed slaves, the *liberti*, who had been deprived of all family connections by slavery. The poor and beggars seem to have found that the road to the sanctuary offered good opportunities for some aggressive panhandling in Martial's (12.32.10) and Juvenal's (4.117) day. Although in Satire 4 Juvenal was writing about the reign of Domitian, his audience read this poem some time after that emperor was dead, and the poet's attack on Blind Catullus as a beggar in Aricia was a slander contemporaries would have understood. Beggars go where there will be something to beg for. Appian, who wrote under Antoninus Pius (138–61), knew Aricia as one of the richest sanctuaries in Italy (*B.C.* 5.24). In Greece, addressing a Greek audience about the sanctuary of Epidauros, Pausanias (2.27.4), speaks of Aricia at length and has no need to explain its location or significance.

There are tile stamps from the reigns of Hadrian, Antoninus, and Marcus Aurelius (Ghini 2000, 55), indicating that buildings were being restored if not replaced entirely through the third quarter of the second century. Yet in Diana's sanctuary at this time, as in so many social institutions that have survived from the Republic, there is a sense of underlying stagnation. The reign of the Five Good Emperors was undoubtedly a time of peace and prosperity (Gibbon had a point here), but there was no dynamism in the institutions. There were no more creative adaptations of practice, myth, or theology in the sanctuary. Preservation, the maintenance of the status quo – that was absorbing all the money, all the creative energies. Beautiful restoration, but no evidence of new construction. By the end of the second century, Diana Nemorensis, whose cult, through innovation and expansion, had overcome so many disasters and crises – Arician loss of autonomy, the civil wars of the Republic, the accession of Octavian – was now simply holding on.

THE CLOSING OF THE SANCTUARY

Unfortunately, the land on which the sanctuary structures had been built was as liable as the politics of the imperial court to shift and become destabilized. By the third century something drastic had happened. At some point there were two destructive events – earthquakes? – in quick succession that severely damaged the buildings in the sanctuary. The damage was not repaired. No artifacts from after that period have been found. Such disasters, following the devastation wrought by the plague throughout Italy in the 160s, would have crippled the sanctuary's functions – those, particularly, that served great numbers of people. There were no more crowds turning off the Via Appia, making their way across the rim of the crater, and descending to the lake. When the crowds vanished, there could be no way to maintain, much less expand, the great sanctuary complex.

Clearly the late second century had brought changes that even the astute and adaptive Aricians found impossible to absorb. Yet the real death stroke had to have been the removal of the *rex nemorensis*. It need not have happened around the same time as the devastation of the sanctuary buildings. The *rex* lived in the wild, and his original service had been to Aricia, not to the pilgrims attracted there. He did not depend on streams of visitors or the wealth pouring into the temple. By Servius's time, the fourth century c.e., however, the priest-king had been removed to Sparta (*ad Aen.* 2.116). Servius does not tell us who was responsible, but by implication he does reveal two other important facts.

First, whatever the state of the sanctuary when it happened, the *rex* was still an impressive religious figure. Even in the heyday of the Republic, it was not unusual for priesthoods to simply fade away – the minor *flamines*, for instance, whose deities no one seemed even to understand. A quiet withering of such a priesthood was both possible and unexceptional. The *rex nemorensis* did not wither away, however. He had to be moved. The *rex* was still a religious figure to be reckoned with.

Second, Servius indicates that the ritual of the priest slaying his predecessor continued to be a potent and dangerously uncontrollable symbol of kingship. He says the *rex* was moved to Sparta because of the cruelty of the ritual. Even Servius finds this perplexing, and he protests that the *reges* were only slaves. Restraint from cruelty is hardly the defining mark of late antique culture – the arena comes to mind as a comparison – and the ritual would normally have occurred, at most, only three or four times in a century.[25] What was being removed from the sanctuary was not the cruelty of the ritual, but its meaning. Relegating the *rex* to Sparta placed him in a society known for its kings, with an important cult of Artemis and a tradition of violent initiation in the *agōge* but located in a backwater even more remote from the center of imperial public life than Aricia.

The center of imperial power was moving north and east, toward Constantinople. Emperors were rising out of every corner of the provinces, and the order of business in the third century was their assassination. The Christians, too, had promoted a man who died violently (and like a slave, for crucifixion was commonly used on slaves) as a human sacrifice to his god. He, too, was both a king (of the Jews, or of heaven) and a despised person. The struggle for authoritative possession of the dying and reborn god-king, the despised human sacrifice, not to mention the ascension to heaven of the divine queen – this was a scenario being fought over by Christianity and the cults of the

---

[25] Caligula's attack on the *rex* (Suet. *Cal.* 35.3) indicates that he was living to a considerable and well-known old age.

Magna Mater, Isis, and Demeter, with several influential variants also being offered through Mithraism. Diana's cult had spread wide – dedications to her have been found in Dalmatia (to *Triviabus*, *ILS* 3271), Cologne (*ILS* 3265), Spain (*ILS* 3260), and Mauretania (to *Dianae deae| nemorum comiti| victrici ferarum*, "Diana, goddess, companion of the forest, victor over the wild beasts," *ILS* 3257).

Yet however widespread her worship, it would never have been a match for the great mystery cults. More important, religious issues of this sort were no longer being decided at Rome, much less at Aricia – something that must have had its effect on the willingness of the Aricians to let their priest go. If the sanctuary had been ruined and never rebuilt, if the cult had become once more a set of rituals performed in a meadow below the woods beside the lake, if there were tumultuous and resolute religious forces changing the very nature of religious ideas, experiences, and expectations, all these would have combined to indicate that letting the *rex* go was somehow acceptable to the gods. The argument must have been made that Orestes' bones had been taken, and Aricia and the cult had survived: surely they could let the priest follow. Whatever the argument, and whoever made it, the *rex*, the quintessential exile, was exiled.

So the woods around the sanctuary were stripped of their priest-king; the number of visitors dwindled; the Christians arrived; the caves along the shore provided homes for hermits (Lenzi 2000, 161–3), and there is a Christian burial ground as well (Lenzi, 162). Diana's sanctuary was abandoned. We would very much like to know in what order these events occurred and how they were related. No doubt the process was neither logical nor swift. Everything, however, was leading to the same end. It is the cumulative effect of these events that matters, along with the multitude of large and small occurrences, now unknowable, that would have affected any sanctuary, dedicated to any non-Christian deity.

Rome itself was decaying. By the end of the fourth century, when even coins were no longer being dropped or lost around the sanctuary (Blagg 1986, 218) and the riches had long since been pillaged from Diana's temple, decay was everywhere at Aricia. The porticoes on the great terrace were collapsing, the marble no doubt being looted for the lime kilns, and whatever bronze that remained was being melted down for sale. As the bricks and cement crumbled, the vines, the trees, and the grasses slowly took over. The little animals – and some big ones – found new lairs; the trees grew thicker. The seasons following one another, the weather, the water running into the lake, the vegetation creeping over the ruins, all were returning the sanctuary to its native wildness. Diana's rule in her kingdom in the crater's hollow was untroubled by any of it. She was the goddess of change, of the decay that must precede renewal, of life, and of death. Wildness was in her nature.

4

DIANA: HER NAME
AND HER APPEARANCE

Her sanctuary tells us the context that her worshippers thought was appropriate for Diana. To know more about the presence Diana brought to this sanctuary, the divine identity of the goddess whom the Aricians and Latins worshipped here, we must turn to other sources: linguistic (for the roots of her name), material (votives, statues, coins, etc.), and written.

THE LINGUISTIC EVIDENCE

Discoveries arising from the linguistics of Indo-European root forms of Greek and Latin words persuaded scholars in the nineteenth century that the analysis of these linguistic roots would allow them to discover the original, and thus supposedly pure, form of Diana's name, with the corollary that this would make clear who, and what, she "really" was. In the end, of course, there was no great discovery, no uncovering of a hidden truth; but the information gleaned is nevertheless of value.

Modern philologists have concluded that Diana's name is a formation that arose from its Indo-European origins within the culture[1] that we identify as Italic. The core syllable is $d\bar{\imath}$. Birt (1890, 1002–3) argued that $D\breve{\imath}ana$ must be related to $d\breve{\imath}es$, "day," or $d\bar{\imath}um$, "the open sky," concluding, predictably, that she was therefore a goddess of the day or the open sky. Solmsen (*Studien zur lateinischen Lautgeschichte*; Strassburg, 1894, 111) then raised doubts as to the true quantity of $d\bar{\imath}$ in Diana.

---

[1] Cf. Smith 1996, 24–83, for a discussion of current scholarly views, and the archaeological evidence on which they are based, on the formation of the Italic world.

In the extant Latin examples Diana is normally scanned with ĭ. He argued that therefore the name *cannot* be related to the *dī* of *dīum*, which would require ī.

The literary evidence certainly offers no evidence for a secure decision one way or the other. A long first syllable is confirmed by Ennius (*Ann.* 240 Skutch) and Plautus (*Bac.* 312), but a short first syllable is indicated by the poetic usage – also early – of Lucilius (Warmington 143–5), and Plautus elsewhere (*Bac.* 307, *Mil.* 411). In the Augustan age *Dĭana* was by far the more popular choice. The reason is not far to seek. The short syllable offers far greater flexibility and grace in the hexameter,[2] although ī still appears, almost always as the final word in a line.[3]

Entirely abandoning the idea that Diana had Indo-European origins, Kretschmer (1924, 111–12) derived Diana's name from Etruscan "Tiv-," the moon goddess, also connecting it with Πανδῖα, the name for Selene in the Orphic mysteries. An Etruscan origin for Diana, however, has found no more support than the related position of Altheim (1930, 93–172), who thought that both the goddess and her name were entirely borrowed from the Greeks by way of the Etruscans. He argued (1930, 142–3) that the name "Diana," coming from *Divia or *Diviana, was a translation of σέλας (brightness, flame *LSJ s.v.*), which as Σελλασία was an epithet of Artemis in Laconia. This theory was fully refuted by Gordon (1932).

Since then, scholars have returned to the view that Diana's name had Indo-European roots and arose from the Italic culture of central Italy. Wissowa (1912, 247, n. 2) accepted the long first syllable of Diana's name but rightly thought it could not really determine her identity. Gordon (1934, 10), Bayet (1957, 20), Latte (1960, 169), Pairault (1969, 434), Schilling (1979, 373), and Scheid (1996, 1997) have all accepted the conclusion that the name has its roots in *dī* with a meaning of "light" or "shining." This root *dī* is found in *dius* ("daylit," "shining," "godlike"), *divus* ("a god") related to *deus* ("a god"), and possibly to

---

[2] Verg. *Aen.* 3.681, 4.511, 7.306, 7.764, 7.769, 11.537, 11.582, 11.652, 11.843, 11.857; Prop. 2.19.17, 4.8.29; Ovid, *Fast.* 1.388, 2.155, 3.81, 3.261, 4.761, 5.141, 6.745; *Met.* 1.487. First syllable short also in Hor. *Odes* 3.4.71; *Carm. Saec.* 75; *Ep.* 5.51; 17.3. Ambiguous, *Carm. Saec.* 70.

[3] ī scanned Verg. *Aen.* 1.499; Prop. 2.28.60.

dies ("day"), although that *ĭ* is short. Dumézil (1966, 407), although agreeing about the derivation, holds most strongly to the view that it is "open sky" (as in the Latin phrase, *sub divo*, under the open sky; *OLD s.v. diuum*) rather than the light of the moon that is reflected in her name.

Birt (1890, 1003), however, had long before confused the issue further and in the process made apparent the real weakness inherent in the use of linguistic evidence. He objected that because other goddesses were associated with the moon, Diana's name could not bear the meaning of "light" or "shining," and therefore (despite the testimony of Greek and Latin writers) she could not be a moon goddess. He was quite correct that other deities (not just goddesses) were in fact associated with the moon: Juno, for instance, has been identified as a moon goddess. In Rome the Kalends of every month, the days on which the new moon was sighted, were sacred to her. She was also known (on the Nones) as Juno Covella (Varro *LL* 6.27, "Juno of the crescent moon").[4] Her epithet was Lucina (Varro *LL* 5.69; Cic. *ND* 2.68), which she shared with Diana; and under that epithet, she, like Diana, was called on by women in childbirth.

In addition to Juno there was also Luna, "Moon" by name, who may or may not have been a separate deity. She had a temple in Rome just below the temple of Diana on the Aventine, and another as Noctiluna ("Night-Shiner") on the Palatine (Varro *LL* 5.68). Varro (*LL* 5.74) and Dionysius of Halicarnassus (2.50.3) both say that Titus Tatius brought the Sabine cults of Luna and Sol to Rome.

Birt was quite wrong, however, to conclude from all this that Diana *therefore* could not be a moon goddess. His argument relies on an unstated assumption that a special function or field of responsibility could belong to one god only: if Juno was goddess of the moon, or Luna, then Diana could not be. Yet polytheism has no such artificial boundaries and in itself encourages multiple divinities with overlapping responsibilities. The Ides of every month, the day on which the *full* moon (officially, according to the old lunar calendar) appeared,

---

[4] Rabinowitz makes an interesting, but ultimately unconvincing, argument that Juno must be the only moon goddess. Like so many scholars, he makes the assumption that there can only be one moon deity among the Latins, and that this deity had to be Roman.

was sacred to Jupiter (Macrob. *Sat.* 1.15.14), quintessentially the deity of day as *Dies Pater* (Varro *LL* 5.66). Jupiter was not as far as we know a deity of the moon[5] or of the night, but that did not prevent him from having authority over the official calendar day of the full moon.

Multiplicity of deities and functions seemed quite natural to Roman writers, and they made little effort to systematize. In the same passage in which Varro says the Sabines brought Luna to Rome, he says they also brought Lucina and Diana – but not Juno (*LL* 5.74).[6] And he also says that some call Luna "Diana," in the same way they call the Sun Apollo (*LL* 5.68). Luna's independent existence, therefore, can be doubted – as can Lucina's. It may well be that these are indeed epithets that were used independently when a very specific function was the purpose of prayer or supplication: Lucina when help in childbirth was needed; Luna when the moon specifically was worshipped. Certainly Luna's name may be no more than a factual referent for the divinity, as Sol, "Sun," is for Apollo.[7] If she was a separate goddess, however, she and Diana coexisted with Juno as moon deities.

Roman etymologists came to much the same conclusion as modern scholars have done about the root meaning of Diana's name: $d\bar{\imath}$ was connected to *dies* (day), to "light." So, according to Cicero, *Diana dicta quia noctu quasi diem efficeret* (*ND* 2.69;[8] "she was called Diana because she made it like day during the night"). Cicero, however, does not start with a disinterested question as to the meaning of $d\bar{\imath}$. His etymology

---

[5] It is worth noting, though, that the Romans seemed to have thought that Jupiter had an underworld (and anti-day) aspect. Varro connected Jupiter to both Dis and Orcus (*LL* 5.66). Jupiter is also a stone – possibly a meteorite from the sky – as Jupiter Lapis (Livy 1.24.8). Stones (even meteorites) have a particular connection to the earth and the "roots" of the earth. The complexity of Roman and Latin deities is an important part of the Latins' experience of religion.

[6] The Sabine influence on Rome will always be difficult to estimate correctly. Varro seems to acknowledge that he is stretching his linguistic evidence here (*paulo aliter ab eisdem dicimus haec*, "With minor alterations, we say the following [deities] are from the same people [i.e., the Sabines]"). What exactly constituted "minor alterations" we do not know.

[7] Or Liber. Macrobius (*Sat.* 1.18 16) quotes the poet Laevius' (fl. 90 B.C.E.) statement that Liber is Sol "because he is free and a wanderer." See Courtney (1993, 143). The "wanderer" (*vagus*), is clearly a translation of the Greek "Πλάνης."

[8] Text of *ND* is that of Plasberg.

simply contrives a relationship between the two facts known to him: Diana was the goddess of the moon, and the root *dī* also appears in *dies*. Similarly, Varro concluded that the variant of her name *Diviana* (*LL* 5.68) or perhaps *Deviana* (Probus, *ap. Verg. Ecl.* 6.31) arose from her behavior. In her wandering as the goddess of the moon "she at once achieves both altitude and latitude" (*in altitudinem et latitudinem simul it*).[9]

Thus the modern linguistic analysis telling us that Diana's name has its origins in "shining," "divine," and "the open sky" strengthens our sense that the ancient evidence identifying her as a goddess of the moon was correct. It also strongly suggests that such an identification goes back into the misty origins of the Italic peoples who worshipped her. This accords well with the nature of her Arician sanctuary because the crater particularly emphasizes the circle of earth and sky, with the sky and the moon reflected in the lake. As the *speculum Dianae*, the "mirror of Diana" (Verg. *Aen.* 7.151; Servius *ad Aen. ad loc.*), this lake accurately reflects one face of Diana, as goddess of the moon.

REPRESENTATIONS OF DIANA IN THE SANCTUARY

From the early archaic period, there is physical evidence for sacred actions having taken place in the sacred setting of the crater (Gierow 1964, 361–3), near where the late Republican terrace was built. Of the votives found, however, not many predate the temple built at the end of the fourth century. One small, and very beautiful, archaic bronze ex-voto of a female was found in Savile's excavations (Blagg 56 no. 650),[10] and another archaic votive, not yet published, has come

---

[9] Since *altitudo* can mean both "height" (*OLD s.v. altitudo*, 1–6) and "depth" (*OLD s.v. altitudo*, 7–8), and the moon goes both up in the sky and down around or below the earth, we should understand Varro's use of *altitudo* in this passage to include both high and low, just as *latitudo* must mean from one side of the horizon to the other. He elaborates on this later, *LL* 7.16. Cf. Cic. *ND* 2.69, where Diana is called *Omnivaga* (wide wandering) because she is considered one of the planets, the "wanderers."

[10] It has, in a typical Etrusco-Italic form, a female body as an elongated triangle, widest at the shoulders and tapering to the feet; on its head is a distinctive headdress or hairstyle. The unusual paddle-type headdress or hairstyle that rises above the head is larger but not unlike the knot of hair worn by Fundilia Rufa (Blagg 1983a, 22–3, plate iii) whose herm was found in what is called the "Fundilia Room." Fundilia was certainly an important

to light in the recent excavations of the terrace (Ghini 1997, 181). The provenience of this votive, in the fill excavated on the terrace, suggests that the earliest temple may have stood on the slope of the crater above and that more finds would come to light were this area to be excavated. However, the nature of the sanctuary itself, as well as later evidence from the cult, make it clear that wildness was always a fundamental element, and that the forest was invariably sacred space. Thus the absence of a temple, and of votives representing the goddess, may merely indicate that Diana was worshipped on altars and presented with offerings that were all perishable[11] and so left no archaeological record.

When she does finally emerge from the forest and her hidden past, and materializes as an anthropomorphic figure, Diana is a huntress, in the style of the Greek goddess of the hunt, Artemis (figure 4). Identifiable votives begin to appear in reasonable numbers at the end of the fourth and beginning of the third century, about the same time as the building of the earliest known temple, the one with the gilded roof (Blagg 1983, 48; Känel 2000, 185). This temple triumphantly celebrated the huntress. There was a terra-cotta sculpture of Diana standing on a gable or ridge. She was shown as a young woman in a chiton, right breast bare, with a strap for a quiver (Blagg 1983, 34 no. 136; Känel 185). Antefixes took the form of the winged "mistress of beasts," the so-called Persian Artemis (Blagg 1983, 30 pl. V; Känel 2000, 185; *LIMC* II [1984] "Artemis/Artumes," 777, 786–7, n. 12).

The subsequent temple, built in the late second or early first century, had an elegant gilded bronze frieze incorporating Diana's attributes, especially the quiver (Morpurgo 1903, 318–30). Some of the antefixes from this new temple carry a representation of Diana with her bow and quiver, and her hair secured with a characteristic bow-knot on top (Morpurgo 1903, 318; Blagg 1983, 31–7). Most interestingly, these antefixes have an unusual triangular shape, which Corelli (1987, 169) suggests may allude to Diana's triform nature: as goddess of the moon,

---

woman, and perhaps a priestess of the cult. It is possible that the headdress, like the *apex* of the Roman *flamines*, was a mark of office, and the sixth-century votive represented a similar female headdresses.

[11] Only perishable offerings were made to the Dea Dia even in historic times, as Gradel points out (2000, 203).

the hunt, and the underworld. Other antefixes from these buildings have scenes of the hunt itself (Morpurgo 1903, 318).

CULT STATUES

The fourth- and third-century temple thus proclaimed an already fully realized incorporation of the Artemis-type for Diana the huntress. The appropriation of Artemis for a visual representation of Diana had probably taken place in Latium as early as the sixth century (Malaspina 1994). As Warde Fowler long ago recognized (1899, 200), the iconographic syncretism of Artemis and Diana was certainly complete in Rome by the time of the *lectisternium* in 399/8 (Livy 5.13), where Diana is drawn into the family of Latona (Leto) and Apollo. Ampolo (1970) regarded this integration of the Greek image with the Latin goddess as due to the influence of the Phocaeans, who in the sixth century were competing with the Etruscans in the Tyrrhenian sea (Hdt. 1.165–7) and were also the founders of Massilia (Strabo 4.1.4).[12] It was also in the sixth century that we see close political and military connections between Aricia and Cumae (Livy 2.14.5–6; DH *AR* 5.36). Connections strong enough to bring a military force north to aid Aricia against Porsenna imply a well-established sense of mutual interest.[13] Such mutual interests will also have furthered the interchange of cultural and religious practices.

It is quite possible, then, that there was, among the Aricians, an Artemis-type Diana long before the gilded-roof temple. One candidate for this image, to be dated around 500 B.C.E., was identified by Alföldi (1960). Alföldi argued that the triple Diana on the reverse of the coin of 43 B.C.E. (figure 5), put out by the moneyer P. Accoleius Lariscolus,[14]

---

[12] Late copies of the famous many-breasted (if they were breasts) Ephesian Artemis have been found (Cassatella 1985, 445) on the Aventine, but neither Strabo's testimony nor the late votives clarify matters much. Lora Holland's work, I hope, will soon illuminate the arguments on this point in regard to the Roman worship of Diana.

[13] There had been close connections between southern Italy (Campania and Calabria) and Latium from the early Iron Age, demonstrated by the pottery and other artifacts (*Protohistory* 2000, 23–35). There was no impenetrable barrier shutting Latium off from the rest of Italy at any time.

[14] This coin (figure 5), dated to 43 B.C.E., is helpfully analyzed in Beard, North, Price 1998, vol. 2. 15. Cf. also, *LIMC* "Artemis/Diana" Diana, no. 193; Alföldi 1960; Jentoft-Nilsen 1985, 89.

was a copy of an early triform statue of Arician Diana. The Diana on the left holds a bow and is thus the huntress; the Diana on the right holds a poppy. The central Diana has no attribute but is identical to the other two. Their skirts are long, as is the skirt of the huntress sculpture on the first temple. The style differs, however.[15] The three are joined by a bar behind their heads, and four cypresses rise behind them. Fullerton (15–22), however, has argued that the image copied on the coin cannot be dated earlier the second quarter of the first century.[16]

A certain barbarism was identified with Diana's cultic image. Even if the triple figure cult image copied on the coin was a late archaizing work, as Fullerton says, this tells us nothing about any image it replaced in the precinct. Established cult images do not, after much time, radically alter and take on unprecedented "barbaric" iconography. Moreover, Strabo claims (5.3.12) that the icon at Aricia was a copy of one from "the Tauric region" (the background is given by Servius *ad Aen.* 2.116 and 6.136). It should thus in some way be connected with material from Euripides' play *Iphigenia among the Taurians*. The adoption of the Euripidean myth of Iphigenia and Orestes would have been a fairly radical change, and so certainly had to have been accomplished long before the first century. It might best be assigned to the same changes that brought about the late-fourth-century temple with its Hellenistic influences. A radically new version of a cult myth and the transformation of the sanctuary are probably connected. The Orestes myth at Aricia and the otherwise strange and atypical cult statue worked together. The statue's peculiar and "barbaric" appearance then was explained by its origin in (Thracian?) Tauropolos. Certainly a triple image would be strange and possibly barbaric-seeming,[17] and it was

---

[15] Diana the huntress could wear the long skirt, as the Augustan coin (11–9 B.C.E., Jentoff-Nilsen 1985, 89 *BMC* 489 [1, p. 84]) shows (cf. *LIMC* 1 216, ca. 200 B.C.E.).

[16] The crisis of the Social Wars may indeed have been the impetus for a new emphasis on barbarism in the cult, but this emphasis still would only have been an exploitation of a long-standing, well-recognized quality of the goddess and her tradition.

[17] The Romans were supposed to have copied their cult statue of Diana from the Massiliote Artemis (Strabo 4.1.5), which was in turn a sacred image taken from Ephesus (Strabo 4.1.4). It is an interesting that tradition firmly reported both the Roman and the Arician cult statues as having been borrowed or brought from elsewhere, in neither case with much plausibility.

exceptional even in the cult. It may also have been fashioned in gold, for Ovid speaks of one such:

> Est nemus et piceis et frondibus ilicis atrum;
> vix illuc radiis solis adire licet.
> sunt in eo – fuerant certe – delubra Dianae;
> aurea barbarica stat dea facta manu.
>
> Ovid *Her.* 12.70–1

There is a grove darkened with leafy oak and pine; the rays of the sun are barely allowed to creep in. There is in it – there once was, certainly – a shrine of Diana; the golden goddess stands there, fashioned by a barbaric hand.

Medea is the speaker of these lines, and she belonged to the same Black Sea regions that were known as Scythia. It is not just possible but probable, given that Augustus was a reader of these poems, that Ovid is here ornamenting his narrative with the statue of Diana at Aricia placed in its "original" home. A few lines later, Medea swears *per triplicis vultus arcanaque sacra Dianae* ("by the threefold-faces and the sacred mysteries of Diana"; 12.79). A triple image of the goddess in the form of an archaizing gold cult statue, and said to be from "Scythia," would indeed have been worthy of notice.

There is no evidence that the triple-figured Diana was ever imitated in terra-cotta votives or copied in any other form. Yet whether or not there had been an archaic statue group earlier, the first-century one copied on the Lariscolus coin tells us a great deal about the self-presentation of the cult. This was an image of the cult the Aricians had consciously chosen and deliberately maintained. Diana, they proclaimed, was a complex goddess who possessed an archaic and partially barbarian identity.

On the obverse of the Lariscolus coin there is a bust of Diana. After the publication of Alföldi's article, Paribeni (1961) suggested that an archaizing marble bust of the first century C.E. found at the sanctuary (Morpurgo 1903, 259 pl. 6; Riis 1966, 71; *LIMC* "Diana" 106) was a *replica* of the head of an archaic statue – indeed, of the triple statue of the coin. Then Riis (1966) made a strong argument that the fifth-century bronze head in the Glyptotek (*LIMC* "Diana" 110) belonged to an early cult statue and suggested that it too might derive from an early triple-form Diana.[18] The resemblance of the bronze head to the bust of Diana on the Lariscolus coin is very striking. Both show a close cap of hair drawn forward into either curls or a roll or braid framing the face. Riis has identified the hairstyle of this bronze head as distinctive for the representation of Diana, pointing out that the bronze bust of the fifth century, the marble head discussed by Paribeni, and the head on the obverse of the Lariscolus coin all share this unusual hairstyle. It appears not just on the obverse of the Lariscolus coin but also on Roman coins representing Diana going back to the beginning of the second century B.C.E. (Jentoff-Nilsen 1985, 17–22 and plates). (This, in addition, confirms the identification of the bronze bust as Diana.) Riis has made a persuasive argument, and the proposed identification of the bronze head as part of an archaic or fifth-century cult statue for Diana remains probable. Still, without other evidence, we cannot be absolutely certain that what we have is the bust of the archaic cult statue.

Finally, the larger than life-size Diana statues appear, contemporaries of the temple constructions of the later second and early first centuries B.C.E. The quality of the marble, Pentelic and Parian, as well as the size, supports the interpretation of them as cult statues. Here, Diana exhibits (figure 6) a dignified and queenly image (Guldager Bilde, 1997b; Guldager Bilde and Moltesen 2002, 20–1 cat. nos. 1 and 2) that is like, and yet distinct from, that of Diana the huntress. She may have been enthroned (Guldager Bilde 2002, 20–2 and figures 4–9). The womanly Diana of these later cult statues may still have carried a quiver and bow, but the evidence is lacking. She was much more like Juno. Because Diana and Juno were both called Lucina and were both worshipped as moon goddesses, these statues may have been the image of Diana the moon goddess.

DIANA AS AN ARTEMIS FIGURE

Despite these very different cult statues of Diana as triple goddess or queenly divinity, it was the girl huntress who won by far the greatest

---

[18] Guldager Bilde suggests that there is also a resemblance to the female in the so-called Agisthus relief (1997, 200).

favor among her worshippers (figure 4). The votive representations of the goddess as huntress are the most numerous.[19] In her most familiar form, Diana is a young woman in a knee-length tunic, boots, and deerskin mantle, wearing a quiver and holding a bow (Moltesen 1997, 154–5 and 157–64; Blagg 1983f, 48–56; Riis 67–74; cf. *LIMC* "Diana," 69). Sometimes she is alone, sometimes accompanied by a hunting hound (e.g., Blagg 1983, 48 N67), and sometimes with a deer or stag beside her (e.g., Blagg 1983, 50 N178: *LIMC* 216). These votives are typical of central Italic practice, and many come from molds which produced votives dedicated at other sanctuaries (Blagg 1983, 46). They disappear in the late first century B.C.E., at Nemi as elsewhere, indicating a shift in the expression of religious devotion. But from the time of the first temple at the end of the fourth century to the end of the Republic, the Artemis-type was the most widely used image of Diana at the sanctuary. The Republican temples had antefixes, as well as roof and frieze sculpture, of Diana the girl huntress, and the theme was reinforced by the use of hunting equipment as decoration.

Diana was a goddess of hunters long before the introduction of the Artemis-type into Italy. What we must try to understand is what the statues, architectural decorations, and votives tell us about how Aricians used the Artemis-type to express religious ideas concerning their goddess.

> Above all, we must break free . . . of the assumption that a unified, freestanding, style is somehow expressive of historical individuality. . . . We can no longer approach works of art exclusively from the standpoint of production, as the expressions of artists or patrons, but we must also examine them as forms of communication – that is, as a factor in the collective life of a society.
>
> Hölscher 2004, 7

Diana as huntress – and the other representations of her – are part of the ongoing communication of the Aricians (and all their visitors) about their religious beliefs. It is extremely important to attend to the religious expression of those who came to the cult.

---

[19] Terracotta votives: Morpurgo 1903, 324; Blagg 1983e, 48–50; Blagg 1986, 214; Känel 2000, 204; bronze: Morpurgo 1903, 318–20, 324–32 and figs. 22, 39–45; Blagg 1983f, 54–6; marble: Guldager Bilde and Moltesen 2002, 24–5, cat. nos. 5–7).

NEGOTIATION OF IMAGE AND SYMBOL

Hölscher rightly points out that the characteristic response of eighteenth and nineteenth-century scholarship was to see Roman culture as a culture of imitators: more specifically, imitators of the Greeks. Twentieth-century reaction against this attitude, however, even as it cast Greek culture as a foreign disruption of the indigenous, and independent, genius of Roman art (Hölscher 2004, 6), still tended to preserve the widely disseminated Romantic belief – so ingrained as often to be taken for granted, without need for words – that originality and individualism were the defining mark of creative genius.

Hölscher is concerned particularly with the visual arts. His observations about the scholarly perception that the Romans are either imitators or were somehow subjugated by the power of Greek myth and art, applies just as well to the study of Roman and Latin religion. If the visible forms of religion, the statues and votives, so the argument goes, were not indigenous and independent, this proves, virtually by definition, the impoverishment of the native religious experience (e.g., Horsfall 1987). What is even more disturbing is the corollary: that if the temple statues and votives, such as those at Aricia, follow Greek prototypes, then the religion of Diana's cult must also be following a Greek prototype. The assumption that visual imagery is the defining characteristic of a cult is inseparable from the idea that only radical originality can express the beliefs of a truly independent society.

Fortunately for the study of religion, new models for understanding and analyzing the Greek impact on religious iconography in Latium from the seventh century on are replacing the old models of Greek versus Roman, cultural versus political conquest. Most significant has been Dench's reformulation of the entire study of Hellenistic Italy (Dench 2003), the crystallization of several decades of work by historians, archaeologists, and art historians (Dench 2003, 289–300). As Dench makes clear, by the late fourth century a clear set of iconographical rules had been developed in south Italy: "the winners are made to occupy the role of 'Greeks,' while the losers are attributed the representational space and posture of 'barbarians'" – even when the "winners" were clearly Romans and the losers were Samnites (Dench 2003, 300). That is, the visual language of self-identification, "Greek," had been appropriated to describe "us," and "barbarian" to describe "them." As we have seen, and will see in more detail, the Aricians clearly required both qualities, the Greek and the barbarian, the Us and Them, to express Diana's nature fully. They were also exceptionally sophisticated in deploying these qualities in both visual and literary expression.

A similar process of appropriation and creative adaptation has been described by Webster, in her study of the "Romanization" of the Celtic religion in the Roman provinces.[20] Whereas Dench presents the political and public aspect of cultural appropriation, Webster provides an excellent analysis of religious appropriation (2001, 219–23), which she describes as a pragmatic process of "negotiation" (2001, 221). Such negotiation is what we should see in the Roman and Latin appropriation of Greek classical representations of deities. While the Greek sculptors provided a new, and very Greek, way of "seeing" the gods, nevertheless the gods were Latin. One legacy of Christianity is the privileging of either-or in religion. Even when scholars have put aside Christian bias, there is still a tendency to suppose that a strong and vital religious tradition must necessarily find "contamination" repugnant, and that any introduction of a new mode of representation, particularly if it is "foreign," must also signal some failure, a crisis, or a lack of conviction in existing religious practice. Certainly religion was always a means of self-identification, a foundation on which to base the description of Us and Them. Yet the Italians, the Latins, and the Romans were far more subtle, and far more inconsistent, in their application of that cultural dichotomy than is acceptable in the inherited context of Christian belief.[21] As both Dench and Webster demonstrate, dominant beliefs and iconographic traditions (whether Greek or Roman) influence and frequently enlarge those of the indigenous cultures, but this does not constitute proof of a fundamental change in belief or in practice. Quite the contrary: it is evidence for a vigorous religion engaging with, and using, new ideas to express itself.

[20] For the place of Webster's comparative colonial approach within the "paradigm shift" currently taking place in Roman material culture studies, see S. James, "Roman Archaeology: Crisis and Revolution," *Antiquity* 77 (2003): 178–84.

[21] Although it must also be recognized that the Christian construct of the "saved" vs. the "damned" is the ultimate application of that old system of Us and Them, Greek and Barbarian.

Such new models are particularly valuable in studying Latin religion. This is particularly the case in the appropriation of an established Greek mythic language as the means of discussing Italic or Latin identity and beliefs, because Dench and Webster provide a much more nuanced approach to the problems presented by the Hellenized appearance of Diana. These models also accord much better with our understanding of what religion is, a living process where human beings interact with each other and the divine, "through symbols, exchanging signs, and reacting to them while working on their own 'reality' which constitutes 'religion'" (Burkert 1996, 5). Religion was not a fixed cultural construct, certainly not in pre-Christian antiquity. When the Artemis type of Diana was first used in sixth-century Latium, it was through conscious choice. Whatever the Artemis figure represents, it must be the result of choices made by the Latin people, a negotiation between their inherited understanding of their own gods and rituals, and the models for representation presented by the Greeks. It was through Greek images that Latin religion began to forge, consciously and deliberately, its own religious expression in terms of material culture.

We must begin now to ask how each cult uses the visual and religious language that the Greeks made available to the Mediterranean world. This will lead us much closer to the elucidation of our evidence. For instance, we know that the Artemis myth was adopted for Diana in Rome from the sixth century and her cult statue was a copy of the Massiliotes' Artemis. What use, if any, we should ask, was made of the accompanying Greek mythic and cultic material, how did the Massiliote Artemis represent that, and what does it tell us about the worship of Diana at Rome, or at Aricia? We know that Romans, by the beginning of the fourth century, had officially accepted Diana as part of the family of Apollo and Leto, and all three were celebrated in the *lectisternium* of 399. Octavian, as we have seen, brilliantly exploited this long-standing Roman divine family, taking on the attributes of Apollo, and celebrating Diana as his sister. Hence Horace's *Carmen Saeculare*, which honors brother and sister almost equally.

The first appearance of the Artemis type at Aricia also probably occurred in the sixth century and was certainly full-fledged by the end of the fourth, a century after the Roman *lectisternium* of 399. Yet

Apollo never insinuated himself into the cult life of the Arician sanctuary. Even after Octavian became Augustus, and Apolline imagery, together with the sibling relationship, became part of the foundation for the principate, Aricia showed no interest in appropriating Apollo. Octavian might import the remains of Orestes from Aricia to Rome, but Aricia never brought the princeps' Apollo to Diana's sanctuary. That is significant for our reconstruction of the cults at Rome and Aricia, and demonstrates just how independently the Greek material could be used. Myth and iconography were adopted only insofar as they gave greater expression to existing cultic (and perhaps civic) constructs; what was irrelevant for those purposes was left out.

There was always an undercurrent of competition between Rome and Aricia over Diana. One curious fact: Romans and Aricians both acknowledged that their cult statues of Diana were borrowed – but not from Greece, except secondhand through semibarbarous Greek colonies. The Massiliote Artemis whose copy was placed in the Aventine temple was itself a copy in turn of Ephesian Artemis, whereas Aricia's Diana came from Tauropolos – a mythical place generally held to be somewhere on the Black Sea. These acknowledgments of barbaric borrowing become even more interesting in that there is no corroborating evidence for either claim.

THE NATURE OF TRANSFORMATION

The independence of Arician use of Greek material can been seen at its clearest when we consider the way in which Greek myth was, and was not, used to discuss cultic figures. At Aricia, the *rex nemorensis* survived, as did Egeria. The *rex* might have gained a Greek founder in Orestes, but, as we will see (Chapter 8), this affected the myth of Orestes rather more than it influenced Diana's priest-king. Virbius suffered *interpretatio Graeca*,[22] but even when he was interpreted through the myth of Hippolytus, he was not lost and his name was not forgotten

---

[22] Perhaps the fact that Egeria was called a "nymph" may be considered *interpretatio Graeca*, but once again it shows us more the degree to which such interpretation was limited. Egeria has a distinctly Latin story, associated with Rome and Numa, with a retirement at Aricia. No Greek myths were attached to her.

(Chapter 9). All this indicates that a vigorous Latin cult continued un-interrupted into the historic period. What is more, only Hippolytus – not Orion, not Actaeon, not Meleager – was borrowed from among the many young hunters associated with Artemis in Greek mythology.

At Rome, on the other hand, the cult of Diana never acquired any kind of young male attendant from Artemis' Greek mythology (or from Aricia). The Romans might have taken Orestes' bones, but that was a historical event; the myth of Orestes remained attached to Aricia. The independence of these two cults is made evident by the fact that when Octavian brought Orestes to Rome from Aricia, he put the urn by the temple of *Saturn*.

In the end it becomes impossible to sustain any theory, for any period, of the domination of Latin religion by imported Greek myth and iconography. What we see, rather, is evidence for a creative nego-tiation between the Greek tradition and Roman or Latin religious concerns. *Use* determines the nature of the cult. It was Artemis' hunt-ing nature that was important at Aricia, and it served to emphasize the religion of hunting in the Arician cult. Ex-votos are a fair guide to popular belief: Diana the huntress was sought, petitioned, and propiti-ated in daily worship. The early and later temple decorations manifestly express the priests', and Arician elders', interpretations of their Diana: Diana was a huntress, but that was not all she was. The evidence for her name as a moon goddess, the possible cult statues (whether they were really cult statues or not) and the triple Diana (whether that was an original statue group, a copy of an original, or a late archaizing invention), all make it clear that Diana was much more complicated. The images of the girl huntress were, and are, only a beginning.

5

THE GROVE, THE GODDESS,
AND THE HISTORY OF EARLY LATIUM

THE LATIN PEOPLE AND DIANA

There is another very early aspect of Diana that we must consider, that of her appearance in the sixth century B.C.E. as the patron goddess for alliances of Latin cities, some (apparently) against Rome, but at least one of all the Latin cities with Rome at its head. Once we understand how she functioned and was used by the Latins in this early period we will know a great deal more about the archaic, Latin identity of Diana before the appearance of the Artemis-type iconography in the fourth century.

To begin with, we must return to Grattius' account of the ritual at the meeting point of paths in the forest, the *discrimen*, which suggests that an old initiation ritual lay behind this Augustan civic religious celebration. At the *discrimen* the participants fling down their weapons. This ritual of disarmament is quite different from the prohibition of arms in sanctuary precincts. Diana's groves and sanctuaries were always in the wild, outside the boundaries of the city. In the archaic period the forest was actively dangerous territory, inhabited by wild animals, lawless men of all kinds (men whom the *rex nemorensis* ritually symbolizes), and enemy warriors. Men would never have approached Diana's sanctuary except under arms. A ritual that controlled these weapons therefore would be among the most important of Diana's concerns.

The ritual served as more than a proof of Diana's power to protect unarmed men in the woods. In the eighth and seventh centuries, Latium consisted of relatively isolated, mostly mountain, communities, each ruled by warrior elites anxious to prove themselves.[1] There must have been a constant making and breaking of local Latin alliances organized against each other. Thus Diana's grove was a place where the leaders of these cities could meet in safety to have their differences settled by the larger group. When differences were beyond settlement, individual cities could meet there to discuss alliances and combined military actions to be taken against mutual enemies. The need for mutual aid would not, obviously, mean that they trusted one another. The absence of arms would have served to prevent violence and treachery at such meetings.

THE CATO FRAGMENT

Lucum Dianium in nemore Aricino Egerius Baebius (Laevius)[2] Tusculanus dedicavit dictator Latinus; hi populi communiter; Tusculanus, Aricinus, Lanuvinus, Laurens, Coranus, Tiburtis, Pometinus, Ardeatis Rutulus.

Cato fr. 58 Peter

Egerius Laevius the Tusculan, as Dictator Latinus, consecrated the Grove of Diana in the Arician forest; and the peoples of the following cities communally: Tusculum, Aricia, Lanuvium, Laurentum, Cora, Tibur, Pometia, Rutulian Ardea.

This passage refers to one such set of alliances. It does not tell us when the alliance was made, nor does it indicate the enemy against whom they were uniting. In order to consider the political implications of this fragment, however, it is important first to gain as much insight into the religious context as possible. It is much to Alföldi's credit to have recognized (1965, 48) that the context of the fragment meant Diana *had* to be a warrior goddess in the sixth century, even though he could not (and did not try to) explain how she later became the Wissowan "women's goddess."

---

[1] See Smith 1996, 77–105, for an excellent summary of the archaeological evidence indicating the fortification of Latin communities from the eighth century or even earlier, the increasing wealth of the élite, the expansion to which this led, and the inevitable resultant tension over disputed territory. Alföldi's postulation of an organized Latin tribal community from the earliest days (1964, 46) cannot be sustained, although tribal connections were clearly recognized. See Cornell 1995, 293–8, for a much more nuanced analysis of the relationship among the Latins.

[2] *Baebius* is the reading of one of the manuscripts, generally accepted instead of *Laevius*, read by Peter.

The first and most important question raised by the dedication is, obviously, whether it marked the religious beginning of the cult of Diana at Aricia. This it cannot have done. As Wissowa (1912, 247–8) argued, the evidence of the sanctuary and the priesthood of the *rex nemorensis* indicates that the cult must date at least from the late Bronze Age.[3] Whatever event the dedication recorded in the fragment of Cato refers to, it cannot represent a *historical* beginning to the sanctuary of Diana. Moreover, the dedication of a grove to Diana by the Latin peoples was not unusual. We are told that the leaders of the Latin communities met in other groves (Corne, near Tusculum, Pliny *NH* 16.242; and the Lucus Ferentinae,[4] Livy 1.50; DH *AR* 3.34.3, 4.45.3),[5] although we have no evidence of cult worship in them. They were places of *numen*, but not of cult. They retained their identification as sacred groves, but how they were distinguished as such, lacking ritual and precinct markers, we do not know. Diana was certainly the goddess of the grove at Corne (*lucus antiqua religione Dianae sacratus*, "a grove consecrated to Diana in accordance with ancient religious belief"; Pliny *NH* 16.242), and it is probable that she was also the patron of the Lucus Ferentinae (Ampolo 1981). In addition, there is the foundation of a shrine to Diana dedicated by Servius Tullius, on behalf of the Latin League, on the Aventine – the only other place in Latium besides Aricia where a grove to Diana[6] is associated in our sources both with the Latin people and with the foundation of a *cult*.

SACRED DISARMAMENT IN THE FOREST

The precinct was dedicated, perhaps with a sod altar, at a meeting of representatives in the Arician grove. Such dedications seem to have been standard among the Latin peoples. A sacred grove, being

[3] The antiquity of the cult was accepted even by Momigliano 1962, one of the few to dispute Wissowa's views on the relationship between Rome and Aricia.
[4] Zevi (1995, 125) argues that such groves were sacred either to Diana (when they were in the wild) or to Aphrodite (when they were in or near cities).
[5] Other groves of Diana were found at Tibur (Mart. 7.28.1) and near Anagnia, where the Via Latina separated from the Via Labicana (Liv. 27.4.12). These are not identified as meeting places of the Latin people, but both might have originated in that way.
[6] It is reasonable to assume that a grove sacred to Diana preceded the shrine which Servius Tullius caused to be dedicated to her (Liv. 1.45; DH *AR* 4. 26).

something more than mere neutral ground, offered distinct advantages for such meetings. It always lay outside the *pomerium*, the sacred boundaries, even of the city that controlled it (e.g., Tusculum and the grove at Corne, the sanctuary of Diana and Aricia). The advantages are quite apparent. When they used a grove outside the city boundaries, warriors did not have to enter the walls of a possibly hostile community and then relinquish their arms. In return, a city did not have to open its gates to armed men sent by a potential aggressor. Diana and her grove provided security for peaceful meetings of rival communities.[7] Because such groves were common in Latium, such a meeting place was both appropriate and convenient for those concerned.

The religious ritual that facilitated these meetings long predated the sixth century and the appearance of the so-called Latin League. There is no reason whatsoever to think that the meetings had to be of all the Latins – whoever *they* might have been. In their original archaic form, the meetings must have included the principal communities concerned in any conflict, together with their supporters. No doubt rival meetings were held in rival groves when that was necessary.

TURNUS HERDONIUS AND TARQUINIUS SUPERBUS

Let us now look at the account of one of those meetings in the late sixth century, reported by both Livy and Dionysius. Although it shows that secularism and political ambition were already undermining the communal religious sense that made the meetings possible, the very transgressions illuminate traditional expectations by contrast.

The incident concerns Tarquinius Superbus and one Turnus Herdonius of Aricia (Livy 1.50–1; DH *AR* 4.45–8). According to these accounts, Tarquinius[8] appointed a meeting of the Latin *proceres*

---

[7] Other deities whose worship traditionally lay outside the city boundaries may also have served the same purpose. There is no exclusive claim to any function by any deity, although by practice, certain deities became favored for specific purposes, as Diana was for meetings under truce.

[8] The location of the grove cannot be determined with absolute certainty. The question turns very much on what might constitute the *aquae Ferentinae*, waters that had to be deep enough to drown a man (Livy 1.51.7–9). Arguments for various locations are surveyed in Ampolo (1981, 221–4). Ampolo (1981, 226–33) persuasively argues for a location very near Aricia, the Alban Mount and the Via Appia, known in medieval times

("nobles" or "men of distinction") at the Lucus Ferentinae. The *proceres* were there by daybreak (*prima luce* Livy 1.50.2), which means they either had traveled several hours in the dark from their respective communities (unlikely) or had actually arrived the day before. Tarquinius, however, demonstrated his arrogance by not appearing until too late for the proceedings that day – a little before sundown (Livy 1.50.2) or even until the next day (DH *AR* 4.45.3–46.1). Turnus attacked Tarquinius for this insult to the assembled Latins, Tarquinius responded with his own charges against Turnus, and the Latin nobles agreed to reassemble the next day, clearly intending to debate the charges and come to some conclusion as to Tarquinius' fitness to lead them. To deal with the problem in his own way, Tarquinius bribed a slave of Turnus' to bring a quantity of swords into his master's "lodgings" (*deversorium* Livy 1.51.2; τήν κατάλυσιν τοῦ δεσπότου DH *AR* 4.47.2) during the night. These swords, revealed the next day, became Tarquinius' proof to the assembled *proceres* that Turnus was plotting an assassination. Turnus was condemned, imprisoned in a wicker cage, and either buried alive (DH *AR* 4.48.2) or drowned in the Aqua Ferentinae (Livy 1.51.7–9).

If the weapons found secreted in Turnus' "lodgings," falsely introduced though they were, counted as proof of his criminal intentions, then the men meeting at the Lucus Ferentinae were clearly expected either to come unarmed or to surrender their arms on arrival. Moreover, as Ampolo has demonstrated,[9] Turnus' punishment is a classic ritual death, a purificatory sacrifice for the violation of the prohibition against weapons. In the same way, a Vestal who betrayed her vows was buried alive (DH *AR* 2.67). This punishment is reserved for only the most profound violations of sacred law. Turnus' alleged

and antiquity as the *lacus Turni*; cf. Zevi (1995, 123–5). Against Ampolo's suggestion, however, is the fact that it stretches the imagination to have a place clearly named as the *Lucus Ferentinae* beside a well-known *Lacus Turni* and yet for Livy to be ignorant of it (Dionysius as a Greek might not know enough about the topography of Latium). Far more likely, it seems to me, is that Turnus was a real person and the connection with the *Lacus Turni* was what made him in Livy's sources (and in Livy's opinion) an Arician. Dionysius, not knowing the topography, probably preserves his actual home, in a corrupt form, as Κορίλλη. It has not been noticed that "Ferentina" may be an epithet of Diana herself.

9 Ampolo 1981, 226.

crime was the equivalent of a Vestal's sexual impurity. The presence of weapons in the sacred grove polluted the entire community of Latin people.[10] The fact that the crime was the introduction of weapons, for which the ritual punishment was death, substantially increases the likelihood that the Lucus Ferentinae was a sacred grove of Diana.

The account by Dionysius of Halicarnassus of the same event (4.45–8) is much richer in (potentially more spurious) detail than that of Livy, but their accounts agree in essence. However, one fact that Dionysius provides about the hiding of the weapons tells us more than has been realized. He says that the weapons were hidden ἐν τοῖς σκευοφόροις, which would normally mean "on the pack animals" or "porters." This has caused unnecessary puzzlement. The need for pack animals has not been understood, because it has not been realized that the participants had to spend the night in tents in the grove the night before the meeting at dawn. Pack animals were required to bring in the tents and supplies.

So Tarquinius laid his plot, remaining in Rome, while the delegates, Turnus among them, spent the night within the sacred grove, where the ritual prohibition against weapons was in force. Each community's delegation – perhaps two or three men at the least, with the appropriate number of attendants[11] – would have had to bring its own tents and supplies. So pack animals (or at least *one* pack animal) would have been necessary for Turnus, as for the other delegates. A pack animal secretly loaded with the forbidden weapons could be led into the grove, and be there, unsuspected among the others, in the morning.

Some ritual would probably have been performed at night, and in the morning the assembled Latin *proceres* could begin their

---

[10] Dionysius was sufficiently struck by the account he received to feel the need for an explanation of what Turnus' "crime" had been. He has Turnus provide the explanation and the justification of his own death, that he should be executed ἐὰν εὑρεθῇ παρεσκευασ-μένος ὅπλα ἔξω τῶν ἐνοδίων· (if he were found to have provided arms more than those necessary for his journey; 4.48.1). This is a feeble and clearly inadequate reason for so speedy and dreadful a punishment. However, Dionysius, lacking knowledge of the ritual under which the meeting was held, has at least *tried* to explain it.

[11] If we begin with the improbable but canonical thirty Latin communities (Livy 2.18.3; DH *AR* 3.31.4; Alföldi 1964, 10–25), that means sixty to ninety *proceres* and at least an equal number of attendants.

deliberations.[12] Then Tarquinius arrived. Any violation of ritual prohibitions would have required the appeasement of the goddess. The
appeasement would be the sacrifice of the one who violated the ritual.

What sharply distinguishes such meetings from, say, the annual celebration of Jupiter Latiaris is their irregularity and the varying number
of cities involved. Such meetings would be invoked by the Latins as
and when needed and would include only those directly concerned.
The communities that gathered at any one time for the ritually protected meeting would thus not necessarily include all those of the Latin
name.[13] The need for such meetings is obvious. A shared ethnic identity and a shared Latin cult of Jupiter Latiaris could never of themselves
have kept them from being contentious and mutually hostile. This is
the context in which the ritual of the grove sacred to Diana became
so important. It, too, could not eradicate the hostility, but at least it
offered a safe meeting ground for negotiation.

By the sixth century, the chief enemies of the Latin communities
were the Sabines and the Etruscans. The greater the external threat, the
greater the potential for federation and the stronger the inducement to
abandon internecine quarrels. As political sophistication grew, some of
these Latin communities – again like Rome or Aricia – would begin to
use the gathering in the grove to consolidate and develop their political
power. Such consolidation must have brought a natural extension of
the ritual, but the notion that consolidation and federation of power
had been the original function and motivation of the meetings in the
grove cannot be sustained. Diana was not a "federal deity." She was
the goddess whose sacral power enforced a truce between men who
bore arms, whether as hunters or warriors. The ritual of her grove
offered a sacred and neutral space where hostile communities could
meet. This early use of the grove was to provide a context in which to
settle peacefully the complaints of one group of Latins against another
or to create an alliance of Latins against a common enemy. Before the
sixth century, there was nothing that could be described as a "Latin

---

[12] By the first century, neither Livy nor Dionysius could be quite sure what "late" meant
in this context, but they were both very certain that Turnus' late arrival was consciously
insulting and that he had deliberately forced a postponement of the meeting to accom-
modate him.

[13] Liou-Gille has counted six different lists of members (1997, 737, n. 46).

League." Nevertheless, the ritual of the grove made it possible for the concept of a League to develop.[14]

THE DICTATOR LATINUS

Cato records that a dictator Latinus made the dedication at the grove of Diana. He could have been, like his Roman counterpart, a magistrate elected when there was special need (Cornell 1995, 299). It is the case that a *Roman* dictator held a magistracy whose power superseded, temporarily, that of other magistrates. It was an appointed or elected position, and it had a specific time limit. The dictator Latinus may have operated under similar restrictions. That is certainly suggested by the fragment of L. Cincius preserved by Festus (*s.v. praetor*, 276 L[15]). The account is not as clear as we would like, but it does indicate that at one time leadership was shared among the Latin cities.[16] A temporary

---

[14] The scholarship on the "Latin League," or various leagues of Latin cities, is enormous. The most recent study of the alliances among the Latins that have been identified by one scholar or another as a Latin League, is Liou-Gille 1997; cf. also the discussion in Cornell 1989, 265 and n. 22.

[15] **Praetor**... *cuius rei morem ait fuisse Cincius in libro de consulum potestate talem: "Albanos rerum potitos usque ad Tullum regem: Alba deinde diruta usque ad P. Decium Murem consulem populos Latinos ad caput Ferentinae, quod est sub monte Albano, consulere solitos, et imperium communi consilio administrare.* "Praetor... Cincius, in his book on the power of the consuls, said that the custom of this office had been the following: the Albans held power up to the reign of Tullus: then when Alba was destroyed, the Latin people customarily consulted each other at the headwaters of the Ferentina, which is below the Alban mount, and administered the *imperium* by mutual agreement, until the time of P. Decius Mus."

[16] Cornell (1995, 299) supposes that the fragment can only refer to a period after the *Foedus Cassianum* and therefore that there cannot be a time when the Romans were not the chosen leaders. Cornell also argues that "Rome was never a member of a general Latin alliance. In fact, the traditional account maintains that the League was a political coalition of Latin states formed in opposition to Rome" (297). Alföldi (1969, 1–46) on the other hand argues for an ancient league of a traditional thirty cities. Like Alföldi, I think the tradition of such meetings goes back to the earliest times and is rooted in Latin cultural identity. Like Cornell, I doubt that it was possible for these communities to create an organization that was not ad hoc, or to formulate a long-term, mutual, political purpose, until the sixth century, and in all likelihood toward its later years. In agreement with Cincius, I suggest that the leadership was irregular, and, in addition, I argue, profoundly religious, and determined by religious means. However, the Lucus Ferentinae cannot have been the only place available for these meetings. If the meetings and the leadership were irregular, determined by necessity and omens, and included only those cities with a direct interest in the issue at hand, the site had to be moveable. I suspect the Lucus

ad hoc position would offer the greatest amount of delegated authority to the dictator, while minimizing any long-term threat to the political autonomy of the cities providing men to the allied military effort.

In any case, the position would have been both religious and military, for the separation of these functions was long in coming in Rome, even after the expulsion of the kings.[17] The dictator Latinus would have been understood to be in the religious service of the gods, from whom his power to command political allegiance or military obedience from the Latin people ultimately emanated. The surrender of several communities' autonomy to the citizen of one of them would necessarily have formidable religious as well as political and military implications,[18] and divine sanction for his power would be essential in a world where leadership was invariably regarded as divinely bestowed.

LEX ARAE DIANAE IN AVENTINO

Further testimony to the ways in which Diana governed political and civic arrangements is presented by the *lex arae Dianae in Aventino*. This antique law illustrates how Diana presided over rituals for those who had to act together but did not belong to the same community and who thus lacked an established and shared civic (also therefore priestly) system capable of making a conventional dedication. We do not have the law itself, only references to it in inscriptions, which record the foundation of temples to other gods in lands controlled by the Romans. The context in which these references occur suggests that the law gave directions on how to establish sacred boundaries. The most complete example runs as follows:

L. Aelio Caesare II P. Coelio Balbino Vibullio Pio cos./ VII idus Octobres, / C. Domitius Valens IIvir i.d., praeeunte C. Iulio Severo pontif.,/ legem dixit in ea verba quae infra scripta sunt:

Iuppiter optime maxime, quandoque tibi hodie hanc aram dabo dedicaboque, ollis legib./ ollisque regionibus dabo dedicaboque, quas hic hodie palam

---

Ferentinae became the fixed meeting place only after the sixth century, probably because it was convenient and near the communal sanctuary of Jupiter Latiaris.

[17] Cf. the excellent discussion by Cornell (1995, 232–6).

[18] It is this that seems to me to argue most strongly against a permanent or even a rotating appointment as dictator.

dixero, uti infimum solum huius arae est:/ si quis hic hostia sacrum faxit, quod magmentum nec protollat, it circo tamen probe factum esto; ceterae/ leges huic arae ea[e]dem sunto, quae arae Dianae sunt in Aventino monte dictae. Hisce legibus hisce regionibus/ sic, uti dixi, hanc tibi aram, Iuppiter optime maxime, do dico dedicoque, uti sis volens propitius mihi collegisque/ meis decurionibus, colonis, incolis coloniae Martia[e] Iuliae Salonae, con- iugibus liberisque nostris.

CIL III 1933 = *ILS* 4907

In the second consulship of Lucius Aelius Caesar and Publius Coelius Balbinus Vibul- lius Pius, on the ninth of October, Gaius Domitius Valens, Duovir for administering the law, with Gaius Iulius Severus pontifex presiding, spoke this law in the words which are written below:

Jupiter Optimus Maximus, when today I give and dedicate this altar to you in accordance with these laws,/ I will also give and dedicate [it] in accordance with these boundaries which I will have named here today in public, namely that it forms the foundation of this altar[19]*:/if anyone makes sacrifice here with a victim which does not produce the* magmentum *[?the entrails?], on that account, nevertheless, let it have been sacrificed correctly; let the rest of the laws for this altar be the same as those spoken for the altar of Diana on the Aventine mountain. In accordance with these laws and these boundaries I thus, as I have said, give, declare, and dedicate this altar to you, Jupiter Optimus Maximus, so that you may willingly be propitious to me, my colleagues, my decurions, the colonists inhabiting of the Martia Iulia Salona colony, and our wives and children.*

The ritual identified here is one in which the boundaries of the sacred enclosure[20] and the proper conduct within the enclosure are defined. The *lex arae Dianae* has nothing to do with federalism. It was not Rome's habit or, indeed in early days, power, to dictate a ritual by which their allies or colonies could make a religious dedication. That power would be exercised by the local priesthood and the oligarchy

---

[19] Mommsen in his commentary on the inscription suggested that *uti infimum solum huius arae est* meant *nam ibi arae termini sunt, ubi solum incipit planum esse* ("for the boundaries of the altar are where the ground begins to be level"). This is logical, but not, I think, correct. *Infimum solum* here should mean "the foundation, the solid ground" – the territory, in the most physical sense – for the altar. It suggests that the sacred space was originally conceived in three dimensions and included the trees and air above the circumference of the boundaries. This would accord both with the use of augury and with the fact that Diana would protect birds and other dwellers in trees as well as those on the ground.

[20] That is, the *regiones* – the same word used by augurs to mark out the sky (*OLD s.v. regio* 6; Livy 1.18.7, 1.34.9).

within the city boundaries in accordance with local religious beliefs, rituals, and laws. The *lex arae Dianae* was a ritual for dedications made in circumstances where civic authority had not been established or did not yet apply. In this example, the dedication is on behalf of the military colonists, the local inhabitants, and all their families. It is a dedication made on behalf of people with potentially conflicting allegiances. This is the fundamental nature of the ritual proper to Diana's grove, applied through the law established in her temple on the Aventine. How that law became part of her Aventine cult is discussed below.

SERVIUS TULLIUS AND THE AVENTINE CULT OF DIANA

The only other Latin cult of Diana was at Rome, on the Aventine, and it was founded by Servius Tullius. The differences and similarities will tell us more about the general religious view of Diana in Latium in the sixth century and perhaps allow us to determine ways in which her cult at Aricia was unique. First, though, it is important to make a careful distinction between three kinds of cult.

1. A conventional civic temple or cult served the city that maintained it and was administered by the citizens for the well-being of the community. That, according to all our evidence, is what the sanctuary of Diana near Aricia was, and that is also what the Aventine cult was at the time Livy and Dionysius were writing.
2. By contrast, a federal cult was participated in equally by all members. It was an expression of their collective piety and offered an opportunity for the resolution of political and military problems on an equal basis between the members, as well as providing a rallying point against outsiders. This was the original form of the "Ionian league" at the Artemision in Ephesus that Dionysius presents as a pattern for Servius' league. However, Dionysius' federal cult at Ephesus never actually existed,[21] although there was a sixth-century federation known as the Ionian league that

---

[21] "...the Artemision, although financed by Ionian subscription, was never the centre of the Pan-Ionian movement. Ephesus never usurped the place of Mycale and the temple of Poseidon Heliconius as the centre of the great confederation which drew all the Ionian cities, Ephesus included [I.G 12.5.444], together in self-defence" (Ogilvie 1965, 181).

centered around the cult of Poseidon and met at that god's temple in Mycale (Hdt. 1.148).

3. Finally, there was the synoecistic cult, in which a particular deity and his or her sanctuary became the gathering place for allied communities under the leadership of the community that controlled that sanctuary.[22] The paradigm (for modern scholars) of this kind of cult is, of course, Athena's Greater Panathenaia, which all Athens' subject allies were required to attend and to which they had to bring tribute.[23]

Servius' cult to Diana on the Aventine (Livy 1.45; DH *AR* 4.25.3–4.26.5)[24] was vowed and dedicated[25] to advertise and to advance the expanding political expectations of Rome in Latium. Servius chose Diana because he was seeking to appropriate for Rome's benefit that religious ritual of hers through which the Latin people met either to settle differences or to make alliances under her power.[26] By appropriating the goddess in this way, Servius clearly hoped to appropriate the Latins as well, and without a war.

Such dedications were neither new nor unreligious, but that of the Aventine requires us to consider what it was about Diana that made her cult a desirable choice for these purposes.[27] A reasonable initial

---

[22] A synoecistic cult is clearly what Livy and Dionysius have in mind in describing the Aventine foundation. That Rome in the sixth century was in a position, or soon would be, to compel such synoecism is now clear. Cf. Cornell (1995, 198–214) and Smith (1997, 208–16).

[23] Parke (45 and n. 28) for the inscriptions recording the requirements. Parke points out that this was simply an extension of the practice of colonies honoring their allegiance to the mother city.

[24] Malaspina (1994–5, 15–35) offers an excellent presentation of the archaeological and literary evidence and an analysis of the scholarly arguments (with comprehensive bibliography).

[25] Both our sources say that he founded a temple to her (*fanum*, Livy 1.45.2; νεὼς DH *AR* 4.26.4), and it is possible that some sort of building was part of his design for the cult. Ampolo (1997) argues that the coin of L. Hostilius Saserna (48 B.C.E.) shows the sixth-century cult statue borrowed from Massilia; a cult statue virtually presumes a temple.

[26] The paradigm of the Greek Amphictiony imported by Dionysius of Halicarnassus (4.25.3–6) can be ignored. The Latins were perfectly capable of developing political and religious alliances without a Greek to show them the way.

[27] This is of particular interest, as Servius was thought to have had a personal devotion to Fortuna (ἣ παρὰ πάντα τὸν βίον ἔδοξεν ἀγαθῇ κεχρῆσθαι, "whose favor he seemed to

assumption is that Servius was taking advantage of the fact that there had long been a grove sacred to Diana on the Aventine, which was outside the *pomerium*. The old religious institution of the meeting under ritual disarmament in Diana's grove was ripe for reshaping as a political organization for ultimate control of the Latin cities. For this purpose a grove to Diana located on the Aventine would have been ideal. Livy's account is the most explicit about Servius' intentions:

> ... [Servius] consilio augere imperium conatus est, simul et aliquod addere urbi decus. Iam tum erat inclitum Dianae Ephesiae fanum; id communiter a ciuitatibus Asiae factum fama ferebat. Eum consensum deosque consociatos laudare mire Seruius inter proceres Latinorum, cum quibus publice privatimque hospitia amicitiasque de industria iunxerat. Saepe iterando eadem perpulit tandem, ut Romae fanum Dianae populi Latini cum populo Romano facerent. Ea erat confessio caput rerum Romam esse, de quo totiens armis certatum fuerat. ...
>
> 1.45.1–3

> *[Servius] attempted to add to Rome's power through diplomacy, and at the same time to add something beautiful to the city. Already at that time the temple to Diana at Ephesus was well-known; report has it that it was built by the cities of Asia in common. Servius in a most remarkable manner praised this harmony and community of worship to the Latin nobles, with whom he had assiduously exchanged hospitality and friendship both publicly and privately. By often repeating the same arguments, he prevailed at last, with the result that the Latin peoples, together with the Roman people, built a temple to Diana at Rome. This was their admission that Rome was the capital, a point concerning which so often there had been an armed struggle.*[28]

As Livy understands it, the cult was not a success. The verb *conatus est* ("he attempted") implies that Servius tried but failed in the end; *perpulit tandem* ("he brought it about at last") indicates that he had to overcome considerable resistance; and *ea erat confessio* ("this was an admission") makes it clear that, even though the resistance had been overcome, the desired implication of the communal temple – that is, that Rome was the *caput rerum* – was one that was only reluctantly made by the people involved.

---

have enjoyed all his life," DH *AR* 4.27.7; cf. Varro *LL.* 6.17; Plut. *Quaest. Rom.* 74). Livy, though, makes no mention of this.

[28] The text is that of Ogilvie. Dionysius' account parallels that of Livy, with the usual elaboration through comparative Greek mythical and archaic history.

Livy is equally clear about Servius' intentions. The Roman king intended to gain *imperium*[29] for Rome; he was not concerned with federation, which implies or makes a gesture conceding equality among all members. He met considerable resistance from his (unnamed) Latin friends and allies, who nevertheless contributed to what was designed to be a symbol of their acceptance of Rome's dominance. Dionysius is even more blunt. He says that Servius himself drew up the laws on mutual rights of the member cities and prescribed the festival and the assembly, leaving a permanent record in the form of a bronze pillar engraved with the decrees and the names of the cities (DH *AR* 4.26.3–4). Rome was in the mood, and in the position, to make the *claim* for dominion through this temple.[30] However, Livy's narrative heightens the significance of Servius' *hospitia amicitiasque*, the hospitality and friendship he had established with the Latin cities, and Dionysius does not offer any challenge to this view. Without the personal authority of Servius, there would have been no communal temple. Livy's narrative suggests that, Servius' persuasive friendships apart, it was doubtful whether Rome was in a position to defend her claim to be the leader of the Latin peoples,[31] whatever the inscription claimed.

Livy's immediately following account of the miraculous heifer illustrates the relationship between the worship of Diana and power over others. As he tells the story (1.45.3–7; Plut. *Quaest. Rom.* 4; Dionysius

---

[29] *Imperium* is a concept more appropriate to the political discourse of Livy's age than to that of Servius. Nevertheless, Rome's intentions were not directed toward a federation, if by "federation" one means a unified organization of equals in the manner of the amphictiony that Dionysius claims (a chronological impossibility). Still, although *imperium* is not quite the right term, it seems in a sense appropriate, especially to mark the contrast between the sort of incipient federation that potentially could have arisen from the meetings in Diana's grove and Rome's idea of her permanent and unchallenged leadership of that group.

[30] Dionysius claims that laws concerning the mutual rights of the Latin cities, the celebration of the festival, and the general assembly of the Latins were inscribed on a bronze pillar and set there (DH *AR* 4.26.4–5) at the time. Livy does not mention this. Dionysius declares that the pillar still existed in his day and that its archaic letters attested to its antiquity. That it was archaic seems certain; that it dated from Servius' time is less so. Gras (52) suggests the fourth century. As a document, it should not be dated earlier than the *foedus Cassianum*, which Cornell puts in the fifth century (1995, 299).

[31] Cornell 1995, 293–8. Servius' wide-ranging *amicitiae* among the Latins could have been an effort to strengthen his position in Rome and to provide himself with outside support against internal opposition.

does not mention the heifer), a certain Sabine thought Diana had offered him a way to counteract Servius' religious claim to hegemony. A heifer born on his land, miraculously beautiful and large, was regarded as a prodigy, and the *vates* predicted that the city of the man who sacrificed it would have *imperium*. The prodigy's place of appearance indicates that *imperium* over the Latins was still very much a contested matter. The Sabine went to Rome to make the sacrifice. That in itself was an acknowledgment of Rome's now superior claim to the gift of hegemony from Diana. It must be balanced against the fact that the means of gaining that gift (the heifer) was conferred on a Sabine.[32]

Having tricked the Sabine into leaving the heifer momentarily to purify himself in running water, the Roman priest at once sacrificed the heifer himself. Rome's *imperium* was thus confirmed by Diana's prodigy. Yet Livy does not encourage his audience to rely too much on this omen. The *true* confirmation of Roman hegemony is provided by his account of the prodigy that accompanied the subsequent foundation of the temple for Jupiter Optimus Maximus by Tarquinius Superbus − a temple that had been vowed before Servius' reign by Tarquinius Priscus.[33] In that prodigy, a human head (*caput*) with its features intact was uncovered on the site of the foundation, foretelling *haud per ambages arcem eam imperii caputque rerum fore* ("unambiguously that this was to be the citadel of empire and the head of the world"; Livy 1.55.6; Varro *LL* 5.41).[34] *Haud per ambages* − "unambiguously" − is

---

[32] This prodigy could well be the source for the idea that Diana was originally a Sabine goddess brought to Rome (Varro *LL* 5.74; DH *AR* 2.50.3).

[33] Livy 1.55.1. The site was leveled and perhaps foundations laid during Tarquinius Priscus' reign (Richardson 221; Tac. *Hist.* 3.72). This may be another indication that the political conflicts between the supporters of the Tarquinii and those who supported Servius were symbolized by the competition between the Aventine (Servius' people) and the Capitoline (the Tarquinii). Such ruthless politicization of religious monuments would contribute to a subsequent public reaction against that kind of display. It is just the kind of reaction that we see in fifth-century Rome.

[34] Dionysius (*AR* 4.59–61) has an interesting variation on the prodigy of the head, which illuminates the deep ambiguity of the earlier prodigy of Diana's heifer being born on Sabine land. As Dionysius tells the story, the Romans were forced to go to Etruria to discover a diviner (τερατοσκόπος) to interpret the finding of the head. The Etruscan diviner tried to trick the Romans. He drew shapes of the Capitoline on the ground, and, pointing a stick at various parts of the diagram, tried to get the Romans to admit

a direct comment on the ambiguous omen of Diana's heifer. Jupiter is the god who confirms Rome's destiny beyond doubt.

Whether the details of these prodigies arise from Livy's interpretation of the evidence or were already part of the tradition he found, they tell us two things of importance for our understanding of Diana's cult on the Aventine. First, Diana was accepted by the people who mattered – the Latins and the Sabines – as a goddess *able*, and *expected*, to confer leadership, especially in contested situations. Second, the foundation of her cult on the Aventine was inextricably associated with Servius' personal qualities.[35] Nevertheless, a challenge to Diana's authority was part of the process of deposing Servius. When Servius was removed as king, Diana was replaced by Jupiter as the divine guarantor of Roman hegemony.

THE AFTERMATH OF THE FOUNDATION
OF THE AVENTINE CULT

So Servius' successor (and possible murderer) Tarquinius Superbus resumed construction of the temple to Jupiter Optimus Maximus on the Capitol, and it was dedicated in the first year of the Republic.[36] The

that the head was found "there." The Romans (having been warned by the diviner's son) refused to do so and continued to say "on the Capitoline" and "at Rome." If the Romans had acceded to the Etruscan's prompting, they would have been admitting that the *caput rerum* would be "there," that is, on Etruscan soil. Thus in Dionysius' account, trickery is attempted and fails. (The tale is also a splendid illustration of a thought process in which the abstraction of a map is in itself a deceit. Cf. the attitude of Strepsiades, who on seeing a map wants Sparta moved further away from Athens for safety's sake; Ar. *Nu.* 206–16).

[35] Levi (1991, 122–34) argues that the two divinities of the archaic divine couple found in the excavation of the St. Omobono temple were, in fact, Diana and Hercules. The goddess, who wears armor, is more often associated with either Minerva or Juno, but the identification of Hercules is as secure as it could be. Levi argues that the pairing of Diana and Hercules in the *lectisternium* of 399 (Livy 5.13.4–6; DH *AR* 12.9.1) indicates the traditional association of these two deities in Rome. If this is true (and I find it very attractive), a cult of Diana in Rome had already been established inside the *pomerium* and was far more important than we have realized.

[36] Dedication of the temple in the first year of the Republic: Livy 2.8.6–8, 7.3.8; Polybius 3.22.1; Tac. *Hist.* 3.72; Plut. *Public.* 14; vowed by Tarquinius Priscus, continued by Servius, and completed by Tarquinius Superbus, Tac. ibid; vowed by Tarquinius Priscus, and built by Superbus, Plut. ibid. Plutarch indicates that the right of dedication was passionately contested and that Publicola was only denied the honor by a ruse.

promised hegemony of Rome was secured by divine approval when the workers discovered on the Capitol itself that buried head (*caput*), its features intact, an unambiguous prodigy delivered to Romans on Roman soil and seemingly without any need for priestly trickery.[37] Diana's guarantee of Roman hegemony had been hedged about with doubts and uncertainty. She had represented the ambition and power of Servius Tullius; she also seems to have shared in the ambiguous reception of this king, who was alleged once to have been a slave.

However – and more significantly for the nature of Rome's future expansion – the Capitoline cult of Jupiter was never a federal cult. The foundation of the great Capitoline temple repudiates the federalizing policies pursued by Servius in favor of unadorned imperialism. Building the temple, and thus magnifying the worship of Jupiter, was not just a religious act. It was an effort to overturn everything Servius represented.

Outside Rome, though, the failure of the Aventine cult did not affect the Latin worship of Diana or the collective meetings in the grove. When Tarquinius Superbus rode to the Lucus Ferentinae to meet with the *proceres* of the Latin people (Livy 1.50; DH *AR* 4.45), neither the Romans nor the Latins seemed to have noticed that they were not meeting on the Aventine.[38] The account makes it clear that at that time the Romans did indeed have presumptive, if not firmly established, control of this gathering. If any federal meeting of the Latins had ever occurred on the Aventine as Servius wished, such meetings had certainly ceased with his death, and the Latins went on meeting, with or without the Romans, in various groves dedicated to Diana.

One lasting legacy, however, was the *lex arae Dianae in Aventino*. No doubt because it was used by Roman colonists, it became a paradigm for the foundation of a cult among people who were, at the moment

---

[37] There was still trickery – if we follow Dionysius (*AR* 4.59–61) – in the way the Romans had appropriated the Sabine heifer to win Diana's approval. It is probable that emerging religious and civic morality rejected prodigies gained by ruse, along with the political maneuvering that inspired them. If so, Servius really did represent the rejected archaic past, and Tarquinius really was trying to ride the wave of the future – which, despite all his efforts, was the Republic.

[38] As Gras (1987, 53) recognized.

of foundation, not yet united in a single civic group, with established priesthoods and rites to authorize the foundation on their collective behalf.

THE FAILURE OF SERVIUS' FEDERAL CULT

Servius had tried to make the sanctuary of Diana on the Aventine the recognized cult center of the Latins, and he had failed. The reasons for his failure lie in the realm of Roman political history. What concerns us here is the effect the foundation of the Aventine cult, and its failure, had on the worship of Diana at Aricia.

The date when Servius established his cult cannot be determined exactly. Both Livy and Dionysius place the building of the temple in their narrative just before they give an account of his death, a strong indication that Servius built the temple late in his life. Livy attributes such success as the federal cult did in fact achieve to Servius' friendly alliances. Because it takes time to establish such connections with surrounding communities, this suggests again a date late in Servius' reign. The nature of his death and the particular events associated with it were, however, thought to be uncannily influenced by his interest in Diana. Was this cause or effect? His murder by his daughter and son-in-law (Livy 1.48; DH *AR* 4.38–9) is presented almost as a sacrifice to Diana (Livy 1.48.6; DH *AR* 4.39.5; cf. Cook 1902, 380 n. 3) and as the result of a contest between Servius, the old king, and Tarquinius, the challenger, in a parallel to the mortal combat between the *rex nemorensis* and *his* challenger.

If the foundation of the cult came late in Servius' reign, there cannot have been many years in which to establish a communal celebration before he died (traditionally in 535). The Capitoline temple to Jupiter was dedicated in 510, the first year of the Republic (Richardson 1992, 221–2). Between 535 and 510 – indeed, for the next hundred and fifty years – Rome had to use force to maintain her leadership among the Latins. There is no record of actual attendance at a communal rite, and at no time in this period could the Aventine cult have ever established a secure claim on religious or political devotion through continued observance by the Latin peoples.

Thus the most far-reaching of all the consequences of Servius' *federal* foundation was its failure. The claim by a city like Rome (or Aricia) to special authority *because* she controlled a particular sanctuary of Diana threatened the neutrality that had made a federalizing cult possible. So Servius weakened the very religious force he was attempting to use. This can be seen quite clearly in the account of Tarquinius' trick against Turnus Herdonius in the Lucus Ferentinae. Tarquinius not only caused weapons to be brought into the sacred grove, but he also planted them on an innocent person. If there was one individual there who was certain Diana would not avenge herself on a transgressor, it was Tarquinius. The goddess neither punished the true violator of her sanctuary nor did she protect an innocent man. Tarquinius may have been a cynical rationalist, or he may have believed in the greater power of Jupiter to protect him. In either case, he provided a perfect demonstration that Diana's wrath did not have to be feared by a Roman.

Turnus' ritual death well illustrates the political realities that were forcing changes in religious attitudes in Latium. The expensive and expansive ambitions of individuals, political alliances, and cities were aggressively appropriating religion to serve their ends. Some attempts (like Servius' federation of Latin cities) may have been noble; some (like Tarquinius' attack on Turnus) certainly were not. Their combined effect, however, was to raise doubts about the efficacy of the very religion that was being appropriated. Nevertheless, it was a period when, despite the well-advanced secularization of politics in central Italy, the potency of the old religious formulations remained a major force to be reckoned with.

THE IDES OF AUGUST IN ROME AND ARICIA

There is one confusing legacy of Servius'. foundation of a cult to Diana on the Aventine. The Roman and the Arician cults celebrate their major festival to the goddess on the same day, the Ides of August. There are two principal interpretations of this. Wissowa (1912, 249–50) firmly argued that the cult at Aricia was far older than that in Rome. Therefore the original festival on the Ides of August belonged to Aricia: Rome must have appropriated the festival date when Servius Tullius tried to establish his cult of Diana on the Aventine. Most scholars have accepted Wissowa's argument.[39]

The contrary view, advanced most thoroughly by Momigliano (1963, supported by Liou-Gille 1997, 760–1), is based on the notion that Statius (*Silv.* 3.1.52–60) proves that the Ides of August was a federal festival to Diana. If so, this would have to be the festival that Servius founded, and the Aricians will have copied it to challenge Rome. However, Statius is not talking about a federal festival. He does indeed say that the entire Italian land celebrates the festival (3.1.60), but it is clear from the context in which he and some companions consider the day a holiday, that the actual celebration is held by individuals in their homes (*pudicis. . . focis* 3.1.59–60). There are no city magistrates from around Italy or even from Latium processing to the Aventine. At Rome, in fact, slaves had a holiday, and women washed their hair (Plut. *Quaest. Rom.* 100; Festus 460 L). Could anything be more domestic, more personal – and less federal?

We must return to the most probable explanation for the celebration of the Ides of August: that Diana was a major goddess at Aricia, a moon goddess with an ancient and complex hunting cult that reached deep into the civic and military life of the city, and that the Ides of August was her festival day. It is extremely unlikely that in this period such a festival day would be *changed* for political reasons – indeed, for any reason whatsoever.

The Ides of August is a reasonable festival date for the cult at Aricia. The location of Diana's sanctuary in the grove on the floor of a crater of an extinct volcano, beside a lake with no outlet (before the *emissarium* was built), meant that in any year with substantial rainfall, and generally in rainy months, the area around the sanctuary would have been marshy or underwater. An annual festival is therefore most likely in a month where dry and rainless conditions could be expected. The middle of August is ideal. Modern rainfall totals indicate that the driest months are June and July, each showing an average of .60 inches. It rains slightly more in August (1.30 inches), but the two dry preceding months would normally lower the lake and dry the marshy areas. Proportionate

---

[39] Most strongly for Aricia's priority: Gordon 1934; Alföldi 1960, 1961. The argument for the priority of the Aventine: Momigliano 1963 (very weak); Liou-Gille 1997, 760–1.

relationships, if not exact measurements, would have been the same in antiquity. Whatever rain did come in August (and 1.3 inches is not a great deal) would not be enough, in most cases, to restore the marsh. The temperatures in August are warm (highs today average 83 degrees Fahrenheit, lows 66 degrees). We know that the festival at Aricia was celebrated partly at night, and a warm night in the forest offers highly desirable conditions.[40]

There are, then, three possible explanations for the fact that the Roman cult of Diana had the same festival date as that at Aricia: (1) the Ides of August was generally, throughout Italy, the day on which Diana was honored, so some festival had always been celebrated there on that date, a fact which Servius acknowledged; (2) Servius chose the Ides of August as a deliberate challenge to Aricia, and in an effort, by focusing on the cult of Diana, to weaken support for that city on the part of the Latin communities; (3) the original foundation date of the Aventine cult was quite different, but what with the subsequent supremacy of Jupiter Capitolinus and the continued strength of the Arician cult, the original Servian foundation date became displaced, and the festival on the Ides of August took its place by attraction.

The first of these explanations seems the least likely. We have no evidence in the archaic period for a single festival day for a particular deity universally recognized and celebrated by all the Latins, much less all the Italians. The second is more probable, because it at least reflects what we know about Servius' intentions and the political situation in Latium when the Aventine cult was founded; it also respects the Roman instinct for conserving even little-used rituals. The third solution is enticing but more problematic. The calendars record Diana's festival in small letters,[41] conventionally regarded as indicating an event introduced after the end of the regal period. By the first century B.C.E., the festival for Diana had become a special day for women and slaves. It is possible that the original federal festival established by Servius, being

---

[40] We can compare the communal festival of Jupiter Latiaris, which was a movable feast celebrated in the spring, before the campaign season got under way. It was a daytime festival, ending with a bonfire on the same night (Lucan *BC* 5.403). Because the ritual took place on top of a mountain, marshy land was not a concern.

[41] *ILLRP* 9. Good reproductions of a complete calendar can be found in Michels (1967, pl. 4) or Scullard (1981, 259–76).

no longer attended by Rome's Latin allies after his death, simply lapsed. Yet there was a temple: women and slaves then filled the resultant vacuum and made the cult theirs. The reputation of the Arician celebration could gradually have drawn celebration to the Ides of August. The real advantage of this scenario is that because the celebration on that date would have become consistent only in the Republican period, it would explain why the festival was recorded in small letters on the calendar, even though the temple had been founded by a king. The absence of any élite interest in Diana in the early Republic and the fact that Jupiter was meant to displace her in both late-sixth-century and Republican religious politics, combined with the appearance of slaves as worshippers, together suggest that the Roman colleges of priests had chosen a strategy of benign neglect for this once potent religious foundation. So I lean toward the third explanation.

We should, in all this, not lose sight of one important point that Servius' foundation, and its subsequent fate, illustrates about Latin religion. Although observance could be commanded, even legislated, personal belief and devotion could not. This is where King Servius went so wrong. Whenever religion was manipulated for political gain, it was weakened. Aricia's remained, in all ages, the stronger, more complex cult, with more widely shared devotion. This quality, of the sacred importance and religious immanence of a place, the Romans called *numen*. No one was able to *make* a place of religious experience, for Diana or anyone else. Aricia unquestionably had the *numen*.

THE CATO INSCRIPTION AND THE POLITICS OF THE CULT OF DIANA

Where then does this leave us as regards Cato's record of the Latin peoples' dedication of the grove at Aricia to Diana? Much has been made of this passage for the purposes of constructing a minimal political history of the Latin peoples during Rome's rise to ascendancy.[42] It

---

[42] For the historical problem, Cornell 1993, 293–301; Liou-Gille 1997; Alföldi 1965, 49; Ampolo 1981, 219–33; Zevi 1995, 128–31. For the religious connection between Diana and the League: Wissowa 1912, 247–8; Warde Fowler 1899, 198; Latte 1960, 469; Pairault 1969, 426–31, 439–45; Dumézil 1996, 409–10; Bayet 1957, 20–1.

cannot be, as we have seen, a record of the historical moment when the sanctuary in the crater was founded, since the probable date of this alliance falls centuries after the origin of the cult. We can be reasonably certain Rome was not included in the list even though it is incomplete. If she had been, she probably would have figured at the top, but this cannot be proved.

It is equally unlikely that the alliance of Tusculum, Aricia, Lanuvium, Laurentum, Cora, Tibur, Pometia, and Rutulian Ardea was arranged in the sanctuary of Diana as a way of challenging Servius' federal cult of Diana in Rome. The last decade of the sixth century is regarded as the earliest any *organized* opposition to Rome began to form (Cornell 1995, 297–8; Zevi 1995, 128–9). A challenge to Servius' Aventine foundation three and half decades after his death, perhaps half a century after the foundation of the Aventine cult, and a decade after the dedication of Jupiter Optimus Maximus on the Capitoline, would have been quixotic. Jupiter, not Diana, was the Roman symbol of power and hegemony at the end of the regal period. If the Latins were trying to use religion to encourage and embolden opposition to Rome, they needed to look elsewhere than the Aventine. They chose Diana as their divine patron, and the grove of Diana for their meeting (despite the fact that the Romans had turned to Jupiter), and for reasons that had to do with Diana's power to bring together uneasy and competitive cities and bind them together for a single purpose. That purpose was to stop Rome and her expansionist policies.

LATIN DIANA IN THE ARCHAIC PERIOD: A SUMMARY

The accounts of the supposedly "rival" Diana cults of the Aventine and Aricia give us a glimpse into the nature of this goddess in the archaic period. Ritual gatherings were held in groves dedicated to her, to allow leaders from (potentially) hostile communities to meet on neutral ground where they could either settle their differences or ally against a third force. The ancient practices, particularly those of ritual disarmament, associated with Diana's cult provided the security essential to make these meetings possible.

By the sixth century, however, purely political forces were beginning to invade and overtake religious practices. Servius Tullius had seen that the ritual also provided a traditional means by which he could accomplish a very untraditional goal: a federation of Latin communities. His foundation of the cult of Diana on the Aventine was a deliberate attempt to create such a federation, with Rome as its accepted leader. Ancient accounts of Servius' actions indicate that Diana's omen guaranteeing hegemony among the Latins for Rome was ambiguous, however. Moreover, Latin acceptance of Servius' federal cult was reluctant, and the alliance he desired ultimately failed. The idea of federation enshrined in the foundation of Diana's cult on the Aventine had been rejected – probably during the same political upheaval indicated in the historical accounts – by Servius' violent death and his usurpation by Tarquinius Superbus.

Thus Diana was a powerful deity whose authority could guarantee hegemony and whose ritual practices could be manipulated to provide divine support for a federal cult led by Rome. This is not a nymphlike goddess of women and children. She is the patron of warriors and leaders and a divine guarantor of hegemony among the Latins.

The dedication at Aricia recorded in the fragment occurred around 500 B.C.E., almost four decades after Servius' death in 535 and perhaps half a century after his foundation of the cult on the Aventine. Both the Arician and the Aventine dedications represent a new understanding of the potential possessed by the ritual in the grove for making a permanent alliance among the Latins. We know that Servius' alliance failed. The sixth-century dedication at Aricia – not to be confused with the far older origins of the cult itself – led to, or was the expression of, the Latin League. This alliance of Latin cities opposed Roman expansion and succeeded in delaying Rome's definitive conquest of Latium; but by the mid–fourth century Rome had finally prevailed. The cult of Diana at Aricia, which had existed long before the Latin League, continued to grow in strength and importance. The Aventine cult was allowed to become the province of slaves and women.

The festival date, the Ides of August, was the same for both the Aventine and the Arician cults. There is no indication that the Arician celebration on the Ides of August was federal at any time, or that the festival of Diana on the Aventine was ever a significant event for the Latins. Servius probably chose the Ides of August for his cult because he wished to challenge, and absorb, the growing prestige of Aricia by appropriating her cult and festival date; but he failed. The most remarkable consequence of what must be considered a series of failures in Diana's name – first by Servius, then by Aricia, and finally by the Latins as a whole – is that the sanctuary at Aricia only became stronger and more widely sought as a result.

6

THE MANY FACES OF DIANA

DIANA: THE PROBLEM

Diana. Her name had its roots in the culture of the early Indo-Europeans, and suggests she was a shining celestial deity. She was worshipped as the moon in all periods for which we have evidence, and it is reasonable to think that it was as the moon that she was worshipped by the people who named her. Her sanctuary in the crater indicates a deity closely involved with nature, especially the wild. The archaic priest who served her in that sanctuary testifies to the antiquity of Diana's worship, and the form of his ritual, in which he was always the hunter who was hunted, suggests a hunting cult was his earliest context. Among the archaic Latins, Diana was a warrior's goddess, the guarantor of leadership and authority. In the same archaic period, when Greek religious iconography was becoming fashionable in Latium, Diana was identified with Artemis, the huntress, and in the first temple (that we know of) built for her in her sanctuary in the crater, she is triumphantly celebrated as a huntress. Later evidence indicates that she was worshipped as a helper to women in childbirth, as the goddess of roads and paths, and as an underworld deity.

The multiplicity of functions, and the Greek iconography, have together been interpreted by modern scholars as unquestionable evidence of syncretism, and the question has always been, as a result, what was Diana *really*, before she began mutating under foreign, especially Greek, influences? With that question came two unexamined assumptions: first, that there had to have been some core identity, some central form, to which the remaining identities and functions were added; and second, that the acquisition of these functions was haphazard and – apart from elemental connections, as between a female goddess and childbirth – lacking any real connection with the core identity.

Thus Wissowa rejected both the moon goddess and the hunting goddess, and concluded that Diana was "a protectress and helper of women in the illnesses of their sex" (1912, 248). The introduction of the Artemis-type iconography, he thought, proved that the cult of Diana had been altered by the connection with the Greek goddess (1912, 251), and all aspects of her beyond the range of a protectress of women, particularly her identity as a goddess of the hunt, were derived from Artemis. In reaching this conclusion he was particularly influenced by Johannes' argument (1907, 59–75) that the Romans (by which he meant the Latins in general) did not hunt (Wissowa 1912, 247–51). In subsequent scholarship, the range of Diana's concerns has been allowed to expand to a vague patronage over the wild, but a conspectus of modern scholarship reveals that in essence her core identity is still seen as that of a nymphlike nature goddess concerned primarily with women.[1] It is silently assumed that almost every other quality attributed to her, especially her hunting aspect, was acquired from Artemis.

The conclusion that Diana was specifically (above all in her earliest, pre-Artemis form) concerned with women simply cannot be sustained. The votives at the sanctuary, on which Wissowa based his argument, indicate that the interests of women and men were equally represented in the cult (Hänninen, 46). The foundation of the rest of Wissowa's argument – that Diana had to have borrowed her form as a hunting goddess because the Romans (i.e., Latins) did not hunt – lacks substance. The Romans and the Latins indeed hunted

---

[1] Scheid (1997); Birt: "Diana ist ursprünglich zwar nicht Mondgöttin, aber Lichtgöttin gewesen und als solche weiter Schützerin und Patronin der Fruchbarkeit im Pflanzenreich, Tierreich und unter den Menschen" (1884, 1002); Altheim: "es is schließlich der Charakter der Diana als Frauengottheit, der . . . als im Mittelpunkte stehend hervortritt" (1930, 94); Latte: "ursprünglich von der Mondgöttin sich zur Schützerin des weiblichen Lebens entwickelt hatte" (1960, 170); Scullard: "perhaps originally a 'wood-spirit' who gradually came to preside over the affairs of women" (1981, 173); Rose: "a goddess of forests who helped women by giving them children" (1948 90); Turcan: "goddess of woods and chastity" (2001, 152); Dumézil: "combines in herself . . . the world of the sky . . . the symbolic conferring of the *regnum*, and the patronage of births" (1996, 409).

(Green 1996a), and the evidence of the archaic period testifies that this goddess had a position in Latin culture entirely congruent with her identification as a goddess of warriors and of the hunt. We must conclude that when the Latins made the original identification of Diana with Artemis, it was based on the fact that the two deities had hunting in common.

In determining Diana's nature, it is necessary, it seems to me, to give the earliest evidence, that of her name, its due weight. We must also seriously consider the evidence of what the Latins, and the Aricians in particular, knew about their own goddess. If she was represented as a huntress, if she had a history as a hunter's and warrior's goddess, it was because they worshipped Diana as such, and that was why she was given the face of Artemis. The great difficulty we are left with once we do this is that we must then reconcile the moon goddess' name with the hunter-warrior goddess' identity.

THE NATURE OF THE HUNTING CULT

Actually, once one considers the nature of hunting as late Bronze Age and archaic age peoples practiced it, the difficulty is not so great. In Latium, by the middle Bronze Age, pastoralism was giving way to agriculture (Smith 1996, 32), a process that continued, with greater concentration in settlements (the population of which still numbered less than a hundred individuals) through the ninth century (Smith 1996, 41–2). Farmers and shepherds hunted to feed themselves and for the fur, hide, bone, and horn that the animals supplied. They also hunted to eliminate pests that ate crops – hare, wild goats and deer, and predators such as foxes, wolves, or boar, that killed animals and destroyed property. Zoö-archeological evidence confirms that the Latins hunted the hare (*Lepus europaeus Pall.*), the deer (*Cervus elaphus L.*), the wild goat (*Capreolus capreolus L.*), the boar (*Sus scrofa fer. L.*), the beaver (*Castor fiber L.*), and birds of various kinds.[2] The continual struggle farmers and shepherds had with wild animals was known to Grattius as the *bellum ferinum*, the "wild-beast war" (*Cyn.* 13).

---

[2] Cf. the graphs in De Grossi Mazzorin 1989, 126–30, and Green 1996a, 228–35.

As settlements grew and were fortified, an élite emerged in the eighth century. Clan or tribal or settlement leaders hunted to display their prowess over dangerous beasts, to demonstrate their fitness against human enemies, to emphasize their right to leadership, and, of course, to reward their followers with the spoils of the chase (De Grossi Mazzorin, 127; Smith 1996, 86–8). Warriors and hunters tend to identify themselves with strong or potent animals. In the historical period, such animals continued to be symbols around which the Latins and the Italic peoples generally constructed military and even civic identity. The Romans originally had boars and wolves as well as eagles (all predator animals) on their military standards (Plin. *NH* 10.16). The standards were sacred (Brand 1968, 91–2). The boar was the theriomorphic patron of Lanuvium (Alföldi 1956, 276–8); the *picus* (woodpecker) led the Picentes; the *(h)irpus* (wolf) led the Hirpini; and the Itali identified themselves with the *uitulus*, the young bull, a pattern that has secure parallels across Indo-European cultures (Alföldi 1965, 275–6).

Such identification is characteristic of hunting religions. Hunting cults – descended from the ancestral hunter-gatherer cultures – are among the oldest of religious phenomena and known worldwide. They are characterized by an intense awareness of nature,[3] arising from intimate involvement with the natural world, and by a mysticism centered on nature, in particular on the animals of the hunter's own region.

Yet, notwithstanding . . . theoretical caveats, a systematic, cross-cultural look at hunter-gatherer religions reveals that underneath all of the contextual and cultural diversity, there indeed is a substrate of ritual, cosmological, and symbolic commonality. . . . They have certain common features: a practical and conceptual consciousness focused on animals, plants, the landscape and seasons, and meteorological and astronomical phenomena. At the metaphysical level, hunter-gatherers regard nature as pervasively animated with moral, mystical, and mythical significance; . . . Foremost of nature's beings are animals, especially the game animals which, for all hunter-gatherers, feed both the stomach and the mind and beguile the heart.

Guenther 1999, 426

[3] "Living within and off nature, foragers have both their practical and conceptual consciousness focused on animals, plants, the landscape and seasons, and meteorological and astronomical phenomena" (Guenther 1999, 426).

In any period, the hunter needed to know everything he could about the animals he hunted, and hunting cults as a result were, inevitably, the repository of a vast range of natural history, and of mystical ideas about animals, especially about what animals "meant" in the cosmos. Of course the hunter worshipped and studied the gods who governed the animals and their existence. It was fundamental to primitive thought that, because of its own waxing and waning, the moon controlled growth and dying or decay. This remained a central belief throughout the Greco-Roman period (Pliny NH 18.321–9). The moon figured both as a mystery and as a familiar, dependable, celestial marker for man to follow. It was the earliest measure of time, marked the seasons, and foretold the weather . Pliny says the moon shamed men who tried to observe her; she was the nearest star and yet the one that they knew least about (NH 2.41), as well as the teacher (*magistra*) of all that they *had* learned about the heavens (NH 2.44). Tavenner (1918) and the aptly named Lunais (1979, 49–74) have collected the extensive evidence for this kind of moon lore in Roman thought.

The ancient hunter had to study the goddess who controlled plants and animals and marked the seasons. Our own experience of the easy superiority of humans over nature, and particularly over animals, cannot adequately convey the experiences of ancient man. Success in hunting was not easy.[4] The ancient hunter was at a marked disadvantage when he entered the wild in pursuit of his prey, particularly because, in the Mediterranean, he hunted on foot (Hull 1964, 71). His prey – even a small animal such as the hare – had the odds very much in its favor. The hunter was often, it would seem, overwhelmed by the challenge to his skill offered by the hare, as, on Greek vases the hunted hare is frequently gigantic, as big as the dog, and on occasion as large as the hunters themselves (Schnapp 1989, 72–5). The hare was the most commonly hunted animal in Greece and Italy, and it is clear that this small furred mammal taught the hunter humility and

---

[4] Modern research has shown that shotgun hunting increases the "take" tenfold over bow hunting (M. Alvard and H. Kaplan, "Procurement Technology" in *Human Predators*, M. Stiner, ed., Boulder 1991, 79–104). The Romans used nets and spears, more productive than bows but bearing no comparisons to the results obtained with guns.

regularly reduced him "to size," as the vases demonstrate.[5] This would be discouraging and even dangerous for the aristocratic hunter seeking to maintain dominance over his followers by impressing them with his skill. For the man who needed to feed himself and his family, it could be disastrous. Dogs were thus indispensable to the hunter and had two functions: they traced the prey by scenting its tracks, and they flushed it, once found, into the nets.

The single element that determined the outcome of the hunt was moisture, because moisture captures scent. Although scent is elusive and even today not entirely understood, moisture was and is the key. Too dry or too wet, and the scent will not hold (Xen. *Cyn.* 5.4–5; Hull 1989, 69), and the dogs will have nothing to follow. Different animals produce scent from different points of their body, and the moisture that will hold the scent must be at the requisite level. Even for the same animal, the track the animal leaves can be on the ground or at varying levels above it, depending on the way it moves (Hull 1989, 69; *Cyn.* 5.3–4, on the irregularity of scent, particularly in the spring when hares are leaping both high and long, ἀντιπαίζοντες, playing with one another).[6] The hunter had to know where moisture would lie and when in the day or night it was present, how long it would linger, and how its presence varied over the seasons. Moisture, ruling the mysterious factor of scent, thus determined the success or failure of the hunt before it even started.

The moon was "feminine" and the cosmic source of all moisture, and was particularly the source of dew, which she brought at night (*NH* 2.223). The nutriment of the moon was contained in bodies of fresh water, as the sun's was contained in salt water (*NH* 2.223). Thus the lake in the crater by Diana's sanctuary, the *speculum Dianae*, was not simply ancillary to her worship. The lake "fed" the moon, even as it reflected her, and by feeding her moisture, served to help her assist the

---

[5] The European hare can make leaps of up to 12 feet or clear obstacles of 5 feet. In bursts it can reach 45 miles per hour, although more commonly it travels up to a quarter mile at 35 miles per hour. It is a good swimmer and will jump into a stream or lake – thus destroying its scent – to lose the hounds, swimming up to a mile (Hull 1989, 67).

[6] Cf. also Xenophon *Cyn.* 3–4 on hounds' habits (good and bad) in following the hare's trail; the behavior of scent and the proper conditions for good tracking (*Cyn.* 5; 6.2), and Grattius on hounds' behavior in tracking (*Cyn.* 230–48).

hunter. The moon was the hunter's goddess because without the dew and the damp to hold the scent of a hare or deer or boar, the hunter and his dogs had little hope of ever finding their quarry. The hunter needed the moon; and the moon, by bringing the damp, captured the scent, and thus "captured" the animal, leading the dogs, who led the hunter, straight to the prey. From time immemorial, the moon *was* a huntress.

Thus there was no time among the Latins when the moon goddess was not also a hunting goddess, or when the hunting goddess Diana was not also the moon. There is no either-or, no decision we must make between Diana the moon goddess and Diana the huntress. Diana was worshipped in the wild, in a crater beside a lake, because that was where her elements – the moon, the wild, the water – could be worshipped together.

There was another way in which the moon affected the hunter. The hunt tested the strength of both hunter and hunted, and led to the death of the weaker. The moon filled or emptied all beings of their breath, the *spiritus* (*NH* 2.221). Aristotle, according to Pliny, said that no animal died except at the ebbing of the tide (*NH* 2.220), which was controlled by the moon. The moon could fill the prey with breath and keep it alive, or it could pull away breath so that it died. The hunter needed a divinity who knew about death and could interpret the cosmic meaning of death to her suppliants. The more humble archaic hunter would have felt no less reverence, and no less anxiety, acutely conscious that his every action, particularly when he was seeking to kill, was also influenced by the moon's changes. Life returned from death, and life and death were connected in the moon's eternal cycle.

All knowledge and belief that concerned the hunter, from the specific (animals, plants) to the more general (the landscape and seasons) to the cosmological (meteorological and astronomical phenomena), are regularly preserved in and passed on through hunting rituals. Ritual, by means of language and performance, provides the means by which "information can not only be acquired, processed, and stored individually, but fully transferred to others, to be processed and recalled in parallel efforts ... [this information becomes] largely independent ... from the accidents of individual death" (Burkert 1996, 24). Such knowledge was essential.

We shall in due course consider each of her further qualities, but all of these can be shown to be related to Diana's essential identity as the moon *and* hunting goddess, her oldest attested forms. A multiplicity of functions is also true of Artemis, *parthenos* and huntress, mistress of beasts (*Potnia Therōn*), goddess of initiation and of certain aspects of war, protectress of women in childbirth (Lay, *Neue Pauly*, cols. 53–9; Sourvinou-Inwood *OCD³* 182–4). Apollo likewise was the god of initiation, of military and athletic training, of warriors, of music and poetry, of healing, and of oracles (Graf *Neue Pauly*, vol. 1, cols 863–8, s.v. "Apollo").

In the third century there is a transformation of Diana's cult at Aricia. This is when the face and iconography of Artemis first appeared to represent her and the temple-complex structures of Hellenistic sanctuaries were first imitated. The Latins were using this new language, one of visual images and structures, to express their ideas about their own goddess. When we turn to the literature, we find that the Latins were also – perhaps at the same time, perhaps later – beginning to adopt and adapt certain Greek myths the better to explicate their cult. This is the religious context in which we must read the literary evidence, our most subtle and nuanced source of information about Diana. We will learn a great deal more about Latin religious thought by attending carefully to the way in which the Latins used (and did *not* use) the Greek religious visual and mythical language to express themselves.

However, the wide-ranging, widely disparate literary evidence presents its own particular problems for the interpretation of the nature of Diana. Can we expect the Roman literary tradition to be accurate, either about Diana of Aricia, or about Diana as she was generally perceived? The answer for the Augustan Age, the period richest in references to the goddess, is emphatically yes. In fact, the personal and political importance of the cult of Diana to Augustus – both at Rome and at Aricia – all but guarantees an orthodoxy in contemporary discussions of the cult unimaginable in any other circumstances in the Latin or Roman world. Our principal poetic witnesses, Vergil, Ovid, and Horace, were so close to the princeps, so dependent on his good will, and therefore so attuned to his expectations (whether approving them or not), that what they say about Diana or her sanctuary must have rested on unassailable cultic authority, reinforced by

Augustus' approval. Grattius, a colleague of theirs and probably also a priest or elder of the Arician sanctuary, can likewise be assumed to have related what was Arician orthodoxy regarding Diana. We may not hear about things Augustus disliked; but what we do hear, we can rely on. Moreover, the cult of Roman Diana was, historically, of lesser importance than that at Aricia. Though Diana, unspecified, might belong to either cult, we can be reasonably certain, unless there is evidence to the contrary, that what applied at Rome also applied at Aricia. As we shall see in later chapters, there is, on occasion, such evidence in regard to cult practices. The differences do not extend to the nature of the goddess herself, however.

As we have seen, an interpretation of Diana and her cult, and especially of the curious phenomenon of the *rex nemorensis*, will have been worked out between the princeps and the sanctuary to support Augustus' imperial ideology. Although later emperors would never have had the same personal involvement in the cult as Augustus, much the same considerations for writers must have been in force at all times. Whatever fell within the framework established in the Augustan Age would have been safe. But because of the *rex nemorensis*, the possibility would always exist that a reference to Diana contained some hidden message about the current ruler. The Aricians in particular would have been particularly careful to encourage only the most traditional and "Augustan" views of the cult. Safety for everyone meant staying carefully within the lines set out by sanctuary interpretations of the Augustan period. If any work mentioning Diana could have been misread by an informer, it *would* have been misread.

Republican authors would not have been constrained by such considerations. In the period of the Republic, a "Roman" view of Diana would have been the collective result of constantly renegotiated, but widely accepted, ideas of who Diana was – as Diana Nemorensis, Diana Aventinensis, Diana Tifatina. Even so, the cult of Arician Diana was *the* Latin cult of this goddess. Aricia actively defined the nature of "Diana" through her wealth and the visual power of her cult presentation, and that would have carried considerable weight in the shaping of popular as well as intellectual opinion. Certainly when Varro speaks of Diana, it is unlikely that he is saying anything about her nature or cultic identity that would have been unacceptable to, or notably inconsistent with, the Arician cult, especially given his fondness for variant traditions where they are significant. Other authors must be assessed individually, but, with one exception (Cicero), they say nothing that is inconsistent with what is known from the material remains of the Arician cult and from later, especially Augustan, authors.

Once we are able to place Diana's many attributes and epithets in the context of her religious identity and to explain *how* they are related, we will be better able to appreciate the way in which the worship of Arician Diana was used in literature. That will allow us, in succeeding chapters, to consider how the cult priest and the attendant sacred figures of Orestes, Virbius/Hippolytus, and Egeria functioned for the Latins. We will see, in fact, the evidence for spiritual depth and a sustained internal consistency in the evolution of the cult itself. It is a consistency that demonstrates this goddess' extraordinary power, as well as the resourceful and imaginative management of the cult by the Arician elders over time.

THE MOON AND THE HUNTRESS

Diana was regularly called on as a goddess of the moon.[7] "Diana" is used as a synonym for the moon in the analytical works of Varro (*LL* 5.68) and Cicero (*ND* 2.68–9, 3.51; 3.58) where she is counted as one of the planets, πλάνητες, the wanderers. Her alteration night by night was an enduring mystery that both fascinated men and eluded their ability to understand.

> nec par aut eadem nocturnae forma Dianae
> esse potest umquam semperque hodierna sequente,
> si crescit, minor est, maior, si contrahit orbem.
>
> Ovid Met. 15. 196–8

And the shape of nocturnal Diana cannot ever be the same or equal to itself, and always, if she is waxing, her form is less today than it will be tomorrow; and if she is waning, it is greater today than it will be the next.

---

[7] Diana as a moon goddess: Catull. 34.16; Cic. *ND* 2.68–9, 3.51, 3.58; Verg. *Aen.* 9. 404–5; Hor. *C.* 4.6.38, *C.S.* 1–2, 33–6; Ovid *Met.* (the Roman book of the *Met.*) 15.196, *Her.* 12.69; Servius *ad Aen.* 4.511; Trivia as the moon: Petr. *Sat.* fr. 20; Sen. *Medea* 787; Martial *Epigr.* 10.70.7. Diana Caelestis (probably encouraged by syncretism with the Carthaginian goddess): Dessau 3248; *CIL* V 5765, VIIII 999, XIV 3536.

The poets regularly use "Diana" by metonomy for the moon (Verg. *Aen.* 9. 404–5; Hor. *C.* 4.6.38; Ovid *Met.* [the Roman book of the *Met.*] 15.196, *Her.* 12.69). It accords with Varro's and Cicero's analytical treatment of her that the two poems that are specifically hymns to Diana (not to Artemis) both refer to her moon aspect (Catull. 34.16; Hor. *C.S.* 1–2, 33–6). To Horace, her aspect as the moon and as the huntress is of equal importance (*silvarumque potens Diana, lucidum caeli decus*, "Diana, ruler of the forests, radiant glory of the heavens"; Hor. *C.S.* 1–2[8]), and he joins her to Apollo in accordance with a cult tradition at Rome going back at least to the *lectisternium* of 399. Catullus, on the other hand, identifies her lunar aspect with her command of the roads as Trivia (discussed later), an epithet that is not attested for the cult of Diana at Rome but commonly belongs to Diana of Aricia. "Trivia" is often used instead of "Diana" when speaking of the goddess in her moon aspect (Petr. *Sat.* fr. 20; Sen. *Medea* 787; Martial *Epigr.* 10.70.7), and we shall come, in a moment, to the reasons for this.

However, when men thought of Diana in relationship to their more personal, daily concerns, in their hunt for love and their need for help or assistance in other pursuits, they approached her as the huntress.[9] This was inevitable, as the hunt is, in and of itself, a metaphor for the pursuit of anything that one wants or needs. The younger Pliny, constrained by social duty to go on a hunt, turns it into a time to pursue his literary goals, and he recommends the same activity to Tacitus when he wants to write (Plin. *Ep.* 1.6). Minerva (art) as well as Diana (hunting) could be found in the woods, he wrote (1.6.3), and Tacitus apparently responded, either then or at another time, by instructing Pliny to honor Diana as well as Minerva, which Pliny

---

[8] The text of Horace throughout is that of Borzsák.

[9] Diana as a huntress: Tibull. 3.9.19–22; Propert. 2.28.60, 2.19.17; Vergil *Aen.* 7.306, 7.761–82 (where Vergil is speaking of the goddess of the Latins, not the Greeks); Ovid: *Am.* 3.2.31, *Ars* 3.43, *Her.* 12.77, 4.87, 4.91; Plin. *Ep.* 1.63, 9.10; Servius *ad Aen.* 1.219, *CIL* 6.124. I have excluded passages where Diana occurs in a specifically Greek myth (like that of Actaeon), which has no demonstrated context, internally or externally, that connects her with the Latin goddess or Roman culture. Thus, although the *Metamorphoses* is in fact a rich source of allusions to Diana-as-huntress, it does not appear in this list.

complained he could not do because of a general dearth of boars (*Ep.* 9.10.1). Tacitus was possibly a great hunter, but in any case it is quite clear that Pliny each time turns hunting from the pursuit of animals to the pursuit of literature.

The erotic poets use Diana to illustrate the state of their personal relationships in a particular way. A tension is always implicit between the morality of Diana, which is quite serious and goes well beyond sexual chastity, and her commitment to help her worshippers seize their prey, even when that prey is sexual. Thus, just as the contrast between military service (Mars) and service to love (Venus) provides the erotic poets with a means of contrasting public service and poetic ambition, so the hunt, and service to Diana, offers them the opportunity to contrast the ideas of chaste fidelity and sexual attraction, faithful love and amorous pursuit. When we turn to the Virbius/Hippolytus myth, we will see just how serious this contrast could be. The Roman poets were not simply working in imitation of Greek originals, for the Virbius/Hippolytus story shows that Diana did not exclude sex entirely from her realm. By so supposing, modern scholars have missed the ambiguity that is, in fact, part of the erotic meaning of the hunt, a meaning ripe for exploitation by the erotic poets. Ovid, after all, recommended Diana's sanctuary at Aricia *specifically* as a prime hunting ground – for tracking down women (*AA* 1.259–60; cf. Green, 1996b). Again, the Augustan connections with Aricia, which would instantly have come into the thoughts of his Roman audience, make it clear that Ovid was choosing his words with care. Even though he *may* have been employing Greek models, what he was describing were the Latin realities of Diana's cult.

The hunt in itself was considered a sacred rite to Diana. So Propertius promises he will take up Diana's rites (*sacra Dianae/suscipere,* 2.19.17–18), that is, go hunting, while Cynthia is off at some religious festival. It is a wry touch, because service to Diana requires him to relinquish his vows to Venus (an oblique admonishment to Cynthia to go and do likewise). At the same time he is fact promising nothing, for there are many *ferae,* "wild beasts," that he might begin to hunt (*incipiam captare feras,* 2.19.19), including, as Ovid pointed out, other women. Ovid (*Amores* 3.2.31 and *Met.,* passim) likes to visualize the girl huntress with her short tunic and bare legs, and to use this portrait of the huntress' seductive chastity as a suggestive contrast to his own pursuits. The huntress was an erotic figure, whose chastity only intensified her erotic appeal (*AA*. 3. 143–4). He, like Propertius, played with that eroticism, and the letter from Phaedra to Hippolytus in the *Heroides* (with its inevitable associations with Virbius/Hippolytus at Aricia) show just how the eroticism functioned even when the female was pursuing the male (*Her.* 4.87–.91). Sulpicia (Tibull. 3.9.19–22) wrote what might be called the mistress' reply to the hunter: in her pursuit of her beloved Cerinthus, her poem is a plea to accompany him on his chaste hunt. Here the lover-hunter is eroticized, while the poetess seeks to take the place of the goddess who accompanies him. Cerinthus, if he is mindful of Hippolytus' fate, would be wise to be afraid of more than boars, and to maintain his fidelity to Sulpicia .

Latin Diana, as we have seen in the historical accounts of the conflict between Arician and Rome, was a warrior-huntress. That image is central to Vergil's presentation of Diana in the *Aeneid*, particularly the second half, when the Latins come together to drive out the Trojan immigrants. Behind this stands the historical association of Diana with the Latins when, with the Aricians at the fore, they organized in the centuries-long struggle to resist Roman hegemony. In historical fact, however, the Latins were compelled to yield to the Romans, just as in Vergil's epic narrative the Trojans will prevail. Because Augustus could be so associated with Diana, it was necessary to distance the goddess from the doomed campaign of the Latins under Turnus without divorcing her from her people. Vergil provided a brilliant substitution for Diana in the figure of Camilla. Camilla is the girl-huntress as a warrior (*bellatrix*, 7.805)[10]; she is the avatar of the hunting goddess who led the great hunting bands that were, on horseback and on foot, the foundation of the military (*agmen agens equitum et florentis aere cateruas*, "leading a squadron of cavalrymen and a host petalled in bronze"; 7.804, 11.432). Camilla is light and swift of foot (*illa uel intactae segetis per summa uolaret/gramina*, "she would fly along the tips of the unmown

---

[10] The text of the *Aeneid* is that of Mynors.

crops"; 7.808–9), a charismatic leader (*agrisque effusa iuuentus/ turbaque miratur matrum et prospectat euntem*, "the youth running out of the fields and the crowd of mothers marvel and watch her approach"; 7.812–13). She wears royal raiment (*ut regius ostro/ uelet honos leuis umeros, ut fibula crinem/ auro internectat*, "as the cloak of royal purple was lightly draped on her shoulders, as the clasp bound up her hair in gold"; 7.814–16) and rides at the head of her regiment (11.498–501). She carries a Lycian quiver, and Vergil closes book 7 with an ominous and weighty line focused entirely on Camilla's weapons ready for use (*Lyciam ut gerat ipsa pharetram/ et pastoralem praefixa cuspide myrtum*, "that she herself carries a Lycian quiver and a shaft of bucolic myrtle with the arrowhead affixed"; 7.816–17). She fights as a hero and gives a heroic speech (*audeo et Aeneadum promitto occurrere turmae/ solaque Tyrrhenos equites ire obuia contra*, "I dare and I vow to meet the forces of the Trojans, and alone I will go to confront the Etruscan cavalry"; 11.503–4). Her *animus*, her mind, like that of Turnus, is on the action required of her (11.509–10). He addresses her as *o decus Italiae uirgo* ("O Maiden, the glory of Italy"; 11.508), and we can scarcely doubt that this was also an invocation of Diana and meant to be heard as such. Diana grieves for Camilla, whose fate, like that of other heroes, is death in war (11.534–8). She has her *aristeia* and a catalogue of the men she defeats fighting on horseback and on foot (11.648–724). Her death is heroic (11.759–831). Camilla, leading the Latins in the *Aeneid*, stands for Diana leading the Latins against Rome and the Etruscans in the sixth and fifth centuries. In every way Camilla is a subtle and carefully constructed compliment (and complement) to the Arician cult traditions, the history of which extended back through the regal period.

THE *TECHNÊ* OF HUNTING: THE NETS

Because Diana and her cult had long provided the hunter with the knowledge, skill, and tools to succeed in the hunt (whether for animals or other men), she was one of the gods of *technê*, of skills of all kinds. Animals could not be captured without nets, so Diana was responsible particularly for the craft of weaving hunting nets.

> Lepusculi timentis hoc quadrangulum
> dedit Diana rete nexile, arcyas,
> viscum fugai lineamque compedam.[11]
> Varro, *Men.* "Parmeno" 385

Diana provided this four-cornered plaited net for the little hare; the purse-net, the bird-lime and the restraining line.[12]

Grattius takes this craft of net making and weaves it into his *Cynegetica*, at line 24, the first line after the proem: *armorum casses plagiique exordia restes* ("the beginnings of hunting equipment [*armorum*] are the nets and the cords of the snare"). *Exordium* is the warp that begins a net on the loom (*OLD s.v. exordium* 1.a), but it is also a beginning in general (*OLD s.v. exordium* 2) and the beginning of a literary work (*OLD s.v. exordium* 4). Grattius thus is announcing that he is beginning a work of *technê*, and in this part it is the *technê* of weaving. The line itself is charmingly interwoven as well.[13]

The weaving of nets is a skill that is at least as old as, if not older than, the skill of weaving cloth. Grattius spends thirty-six lines describing the material to be chosen for the net and compares the properties of flax and hemp from across the Mediterranean (*Cyn.* 34–60). Even here, the *technê* is dependent in part on the knowledge of the effects of moisture, for the proper time for collecting the flax is in the driest part of the summer, after the rising of the Pleiades (*Cyn.* 57–9). Grattius does not, like Xenophon (*Cyn.* 2.4–6), give the precise dimensions, thickness, mesh size, and types of knots needed in nets for catching different animals, but he spends some time on the scares, feathers, or other means of frightening the prey, which had to be worked into the net (*Cyn.* 75–94). Nets are not just objects; they quickly become metaphors. The *technê* of the hunt is, therefore, always capable of expressing and characterizing the *technê* required to pursue any object of desire. There were as many kinds of "nets" as there were kinds of prey, as Ovid said

---

[11] The text of Varro's *Menippeans* is that of Astbury. As a group they are dated to between 80 and 60 B.C.E., but any individual satire could have been written later (Cardauns 2001, 40).

[12] Even though Varro, with his Pythagorean tendencies, distinctly disapproved of hunting (*Men.* "Meleagri" 294–7), he nevertheless understood its principles.

[13] Note that when Pliny is out hunting and writing at the same time, he is sitting by the nets – weaving the net of his own prose, as it were (*Ep.* 1.6.3).

(*mille animos excipe mille modis*, "trap a thousand hearts with a thousand devices"; *AA* 1. 756).

From weaving nets to weaving cloth is a natural step, and well-woven cloth as a gift was a traditional method of gaining the favor of female goddesses. It is thus not surprising that in historical times several cults of Artemis, as well as the cult of Diana at Aricia, were closely associated with textiles (Kleijwegt 2002, 100–5)[14] in particular with the production and merchandising of religious textiles – that is, cloth, clothes, and materials worn by the worshippers or dedicated by them to the goddess (Kleijwegt 2002, 116–24).

The making of cloth to provide clothing then forms an essential component of civilized human identity, and clothing thus functions as a signifier of civilization. The *technê* of weaving became the metaphor for the gifts of civilized knowledge in general that Diana brought to her worshippers. The clothing she taught them to make to cover their nakedness symbolized all the knowledge and the skill she provided.

> Dona cano diuom, laetas uenantibus artis,
> auspicio, Diana, tuo. prius omnis in armis
> spes fuit et nuda siluas uirtute mouebant
> inconsulti homines uitaque erat error in omni.[15]
>
> Grattius *Cyn.* 1–4

Under your auspices, Diana, I sing the gifts of the gods, the arts joyful to hunters.[16] *At one time all hope was in weapons, and without guidance men used to move about the forests with naked prowess and there was error in every life.*

Man's willingness to accept clothing and to wear it, Grattius indicates, was a gesture that recognized the error of wildness. It was as well an

---

[14] It is, perhaps, also significant that the process of cloth production is dependent on a good and abundant source of water (Kleijwegt 2002, 112).

[15] The text is that of Formicola.

[16] It is important to note here, and it will be repeated elsewhere, that in no way does any deity in the ancient world claim to be the sole source for any benefit to mankind, any more than she or he insists on functional exclusivity. Cults were responsible for collecting and formalizing information (this includes medical knowledge). They were not in competition with each other to be "first." Thus, the arts of hunting were, in a general sense, divinely bestowed – under the auspices of hunting deities such as Diana. Attributing cloth weaving to Diana does not affect Minerva's claim to be the goddess of weaving.

acknowledgment of the goddess' power to guide men on the path toward civilized behavior.

DIANA TRIVIA, GUARDIAN OF THE ROADS

Diana was the guardian of the roads (Varro *ARD*, Cardauns 276 = Aug. *CD* 7.16), and she watched over the paths, particularly the *trivium*. "Trivia" is the earliest attested epithet for Diana (Ennius *Tragedies* fr. 127 Warmington = Varro *LL* 7.16). There is a certain darkness or danger that accompanies the use of this name for her, no doubt because Trivia also stood for the aspect of Diana that pointed the way to the underworld and the dead (Servius *ad Ecl.* 3.26; Wissowa 1912, 174). *Trivium* is commonly translated into English as "cross-roads" (e.g., *OCD s.v. Trivia*, rightly avoided in *OLD s.v. trivium*), which is misleading if not actively incorrect. "Crossroads" suggests a four-way meeting of two roads, an urban junction, which in fact is properly called a *quadrivium* and was the creation of Hellenistic city planners and road engineers.[17] In nature, neither humans nor animals in their movements create a t-junction naturally, as observation of traffic patterns in parks or around large campus buildings reveals. Paths tend to converge or diverge in y junctions – the three ways. It was this older and more natural y junction that Diana Trivia watched over. *Trivium*, as its two elements indicate, referred to a point where the path split into "three-ways" (*tri* = three; *vium*, from *via*, way or path).

The concern for this junction, and its ominous nature, originated in the hunting cult. The intersection of paths was a good place for

---

[17] The *quadrivium* (*OLD s.v. quadrivium*, with citations from Catullus and Juvenal) is the junction of two intersecting and crossing roads. As I work on these pages, I am sitting in the ancient village of Methymna (now Molyvos) on Lesbos, where Orpheus' head was said to have washed up. The Genoese, Byzantine, and Turkish cobblestone roads that lead everywhere up to the castle and around the village show the myriad forms of the y junction. Most t junctions are where the new (second half of the twentieth century) harbor road beneath the village cuts directly across the old roads. Regarding the *trivium*, it is impossible to say whether the quality of "three" was what was significant to the archaic worshipper or the shape of a y junction, which happens to have three arms. No doubt each reinforced the other.

the hunter to put his nets. Road nets "were set up across paths and roads, both the paths made by humans and the game paths made by animals" (Hull 1989, 72–3). Paths were places of danger, where hare or human could be caught because the path itself was a sign of the animals' presence and of their movement.

The Lares Compitales were also worshipped at the intersection of paths and roads, and their cult offers an illuminating contrast to that of Diana. The Lares, as our evidence shows, were more closely connected to the home and the farm, particularly through the family festival of the Compitalia (Wissowa 1912, 167–71). The Lares belonged to specific places. It is probable that there was an understood distinction between the meeting of paths in the wild, the *trivia*, where Diana held sway, and a meeting of paths leading to and from farms and rural homesteads, which would be marked by the Lares Compitales. In the wild, the danger came from presumed enemies; in the civic and domestic sphere, conflict would be between neighbors and fellow citizens.

However, although the source of the danger implicit in the *trivium* can be found in the practicalities of hunting, the religious significance of the *trivium* was in its symbolism. The innate mysticism of the hunters' religion, with its intense preoccupation with natural phenomena, was a powerful creator of metaphor (Guenther 1999, 426–7). The point where a path split represented the moment of decision in wild surroundings and unknown circumstances. The fact that "Trivia" is often associated with Diana as moon rather than as huntress also suggests that particularly dangerous circumstances were equated with reaching a split in the road at nighttime. One had to make a decision, take an action, by the deceptive light of the moon. Trivia would then be particularly called on in moments of danger, moments when death could threaten.

> Tu potens Trivia et notho es
> Dicta lumine Luna.
> Catullus 34.15–16[18]

---

[18] The text of Catullus is that of Mynors.

> *You are called the powerful "Trivia,"*
> *and "Luna" for your borrowed light.*[19]

Trivia is an epithet used for Diana by Ennius, Catullus, Propertius, Vergil, Horace, and Seneca, and it is also found in inscriptions.[20] Heracles was the most famous *exemplum* of this moment of crisis. As a young man, Heracles had to choose between the paths of virtue and vice. It was a parable that was said to go back to Pythagoras (Servius *ad Aen.* 6. 136), although Xenophon (*Mem.* 2.1) offers the earliest surviving record of it. Xenophon attributes the myth to Prodicus, a contemporary of Socrates. The choice at the y-juncture must be made in a quiet place that is clearly outside the city. Persius (3.56; 5.35) shows just how familiar it was as a philosophical topos.

In Diana's cult at Aricia, however, Heracles was not the figure through whom these ideas were expressed. The bough of the *rex nemorensis* and the Pythagorean Y (Servius *ad Aen.* 6.136) are here the symbols of the *trivium*. Once again we see the enormous adaptability of the cult and the wealth of creativity invested in the religion practiced there. The bough could function as a philosophical symbol. In the parable, Heracles had to choose between (seductive) vice and (harsh) virtue. The choice for the *rex* was perhaps between the freedom of a fugitive outside the law or obedience to the harsh requirements of life as Diana's priest within the sanctuary. To lend this force, there was a certain similarity between the *rex* and Pythagoras. Pythagoras, after all, had been a fugitive from Polycrates, the tyrant of Samos (KRS^2 p 224). Empedocles, Pythagoras' follower (KRS^2 259), also celebrated himself as a fugitive and exile (KRS^2 401). The man in search of truth was an exile set to wander in the world. Diana's cult clearly found the mysticism of the South Italian religious philosophies sympathetic.

---

[19] Note that although the moon does "borrow" light from the sun, the gold-roofed temple would also "borrow" light, reflecting the sun or moon. Catullus may or may not be actually referring to the sanctuary at Aricia, but any reading of this poem must at least consider the possibility.

[20] Diana Trivia: Ennius *Tragedies, Andromeda* fr. 127 Warmington (= Varro *LL* 7.16); Catull. 66.5; Prop. 2.32.10; Verg. *Aen.* 6.13, 11.566 (*triformis*, but in the woods); Verg. *Aen.* 7.774, 7.778; Hor. *C.* 3.22; Seneca *Ag.* 367; Ps.Sen. *Octavia* 977; Statius *Theb.* 10.365–6; Apul. *Apol.* 31.32; *CIL* X 3795.

For Diana's worshippers, their choice lay between straying from the path into the barbarism of the wild and following the way indicated by the goddess toward knowledge and so to civilization. Thus the y junction was profoundly religious; but it was also a very real part of daily life. These junctions were everywhere, a persistent reminder that no doubt reinforced the power and relevance of the metaphor for those who sought Diana's help.[21] The goddess guided men – and women – in these moments of crisis. The early hunter, the young initiate, and the man who went to unknown territories to sell his goods, to make war, or to learn about the world, turned to her. So did the women who were embarking on the experience of pregnancy and birth, which could easily take them into the territory of death, as Catullus makes clear. They would not go on their journey, as primitive men had, *inconsulti* – without guidance.

DIANA AND THE UNDERWORLD

For primitive man, the "death" of the moon once a month has to have been one of the most dramatically significant occurrences in the heavens. Yet curiously, Diana's identity as a goddess of the underworld is the most often denied or displaced to a late Hellenistic period, and attributed to the Grecizing of the goddess (Wissowa 1912, 251–2). This cannot be sustained. *Hinc Epicharmus Ennii Proserpinam quoque appellat, quod solet esse sub terris* ("From the fact that she is accustomed to be under the earth, the Epicharmus of Ennius also calls her Proserpina"; Ennius fr. 40 Courtney = Varro *LL.* 5.68).

---

[21] Away from civilization and the cities that secured it, violence and barbarism could easily lurk, a constant reminder of how important it was to rely on Trivia's assistance. Even in historical times, even after the Romans had provided the empire with well-constructed roads, there was little or no signposting in the modern sense. Anyone who has traveled in the hinterlands of Italy or Greece will at once recognize how uncertain the process would be on foot. Laurence (1999, 84–90) provides the detailed evidence for the difficulty, indeed the danger, of travel across the Roman empire even in the high period of the Antonines. This was a world without road maps and the only direction the itineraries could give was by cities that were stations on the way. Note how, in Ter. *Adelphi* 581–4, an unspecified temple to Diana is used as the signpost that clarifies directions.

The goddess of the moon must have had a presence in the under-world from the moment of her earliest worship, because the moon's monthly disappearance into the cosmic dark, and her less frequent but even more dramatic eclipses, were always a critical matter for ancient society. Even after the rationalist discoveries of the seventh and sixth centuries, great events – such as Nicias' refusal to move his army for three weeks after an eclipse of the moon, which led to the destruction of the Athenian forces at Syracuse (Thuc. 7.50.3–4) – were still at the mercy of an intelligent, educated man's fearful reverence before the power implicit in the moon's vanishing (as Pliny notes, *NH* 2.54).

Lunar Diana's aspect as a goddess of the underworld – frequently called, in that form, Proserpina – was already well worked into the Hellenistic theogonies long before Ennius wrote, as the genealogy provided by Cicero indicates. In one of these theogonies, Proserpina had become Diana's mother: *Dianae item plures: prima Iovis et Pros-erpinae, quae pinnatum Cupidinem genuisse dicitur* ("There are likewise several Dianas: the first the daughter of Jupiter and Proserpina, who is said to have borne the Winged Cupid"; Cic. *ND* 3.58[22]). "Prima" as it refers to Diana here probably means "the first," cosmologically speaking. Jupiter and Proserpina would be her parents, because Diana belonged both to the realm of the sky and day (Jupiter) and to the night, darkness, and the underworld (Proserpina). It is a pedigree that may well have Orphic connections and thus go back to the sixth or fifth centuries.[23] Such Orphic interpretations would have been very much at home at Aricia.

Diana's monthly journey to darkness and back was the *exemplum* for that most dangerous journey of all: the journey in which one must meet death. Vergil provided a profound exploration of this aspect of Diana's religious identity in *Aeneid* 6, where his epic recasting of the ritual of the *rex nemorensis* leads Aeneas to the underworld. In this context, the goddess was dangerous and ominous. Her triple form became particularly important in this context, as though writers felt the

---

[22] The edition is that of Pease.

[23] Pease 1958, 1119. The Orphic interpretation would have enriched the meaning of Diana in the underworld, but it cannot be regarded as the source of Diana's connection to it. That is, of course, dependent entirely on her identity as a moon goddess.

need to assert the continuing existence of her other aspects. Ovid says that Hecate's three faces guard roads where they branch in three ways (*Fasti* 1.141). In the book of Dido, the Diana figure who almost draws Aeneas from his destined path (Dyson 2001, 148–54), Vergil invokes Diana as Hecate – *ter geminamque Hecaten, tria virginis ora Dianae* ("and Hecate, treble-formed, the three faces of Diana the virgin"; *Aen.* 4. 511) at Dido's funeral pyre (cf. Val. Flac. *Arg.* 5.235–44; Pomp. Porphyr. *Comm. in Hor. Carm.* 3.22.4).[24]

For Statius the Ides of August, the first day of Diana's great festival, was the *Hecatean Ides* (*Silv.* 5.3.60). In journeys to the underworld, Diana's aspect as Trivia was often invoked, because this epithet again provided a reminder that this was not all there was to Diana. Apuleius calls her *manium potens Triuia* ("powerful Trivia of the shades"; *Apol.* 31.32). Servius (*ad Ecl.* 3.26) reported that *rustici* mourned *per trivia*. It was as though the splitting off of a path, like a tomb, was the gateway to the underworld.

Servius (*in Georg.* 1.5) also relates the Stoic view that Luna, Diana, Ceres, Iuno, and Proserpina were all names used for the same goddess: in this philosophical view, there was only one deity, although she was known by many titles. Yet there were distinctions that could still be observed.[25] Vergil uses "Hecate," Servius says (*ad Aen.* 6.118), because "Proserpina" is inappropriate while they are still in the grove – that is, although they are removed from the ordinary world, they have not yet descended to the underworld. But because they are in Avernus, which is earthly yet belongs to the underworld, Vergil cannot use "Diana" either. In this connection we should, of course, always bear

---

[24] Hecate was, at least in the Greek theogonies, a separate goddess (Hes. *Theog.* 411–52). The name, like that of Proserpina, was used to express Diana's underworld character. This is not to argue that Hecate was Artemis (or Diana), only that it was useful for speakers to employ the name when speaking of the goddess in the underworld.

[25] A different but related set of distinctions led Vitruvius to join Juno, Diana, and Liber Pater (Bacchus) as deities needing a "middle" architectural form (*ratio mediocritatis*, Vitr. 1.2.5. cf. *OLD s.v. mediocritas* 3b, "the fact of being neither one thing nor the other," where this passage is quoted). Previously, in the same section, Vitruvius has said that Jupiter of the Lightning Bolt, Earth, Sun, and Moon should have buildings *sub divo*, in the open, whereas Venus, Flora, Persephone, and Fountain Nymphs should have the Corinthian style on account of their gentleness. Note that Persephone is gentle, which is a distinction from Hecate, the goddess of the underworld in her horrifying aspect.

in mind that such distinctions were flexible and encompassed a general understanding of qualities, not specifics of theological argument.

It is unlikely that we shall ever know the real Latin name of Diana in the underworld – if indeed there was one. The moon at the dark was called *silens* – not by the poets but by the technical writers, such as Cato (*luna silenti, Agri.* 40.1), Columella (2.10.12), and Pliny (*NH* 16.190, 18.314, 18.318, 28.77, 37.155). The dead were known as the *silentes* ("the silent ones"; *OLD s.v. silens* 2; Verg. *Aen.* 6.264). This pervasive silence indicates not just that there was a reluctance to name these deities among the Latins but that, for the Latins, the very silence of the underworld precluded naming. Ovid appropriated epithets like *Tacita* ("The Silent One," Ovid *Fast.* 2.571–82) or *Dea Muta* ("The Mute Goddess," Ovid *Fast.* 2.583–616) for underworld feminine deities. He also seems to suggest that the ghosts of the dead could only moan, not speak (*Fast.* 2.551–4). Lucan's Erichtho makes much of the fact that she needs a just-killed corpse for her predictions, possibly on the grounds that summoning up those who had been dead longer would do no good because they were unable to communicate *(B.C.* 6.619–23). In the *Aeneid*, Vergil makes much the same point with the silence of Dido (6.469–74), the moaning (6.426–30), and the wordless whimpering (6.337–83) of the Trojan shades (6.492–3). Aeneas *is* allowed to speak with Palinurus, who has not crossed over the river, and Anchises, who dwells in the Elysian Fields (6.637–78). One characteristic of Latin religion is that it uses Greek mythology as a rich source of protective euphemism. Thus Hecate or Proserpina (the Latin form of Persephone) are used as names for Diana in the underworld.

Lastly, as we saw in Chapter 3, the actors in the theater in Diana's sanctuary had their own well-designed pit and corridor to allow them to descend and ascend to stage level. In some fashion, the performances at the theater must have illustrated the journey below, and perhaps the return, that was part of the religious identity of Diana the moon goddess.

THE TRIPLE DIANA

Diana, then, was *Diana triformis: Luna, Diana, Hecate.* These were neither different goddesses nor an amalgamation of different goddesses.

They were Diana,[26] well represented by the triple statue of Diana on the coin of P. Accoleius Lariscolus (fig. 5),[27] Diana as huntress, Diana as the moon,[28] Diana of the underworld. Three seems to have been a number closely associated with her, perhaps inevitably, as the moon goddess who has three stages: full, dark, and the changes between. Perhaps inevitably she had three faces because she was in the sky, on earth, and in the darkness with the dead. She may have been addressed as *Luna* when her lunar aspect was alone significant; as the huntress she was always Diana; as the goddess who went to the underworld and returned, she was addressed only through the safety of assumed names, such as Hecate and Proserpina.

DIANA LUCINA: GUARDIAN OF WOMEN IN CHILDBIRTH[29]

When Catullus wrote his hymn to Diana, he called her *potens Trivia* (34.15), *Luna* (34.16), and *Juno Lucina* (34.13–14). Diana the goddess of the moon, the hunting goddess (and, traditionally, a virgin), was also a goddess of childbirth. Cicero provides one of those rationalizing explanations that explain very little but are illuminating in that they show us that the Romans did not ask quite the same questions we do.

[Diana] adhibetur autem ad partus quod ii maturescunt aut septem non numquam aut ut plerumque novem lunae cursibus, qui quia mensa spatia conficiunt menses nominantur.

Cicero ND 2.69

She [Diana] is invoked at childbirth because the period of gestation is sometimes seven or, as more often, nine revolutions of the moon, which, because they complete measured spaces [mensa spatia] are called months [menses].

There is no doubt in Cicero's mind (and presumably no question had been raised in any of his sources) that Diana was properly called on by

---

[26] Clearly and forcefully stated by Zevi (1995, 129–31).

[27] See Chapter 4.

[28] Beard, North, and Price 1998, vol. 2, 1.5c [ii].

[29] Diana Lucina, goddess of birth: Cic. *ND* 2.68; Diana as goddess of birth (without reference to Lucina): Ovid *Fasti* 2.447–52; Seneca *Ag.* 367; Martial *Spect.* 12.1, 13.5–7 (where he is clearly disturbed that the goddess of birth is also the goddess of death, cf. Zevi 1995, 131).

women in childbirth. When Romans asked why this was so, they were not prompted by a sense that a virgin goddess was an inappropriate guardian of birthing mothers. Cicero's answer, that the months measure out pregnancy and Diana as the moon measures out those months has a certain point, of course. Menstruation in females recurs in a monthly pattern, and for the ancients conception and birth were, as we have seen, intimately connected to the moon (Pliny NH 7.38,16.190–1, 18.321–3). The number of months of gestation, however, was a matter more of theory than observation. Observed events were rarely allowed to discredit any explanation that was on other grounds regarded as sound theory. From astronomy to zoology, the ancients were expert at reconciling appearances (and their anomalies) with scientific theory (Lloyd 1991, 248–53). Any specifics that might detract from or call into question central scientific principles were thus conveniently circumvented. Diana's virginity was not even such a specific – it simply did not create doubt about her guardianship of pregnant women. In the end, the moon goddess was called on at the birth of a child because the moon governed birth, death, growth, and decline.

> rite crescentem face Noctilucam
> prosperam frugum celeremque pronos
> volvere menses.
> Horace Odes 4.6.38–40

[maidens and youths] . . . in ritual sing the hymn to the waxing moon, the lamp of the night, with her torch, ripener of crops, and swift to turn the advancing months.

In the sense that the moon was indeed the source of all moisture, essential for successful reproduction, Diana was, as both Horace and Frazer (2.128–9) say, a fertility goddess. More important for expectant mothers was the fact that the moon was a visible and cosmic paradigm of birth and death. Because a child's birth was all too frequently the cause of its mother's death, a pregnant woman would not have been in doubt that at the moment of birth, the path divided: one branch led to life and the other to death. Medea swore she would rather go into battle three times than give birth once (Eur. *Medea* 250–1). Pregnant women would pray to Diana Lucina for all the divine assistance and protection she could give.

Which brings us to a new problem: why did they call on her sometimes as *Juno* Lucina?

Quae ideo quoque videtur ab Latinis Iuno Lucina dicta vel quod est et Terra,
ut physici dicunt, et lucet; vel quod ab luce eius qua quis conceptus et usque
ad eam, qua partus quis in lucem, ficta ab iuvando et luce Iuno Lucina. A
quo parientes eam invocant: luna enim nascentium dux quod menses huius.

Varro LL 5.69

*She [Diana][30] seems therefore to be called by the Latins Juno Lucina, either because
she is also the Earth, as the natural scientists say, and [lucet] "shines"; or because
on account of her light – ranging from that marking a conception to that accompanying
a birth into the light of day – she was termed "Juno Lucina," Juno from* iuvo *("to
help") and Lucina from* lux *("light"). Because of this fact women in childbirth invoke
her; for the Moon is the guide to those being born, since the months belong to her.*

Lunais (1979, 168–74) has argued that Diana, as the moon, was
originally the one concerned with childbirth, and this concern was
only gradually yielded to Juno. Yet as Varro makes clear, in this case,
"Juno" was an epithet of Diana, not the name of the goddess worshipped on the Kalends of the month at Rome. Catullus (34.13–14)
says that when women cried out to Juno Lucina, it was Diana that they
meant. It seems to me that Lunais errs in not trusting the very clear
ancient evidence. Whatever cultural and linguistic process turned the
name of one goddess, Juno, into the epithet of another, "Juno Lucina"
was indeed used by women to summon Diana's aid in childbirth.

At her sanctuary in Aricia votive offerings of swaddled infants and
terra-cotta representations of wombs have been found (Blagg 1983e;
Blagg 1986, 214–15; Blagg 1993, 107; Lesk, 80–9). As Grattius shows,
the sanctuary offered sound, careful advice for the care of pregnant
dogs and the nurture of their pups. We can expect that women who
wanted to know how to take care of themselves or another in pregnancy could go to the sanctuary to learn. Good food, kind attention,
and comfort constitute enlightened maternity care. As in hunting, the
practical side always offered a grounding in reality that supported the
religious metaphysics. Diana's priests gave sensible advice on prenatal
care, yet Diana represented what was much greater: the sum of the

---

[30] The passage is an extension of Varro's discussion of Diana.

cosmic process of birth, of waxing and waning, growing and dying.
Each reinforced the other. Women would have accepted both with
gratitude.

TEACHING AND TRAINING THE YOUNG

Catullus' hymn to Diana is sung by a chorus of boys and girls, *puellae et
pueri integri* ("girls and boys unblemished"; 34.2) and Horace's *Carmen
Saeculare* was also written for young people to sing to Diana (*virgines
lectas puerosque castos*, "chosen maidens and chaste boys"; Horace *C.S.*
6).[31] It seems likely that such hymns were regularly performed for the
goddess by young people. Propertius promised that Cynthia would
perform dances to Diana (2.28.59–60), which may have been traditional among maidens, that is, among unmarried women. Because
Diana was a goddess who cared for animals in their conception and
for their mothers at their birth, she also presided over the training of the
young. Grattius describes at length the proper care for hunting dogs,
care which he says was learned under Diana's auspices (*Cyn.* 283–304).
She was just as concerned for the training and care of young humans.
This aspect of her function was related more to Diana Trivia than to
Diana Lucina, for the young are prone to error, to wandering off the
path.

Iuvenalia fingebantur Dianae simulacra, quia ea aetas fortis est ad tolerandam
viam. Diana enim viarum putabatur dea.

Festus (L 92)

*Images of youths are made for Diana, because that period of life is hardy for enduring
travel [the road]. For Diana was thought to be the goddess of the roads.*

In the earliest hunting cults, when initiation of the young into
the community of hunter-warriors was a preeminent concern, this
moment of decision would have been framed in the ritual of initiation.
Such rituals articulated a passage between one identity and another
for individuals and confirmed the new integrity of the society that
had admitted them. In the imperial period they were increasingly

---

[31] Diana and ceremonies of the young: Catull. 34; Verg. *Aen.* 1.499; Hor. *C.* 1.21.1–4,
2.12.17–20; *C.S.* passim; Diana as protectress of the young male and female, Hor. *C.S.*
69–72.

abstracted from their physical context and turned into a trope about education. The y junction and the branch were integral symbols of that moment of decision, so that Persius in his fifth satire could praise Cornutus as a mentor:

> cumque iter ambiguum est et vitae nescius error
> deducit trepidas ramosa in compita mentes,
> me tibi supposui.[32]

> Persius 5.34–6

And since the journey is uncertain and the uncomprehending wandering of life leads anxious minds to the branching junction,[33] I put myself in your care.

This passage of Persius is quoted by Servius in his discussion of the golden bough (*ad Aen.* 6.136), no doubt because, by Persius' time, Aeneas in *Aeneid* 6 firmly represented a young man at the point of choosing the direction of his life and had displaced the Xenophontic Heracles version. The *Aeneid* would have been taught that way in the schools. In Festus' view, Diana was the goddess of the young *because* she was the goddess of the paths.

As we have seen, Grattius (*Cyn.* 483–92) described a procession that must originally have been an initiation ritual. There the young men strew their weapons among the flowers "at the turning point in the middle of the forest" (486) where there was clearly an altar to the goddess. The turning point, *discrimen*, was also a dividing line (*OLD s.v. discrimen* 1) that separated the young from their previous lives, as well as the *process* for deciding, a test (*OLD* s.v. *discrimen* 3b). A *discrimen* was also a decisive stage, critical point, crisis (*OLD* s.v. *discrimen* 4).

According to Grattius, the offerings – an urn with funeral associations, a green-wood bier with steaming cakes, and a young goat, and fruit still clinging to the branch (488–90) – symbolized youthful sacrifice, when the initiates must make their transition into the community as adults. In Grattius' account, the youths offer sacrifice for the bounty of the year (491–2), and the goddess responds according to their

---

[32] The text of Persius is that of Jenkinson.
[33] *OLD s.v. compitum* 1c: "of a point where a choice of courses, actions, etc. has to be made," with this line cited; also *OLD s.v. ramosus* 2, where this line is cited as well, with reference to *ramus* 2d: "the branches of the Greek letter Υ, used by Pythagoras to illustrate the image of the two ways."

request for help (493). They may have been asking *vincere silvas*, "to master the forest" (the original hunting function of the initiation) or *fatorum labes exire minasque*, "to escape the marks and threats of fate." These "marks" may once have been the result of blows or injuries from various trials the boys were originally required to endure, for it is characteristic of initiations that "group aggressions are vented through various torments and threats, as if the young people were to be killed or devoured by a monster. In this way a dimension of death and new life is introduced" (Burkert 1985, 260). In the historical period, no doubt, there were no more endurance tests, and all this had become symbolic.

Nevertheless, the message remained that Diana was the *tutela* of the young, "a source of safety" (*OLD s.v. tutela* 2b). There is a third-century C.E. wall painting (*LIMC* "Artemis/Diana," 55) that may be an illustration of the contemporary views of that ritual. It shows adolescent boys with torches before an altar of Diana. Two of their compatriots bear long poles with fruit hanging off a crossbeam. Others are carrying baskets of fruit. The altar they approach is round, and a statue of the goddess is mounted on it. Torches, joined by a crossbeam, stand on either side of the goddess. The traditions associated with her cult had been deeply absorbed into the greater Roman consciousness even though the sanctuary of Diana at Aricia was closed by the time this was painted.

DIANA AS *VICTRIX, OPIFER,* AND *CONSERVATRIX*

Propertius thought Cynthia owed dances to Diana because the goddess had brought Cynthia safely through some dangerous illness (2.28.59–60). Certainly she had a healing function (see Chapters 10 and 11), but her aid to her suppliants would not have been limited to healing. Here we see Diana as a very personal deity, one whom men and women involved closely in their lives, one with whom individuals felt they had a most particular relationship. Those who received help made dedications to Diana Opifer, the bringer of aid (*CIL* XIV 5537 = *ILS* 3238), Diana Victrix (*ILS* 3251), and Diana Conservatrix (*ILS* 3250). These epithets do not enter the literary record to any degree; they are simply the testimony of individuals whose gratitude required expression. Thus the goddess who could lead hunters, warriors, and the Latins against the Trojans or the Romans could also bring assistance, preservation, or victory to an ordinary human being trying to overcome adversity in all its forms. The dangers of the wild were a natural metaphor for what human beings in their lives had to confront. In this way hunting cult ritual was universally applied to the ordinary cares and misfortunes of daily existence.

DIANA AND SEXUALITY

So we return to the misfortunes of those who were in the hunt for their beloved. They may seem a surprising group to have been among Diana's concerns. She was, after all, a virgin, and that, as Ovid seems to say, made her hostile to love (*Illa, quod est uirgo, quod tela Cupidinis odit*, "because she is a virgin, because she hates the weapons of Desire"; *AA* 1.261). This is where the (supposed) Greek models are so potentially misleading, for the Latin deities have their own way of distinguishing – or not distinguishing – their area of concern. Diana and Venus were not by any means regarded as polar opposites. Zevi (1995, 136–42) has argued, for instance, that the opposition between the sanctuaries of Diana and Venus/Aphrodite in early Latium was the distinction between *silva* and *hortus*, between the wild nature that must stand away from the city, and cultivated and controlled nature, which is part of it. By the high empire, as L. Bianchi (1997) has observed, many of the attributes of Venus – including attendant Erotes, the baby winged "Cupids" – had been acquired by Diana *particularly* in the representations of the myth of Actaeon. This may seem to be one of those rather baroque developments that we are only too ready to accept from the second or third century C.E., but in the late Republic Cicero knew a genealogy that made Diana the mother of the winged Cupid (Cic. *ND* 3. 58). She may have hated "Cupid's arrows" in one of her aspects, but that did not mean they were unfamiliar to her – quite the opposite. Although the genealogy was probably a Hellenistic philosophical construct, as Cicero says, it cannot have violated some essential characteristic of Latin Diana as it was understood – or Cicero would have been careful to distinguish the deity as Artemis.

There is no evidence that the myth of Actaeon was ever of interest at Aricia, but even so, the hunt and sex were closely allied, as we know from the story of Virbius/Hippolytus, the narrative that *was* integral to the cult (for the evidence, see Chapter 9). As Barringer (2001, 171) says, "contrary to scholarly claims, hunting and sex do overlap. The hunt can exist without sex (and it is worth noting that literal hunting myths are rare), such as Odysseus' boar hunt, but sex, mythological or actual, cannot exist without the hunt." That is, the sexual urge sends the male in pursuit of the object of desire – on a hunt, in fact. A female in rut will draw her suitors, who will fight each other to the death and be impervious to any kind of danger.

The primitive hunter, being only too aware of this, feared first of all that men who hunted could be drawn to sex with female animals, particularly deer, and then that their mating would result in offspring that would be part human and part animal, producing an accompanying guilt at potentially killing a fellow human disguised as an animal (Luckert 1981, 141–2, 149–50). This mixing of wild and civilized, animal and human, was regarded with horror and was one reason hunting deities set powerful prohibitions that required human hunters to be absolutely celibate during the hunt. That a central concern of the hunting cult was sex is shown by the Greek hunting myths, as Fontenrose has well demonstrated (1981, 251–60; cf. Barringer 2001, 125–74; Schnapp 1989; Green, 1996b). In these myths the hunter, or huntress, commits some sexual violation, for which the swift and terrible punishment is either a violent death comparable to that visited by the hunter on his prey (e.g., Actaeon, who was torn apart by his own hounds) or an eternal loss of human identity (Callisto becomes a bear, Orion a star).[34] Some hunters, like Orion, Virbius and Hippolytus, were then rescued by the goddess, but they never returned to their original human form and life.

What is preserved in both the Artemis myths and the Arician story about Virbius is the goddess' love for the young male hunter, a divine love that proves fatal for him. This is what makes for so much erotic ambiguity when Propertius decides to go hunting when Cynthia is

---

[34] Cf. Luckert's discussion of virginity and the hunter in relation to the Navajo deer deity, 140–5.

away or when Sulpicia asks to accompany Cerinthus. Entering Diana's
forest made a certain kind of love dangerously possible. Catullus, when
he retells the story of Endymion, the moon's lover, is willing to use one
of Diana's most popular epithets, and call the moon "Trivia" (66.5–
6).[35] The hunter's path could take him toward desire – and the goddess
who loved Virbius was not in the least unfamiliar with this fact.

That she loved Virbius cannot be questioned. Virbius was to Diana,
Servius says, as Attis was to Cybele (Servius *ad Aen.* 7.761). This comparison is quite extraordinary and must come from real knowledge of
the cult, for Attis and Cybele were hardly the most natural paradigms
for a Latin deity and her companion figure. An analysis of this passage must wait until we focus on Virbius particularly, but it clearly
places Diana and Virbius in a relationship based on an erotic connection between the two which then led to Virbius' violent death. It
would have been some narrative close enough to the Hippolytus story
to make it possible to use Hippolytus in the cult. Diana, as we have
seen, was concerned with fertility in her lunar aspect, and that kind
of natural fertility would be both expressed, and controlled, through
the cult rituals. It was this that led Frazer to suggest that there was a
hieros gamos between the goddess and her priest, who represented Virbius as the paradigmatic youthful male consort (1.19–21, 1.40, 2.129,
5.45). That she was a virgin need not be an insurmountable problem. Venus/Aphrodite regularly renewed her virginity, and there is no
reason that renewed virginity may not have also characterized Diana,
whose moon image continually recreates itself.

So when it seems to Propertius (2.32) that Cynthia has run off
to an illicit love affair, he justifies his suspicion by the fact that she
is taking part in a procession for Trivia at the sanctuary (2.32.1–
10[36]). This is not just any festival, not just any cult a girl could
use as excuse for a night out. The cult of Trivia was one in which

---

[35] The Endymion story was quite familiar to audiences in the late Republican and early
principate. Varro wrote a satire titled "Endymiones" (*Men.* 101–108 Astbury), and Prop.
2.15.15 used it as well. For the Greek account of the story, see Apollodorus 1.7.5 and
Paus. 5.1.4–5.

[36] Goold has reordered the lines to make 2.32 an extension of 2.31. I find the reordering
convincing, but it does not affect my argument. Propertius says plainly that Cynthia's
participation in the procession is reason not to trust her (2.32.8–10).

sex could potentially become part of the hunt, with very dangerous results.

DIANA: THE RESOLUTION

Separating the Latin goddess Diana from her identity as a moon goddess and a huntress, as scholars have done now for far too long, has unnecessarily impoverished our understanding of Latin religion in general and the religion of Diana in particular. The moon goddess and the huntress were inseparable aspects of the same deity. From this identity flowed all the forms in which she was specifically worshipped: goddess of culture and civilization; goddess of the roads and paths, of the young and their education; goddess of life and death, growth and decay; goddess of women in childbirth and protectress and rescuer of men and women in all their multitudinous disasters; the virgin and the beloved of Virbius. The elaborations, the literary flourishes, and syncretic furbelows did not create this multiformed goddess but were made possible by the essential and original complexity of the lunar deity who was also – who had to be – a hunter's goddess.

PART II

FUGITIVES AND KINGS, GREEKS AND SLAVES

1. The Mirror of Diana (Lago di Nemi): author's photograph

2. Il Giardino, site of the sanctuary: (modern museum, upper left) author's photograph

3. Relief of Actor's Masks: Satyr and Maenad: University of Pennyslvania Museum, Philadelphia (with permission)

4. Bronze votive statue of Diana the huntress: Nottingham City Museums and Galleries (with permission)

5. Triple Diana, the Denarius of P. Accoleius Lariscolus (43 B.C.E.): British Museum (with permission)

6. Acrolithic Head of Diana: University of Pennsylvania Museum, Philadelphia (with permission)

7. Votives of body parts: wombs, feet, heads: Nottingham City Museums and Galleries (with permission)

8. Medical votive, woman with her intestines displayed: Nottingham City Museums and Galleries (with permission)

7

THE NECESSARY MURDERER

> . . . From the still glassy lake that sleeps
> Beneath Aricia's trees –
> Those trees in whose dim shadow
> The ghastly priest doth reign,
> The priest who slew the slayer,
> And shall himself be slain.
>
> Macaulay, *Lays of Ancient Rome*, "The
> Battle of Lake Regillus," 19–24

The great challenge the *rex nemorensis* presents is to explain what this strange and violent ritual meant as a religious event central to the identity of Diana's sanctuary.[1] As Burkert observed (1985, 254), "the practice of ritual is more than a casual encounter, it is participation: *hieron metachein*. The ground-line is the animal sacrifice with its two poles of bloodshed and eating, death and life." Yet *human* sacrifice in this ritual of the *rex nemorensis* is the ground-line of participation. How did it function as a sacrificial embodiment of the death and life of the priest-king, and what did it mean for the goddess and her people?

FRAZER AND THE *REX NEMORENSIS*

Diana's priest-king has rarely failed to fascinate even the most prosaic mind, as we know from Strabo (5.3.12). Yet the *rex* and his challenger were not always considered significant, as we know from Cicero

---

[1] An earlier version of this chapter appeared in *Arion* (Green 2000).

(*Ad Att.* 15.4 = Shackleton Bailey 382). In the eighteenth century academic interest centered on Orestes and Hippolytus (Lucidi, 80–98), the Greek *aitia* offered by the ancient sources. The *rex* himself seemed less important. It was in the nineteenth century that the golden bough and the priest very quickly took on their high Romantic glow, as Turner's paintings[2] in the early decades of the century and Macaulay's *Lays of Ancient Rome*, published in 1842, so vividly demonstrate. Lord Savile, while serving as ambassador to Rome, began the first scientific dig in the early 1880s. Later in the decade, James George Frazer in his turn became intrigued by the ritual, and *The Golden Bough*, his monumental twelve-volume magnum opus, grew from there. In royally purple prose Frazer set before the world the image of the *rex* in his wood forever on guard against his murderous successor. From that point on, the reputations of the *rex* and Frazer have risen and fallen together. It has become impossible to talk about the one without discussing the other.

Purple prose aside, Frazer's actual conclusion about the *rex* was mundane, if somewhat convoluted. He argued that the *rex nemorensis* was a priest of the oak spirit identified with the sacred oak tree which he guarded (1.11), and that his death, and the burning of the bough, had originally been a annual sacrifice in the summer for the success of the crops (1.1–2, 11.285–7). He also suggested that the king of the wood had the goddess herself for his queen, perhaps through a sacred marriage (1.40–1). The priest represented the mythical Virbius and had the same relation to Diana that Adonis had to Venus or Attis to Cybele (1.41). Virbius, in addition, was a local form of Jupiter, and the *rex* was a human Jupiter, a god of the greenwood (2.379), which thus linked him to the common European figure of the Green Man, Green George, and Jack-in-the-Green, as well as to other woodland rituals of life-in-death like that of the cutting of the Christmas tree (2.7–96). His explanation was persuasive for some, controversial for many, and has so remained to this day.

[2] J. M. W. Turner, *The Golden Bough*, originally titled *The Sibyl gathering the golden bough*, oil on canvas, painted 1834, now in the Tate Gallery, London. Turner had made two earlier studies of the same subject, c. 1798 and 1814–15. See "The Golden Bough," Marvin Butlin and Evelyn Joll, *The Paintings of J. M. W. Turner*, 2 vols., 1977, 2nd ed. 1984, catalogue entry 355; and for the two earlier studies, Butlin and Joll, 34 and 226.

Frazer's account had the great merit of organizing the relevant details of the ritual and the priest and offering an explanation that normalized it within traditional European, and indeed worldwide, ritual practices. That does not mean he had the correct explanation. Nevertheless, the fury of opposition to Frazer has been directed at his use of the *Aeneid* and Servius' commentary as evidence, because Frazer thus made an unavoidable, and highly unpopular, connection between the *rex*, Vergil, and Aeneas. The result has been an unfocused (although sustained) attack on Frazer, to the neglect of any serious discussion of the *rex*. For all their intensity, his opponents have failed to identify, much less address, the flaws in his central argument.

WISSOWA

In his *Religion und Kultus der Römer* Wissowa responded to Frazer's analysis by politely noting that he was among those unpersuaded (1912, 248 n. 3), without actually discussing the reasons for his disagreement. He acknowledged that the dedication of the Grove by the dictator Latinus[3] was certainly connected to the fact that the priest of Diana bore the unusual title of *rex nemorensis*.[4] He did not, however, consider what the connection might have been, and it is difficult to see how it relates (after a brief resumé of the *rex* and his ritual as described by Servius, *ad Aen.* 6.136) to his subsequent discussion of Diana, the women's goddess, and his assertion that the dedication by the dictator Latinus only marked Aricia's leadership of the Latin League itself. Unlike subsequent critics, Wissowa did not discard Servius' evidence. He did not, however, elucidate just how a woman's goddess became the patron of the Aricians, and the divine leader of the Latin political and military rally against Rome. More important, although he acknowledged the connection linking the woman's goddess, the *rex*, and the dictator, Wissowa left it unexplained. Like Frazer, Wissowa concluded (1912, 248) that combat to the death was an integral part of

---

[3] Cato fr. 58 Peter.

[4] "Es hängt gewiß damit zusammen, daß der Priester der Diana Nemorensis den außergewöhnlichen Ehrentitel rex Nemorensis (Suet. *Calig.* 35) führt," Wissowa 1912, 248.

the original ritual and that the weapon was the bough. Both Frazer and
Wissowa discarded without comment the testimony of Strabo (5.3.12)
and Ovid (*AA* 1. 260) that the *rex* carried a sword. Wissowa then set
out his own thesis of evolutionary decadence, suggesting that a once-
honored priesthood had so far declined that only escaped slaves were
willing to participate, with the result that the ritual had become much
lowered in Roman estimation.[5] And there the matter has remained.
Wissowa, while rejecting Frazer's explanation of the *rex* and his ritual, provided no counter-interpretation and encouraged none. The
shadow of Frazer's tree spirit lingers, despite all the ferocious criticisms,
because Frazer at least made some kind of sense of the evidence.[6]

THE ERRORS OF FRAZER AND WISSOWA

Our most substantial sources for evidence about the *rex* and his ritual are Strabo, *Aeneid* 6, Servius' *Commentary* on that book,[7] and
Lucan, who is clearly reflecting the Vergilian tradition through his own
inversions of that tradition. When Servius says that Vergil bestowed
Aricia as a mother on Hippolytus as a compliment to Augustus and
his lineage (*ad Aen.* 7.762), there was a long and very public tradition behind his statement. Octavian had appropriated the remains

---

[5] "Ein offenbar uraltes Sakralgesetz schrieb vor, daß diese Würde nur durch einen
Zweikampf mit dem bisherigen Inhaber, bei welchem ein Zweig von einem bestimmten
Baume des Haines die Waffe bilden mußte (Serv. *Aen.* VI 136), errungen werden kon-
nte, und dieser Brauch führte römischer Zeit dazu, daß nur flüchtige Sklaven sich der
Gefahr dieses Duells aussetzten und durch Tötung ihres Vorgängers das natürlich in
seiner Schätzung sehr gesunkene Amt erwarben," Wissowa 1912, 248.

[6] See the excellent summaries – as far as they go – of Sørensen and Spineto (2000, 17–24)
each recognizing, with some diffidence, the *rex nemorensis* as a vegetation god, another
Frazerian variant of the tree spirit.

[7] That specific section of Servius (*ad Aen.* 6. 136) connecting the bough, the *rex*, and
Aeneas has often been dismissed as virtually an invention of Frazer's. This dismissal was
a task made easier by the absence of a translation of Servius' Latin. I have provided
(see Appendix) both the text and a translation, with a discussion of the only previous
English translation, that of J. Z. Smith, who rightly saw that this passage of Servius was a
problem that had to be addressed. His discussion incorporates the best of the arguments
to disconnect the *rex* from Vergil's Golden Bough; even so, the argument will not stand.
Servius' Latin makes it clear that the ritual of the *rex nemorensis* was widely understood
to lie behind this portion of the *Aeneid*, and this is why he provides the description of
the ritual of the taking of the bough by the challenger to the *rex*.

of Orestes, as we have seen, and Orestes was the founder of the ritual of the *rex nemorensis*. That Vergil might have *inadvertently* created a ritual for Aeneas that could be read as an allusion to the *rex nemorensis* beggars belief. Vergil must have intended his Roman audience to read the Arician cult behind the text of book 6,[8] and from Servius' commentary we know that it was so understood. The *Aeneid* and Servius' commentary therefore have to be, as both Wissowa and Frazer saw, central to the discussion of the *rex nemorensis*. Vergil clearly used the ritual with a sensitive awareness of its religious meaning, even when he chose, rightly, to adapt it to serve his poetic ends. It was Wissowa's error of interpretation to accept Servius' account of the *rex* in substance but to pass over its relationship to the *Aeneid*.

Frazer, on the other hand, made several serious errors in dealing with the *rex nemorensis*. The first was that despite his recognition of Diana as a hunting goddess (1.6–8), he could not see that hunting had anything to do with fertility or the security of a primitive society. He therefore treated Diana's priest as a manifestation of a fundamentally *agricultural* religion and postulated an annual death by fire of the priest and the bough (although there is no evidence for either a fire or an annual death).[9] Hunting had its own contribution to make to fertility, security, and the preservation of an ancient community, but its organization, ritual, and metaphysics were quite distinct from those of agricultural religion. Agricultural religion served the citizen-as-farmer. Hunting rituals, on the other hand, were meant for the

---

[8] Julia Dyson, in *The King of the Wood* (2001), has begun the process of reintegrating the *rex nemorensis* into a reading of the *Aeneid*. In making her argument, she has demonstrated just how deeply Diana and her Arician cult were interwoven into the poem.

[9] Frazer (2. 376–87, 11.285–6) argues that the *rex*, being identified with the oak as its spirit, was originally burned each summer. "At a later time," Frazer continues, "his annual tenure of office was lengthened or shortened, as the case might be, by the rule which allowed him to live so long as he could prove his divine right by the strong hand. But he only escaped the fire to fall by the sword" (11.286). Interestingly, Frazer does not include the *rex nemorensis* in his analysis of kings killed when their strength fails (4.1–46), because, in his view, the fundamental purpose of the *rex* was to guarantee fertility to the community, and thus he had to die every year. This follows the agricultural model, but, as we have seen, what we have is a hunting cult. The hunter does not have to die every year – though, of course, he must die eventually – and he always had to die as he lived, by the violent taking of one life to ensure the survival of another.

citizen-as-hunter and warrior. Agriculture was directed toward the creation and sustenance of life; hunting ritual necessarily celebrated the mystery of death, especially death as a source of life. Most male citizens in Latium would have been both hunter-warriors and farmers, and would have required both forms of religious participation in their lives. Frazer's mistake was reinforced by Wissowa's rejection of Diana as a hunting goddess.

Frazer's second error was to postulate that the *rex* was the goddess' protector and had to defend the sacred tree from the challenger, fighting him to the death to keep him from taking the bough. Yet Servius says that the challenger had to take the bough to *gain* the privilege of fighting, which indicates that the fight was not merely an expression of the challenger's will and that the bough marked the beginning of the combat, not its end. The fact that it was necessary for the challenger to gain permission to fight was ignored by Frazer entirely. His explication of the *rex* was so persuasive in itself that not even his most passionate critics noticed this rather important flaw. The more romantic view that the *rex nemorensis* lived night and day in fear of an unexpected attack by a new challenger has proven irresistible. As we shall see, this misrepresents not only Servius' evidence but the primitive beginnings of the *rex*, the very nature of ritual, and the character of the priest who was, in historic times, regarded as the living representative of Orestes as well.

Ultimately, however, Frazer's most damaging error in argument was his failure to defend the connection that he, following Servius, made between Octavian/Augustus, Aeneas, and the *rex*.[10] It left his argument open to debilitating attack. As we have seen, Octavian's Arician ancestry, the contumely he had suffered in his youth as a result of that ancestry, and the high probability that he was the one who brought Orestes' remains from Aricia to Rome all justify the use of the *Aeneid* to understand the ritual. It does not therefore follow, as I have said before, that Frazer came to the right conclusions when he did use it.

Not least on account of the scholarly confusion surrounding the whole episode of the Vergilian golden bough, therefore, it is essential

[10] Frazer 1.22, 2.379, 11.285, 293–5.

to begin by reconstructing, as fully as possible, the *rex's* priesthood and its accompanying ritual. This has not been adequately done hitherto, even though both the *Aeneid* itself and Servius' commentary (*ad Aen.* 6.136[11] in particular) provide crucial and authoritative evidence for the ritual. In the case of Vergil, indeed, this testimony must have been approved both by the princeps and by the sanctuary authorities. Now it remains to read it as such.

THE *REX NEMORENSIS*

Let us begin with the most prosaic account of the *rex nemorensis*, that by the first-century B.C.E. geographer, Strabo.

μετὰ δὲ τὸ Ἀλβανὸν Ἀρικία ἐστὶ πόλις ἐπὶ τῇ ὁδῷ τῇ Ἀππίᾳ· ... τῆς δ᾽ Ἀρικίνης τὸ ἱερὸν λέγουσιν ἀφίδρυμά τι· τῆς Ταυροπόλου· καὶ γάρ τι βαρ-βαρικὸν κρατεῖ καὶ Σκυθικὸν περὶ τὸ ἱερὸν ἔθος. καθίσταται γὰρ ἱερεὺς ὁ γεν-ηθεὶς αὐτόχειρ τοῦ ἱερωμένου πρότερον δραπέτης ἀνήρ· ξιφήρης οὖν ἐστιν ἀεί, περισκοπῶν τὰς ἐπιθέσεις, ἕτοιμος ἀμύνεσθαι. τὸ δ᾽ ἱερὸν ἐν ἄλσει, πρόκειται δὲ λίμνη πελαγίζουσα, κύκλῳ δ᾽ ὀρεινὴ συνεχὴς ὀφρὺς περίκειται καὶ λίαν ὑψηλὴ καὶ τὸ ἱερὸν καὶ τὸ ὕδωρ ἀπολαμβάνουσα ἐν κοίλῳ τόπῳ καὶ βαθεῖ. τὰς μὲν οὖν πηγὰς ὁρᾶν ἐστιν, ἐξ ὧν ἡ λίμνη πληροῦται· τούτων δ᾽ ἐστὶν ἡ Ἠγερία καλουμένη, δαίμονός τινος ἐπώνυμος· αἱ δ᾽ ἀπορρύσεις ἐνταῦθα μὲν ἄδηλοί εἰσιν, ἔξω δὲ δείκνυνται πόρρω πρὸς τὴν ἐπιφάνειαν ἀνέχουσαι.

Strabo 5.3.12

The city on the Appian Way next after the Alban Mount is Aricia; ... they say the sacred image of Aricia is a copy, taken from that of Tauropolos. And indeed a certain barbarian and Scythian custom prevails in the sanctuary. For a runaway slave is established as priest after he has slain with his own hand the man previously consecrated to the priesthood. As a result, he is always armed with a sword, looking around for attacks, ready to defend himself. The temple is in a sacred grove and before it is an overflowing lake, and an unbroken and very high mountain ridge encircles it, enclosing both the temple and the water in a hollow and deep spot. Thus it is possible to see the springs from which the lake is filled; of these one is called Egeria, named for a certain deity. Their outflow is undetectable on the spot [at the sanctuary], but can be seen at a distance, emerging into the open.[12]

---

[11] The text and translation on which the following discussion is based are presented in the Appendix.

[12] Text is that of H. L. Jones.

Although he may not have seen the sanctuary and almost certainly did not see the *rex*, Strabo's description of the priest agrees with all the other available evidence.[13] The essential profile is this: the *rex* was a fugitive slave who gained the priesthood by slaying its current holder. He always went armed, had to be permanently on the alert against the attacks of predators (animal and human), and was the only one (except for his challenger) who was ever allowed to carry arms in the sanctuary, where weapons were normally forbidden. That the *rex nemorensis* went armed was a sign of his extraordinary nature. His sword formed part of his ritual image: he ruled the sanctuary "and a kingdom obtained by the sword with an injuring hand" (*partaque per gladios regna nocente manu*; Ovid *AA* 1.260). Another part of that image was the convention that, as a *fugitive* slave, he was a fast runner: the *reges nemorenses* were "strong of hand and swift of foot" (*fortes manibus pedibusque fugaces*; *Fasti* 3.271). It is a fair assumption that at least in some cases he was expected to flee danger, like any wild animal, rather than face it.

There is a lingering idea, left over from Frazer, that all attacks against which he had to defend himself were attacks from his inevitable challenger. The *rex* lived in the wild and ritually represented the law of the wild – no one, man or animal, is ever safe. It was part of his ritual identity that the *rex* must always display his readiness for such an attack. This would not (as it obviously did not) translate into a daily stream of new potential challengers. This was an ancient and significant ritual, not an entertainment. Certainly there cannot have been more than two *reges nemorenses* from the Augustan period to Caligula's reign. It is entirely possible, for instance, that the *rex* who was alive when Strabo traveled along the Via Appia to and from Rome was the aging *rex* whom Caligula forced to fight his handpicked challenger (Suet. *Cal.* 35.3).

Nevertheless, because the *rex*'s life, and particularly his death, were part of a ritual, they would have been strictly regulated. He carried

---

[13] Apart from Strabo and Servius, the other references to the *rex nemorensis* are Ovid *AA* 1.259–62; *Fasti* 3.263–72; *Met.* 15.487–90, Val. Flacc. 305; Suet. *Cal.* 35, Statius *Silv.* 3.1.52–60; Plut. *Quaest. Rom.* 91; Paus. 2.27, 4.

a sword because his ritual function was to live in the wild, to be the hunter who was always hunted. The religious authorities would have determined at what point ritual combat had to be performed. They needed to provide the proper words to be spoken and determine the proper forms and actions to be observed at each stage. They had the formula by which a new challenger could be recognized and approved. Until the bough was taken, however, there could be no ritual fighting.[14] So the ambitious challenger would not be able to attack the *rex* before he had the bough.

Could the *rex* attack the potential challenger? Surely. Would he have known that the ritual had been inaugurated? The elders of the sanctuary need not have told him directly. His survival depended on his ability to read the signs of the wild – including the indications that a new challenger was being selected and a new ritual prepared. If he missed the signs or read them incorrectly, he was ready to be replaced.

This would mean that the *rex* and the elders lived in a kind of impasse. The elders could not anticipate a successful new ritual until the incumbent had fallen into a condition in which he would be unable to preempt the proceedings – until, that is, he could no longer attack and could only run and hide to protect himself. It is necessary to recognize that the *rex*'s daily display of his fighting capacity functioned as proof of his continued vigor to the sanctuary elders quite as much as it was intended to deter any ordinary predators. Monarchs of all sorts frequently make such warrior displays as both threat and promise. Ultimately, however, as long as the *rex* fulfilled the function expected of him on behalf of the city, there is no reason why the elders would want to supplant him.

THE RITUAL: MEETING THE CHALLENGE

We have no evidence as to what signs persuaded the religious authorities of the sanctuary to anticipate the need for, or recognize the arrival

---

[14] Servius *ad Aen.* 6.136: dabatur autem fugitivis potestas, ut si quis exinde ramum potuisset auferre, monomachia cum fugitivo templi sacerdote dimicaret. See Appendix.

of, a suitable challenger. We can postulate, however, that whenever the reigning priest ceased to be able to display his vigor – whether because of illness, age, or any other inadequacy – the sanctuary authorities then began to watch for the approach of the new challenger. Certain disasters befalling the city, meteorological events, earthquakes perhaps, may also have been understood as signs requiring the ritual to take place. Once those signs were seen and acknowledged, a fugitive was needed to make the challenge.

Any fugitive or would-be fugitive in central Italy could be a potential challenger, and no doubt the outline and requirements of the rite were widely known. Nevertheless, except for the sanctuary priesthood, no one would have knowledge of the specific ritual requirements, prayers in particular. The rite would have to be inaugurated by a religious official with some prayer invoking Diana and, for the benefit of the challenger, stating the conditions under which he must proceed. Grattius, Vergil, and Lucan each offer what might be a pattern for such a speech. Grattius records a ritual that has been displaced to Sicily, performed by a priest who shakes an olive branch (*Cyn.* 447–9) before announcing:

> ... procul hinc extorribus ire
> edico praesente deo, praesentibus aris,
> quis scelus aut manibus sumptum aut in pectore motum est.

In the presence of the god, in the presence of the altars, I ordain that all go out of the land far from here, who have put their hands to crime or contemplated it in their heart.

Exiles and fugitive slaves were by definition generally excluded from civic ritual involvement and protection. Because the challenger and the *rex* were themselves, by definition, *extorres*, exiles from their homeland, this cannot be the precise prayer for the *rex*. Obviously, the ritual of the *rex nemorensis* did not exclude exiles. Aeneas, however, is one who is *extorris* (*Aen.* 4.616), so it is to the *Aeneid* we must look for the terms of the ritual that accepts the exile as participant. When Aeneas has gained the golden bough in book 6 and prepares to enter the cave, the Sibyl and he both make sacrifices to the deities of the underworld. After these sacrifices, the earth groans, and the mountain ridges shake the trees; the howling of dogs signals the approach of the goddess (*canes ululare per umbram/ adventante dea, Aen.* 6.257–8[15]). At this point Vergil has the Sibyl speak these words:

> ... "procul, o procul este, profani,"
> conclamat vates, "totoque absistite luco;
> tuque invade viam vaginaque eripe ferrum:
> nunc animis opus, Aenea, nunc pectore firmo."
> *Aen.* 6.258–61

> ... *"Away, oh stand away, you who are uninitiated,"*
> *cries out the seer, "leave the confines of the forest;*
> *you, Aeneas, begin your journey and unsheath your sword:*
> *now there is need for courage, now for an unshaken heart."*

The form recalls Grattius' prayer, without the prohibition regarding exiles or criminals. We cannot, of course, take these for the exact words of the priestess of Diana, but they at least suggest the terms we might expect for the ritual of the *rex nemorensis*. *No one* was allowed to be in the forest except the initiated and the young man about to enter on the ritual. The initiated would be the reigning *rex nemorensis* and perhaps a priest or priestess who was there to say the requisite prayers. If it was a priestess (on whom Vergil's Sibyl would have been based), her function was to say the prayers and provide the challenger with directions on what he was expected to do.

These terms are reinforced by Lucan through an inversion characteristic of his epic throughout.[16] The Massiliotes speak to Caesar just before he marches into the sacred grove to deliver the first violent blow against the oak tree. He is *extorris* twice over, as an enemy of Rome (*BC* 1.203, 225) and of Massilia (*BC* 3.305). The Massiliotes demand,

---

[15] An interesting, and surely not accidental, echo, in *adventante dea*, of Grattius' *praesente deo*, *Cyn.* 448.

[16] Lucan, as Conte says, "seems to propose a systematic refutation of [Vergil's] model" (Conte 1994, 444). In the *Bellum Civile*, the centrality of the grove and the bough to Aeneas' discovery of his destiny, and Rome's, is subjected to the ruthless unmasking of Augustan pretence that characterizes Lucan's powerful "antiphrastic" (Conte's term) attitude. For the analysis of this passage, and that of the grove as part of Lucan's *aemulatio* and *imitatio* of Vergil, see Green 1994.

in vain, to be counted among the *profani* who *should* be kept apart in this combat between Pompey and his challenger Caesar:

> at, si funestas acies, si dira paratis
> proelia discordes, lacrimas civilibus armis,
> secretumque damus. Tractentur vulnera nulla
> sacra manu. Si caelicolis furor arma dedisset,
> |aut si terrigenae temptarent astra gigantes,
> non tamen auderet pietas humana vel armis
> vel votis prodesse Iovi, sortisque deorum
> ignarum mortale genus per fulmina tantum
> sciret adhuc caelo solum regnare Tonantem.[17]
>
> BC 3.312–20

But, if you are preparing murderous battlelines, if you,
so divided, prepare ill-omened conflicts, we weep for civil war,
and set ourselves apart. Sacred wounds may not be touched
by any hand. If insanity had given weapons to the heaven-dwellers
or if earth-born giants were to attempt the stars,
human piety would not, even so, dare to aid Jupiter
with arms or with prayers, and the human race,
not knowing the fates of the gods, would know only
by thunderbolts that the Thunderer alone reigned in the sky.

Through the Massiliotes, Lucan confirms the terms of the conflict between the *rex* and his challenger. The battle must be conducted by the sacred combatants alone, and they must be set apart from all witnesses. Once the prayers were completed and the ritual combat underway, the priestess would withdraw. No one could assist, either with prayers or arms, and, above all, no one could touch the sacred *vulnera*, which are both the weapons used and the wounds inflicted.[18] In such a conflict, even if Jupiter, the ruler of

---

[17] The text is that of Shackleton Bailey.
[18] Cf. Hunnik 1992, 149, *ad loc* 3.314, who gives a list of other instances of the use of *vulnera* for *arma*, particularly common with the verb *tractare*. In this particular context *tractare* has a layered meaning, for while it *can* mean to manage, hold, or handle, as with a weapon (Ovid *Fasti* 5. 397; Seneca *Tro.* 775), it also means to handle or heal a wound (*OLD s.v. tractare* 2d). It is correctly understood (cf. the translations of Duff, Joyce, and Braund ad loc.) that *nulla manu* means "no Massiliote hand," that is, no hand except that of the chosen combatants. However, the enjambment of *sacra* (which grammatically

the gods, were a participant, he could not have accepted help. The entire battle had to be conducted in secrecy, and the winner would be known only at the end, when he emerged victorious. Lucan uses the Massiliotes to prove that the Roman civil war has wholly overturned the established order: the entire *world* is now part of the ritual. Whereas before no one could stay, now no one may withdraw (*BC* 3.358–74).

The Sibyl begins the ritual with the invocation *procul, o procul este, profani* after Aeneas delivers the bough. Lucan, however, has the Massiliotes assert their identity as *profani* who should withdraw before Caesar assaults the tree with an axe. Were the *profani* sent away before or after the taking of the bough? The most probable answer is that the prayer was repeated at both points. Ritual repetitions of important commands or criteria are to be expected. A command excluding the *profani* may well have been uttered at every major stage in the rite, which had to have taken days to complete.

TAKING THE BOUGH

Aeneas approaches the Sibyl to ask for one thing only (6.106–9): that she should show him the way to the underworld, so that he might go there to see his father. The Sibyl responds that if his desire for this insane task (*insano . . . labori . . .* 6.133–5) is so great he must accomplish three things: take the golden bough, bury a dead man (the lost companion Misenus), and make the sacrifice of black victims appropriate to the dead and to the underworld (6.136–55). This marks (Servius *ad Aen.* 6.136[19]), the point at which Vergil takes over the ritual of the

---

modifies *vulnera*) with *manu*, creates the implications of a "sacred hand." The combatants were a priest and a would-be priest, both of whose lives and deaths were dedicated to the goddess, so the enjambment has particular point. Compare Vergil's extended dramatization of the rules forbidding anyone to aid the combatants in the single combat between Aeneas and Turnus, *Aen.* 12.672–952. Cf. S. P. Oakley, "Single Combat in the Roman Republic," *C.Q.* n.s. 35.2 (1985): 392–410, for historical manifestations of single combat in the Republican period, esp. 406–7 on the requirement that the Roman soldier ask permission to fight; 398–9 on the *spolia opima* as purification of blood guilt; and 409–10 on scars as *dona militaria*.

[19] See Appendix.

rex nemorensis for his glorification of Aeneas and Aeneas' descendant Augustus.

The three tasks mark three major points in the ritual: the taking of the sacred bough,[20] which permits the challenger to engage in combat; the funeral of the dead man; and the sacrifices necessary before entering the cave that is the entrance to the underworld. There is one task obviously missing in *Aeneid* 6, and that is the combat between the *rex* and his challenger, which provides the essential funeral. Vergil has displaced this essential act, which becomes the combat between Turnus and Aeneas in book 12 (Dyson 210–27). Vergil has his poetic reasons for the displacement, which do not in the least obscure the fundamental pattern. Poets are not required to create an exact, point-by-point replication of a ritual that has inspired their work.

As we will see, however, Vergil has in any case inserted a telling substitution for the combat. Aeneas begins his search for the bough alone, after he has set in motion the great preparations for Misenus' funeral (6.156–82). The grove is so large (*silvam immensam*; 6.186; *nemore in tanto*; 6.188) that he must pray for assistance in finding the bough. Vergil does not say specifically to which deity Aeneas' prayer was addressed, but guidance comes from his mother, Venus. Augustus' mother, Atia, like all the Julians, was officially Venus' descendant, but she was also an Arician, thus also identifying her with Diana.[21] It is Venus who sends two doves to lead Aeneas to the bough, perching in the treetops above it (*Aen.* 6.187–211). Vergil says it was like mistletoe (*viscum*; 6.205) and, like mistletoe, was *unlike* the tree that bore it (*quod non sua seminat arbos*, "which its own tree did not seed"; 6.206). Aeneas sees the bough and seizes it (*corripit*[22]; 6.210). He is eager (*avidus*; 6.210)

---

[20] Cf. Dyson 2001, 184–94, on the theme of tree violation in the *Aeneid*.

[21] Dyson 2001, 148–67, points out that both Venus and Dido make their first appearance in the poem in the guise of Diana the huntress, and analyzes the significance of Diana throughout the poem. See also de Grummond 1998. The identification of Augustus' mother, Atia, with Aricia and therefore with Diana would only have added force to the syncretism between Venus and Diana. Varro in the *Antiquitates Rerum Divinarum* identified Diana, Luna (276 Cardauns; cf. also Varro *LL* 5.68), and Venus as the moon (279 Cardauns).

[22] *OLD s.v. corripio* 1a, "to seize hold of, snatch up, grasp"; 3a "to seize unlawfully, appropriate"; 5a "to attack suddenly, seize, or overcome."

as he breaks it off (*refringit*; 6.210), although the bough does not respond with equal eagerness (*cunctantem*[23] 6.211).

In Lucan we once again find the inversion, the "antiphrastic" mode[24] that is in part his systematic refutation of Vergil's model. So in the *BC* the grove is Massiliote, "unviolated" since ancient times (*lucus erat longo numquam violatus ab aevo*; 3.399). The gods worshipped in this grove have no names, but their rites are barbarian and the trees are sprinkled with human blood (3.404–5; cf. Strabo 5.3.12). As always in Lucan, everything, including the barbarism, is more extreme. In Lucan's grove there are no birds to perch on the treetops, because they are terrified (3.407–8). The soldiery, out of fear, will not cut down the trees at Caesar's command (3.426–31), so Caesar himself is "the first" to dare to seize the double-bladed axe, raise it aloft, and drive it into a towering oak (*primus raptam librare bipennem / ausus et aeriam ferro proscindere quercum*; 3.433–4). Lest anyone doubt the nature and the purpose of his act, Caesar defiantly claims the violation: *iam ne quis vestrum dubitet subvertere silvam, credite me fecisse nefas* ("now, that none of you may hesitate to overthrow the forest, believe that I committed the crime"; 3.436–7).

Lucan's subversion confirms what is significant about Vergil's account. In their different ways, both Aeneas and Caesar must enter the groves without companions. Their ritual task must be performed alone. Either the tree itself is high or the bough is elevated, not near the ground or even at eye level. The Sibyl tells Aeneas to keep his eyes up (6.145), and then the doves perch on the top of the tree (*super arbore*; 6.203). The oak is tall (*aeriam . . . quercum*; 3.434). The bough must be grasped by hand (*carpe manu*; *Aen.* 6.146) and cannot be taken unless willing (*namque ipse volens facilisque sequetur, / si te fata vocant . . .*; *Aen.* 6.146–7). Caesar violates this, as he violates every other ritual prohibition, by using an axe.

Frazer (1, 8–9) argued that the core of the ritual was that the *rex* was required to defend the tree against the challenger, and that this was the cause of the combat. There are, however, good reasons to

---

[23] *OLD s.v. cunctor* 1a "to be slow in taking action"; 2a "to remain overlong, tarry"; 3 "to move slowly or hesitantly, dawdle"; 4 "to hesitate in deciding, doubt."

[24] Conte, 444.

think this was not the case. The simplest one is that Servius says that the taking of the bough gave the challenger the power to enter combat.[25] In other words, the taking of the branch was a condition that had to be fulfilled *before* the combat could occur. Servius, by using *potestas*[26] (*dabatur autem fugitivis potestas*, "on the other hand, the right was given to any fugitive" *ad Aen.* 6.136), indicates that by taking the bough the challenger *gains* a power associated with a legal or religious privilege. The *religious* (rather than legal) nature of the act is signaled by the fact that the bough had to be taken without weapons (*rite repertum carpe manu*, "pluck the bough ritually once found with your hand"; 6.146). It was, in fact, a ritual violation, and some violence was required in separating the bough from the tree (Servius' *de qua infringi ramum non licebat*, "from which it was not permitted to break off a branch," echoes Vergil's *refringit*; 6.210). The bough's initial resistance to Aeneas was as necessary as its ultimate yielding (6.211). As an augury of the gods' intentions, it answers a question with a proof. The question: is *he* the one? The proof: he is *able* to pluck the bough.

But if the challenger could not use a weapon, we know that the *rex*, as Strabo and Ovid say, carried a sword. The most economical way to understand this is to suppose that the *potestas* the challenger had to earn by taking the bough was the privilege of carrying a sword in the sanctuary. Having taken the bough by his bare hands, he had won the right to have a weapon, and thus the power to fight the armed *rex nemorensis*.

THE TREE

But how did the challenger know which tree was the sacred tree and which bough of that tree to take? As far as we know no particular tree was more sacred to Diana than any other. Vergil says the tree to

---

[25] *dabatur autem fugitivis potestas, ut si quis exinde ramum potuisset auferre, monomachia cum fugitivo templi sacerdote dimicaret* ("On the other hand, the right was given to any fugitive who contrived to remove a branch thence to contend in single combat with the fugitive priest of the temple").

[26] *OLD potestas* 5 "the power of doing something, a chance, opportunity, or right to do it; (spec.) the right of legal or judicial decision" (*w.* ut + *subj.*).

which the golden bough was attached, like mistletoe, was oak (*Aen.* 6. 209). The tree sacred to Diana in the grove near Corne was a beech, even though a more distinguished oak was nearby (Pliny *NH* 16.242). Frazer argued that the sacred tree was an oak,[27] and it was the one that the *rex* protected. As we have seen, however, the battle came *after* the challenger had taken the bough. In any case, all trees in the grove, and all animals, would have been sacred to Diana. Servius' account does not make it clear whether there was one particularly sacred tree in the sanctuary, or if – as with other kinds of augury – it was a matter of choosing the right tree each time a challenge occurred.

Vergil specifically names the tree on which the bough grows as an oak (*Aen.* 6.208–9), and Lucan has Caesar cut down a towering oak (3.434). Moreover, Lucan memorably portrays the failing Pompey as an old oak, barren of leaves and about to fall (*BC* 1.136–43), so that Pompey is symbolically the oak to which Caesar as the challenger takes his axe. No doubt there was an oak in the Arician sanctuary that was particularly sacred, well known and revered, "decked with a nation's ancient trophies, gifts her leaders have consecrated" (*exuvias veteris populi sacrataque gestans / dona ducum*; Lucan *BC* 1.137–8). It may have been encircled with mistletoe. If so, the parasitical mistletoe would have contributed to its weakness and would have portended impending death, just as Lucan, when he compares Pompey to a tottering oak, portends the death of Rome's current leader (*BC* 1.136–43). However, it is not necessary to suppose that because there was a particularly honored oak in the sanctuary, the ritual bough had to be taken from it.

Indeed, given the nature of the ritual as a trial, is it not more likely that the identification of the sacred tree was part of the test? A ritual so critical to an archaic community certainly would not be constructed

---

[27] Frazer comes to this conclusion from an analysis (1.42) of the double-headed bust (second century C.E.) found at Nemi (and then lost again, but only after a cast had been taken; cf. Blagg 1983e, 40–1, where it is identified as a "double bust of aquatic monsters") and, given the importance of the oak in European religion, from a comparison to the myth of Baldur (11.285). Where Frazer sees oak leaves at the mouth of the younger man (monster?), Blagg sees fins. Both figures have curious horns or perhaps animal ears on their heads. That there is a necklace of leaves around the neck is undeniable, but whether they are oak leaves is open to interpretation.

so as to let the challenger choose the sacred tree. It is the Sibyl who describes the golden bough to Aeneas (6.136–48), and Venus' doves actually lead him to it (6.190–203). A formulaic identification[28] may well have been preserved in the form of a riddle, its essential quality perhaps preserved by Vergil: it was a bough *on* a tree, but not *of* a tree; it has new leaves in the winter when it also has berries wound about it (6.205–7). If the bough was indeed mistletoe, the riddle was not concerned with a sacred tree but rather with a sacred *bough*. Given that a sacred tree might die or be destroyed, this is sensible.[29] The challenger's test was to answer the riddle and demonstrate that he knew which birds, which natural signs would lead him to that bough in the immense forest.

THE BOUGH

Was it mistletoe? Mistletoe certainly would suit the requirements for a riddling task, and, because mistletoe is a branching plant foreign to the parent tree, it would undeniably also be an appropriate symbol for the foreigner who is trying to attach himself to the sanctuary. Frazer's critics have believed that if they could prove Vergil's golden bough was not mistletoe,[30] Frazer's entire thesis would fail, and they have spent much ink on the matter.[31] However, the weight of Vergil's

---

[28] Cf. Linderski (1986, 2226–41) on *observatio* (established signs with fixed meaning) and *coniuntura* (new signs). "The expression *veteres res* ([Cic.] *de Div.* 1.34), the 'old' signs, refers to such signs which *eventis animadversa ac notata sunt* (*de Div.* 1.72). They are the 'known' signs. Their meaning had been established in an empirical ways (*eventis*) through the process of long-continued observation. Such an empirical observation of the phenomena is the foundation of the divinatory knowledge . . . The results of the observation are preserved in the tradition of the *disciplina*, and, above all, are recorded in *monumentis* . . . such as the *libri* of the Etrusca *disciplina* or the *libri augurales*" (2233).

[29] Compare the *ficus ruminalis* in the forum, whose withering was a portent and whose replanting a ritual responsibility of the priests (Pliny *NH* 15.77). A sapling, however, could not possibly be guaranteed to supply the sacred bough that set the combat into motion.

[30] West (1990, 228) is quite certain that the comparison implies nothing symbolical or mystical (229), but is a merely visual description. "The mistletoe simile is about the appearance of gold shown up against the dark evergreen leaves of the ilex" (229–30). In fact, Vergil's *visual* comparison is as much about the new green leaves of the mistletoe in the winter as it is about the gold berries.

[31] Cf. West, 224–38, for a spirited defense of the anti-mistletoe position.

comparison is less on any botanical similarity to mistletoe than on the fact that the branch is *unlike* the parent tree (6.206), gold being unlike wood.[32] There is an additional likeness between the golden bough and one kind of mistletoe, which is that both had yellow berries (6.207–8).[33]

> ... sedibus optatis gemina super arbore sidunt
> discolor unde auri per ramos aura refulsit.
> quale solet silvis brumali frigore viscum
> fronde virere nova, quod non sua seminat arbos,
> et croceo fetu teretis circumdare truncos,
> talis erat species auri frondentis opaca
> ilice, sic leni crepitabat brattea vento.
>
> *Aen.* 6.204–10

... [the doves] alight on the hoped-for roosts on the tree with two kinds of foliage, from where, tinted with reflected gold, the air gleamed through the branches. Just as in the winter cold mistletoe is wont to grow green with its strange[34] leaf among the trees, which its own tree did not seed, and it embraces the smooth trunks with its saffron fruit, so was the appearance of the golden bough on the dark ilex, thus were its gold-foil leaves rustling in the light wind.

The ritual bough and Vergil's golden bough unquestionably share one quality: they both function as an omen. Omen-bearing trees were

---

[32] Compare *Georg.* 2.78–82, where Vergil also describes a grafted slip growing on the host tree, causing the tree to "marvel at the unexpected leaves and the fruit not its own."

[33] Only the berries of the mistletoe can be yellow. Butler's note (1920, 123) is worth quoting at length: "There are two kinds of mistletoe. (1) *Viscum album*, the common mistletoe, an evergreen. The fruit is white, and it is rarely found on oaks (never in Italy, according to Pollini, cited by Lenz; Botanik der alten Griechen und Römer). (2) *Loranthus Europaeus*, a S. European species, deciduous with golden berries, and so frequently found on oak as to be called *visco quercino* (cp. Soph. F. 370 ἰξοφόρους δρυάς. Plin. 16.245, *uiscum in quercu robore ilice*). Here the golden bough is found on an evergreen oak (ilex) and has golden berries. This points to *Loranthus Europaeus*. On the other hand, *Loranthus Europaeus* is leafless in winter, while *Viscum album* is not. This is a point in favour of the latter species (cp. *fronde uirere noua*). The probability is that Vergil does not accurately distinguish between the two plants, which closely resemble each other."

[34] The implication in *fronde ... noua* is that the leaf is both "new," "fresh" (*OLD nouus* 11, 12), and "strange," "out of the ordinary" (*OLD nouus* 2, 3, 4). In translating, one is often forced to choose between equally important ideas. Following Day-Lewis (ad loc.), I have chosen to emphasize the strangeness, because the comparison of the mistletoe to the golden bough is based on that.

a commonplace of ancient natural history. According to Pliny, whole books had been written, in both Greek and Latin, about prodigies in and from trees, including trees that spoke (*NH* 17.243[35]). There was so much material on tree portents that he regarded the subject as potentially infinite. A strange metal tree, patently an omen, had already appeared in the *Aeneid*. In book 3, Aeneas had confronted a bleeding sapling (3.27–46), a tree (*arbos*, 3.27) that oozes blood (3.28–9, 33, 43), and yet is an iron hedge spouting sharp javelins (*confixum ferrea texit/ telorum seges et iaculis increvit acutis*, "The spears that nailed me down here have sprouted/ an iron crop above me, a thicket of sharp javelin wood"; 3.45–6). So when Vergil describes this metal part of the tree as being *like* a mistletoe,[36] the contemporary connotations of mistletoe must enter into the narrative (quite apart from what the ritual bough at Aricia was like). The most significant is that the mistletoe was thought to be indestructible by fire or water (Pliny *NH* 33.94) and thus impervious (at least as reputed) to common destruction. Gold does not tarnish, the common sign of decay for metals. Because Aeneas will use it to gain entrance to the underworld (6.399–407), a bough of imperishable material seems an appropriate offering to be affixed to the sacred threshold (6.636).

There are good reasons to think that the ritual bough may have been mistletoe.[37] The first is that though mistletoe cannot be easily detached from its host, it is, nevertheless, a parasite, and thus would be more easily removed than a living branch. Knowing how to identify the parasite and to use whatever was available naturally in the forest to

---

[35] Pliny mentions specifically the works of Aristander in Greek and C. Epidius in Latin.

[36] Austin's comment (1986, ad loc 205) that "the appearance of the Bough . . . – not the Bough itself – is likened to the mistletoe," if I understand it correctly, suggests that the point of Vergil's comparison is to liken the strangeness of mistletoe in the winter forest to the strangeness of the golden bough in the forest where Aeneas sees it. At the most straightforward level of reading, this is indeed true.

[37] Cf. Préaux 1960, 151–67, who identifies many of the constituent elements that the bough must have (it must be a parasite, have a yellow color, be permanently in leaf) and suggests that *artemisium sempervivum* would be a further acknowledgment of Diana's importance in this context. Préaux recognizes the importance of the ritual at Nemi (165 n. 2) as the source for this part of *Aeneid* 6, and suggests the *aizoüm*, or *sempervivum* (known also as the houseleek). This is a tempting identification, although it remains to be explained why Vergil compares the golden bough to *mistletoe* if the *sempervivum* was in fact what he meant.

remove it, may have been part of the test, one not so much of strength as of forest wisdom. The second reason it probably was mistletoe is that the ritual could not be specific to a particular season of the year. A healthy and vigorous *rex* could expect to live at least several decades after his initiation, and because the Aricians would have no reason to renew the ritual unless he began to fail, there was no way to be certain at what time of year his replacement would have to be sought. The need was for a ritual bough that was in leaf, growing, and available at any time of the year.

There is one more point, rather harder to define. The bough had to be "special" in some distinctive way, or it would be ineffectual as a portent.[38] The bough had to be recognizable in itself as a sign, and the taking of it must be a sign as well.

Mistletoe is in leaf and growing at all times of the year, and it can be found on many types of trees. Its greenness when deciduous trees have lost their leaves is the promise, as Frazer saw, of life in death. It would lend itself wonderfully to a riddling identification, and its presence *on* the tree, while not *of* it, would have provided the quality that made it "special." Moreover, as mistletoe was to the parent tree, so a fugitive seeking this priesthood was to the sanctuary: part of it, but not born from it. Having plucked the bough from the oak, Aeneas immediately takes it into the shrine of the prophetess-Sibyl (*vatis portat sub tecta Sibyllae*; 6.211). It is a reasonable conclusion from this that once the bough was taken, it had to be brought to the priestess and acknowledged by her as the correct one.

THE COMBAT

Vergil then has Aeneas turn to the matter of the funeral of Misenus (6.212). Misenus represents the essential figure who, out of his wits (*demens*, 6.172), through vaunting confidence in his skill (6.164–5;

---

[38] The point is made by Pliny's list of tree portents (*NH* 17.243–5). Trees offer portents by changing color, bearing the wrong fruit, or fruit in the wrong place; when they talk, and when they grow in the wrong place (as on the heads of statues, altars, or other trees). Pliny also regards as the greatest tree portent of all that which was said to have occurred at Nero's death: an entire olive grove moved itself across the road and exchanged places with the crops growing on the other side.

171–3) engages in a sacred combat. His was a *musical* combat (*cantu vocat in certamina diuos*; 6.172) with Triton. The god won, of course, and Misenus was caught and drowned among the rocks (6.171–4).

Trials of skill are well-known in the ancient world, and they follow a certain pattern. There is a striking structural similarity of both Misenus' combat and the ritual of the *rex nemorensis* to that of the Black Hunter (performed in territory "in the wild," "at the edges," dependent on tricks and deceit as much as on strength) as analyzed by Vidal-Naquet (106–28). Vidal-Naquet emphasizes in particular the young man's *furor, lussa, celeritas, menos* (madness, frenzy, speed, battle-rage; 122) and points to the similarities implicit in Roman accounts of Horatius' combat with the three Curiatii. The *rex nemorensis* simply lived out himself what had become ritualized for young men in general in the rites of initiation. "Long before the introduction of hoplite warfare into Greece and Rome, the warrior's function in Indo-European society was twofold. On one side was order, which later led to the development of the phalanx and the legion, and on the other, disorder and the exploits of the individual" (Vidal-Naquet, 122). The *rex nemorensis* is the quintessential individual set part from the community, the ruler of the disorder of the wild. Because Vergil wished to displace the actual combat to the end of the epic and make Turnus (the Latin) the ruler whom Aeneas challenges, he has put in its place the death of Misenus, who died in combat with a god. The elements of Misenus' death, then, will tell us much about the ritual of the combat.

We can deduce that the challenger had to vaunt himself and to issue a challenge to combat with the *rex*, as Misenus challenged Triton. The *rex*, being *sacer*, belonged to the goddess (*OLD s.v. sacer* 1) because he violated the sacred tree and was forfeit to the goddess by reason of an offense against a divine law (*OLD s.v. sacer* 2a). As he was thus sacrosanct (*OLD s.v. sacer* 5), the killing of him by the challenger is both vengeance for the earlier violation of the tree and an extension of the challenger's own similar transgression. The ensuing battle would have taken place in the forest, among the trees.

The forest was the natural habitat of the *rex*. This was a hunt. The *rex* would often (although not inevitably) have been enfeebled – by old age, illness, injury – but he would have known his forest intimately, and he would have had years to plan and practice his skills in eluding pursuit; leading a pursuer into dangerous ambushes; setting traps such as falling rocks, falling trees, concealed pits; leading him on; exhausting him; confusing him; and wounding him. The challenger would have been young and strong, with good eyesight and hearing for tracking his prey – but he would not have known *this* forest. If he could find the *rex* and force him to the point of direct combat, the challenger might then, but only then, gain the advantage.

Once the challenge had been issued, eating, like sleeping, would have been dangerous. Fasting was characteristic of rituals of initiation and of trial and, in any case, neither individual could have taken significant time or risked such vulnerability to eat during the contest. The contest was one of endurance as much as of strength, of forest cunning far more than of sword play. It was a hunt for survival without the possibility of truce or retreat. If eating was not absolutely forbidden, the *rex* would have the advantage, having been able to set up caches of food in advance. Yet eating and sleeping and other bodily needs may be put off only so long. The longer each had to wait to sleep or eat, the more vulnerable to error he became, and the slower to respond to surprise.

No one but the *rex* and his challenger could have gone into the forest once the ritual was under way. The combat would not, could not, have been observed. In the most primitive form of this ritual, it is difficult to imagine that any territory in the wild would have been forbidden to the contestants, although the rim of the crater must have acted as a powerful symbolic boundary keeping them within that circle. Otherwise, they could have ranged as far through Diana's forests as their powers would take them. Even in later ages, when the sanctuary itself had taken up much of the space inside the crater, it is unlikely that the ritual was conducted in public view like a gladiatorial game. The *rex* received the challenge and retreated to his forest home, to lie in wait for the challenger who came after him into the woods.

And there the battle raged. Only one could come out of the forest alive, and he would have had to bring the body of the other as proof of his victory. This is the purpose of the hunt: to pursue another to the death, to survive oneself.

THE FUNERAL

Despite our romantic predilections, the combat itself was not the central act of the ritual. The central act, as in all ritual, was the sacrifice: the funeral of the dead priest-king.[39] The taking of the bough *required* this death.

> ... nunc ergo istum inde sumpsit colorem. ramus enim necesse erat ut et unius causa esset interitus: unde et statim mortem subiungit Miseni: et ad sacra Proserpinae accedere nisi sublato ramo non poterat. inferos autem subire hoc dicit, sacra celebrare Proserpinae.
>
> Servius ad Aen. 6.136

> ... *it follows that, at this point in his narrative,*[40] *he [i.e., Vergil] has taken that material*[41] *from here. For it was essential that the bough should also be the cause of one death: this is the reason why he [Vergil] also immediately appends the death of Misenus; and it was not possible to gain access to the rites of Proserpina except through the removal of the branch. And indeed, he says this: that to go to the underworld is to celebrate the rites of Proserpina.*

In the *Aeneid*, the death is that of Misenus. In the ritual, it is the death of the priest-king. The death is a necessary element beginning with a ritual crime and ending with a return from the underworld. The *Aeneid* has much to tell us about this funeral and its meaning. After the Sibyl's advice, Misenus' body is recovered, and then, by her orders, an altar for a sepulcher is straightaway built up from tree boughs (*tum iussa Sibyllae/ haud mora, festinant flentes aramque sepulcri/ congerere arboribus;* 6.176–8). I return in a moment to this interesting phrase, "altar for a sepulcher," which considerably puzzled Probus and Donatus as well as Servius.

On the pyre, Misenus was draped in purple, *purpureas vestis* (6.221). Servius says the purple was an imitation of blood,[42] which was where

---

[39] The ritual clearly supposes that the king might be victorious, and then it would be the challenger who was sacrificed. This should be understood at every point.

[40] For a discussion of the translation, see Appendix.

[41] See Appendix for a discussion of the translation of *color* in this passage, and Cic. *ad Att.* 2.1.1–2; Seneca the Elder *Contr.* 9.2.20–1, 7.2.10–13, both discussed by Wiseman 1979, 3–7.

[42] Pvrpvreas ad imitationem sanguinis, in quo est anima, ut diximus supra <V 79> (*ad Aen.* 6.221).

the soul was understood to reside.[43] The connection between the color purple and blood, and the symbolism of purple flowers for blood, are both familiar. Yet Misenus had not shed any blood; he was drowned. The purple coverings may well have been seen as symbolic of blood, but the nature of the priest-king who has died – bloodily – suggests that Misenus' vestments reflect *both* the kingship and the blood of the sacrifice by combat.

Misenus is placed on a funeral pyre, which Vergil also calls an altar.[44] While Aeneas searches for the bough (6.183–211), his associates move into the forest to cut down boughs and even trees for Misenus' altar-pyre (6.179–82). Vergil, vividly, makes this gathering of fuel a matter of *cutting down* living wood.[45] They are not gathering deadwood, even though green wood is notoriously difficult to burn. Living wood has its parallel in the perpetual greenness, the newness of the mistletoe to which the golden bough is likened (*Aen.* 204–7). Grattius in his turn says that piling fruit-bearing branches on the altar of Diana (*struitur ramis felicibus ara*; *Cyn.* 442) was part of the ordinary ritual of consulting the god. If the branches bore fruit, the wood was green. The fire on which the incense is placed was also on the altar (*ter pinguia libant/ tura foco*; *Cyn.* 441–2), and therefore we must suppose that the fruit-bearing branches were also burned. More significant still, Grattius says the offerings were placed on a *greenwood bier* (*viridi...feretro*; *Cyn.* 488). *Feretrum*, "bier," is an unusual word, and the one Vergil uses for the altar-pyre on which Misenus' body is placed (*ingenti...feretro*; 6.222). Again, the greenwood bier must have been burned as part of the sacrifice. Grattius in fact suggests that the sacrifice is an imitation of a funeral, with the sacrificial fire the equivalent of the fire under the bier.

This turns our attention to Misenus' bier, the *feretrum* that Vergil also says is an *ara sepuchri* ("the altar of the sepulcher"). Servius explains

As Vergil says of Rhoetus' death: purpuream vomit ille animam, "he spews up his crimson soul" (*Aen.* 9.349).

[44] The tomb itself, but not the pyre, is sometimes called an altar (Lattimore 1942, 132–3).

[45] ...procumbunt piceae, sonat icta securibus ilex/ fraxineaeque trabes cuneis et fissile robur/ scinditur, aduoluunt ingentis montibus ornos; "pine trees fall, the oak resounds with the blows of axes and the mighty strength of the trunks of ash trees, easily cleft, are split, they roll flowering-ash trees down the huge mountains" (*Aen.* 6.180–2).

his puzzlement with Vergil's use of this phrase.

ARAMQUE SEPVLCRI pyram dicit, quae in modum arae construi lignis solebat . . . et aram, quae ante sepulcrum fieri consuevit, intellegere non possumus, ut <III 63> stant manibus arae, cum nondum facta sit funeratio, quae praecedit sepulcrum. Probus tamen et Donatus de hoc loco requirendum adhuc esse dixerunt.

Servius ad Aen. 6.177

He [i.e., Vergil] says "the altar of the tomb" for "pyre," which was customarily constructed from wood in the form of an altar . . . and I am not able to understand "altar," something ordinarily set up in front of the tomb, as (in Aen. 3.63) altars are set up to the manes, since the funeral, which precedes the tomb, had not yet been performed. Nevertheless, Probus and Donatus said an explanation for this passage was still to be sought.

When Servius says the altar is customarily constructed *ante sepulcrum*, "before the tomb," "before" is locational, not temporal. The reference to *Aen.* 3.63 clarifies what Vergil and Servius mean by this. There, Aeneas is describing the rites for the murdered Polydorus, whose body the Trojans do not have. Polydorus receives a tumulus of earth, and altars are set up to his Manes (*stant manibus arae*, the line Servius quotes). Blue ritual headbands and cypresses are draped on this altar in front of his tumulus, and on it is poured milk and the blood of sacrificial victims.

Polybius (6.53.4), in his description of a Roman aristocratic funeral, indicates that there were indeed additional rituals performed at the tomb *after* the burial (μετὰ δὲ ταῦτα θάψαντες καὶ ποιήσαντες τὰ νομιζόμενα τιθέασι τὴν εἰκόνα τοῦ μεταλλάξαντος εἰς τὸν ἐπιφανέστατον τόπον τῆς οἰκίας; *next, after they have buried him and have performed the customary rituals they place an image of the deceased in the most conspicuous position in the house*). Servius' comments, then, must indicate that Romans normally understood the phrase *ara sepulchri* to mean the altar set up in front of the tomb to receive the concluding sacrifices to the Manes of the deceased after the burial.[46] It was the custom, then, that the altar was set up in front of the tomb, and *after* the funeral and

---

[46] As Ovid *Met.* 8.480 and *Tr.* 3.13.2 tend to confirm (despite Austin's assurance that these have nothing to do with Vergil's phrase). Cf. also Servius, who says that "farewell" was

after the burial in the tomb, sacrifices were made to the *manes* of the deceased there.

So that was what was expected. But as Servius points out, Vergil uses *aram sepulchri* for the pyre on which Misenus' body was burnt *before* burial. As Misenus' tomb is on Cape Misenum (*Aen.* 6.232–5), and Vergil makes it clear that it is set apart from the funeral site, this pyre could not have been in front of *his* tomb. Then whose tomb *was* it set before? Clearly in the sanctuary of Diana there had to be a burial place for the deceased *reges*, and that burial place would have been deeply numinous. It is reasonable to conclude that the sanctuary ritual (for which Misenus' funeral is a substitute) required the funeral pyre of the dead *rex nemorensis* to be set up in front of the collective tomb for deceased *reges* and that the pyre was known as an *ara sepulchri*. This is significant for what is to come, because, as Ogden in his study of Greek and Roman necromancy (2001, xxiii) observes, "the basic rites of necromancy in the historical period closely resembled observances paid to the dead at their tombs."[47]

The bough has been found, the dead man's body retrieved and burnt on the pyre. Now the third task the Sibyl has set Aeneas is at hand. The Sibyl performs a second sacrifice to Hecate in preparation for Aeneas' descent before the entrance to the cave (6.236–49). Aeneas then (6.249–54) himself makes sacrifices to Night, Earth, and Proserpina. These sacrifices clearly function in the same way as do, in an ordinary funeral, the final sacrifices which are made before the tomb on behalf of the *manes* of the deceased. Misenus' pyre was indeed an *ara sepulchri*.

There were, and are, caves around the lake in Diana's sanctuary,[48] and it seems very possible that one of these was a traditional

---

said after the ceremonies of the tomb had been performed (*nam "vale" dicebatur post tumuli quoque peracta sollemnia, ad Aen.* 6.231).

[47] Ogden regards most of *Aeneid* 6 as purely "literary," even though he believes that the ritual referred to in book 6 is conducted at Avernus (2001, 21–22, and particularly 61–74), and though he also says that the *nekuomanteion* at Avernus was a mere precinct beside a lake rather than a cave (18).

[48] It can hardly be accidental that some of those caves became retreats for hermits in the Christian era (Lenzi 2000, 162). In lifestyle and detachment from ordinary life, the hermit had certain similarities to the *rex nemorensis*.

tomb-entrance to the underworld.[49] Whether or not the tomb was in fact a cave, once the old *rex's* body was burnt, the new *rex* would have carried the bones and ashes into the entrance and – in the company of the *manes* of the dead man – have begun his "descent" (*katabasis*). The new *rex* would place the bones of his predecessor in the cave-tomb, and then await his vision of the underworld there.

However, according to Vergil, after the burning of the body the Sibyl and Aeneas plunge into the cave – and yet there is still a journey through a forest. The Sibyl and Aeneas walk through this night forest, a passage that begins with the haunting phrase *ibant obscuri* (6.268–81). They come to a point *in medio* (6.282) where an elm marks the beginning of the way to Tartarus (6.295). If we take this absolutely literally, the entrance to the underworld must be somewhere other than the cave before which the Sibyl and Aeneas made their sacrifices to the gods of the underworld. Yet Vergil is oddly unspecific with *in medio*, and this suggests that what was required was the *performance* of such a journey in ritual form. Such a journey is through *ritual* geography, rather than earthly territory, and is often performed as a walk through a maze or a series of concentric circles to "the middle," which is the ritual point of entrance to the underworld.[50] It is not possible to simply *be* at the entrance to another world; one must *arrive* there through a formal religious process.[51] Along the way Aeneas passes figures of disease and misfortune, war and madness (6.270–81) who have put their beds there (*posuere cubilia*; 274), like weary and enduring

[49] It is significant that there was no cave in historical times at Avernus, the ostensible and heroically allusive site for this section of the *Aeneid* (Ogden 2001, 61–8). Ogden (68) suggests that the myth of there once having been a cave at Avernus once was encouraged by the existence of caves at some other *nekuomanteia*, such as Herakleia or Tainaron. Equally, it could have been suggested by the use of the cave as the tomb of the *rex nemorensis* at the Arician sanctuary. In Ogden's categorization, the ritual at Aricia would not qualify as a *nekuomanteion*, as we have no text which calls it that.

[50] "The true world is always in the middle, at the Center, for it is here that there is a break in plane and hence communication among the three cosmic zones" (Eliade 1959, 42, and cf. his discussion of sacred space, 20–65).

[51] Cf. Servius' cool remark on *in medio* (*ad Aen.* 6.282): *si et ingressus et exitus simulatus est et falsus* ("and if the entrance and exit [to the underworld] are simulated, they are also false"). That is, this is a ritual performance of the entrance to the underworld and its exit and not a real entrance and exit.

patients.[52] Aeneas and the Sibyl need not – indeed should not – have moved away from the cave. They have moved further into sacred space, and into sacred time.

THE DESCENT TO THE UNDERWORLD

The tombs of the just-buried always created an opening to the under-world, and these openings "did not *lead to* the underworld: they *were* the underworld, and they were all simultaneously the same under-world" (Ogden 2001, 253). In the company of the bones and the *manes* of the dead *rex*, the new priest went to meet Diana in her third, her dark, form, known variously to the Romans as Juno Inferna, Proserpina, or Hecate. The appropriate time for the approach to the dead is at night.

At night in the depths of the cave the priest-initiate would have been surrounded by the reliquaries containing his predecessors' bones. He had begun this ritual as an exile, a fugitive slave, a man on the run and without resources. He had been received by the priestess and embarked on a ritual whose requirements he then had to learn. The penalty for failure was death. He had answered a riddle, searched for the bough, and begun a desperate, days-long hunt through an unfamiliar forest knowing that he himself was being hunted at every step of the way. A priest had tried to kill him, and he had killed the priest. He then conducted the funeral rites for the man he had killed. At the conclusion of the funeral and the sacrifices, he was required to perform a ritual leading him to the entrance to the underworld. He had entered with the bones and ashes of the dead man, knowing that this was where, in the course of time, he himself would be buried. He remained there in the cave in the dark for some time. At this point, he would have been physically exhausted, possibly wounded, sleep-deprived, and without adequate food for several days. Such extreme, unrelenting pressures on

---

[52] Note in particular the juxtaposition of the Eumenides and Insane Discord in line 280. The first recalls Orestes, who was pursued by the Furies (before they were euphemistically renamed the Eumenides), and the second recalls Octavian, who was propelled into the insane discord of civil war and for whom the process of healing the wounds of that war included bringing the bones of Orestes from Aricia to Rome.

the body and the mind over time will produce extraordinary states of altered consciousness and great receptivity to visions.

A better understanding of the issues at stake can be gained from Glucklich's study of "sacred pain," particularly his discussion of the Native American "Sun Dance," a generic term applied to a number of rituals. The Sun Dance is a well-known and frequently studied ritual, with many variants, which lasts all day for many days in succession. The performers fast and avoid water and often endure the piercing of their chest muscles by sticks or claws that are fastened by rope to a central pole. The end of the dance requires the performer to rip himself loose from the pole by main force, tearing himself free from the pins or claws embedded in his chest. "A pain-induced subservience to a greater telos turns the torture into a ritual of self-sacrifice. That greater cause is then 'internalized' in the sense of uniting conscious emotions with somatic feelings" (Glucklich 2001, 149). Such rituals lead to visions and produce individuals who are thought to be endowed with wisdom and the capacity to heal (Glucklich 2001, 145). The Sun Dance has became an object of curiosity to those who have no religious interest in it at all, much as the ritual of the *rex nemorensis* became a "sight" for travelers like Strabo.

Aeneas is accompanied throughout by the Sibyl (at 897–8, Anchises leads both to the Gates of Ivory), which suggests that the priestess remained throughout with the *rex*, perhaps to be the recorder of his visions.[53] What Aeneas sees, the Sibyl also sees. In any case, what the new *rex nemorensis* experienced there, what knowledge he gained and brought back with him when he returned to the upper world, would have been understood as a gift of the gods. It was as real as any experience of daily life. He was now fully and completely Diana's servant and priest. All normal connections that defined a man in this world – ancestors, family, city, inherited gods and rituals, children – had

---

[53] This raises an interesting question. When Octavian wanted the "bones of Orestes," who went into the cave to identify and collect those bones? Given Octavian's chosen identification with Orestes, and the purification implied by the myth that Orestes was the founder of this ritual, it must be considered a possibility that this scion of Aricia himself sought purification at the sanctuary and gained permission from the goddess, or, more specifically, her representatives, to take the bones that he then brought back to Rome.

been obliterated for the new *rex nemorensis*, first by his fugitive state and then by his priesthood. He had no *personal* future whatsoever. His future belonged forever to the goddess.

He was, however, as his title shows, a leader, a *rex*. Trials of strength to the limit of human endurance create individuals who are thought to have exceptional understanding. Such individuals may be thought to have insight into the needs of ordinary men and women, but it may be that the *rex* was to endure his journey to the underworld and return with an idea, a vision, of the *community's* future. There was a *vaticinator* at the sanctuary, that is, one who uttered divinely inspired predictions (Ovid, *Ex Pont.* 1.1.41–2), and it seems likely that it was the *rex nemorensis*.[54] Certainly Aeneas, through *his* journey to the underworld, learns, not about himself, but about the future of his people. Austin (1986, 232, ad loc 756–853, summarizing a widely held view) says "this inspired vision of Roman history has no really logical connexion with the eschatology that precedes it." This is, as we can now see, clearly mistaken. The inspired vision of Rome as it shall be is only possible through the pain and endurance of the ritual. That is how the *rex* became master of the knowledge he had to provide for his community. He would have emerged after his initiation with a heightened understanding of the gods' intentions for the Aricians. This function is not quite the same as that of a Sibyl or a Pythia. He was an Aeneas figure, a man who had achieved exceptional wisdom through his trials and who advised his people when they needed him.

SUMMARY OF THE RITUAL

Some sign – certainly any failing on the part of the incumbent and perhaps other omens or portents – would tell the officials of the sanctuary that the time was approaching for a challenge to the reigning *rex nemorensis*. An exile, a fugitive slave, would appear and be recognized as the legitimate challenger. He would be forbidden to receive help or be observed. He was, probably, required to answer a riddle about the

---

[54] The alternative possibility is that the *vaticinator* was a priestess of Egeria, because Egeria in particular, and springs in general, were sources of inspiration.

sacred bough and then, having found it, to take it with his bare hands, an act which became another augury.

Vergil likens the golden bough to mistletoe, and the ritual bough probably *was* mistletoe. Mistletoe has one *essential* quality, which is that it would have been abundant and available at any time of the year. The act of taking the bough gained the challenger the power, the *potestas*, very probably to carry a weapon, and certainly to fight the current *rex nemorensis*. Although required, the taking of the bough was a violation of the goddess' protection of her sanctuary and required an expiatory death, which was achieved through the mortal combat between the challenger and the *rex*. The *rex* was armed at all times.

The combat, a ritual hunt, took place in the forest. The combat was between an aging and perhaps ill priest and a young challenger. The challenger and the *rex* would fight until one emerged from the forest carrying the dead body of the other. The vanquished became the expiatory sacrifice, and his funeral was the central event in the cultic ritual involving the *rex*.

Outside one of the caves in the sides of the volcanic crater, the funeral pyre, which was also the ritual altar before the tomb, was erected. Once the body was burned, the new *rex nemorensis* would gather the ashes and bones, enter the cave, and perform a ritual journey, probably walking through a maze or set of concentric circles, which translated him from the world of the pyre and the sanctuary to the entrance to the underworld. He was in a condition readily susceptible to visions. On his return, informed by these visions, the new *rex* became a leader of some sort (as his name indicates), as an advisor or a guide to the community of the Aricians.

When he failed, a new challenger would be expected. The community could not afford to be profligate in risking its priest or the goddess' good will. In most cases, the strong likelihood is that the challenger would also be the victor.

THE EVOLUTION OF THE MEANING
OF THE *REX NEMORENSIS*

At the heart of the ritual of the *rex nemorensis* is the embodiment of the hunter's great fear: that when he enters the wild, which is the goddess' territory, he might in some way violate her or her laws.[55] To hunt, men must become predators, enemies to all before them, and this wildness belongs to the animal nature in every human being. The animalistic side of humans must, on the one hand, be given expression for the hunt to be successful, yet on the other hand, be controlled so that the hunter can safely be let back into society. Thus hunting ritual is concerned with wildness, but its ultimate purpose is to protect civilization from that innate wildness in humans. Hunting laws seek to control and channel human aggression.

In Greek myth, the fear of uncontrolled wildness is crystallized in the hunting myths of Orion, Meleager, Callisto, Atalanta, Actaeon, and Hippolytus. The hunter (whether male or female) sees or does something that violates the goddess. The punishment is personal death, often through transformation into a figure completely wild, either an animal or a tree. The hunter loses his humanity or his life – or both. In some cases, though, the goddess, having demonstrated her absolute power in the wild, then brings the hunter back to life (as with Hippolytus in the form of the myth so closely associated with Aricia) or gives him a kind of eternal life (as with Orion).

The original function of the rite of the *rex nemorensis* is therefore a ritual enactment of what appears in Greek religion as a myth. The *rex* is the young hunter who violates the goddess, first by taking the forbidden bough and then by enacting the brutality and finality of the hunt in pursuit of Diana's priest. The descent to the underworld, carrying the bones of his predecessor, enacts the ritual death of the young hunter. Diana's restoration of the beloved hunter to life is performed through the return of the hunter-priest from the underworld. The attachment of the Hippolytus myth to Diana's cult here is hardly surprising. It was a useful externalization of a complex and secretive ritual.

Greek myth, however, was not the only means of interpreting the ritual to the outside world. The rites of Persephone, as well as the esoterica of Orpheus, the Pythagoreans and other magical/

---

[55] Cf. Fontenrose 1981, 250–61, who also compares the Greek myths to their eastern relatives.

philosophical schools,[56] had similar *katabases*,[57] and they arose from, or were closely related to, Apollo's hunting cults. Such cults, indigenous to southern Italy and Sicily, undoubtedly had connections to other early, prearchaic, central Italic cults with characteristics like those of Diana's. Empedocles did not borrow the fugitive as a metaphor for life from Aricia, nor did Aricia gain its real fugitive in imitation of Pythogorean/Empedoclean sources; but the vitality of such Italic mystical experiences must not be overlooked in the discussion of the *rex nemorensis*. The sanctuary authorities at Aricia had rich sources of religio-philosophical thought to draw on.

Thus it is only a few steps from the underlying sympathies uniting Aricia and the southern Italian mystery religions and religious philosophies, to the *interpretatio philosophica* in the last section of Servius' commentary on the golden bough:

> . . . *it was not possible to gain access to the rites of Proserpina except through the removal of the branch. And indeed, he says this: that to go to the underworld is to celebrate the rites of Proserpina. However, concerning the return of the soul, this is the case: we know that Pythagoras of Samos divided human life in the manner of the letter Y, meaning that the first period of life is undetermined, in that it has not yet given itself either to vices or to virtues; however, the bifurcation of the letter Y [he says] begins from youth, at which time men either pursue vices, that is the left branch, or virtues, that is the right branch. This is why Persius says, "it leads fearful minds to the branching crossroads."*[58] *Therefore he [Pythagoras] says virtues must be pursued by means of the branch, which is an imitation of the letter Y, which therefore he says lies hidden in the forest, because, in the confusion of this life and among the greater part of vices, virtue and integrity truly lie hidden. This is why others say that the underworld is*

---

[56] They were often associated with volcanoes – and the cult at Aricia is in the crater of an extinct volcano.

[57] Empedocles considered himself a human transformed into a god (*KRS²* 399), and he called birth a "sojourn abroad" (Plutarch *de exilio* 17, 607d), because the soul was a fugitive and a wanderer banished by the decrees and laws of the gods (*KRS²* 401).

[58] Persius' subject is *vitae nescius error*, "the ignorant straying of (that time of) life." *Error* has a double meaning, of "departure from right principles" (*OLD* s.v. *error* 6) and "going astray" (*OLD* s.v. *error* 3). *Nescius* is "ignorant" both in the ordinary sense of not knowing and in the specific sense of not knowing philosophy, which is why the conclusion of the sentence has Persius putting himself under the tutelage of a Socratic philosopher-teacher, Cornutus. Persius' MSS read *diducit* rather than Servius' *traducit*. I have translated what Servius wrote.

approached by means of a golden bough because mortals easily die as a result of their wealth.

Servius, *ad Aen.* 6.136[59]

The ritual of the *rex nemorensis*, in Servius' Pythagorean interpretation, is presented as a paradigm of the young man's death to his childhood followed by initiation into a life of conscious moral choice between good and evil. The branch the *rex* takes represents life itself, the life of young men who must be brought to the *discrimen*, the point of decision that Grattius celebrated in his poem (*Cyn.* 486). No doubt the branch and the letter Y had even more esoteric meanings, known only to initiates. *Error*, which means both wandering astray, and a mistake, finds its double sense in the ritual, for the *rex* as a fugitive has indeed both "wandered" and he has made a "mistake" that involves the violation of the goddess. These *errores* have led him to the experience of death from which he emerges with wisdom and knowledge. Wisdom and knowledge, after all, were what the philosopher pursued with as much dedication as any hunter.[60]

Pythagoreanism would almost certainly have been introduced to Aricia through Cumae in the late sixth century. Cumae, like other south Italian cities, was reacting both to the expansion of the Etruscans into Campania and to the Pythagorean revolution at Croton, followed by the expansion of Crotoniate power (von Fritz, 80–6) in the toe of Italy. Pythagoreanism was profoundly oligarchic, and Aristodemus of Cumae was a leader of democratic resistance to the Cumaean oligarchy (DH *AR* 7.4–8; Pallottino 87–8). Pythagoreanism was exhilarating or frightening, depending on one's status and political convictions; but it was undoubtedly a significant intellectual and political force exactly at the time that we know Cumae and Aricia to have had a military alliance (DH *AR* 7.6)

As Servius indicates, Pythagoreanism provided a rich system for the interpretation of what remained a secretive and very mysterious

---

[59] See the Appendix for an analysis of some of the more contested details of this passage.
[60] Cf. Green 1996, 221–31, for a discussion of the widely used metaphor of hunting for the pursuit of philosophy as well as for various kinds of *technê*.

rite.[61] The *rex nemorensis*, as his name never lets us forget, was more than the religious representative for men who had to enter the forest. Fugitive though he had been, he was king as well as priest, a leader of the community as well as a servant of the goddess.[62] Pythagoreanism offered a new political and philosophical construct for his leadership, as a complement to the ritual's original function.

This is particularly significant, as the position of the *rex* was not without parallels elsewhere in archaic Latium. There was a substantial tradition in Roman history of exiles acquiring positions of power in other cities.[63] Because the cult was about kingship, with or without Pythagoreanism, it provided a religious grounding for Italic ideas concerning kings and their power. The *rex* was identified with barbarism, and that, then, defined kingship in terms of barbarism. The *rex* was no more Scythian than Diana, but "Scythian," of course, necessarily connected him to the imperial kingships of the barbarians. In the late sixth century, discussions were becoming increasingly passionate on the nature of power, of kings, of barbarism and civilization. When these discussions reached central Italy, the *rex nemorensis* appeared as a vivid *exemplum* of the essential barbarism of monarchical power.

It is with Servius Tullius, Tarquinius Superbus' predecessor as king of Rome, that the ritual of the *rex nemorensis* is thrust without question into *political* history, where it could never again be ignored. Servius Tullius was the storied war-captive slave (son of a nobleman killed in war and a noblewoman captured and enslaved, who rose to the highest power in Rome: Livy 1.39; DH *AR* 4.1–4). Whoever Servius was, and for whatever reason his history was fashioned as it was – either by himself, by King Tarquinius and his wife Tanaquil, or by popular belief – he defined kingship at Rome in terms that mimicked those

---

[61] In Ovid's *Metamorphoses*, the speech of Numa on the teachings of Pythagoras is followed immediately by the entrance of Egeria (Numa's putative wife) and Hippolytus, and the stories of how they were brought to Aricia (*Met.* 15.60–478 [Numa/Pythagoras]; 479–96 [Egeria]; 497–546 [Hippolytus]). The stories of Pythagoras, Egeria, and Hippolytus occupy nearly half this last book.

[62] In the next chapter, the nature of slavery and enslavement, particularly that of warriors, in archaic Latium will be examined to understand better how a fugitive slave might originally have been considered a suitable candidate.

[63] The Roman kings in general show this pattern, particularly Tarquinius Priscus, the son of the Corinthian exile Demaratus.

of the *rex nemorensis*. He was named (or had named himself) Servius, which was understood to be evidence that he had been born a slave or to a slave. If, as the emperor Claudius believed (and it is indeed most probable[64]), Servius was in fact an Etruscan warrior named Ma(c)starna, the name and the assumed biography of Servius Tullius created an allusion to the *rex nemorensis*. If it was not intended, the allusion still cannot have escaped Servius' notice, given his interest in Diana and the importance of Aricia at this time. Mastarna/Servius claimed to have been selected by the gods for the kingship of Rome after the previous king, Tarquinius Priscus, had been killed by assassins. When King Servius determined that he could make Rome the unquestioned leader of the Latin peoples, he adopted the cult of Diana from Aricia. If the connection between Servius, the putative son of a slave, and the fugitive slave who became priest-king at Aricia had not been made before, it was certainly made then. And clearly Tarquinius Superbus saw that this validated – indeed, virtually predicted – the necessary murder of the king by his successor. Thus, in central Italy the connections between King Servius of Rome and the *rex nemorensis* would have made the Arician ritual a catalyst in the heady mix of traditional culture and the radical political ideas of the Greek world.

The men who expelled Tarquinius from Rome must surely have taken note. Brutus and his allies expelled the king; they did not try to kill him. In the context of the *rex nemorensis*, politicized as it had been for the Romans by Servius Tullius and Tarquinius Superbus, whoever killed Tarquinius Superbus would himself have always been suspected of being, or wanting to be, the next king. To refuse to kill the king, as Brutus and his fellow Romans did, was a rejection of *kingship*, rather than of the man.

So the expulsion of the kings at Rome, followed by Rome's conquest of Latium, settled the political question of monarchy for several centuries. Philosophers and political thinkers, poets and playwrights, reworked the old themes of kings and their killers, barbarians and

[64] See R. Thomsen, the modern authority on Servius Tullius, for a thorough discussion of the evidence. He considers it as established that "after the killing of Tarquinius Priscus a conqueror from Vulci called Mastarna became king of Rome" (1980, 95), and concludes that "the central point of this tradition, the identification of Servius Tullius with the Etruscan conqueror Mastarna . . . has . . . a great inherent probability" (103).

monarchs, and students in the schools learned the lessons by rote. If anyone needed a reminder of the reality of kings, there was the *rex nemorensis*, who continued to serve the goddess in her forest near Aricia. Each priest-king was the ritually necessary murderer of his predecessor, and one day in the forest he would in turn meet his own murderer. Roman attitudes toward kings can never be divorced from this *exemplum* who lived out his life not a dozen miles from the Capitoline hill.

Changes in culture and in the nature of leadership continued to be refracted through Diana's priest-king. A potent mixture of hunting-cult mysticism (the original ritual), philosophy (Pythagoreanism), politics (Servius Tullius, with everything he stood for), and Greek myth (Orestes, Hippolytus) made certain that the *rex nemorensis* offered an immensely flexible mediation for ideas of kingship. So when the young Octavian decided to bring the bones of the founder of this ritual, Orestes, to Rome, he brought the supposed origins of religious kingship in Latium along at the same time. Octavian, with the help of these bones, could seek the leadership that Romans so desperately needed after a century of barbaric, murderous, civil war. All concerned must have understood what he was trying to do, whether they agreed with it or not.

8

"WE ARE FUGITIVES"

Fugitives and exiles were an integral part of the ritual identity of the Arician cult of Diana.[1] The challenger to the *rex nemorensis* had to be a fugitive from slavery before he was qualified to take the bough. His fugitive status, if not his slave status, must belong to his earliest identity. Sometime between the sixth and the third centuries, the cult appropriated the Greek accounts of Orestes and Iphigenia, and the fugitive and exile was identified as a hero. Orestes had committed the terrible crime of killing his mother – as well as King Thoas[2] – and this was invariably presented as a necessary murder required or directed by the gods. Iphigenia had sacrificed strangers to Diana in her capacity as the goddess' priestess. Both had stolen the *xoanon* of the goddess from its temple and were forced to flee to escape punishment for their deeds. According to the cult account, they escaped to Aricia, where Orestes founded the rite of the *rex nemorensis*.

The Greek myth was in this way used to explicate the ritual of the *rex nemorensis* in a form that was popular and widely understood.[3] Once again, it is apparent that the Arician leadership controlling the

---

[1] *...fugimus qui arte hac vescimur* ("We are fugitives who employ this skill" Pacuvius, *Chryses*, fr. 290 Warmington). Chryses is the priest (or child of the priest) whom Iphigenia and Orestes sought out when they were escaping Thoas.

[2] Thoas and Aigisthos, as rulers Orestes had to kill, occupy the same narrative space in the myth. Once Thoas takes on his significant role, Aigisthos fades into the background at Aricia.

[3] The existence or nonexistence of native Latin myth is not the issue here. What is important is the use made of Greek myth by the cult.

cult was exceptionally interested in innovative ways of presenting itself to the widest possible public. At the same time, inherited rituals were maintained. Orestes and Iphigenia are able to show us how, in the later Republic, the religious elders chose to contextualize the figure of the priest-king, either by deciding to import the myth, or perhaps merely by encouraging the popular adoption of Orestes as a way to make the rite meaningful for Diana's suppliants.

However, before these explanatory myths can be examined, the cultural context in which the priesthood of the *rex nemorensis* took shape must be established. The fugitive slave who becomes Diana's *rex nemorensis* presents us with one of the most seemingly conflicted and socially destabilizing problems in the Arician cult. How can this figure be a slave and yet a king; a king in the woods and yet a priest of the goddess? In fact, our evidence for the archaic culture of Latium suggests that the *rex nemorensis* represented a by no means improbable pattern of leadership for the regal period.

FUGITIVE SLAVES IN THE LATIN WORLD

It is essential to our understanding of this slave who became king of the woods to keep in mind that the ownership of one human being by another can only exist where there is a civic structure to enforce that ownership. Nature has no part in slavery. As the Roman jurists held, the law of slavery was a law *against* nature.

Seruitus est constitutio iuris gentium, quo quis dominio alieno contra naturam subicitur.

Digest 1.5.4.1

Slavery is an institution of the law of nations, whereby someone is against nature made subject to the ownership of another.[4]

---

[4] "This is the only instance in Roman law in which a rule of the law of nations – defined as the law 'which all nations obey' (J 1.2.1) – is said to be contrary to nature. No important practical consequences flow from the conflict – an indication of the lack of interest in, and unimportance of, an ideal law for the Romans," Watson 1987, 7. Watson's citation is not from the *Digest* but from Justinian's briefer *Institutes*, the "textbook for first-year students" (6).

Without law enforced by civic power, there are no slaves,[5] any more than there are citizens. Slavery, furthermore, is able to exist only so far as the enslaving civic power can effectively reach.[6] Because Diana's realm lay beyond civic rule, slavery was impossible within it.[7]

Thus in Roman legal principle men had a natural freedom (as distinct from the freedom associated with the condition of citizenship), a freedom that was shared with wild animals. By law, domestic animals could be owned and, if lost or stolen, reclaimed. They were possessions. In contrast, a wild animal was a *res nullius*, a possession of no one, and it had a natural freedom limited only by its ability to survive and escape capture. If a hunter captured a wild animal, it belonged to him, but if the animal escaped, it became a *res nullius* once more, and regained its natural freedom.

Omnia igitur animalia, quae terra mari caelo capiuntur, it est ferae bestiae et uolucres pisces, capientium fiunt.

Digest, 41.1.1.1.[8]

So all animals taken on land, sea, or in the air, that is, wild beasts, birds, and fish, become the property of those who take them.

This was a concept grounded in the earliest hunting practices, where the rules governing the status of men and animals were of the highest importance to those whose life, success, or status depended on the hunt. They were, of course, part of ritual knowledge. But not all wild creatures – bees, for instance, or doves – were killed when they were captured.

---

[5] Slaves, that is, as defined by law. Control of one person by another through physical dominance, charismatic fascination, or magic (Prospero and Caliban come to mind) was quite another matter.

[6] In the history of American slavery, the Dred Scott case and *Huckleberry Finn*, each in its different way, reflect the legal, social, and moral crisis turning on this point: were slaves still enslaved when they had crossed the boundary out of the state that legally identified them as slaves?

[7] Practices of the Roman empire, when, as in a modern society, virtually all territory was under Roman power, must not be allowed to mislead us when we consider early Latium. Civic power was very limited then.

[8] The text and translation of Justinian's *Digest* are those of the Mommsen, Krueger, Watson edition, 1985.

Quidquid autem eorum ceperimus, eo usque nostrum esse intellegitur, donec nostra custodia coercetur: cum uero euaserit custodiam nostram et in naturalem libertatem se receperit, nostrum esse desinit et rursus occupantis fit.

Digest 41.1.3.2

Any of these things which we take, however, are regarded as ours for so long as they are governed by our control. But when they escape from our custody and return to their natural state of freedom, they cease to be ours and are again open to the first taker.

If the wild creature was not killed but confined or maintained by its captor, it retained its natural freedom. The law recognized that certain ones, such as doves and bees, habitually returned to a "home" where they were kept by men. As long as the animal retained the desire to return to that home (*revertendi animum*), it belonged to the owner. When it did not return, it ceased to have an owner. The *Digest* makes it clear that this law applied to bees, and birds such as doves, that were regularly "kept" by men and made a distinction between domesticated animals, such as chickens, and their wild counterparts.[9] A similar distinction seems to have been made about men, for in the same section of the *Digest* the discussion of the status of free men who have been captured follows from the discussion of the capture of wild animals:

adeo quidem, ut et liberi homines in seruitutem deducantur: qui tamen, si euaserint hostium potestatem, recipiunt pristinam libertatem.

Digest 41.1.7

so that free men too may be reduced to slavery; but if these escape the mastery of the enemy, they regain their original freedom.

---

[9] "The wild nature of peacocks and doves is of no moment because it is their custom to fly away and to return; bees, whose wild nature is universally admitted, do the same; and there are those who have tame deer which go into and come back from the woods but whose wild nature has never been denied. In the case of these animals which habitually go and return, the accepted rule is that they are held to be ours so long as they have the instinct of returning; but if they lose that instinct, they cease to be ours and are open to the first taker. They are deemed to have lost that instinct when they abandon the habit of returning. Poultry and geese are not wild by nature; for there obviously exist other species which are wild fowl and wild geese" (*Digest* 41.1.2.5–6).

"Their original freedom" should be understood first as the recovery of the natural freedom possessed by any nondomesticated animal. Then it is extended to the recovery of the status of an *ingenuus*, a freeborn man, in a community. The development of the laws of *postliminium* indicate how difficult and complex the return to civic space became. So, in respect to the *rex nemorensis*, we must make a distinction between natural freedom, which men shared with wild animals, and the liberty (or lack of it) established by the laws of a community. Outside a community, all men were as free as birds, bears, or bees. This freedom was coterminous with the wild, and with the intention of staying in the wild.

Thus, when a man fled slavery or criminal charges or was exiled, he left behind everything associated with his civic status. The legal condition of a man exiled, based on the *interdictio aqua et igni*, was the same as that of a man captured by the enemy (Amirante, 26– 32). In either case, the man was legally dead to his community. Law was concerned, naturally, with the consequences of *capitis deminutio* for those left behind. The cult of Diana was interested, on the other hand, in those who did the leaving. In the late Bronze and early Iron Ages, communities were small, and relationships between them were by no means clearly defined, even by the most primitive of treaties. A man was a fugitive, an escaped slave, or an exile, *only* in his former city. Reciprocal recognition of laws was far from customary when the ritual of the *rex* was taking shape, so that his status, whether good or bad, in his former home might well not be recognized in a new community. Legal relationships had to be established: they could not be assumed, even between the Latins (see, e.g., Livy 1.9 and DH *AR* 2.33 on the refusal of neighboring cities to permit intermarriage with Roman citizens). A captured warrior who escaped his captivity or a man exiled from his city and thus rendered stateless could thus both approach Diana's sanctuary as free men, who, like wild animals, had regained their natural freedom.

Yet the challenger to the *rex nemorensis* had been – indeed, was required to have been – a slave. What did that mean to the early Latin communities? It was the understanding of the legal scholars of the *Digest* that slavery originated when men were captured in war. They recorded one of those etymologies that has no linguistic justification but tells us a great deal about inherited cultural perceptions – the same perceptions that shaped the institution of the *rex nemorensis*.[10]

Serui ex eo appellati sunt, quod imperatores captiuos uendere ac per hoc seruare nec occidere solent: mancipia uero dicta, quod ab hostibus manu capiantur.

Digest 1.5.4.2

Slaves (serui) *are so called, because generals have a custom of selling their prisoners and thereby preserving* servare *rather than killing them: and indeed they are said to be* mancipia (manus + capio), *because they are captives in the hand* (manus) *of their enemies.*

On legal principle, then, slaves were originally war captives, and taking them was like taking a wild animal. Moreover, *every* man captured by the enemy was considered the enemy's slave.[11] This is understandable for the early period before slaves were imported, when "war" was, in fact, very like a hunt: it was a series of border raids, cattle raids, and predatory attacks on vulnerable travelers and outlying farmsteads. Anyone could be captured and enslaved. It was not necessary for a state of war to exist between the city of a potential captive – whether warrior, farmer, or traveler – and that of his captors. It mattered only that there existed no treaty of friendship, no official ties of hospitality.[12] According to the law, any man who was so captured ceased to be a legal person and was regarded as having died at the moment of capture (*Digest* 49.15.18), and *postliminium* law was developed to regulate his return.[13] Yet it was not just the citizen, captured,

---

[10] It seems likely that they are also behind the Roman practice of giving citizenship to slaves manumitted by citizens (Watson 1987, 23–5; Watson argues that manumission by *vindicta*, and perhaps even manumission by census, worked by a "dodge," using the legal process that freed a man wrongfully enslaved, 24–5). This would also explain how the Romans came to settle captive populations in Rome (as they did with Alba Longa, Livy 1.29; DH *AR* 1.66.2; Politorum, Tellenae, and Ficana, as well as captured soldiers of the "Ancient Latins," Livy 1.33; DH *AR* 3.43) which were eventually accepted as citizens.

[11] Gaius *Institutes* 1.129; Amirante 1950, 25.

[12] Watson 1987, 20. In the early period it must have been difficult to tell the difference between "enemies" and "brigands," as the account of Romulus and Remus (Livy 1.4.8–9) and the Sabine women (Livy 1.9) indicate. Technically, persons captured by brigands or pirates continued to be free (*Digest* 49.15.19.2).

[13] If he returned, having escaped his capture and slavery, such a man had the right not only to his natural freedom but also to his *libertas* as a citizen (*Digest* 49.15.5.1–2) as if

who was governed in this way. A man who was exiled was also "dead" to his former home, and *postliminium* law applied to his reentry, as Aelius Gallus (writer on various subjects and prefect of Egypt under Augustus, though not the poet) held, to those who had simply gone over to another city, that is, presumably exiles, colonists, and others (Festus 244 L). It was entirely possible that a wellborn man, a man of high status and family connections, once captured, could be enslaved. So in the earliest Latin communities the man who arrived to challenge the *rex nemorensis* was a man who was considered dead by his community. It made no difference whether he had been exiled, enslaved as a captured warrior, or was on the run because of some crime he had committed.

That the cult of Diana should accept such a man was in no way exceptional. There is good evidence that in Latium generally it was acceptable to receive men who were, for any reason, *extorres* (exiles or fugitives). Moreover, upon acceptance they could be quite quickly elevated to important positions of religious and political leadership. Examples of this are particularly clear in the histories of the kings of Rome. One such example, and a distinguished one, is to be found in the accounts of Tarquinius Priscus (traditionally 616–579), who left his own home of Tarquinii for Rome.

Livy (1.34–35) reports that Tarquinius chose to leave for Rome (at his wife's instigation) in the hopes of bettering himself; but Dionysius (*AR* 3.47) speaks of Tarquinius having been expelled (ἀπελαυνόμενος) from Tarquinii. Moreover, Dionysius (3.46.2) says *specifically* that he was reporting Tarquinius' history ὡς ἐν ταῖς ἐπιχωρίοις συγγραφαῖς εὗρον, "as I found [it] in the local archives."[14] Dionysius is emphasizing the authority of his source. He must have supposed that, first, authority was needed, and second, that what he had *was* authoritative.

---

he had never been enslaved. The legal principle of *postliminium*, the return of a soldier captured and made a slave, governed this difficult eventuality. *Postliminium* law "was highly complex, sophisticated, and developed, even at an early date" (Watson 1987, 21). As Amirante (1950, 24) observes, in the archaic period, *postliminium* in its origins was inseparable from the fact of return. A man had to reenter his city physically to regain his citizenship.

[14] Probably these are the *Libri Annales* (Frier 1999, 109–14), the information and accuracy of which Frier has challenged, considering the material contained in it "jejune" (e.g., 277, 284). Frier says that Dionysius did not claim to have seen the chronicle himself (277).

He appears to give the facts accepted by Roman officialdom (*AR* 3.46–9, obviously expanded by rhetorical narrative detail), while Livy has left us an ameliorative account. The ameliorization is significant. Livy's Tarquinius is not a better man – he is greedy, ambitious, and goaded by his wife (1.34) – but his civil status is more respectable.[15]

It does not appear that any part of the traditional accounts of the regal period found it surprising that a stranger could come to Rome and be made king. The kings of Rome *did* tend to be outsiders. As Cornell says (1995, 143), "from the sources, then, we can gather that the king was an outsider, sometimes a foreigner, but in any case chosen from outside the patrician aristocracy, and that his election was a complex process involving the previous king, the patricians, the people, and the gods." Livy acknowledges this by bestowing on Tarquinius a speech which actually bases his claim to the throne on the tradition of non-Roman kings of Rome (Livy 1.35.3–5).

Another example of leaders coming from outside, from a slightly different but still dubious background, is provided by Tarquinius Priscus' impoverished nephew, Egerius, who was used by Tarquinius, once he was king in Rome, as an agent to gain control of Collatia. It is a muddled account (Livy 1.38; DH *AR* 3.50.1–3). Dionysius is clear that Egerius was leader with absolute power for life (DH *AR* 3.50.3); that is, he was king of Collatia. Whatever the political situation that brought Egerius there, his total impoverishment was legendary, the result of virtual disinheritance by his family in Tarquinia, and inextricably associated with his name Egerius (Livy 1.34.3), which Dionysius indicates was a common Latin appellation for a man without resources (... Ἡγέριος ἐπωνομάσθη, τοὺς γὰρ ἀπόρους καὶ πτωχοὺς οὕτως ὀνομάζουσι Ῥωμαῖοι, "he was named Egerius, for the Romans so name men who are without resources and are beggars"; DH *AR* 3.50.3). We may recall at this point the fact that at Aricia a certain

---

[15] His ambition and need for a new city is also motivated further by the exile of his Greek father, Demaratus, who was a "stranger and an exile" from his own home (1.34.5). Demaratus himself had been an exile, for political reasons, from Corinth, but was accepted at Tarquinii (DH *AR* 3.46.4–5; Livy 1.34.1–2).

Egerius Baebius was the dedicator of the sanctuary of Diana, as well
as being the dictator Latinus.

The social and political practice behind all this is made clear by an
account from a slightly later part of the regal period. Tarquinius Superbus seems to have learned his elder's lesson and improved on it. In a
later war against Gabii, like that against Collatia, the people of Gabii
were proving themselves able to stand up to Roman military assault
(Livy 1.53.4–5; DH *AR* 4.53–4). A frustrated Superbus had to devise
another strategy to take the city. He *faked* the exile of his youngest son,
Sextus Tarquinius (Livy 1.53–4; DH *AR* 4.53–8), who, we are told,
"deserted by pre-arrangement to Gabii, complaining of the intolerable savagery of his father against him" (*Sextus ... transfugit ex com-
posito Gabios, patris in se saevitiam intolerabilem conquerens*; 1.53.5; he
was scourged in the Forum on his father's orders, DH *AR* 4.55.1–2).
Sextus told the people of Gabii that his father wanted no descendant
to inherit his kingdom (thus, like Egerius, he was without resources
or any expectation of resources) and that if he were not taken in at
Gabii he "was prepared to wander all over Latium, and from there to
seek out the Volsci and the Aequi and the Hernici" (*pererraturum se
omne Latium, Volscosque inde et Aequos et Hernicos petiturum*; 1.38.8). The
implicit context of this statement or threat is that he would take his
knowledge of Rome and Latium to their enemies – and he expected
to be welcomed by them. The Gabinii *did* take him in,[16] and he
quickly got himself made the leader on the grounds that he had special knowledge of the practices of the city he came from, Rome (Livy
1.39.1–3). After a few military successes against Rome, the Gabinii
acclaimed him a leader sent to them as a gift of the gods (*dono deum
sibi missum ducem*; Livy 1.54.3; DH *AR* 4.55.4). As Livy says, Sextus
could claim he was king in effect, if not in name.[17] Then, in a passage
Livy adapted from Herodotus, a classic account of a tyrant's advice

---

[16] He brought with him, according to DH, a band of men supposedly fleeing from
Tarquinius' tyranny (*AR* 4.55.3). The Gabinii welcomed these young men as well, as
reinforcements, but of course, they were loyal to Sextus once they were in Gabii. Quite
possibly a similar band of young men was the "garrison" Livy refers to in the earlier
account of Egerius and Collatia.

[17] "... the elder Tarquinius was not more truly master in Rome than was his son in Gabii"
(*non pater Tarquinius potentior Romae quam filius Gabiis esset*; Livy 1.39.5).

(Periander of Corinth, Hdt. 5.92),[18] Tarquinius sent a message to tell Sextus to kill the leading men of Gabii. Sextus did this, and then handed the city over to his father (Livy 1.39.6–10; DH *AR* 4.56–8).

Tarquinius' ruse depended entirely on there being a well-known and well-established practice of accepting exiles and fugitives from crime and making them leaders.[19] Many of them seem to have been called "Egerius," perhaps as a derivation from *e-gero*, as one who has been removed from a place, expelled, or discharged (*OLD s.v. egero* 2c; 3b). Livy and Dionysius both bring out the underlying pattern in their accounts of Sextus. They also reveal the reasons why, in the more sophisticated age of the late sixth and early fifth centuries, the system had to be brought to an end. Tarquinius, cynically, and inevitably, misused the custom for his own ends, by a manipulation of existing practices not unlike his treatment of the prohibitions against weapons in the sanctuary at the Lucus Ferentinae.

This, then, is the pattern: a man of distinction, unable or unwilling to remain in his own city, becomes an exile and finds a position in a new community where he is welcomed as a leader and warrior. Obviously this will have happened only rarely, and then only to men of some very particular, individual distinction. His leadership is received as "a gift of the gods" (*dono deum sibi missum ducem*). In the sixth century and earlier, "gift of the gods" was not just a turn of phrase. There had to have been something that was understood to be a sign from the gods to validate him. As leader, whatever he may have been called, he had the powers of a king. For all that to happen, his final severance from his original home needed to be convincing – that is, it had to be clear that he could *not*, under any circumstances, go back. A crime in these circumstances was a validation rather than an impediment. A man like Sextus, it could not be doubted, was indeed an exile, a man without a city.

---

[18] The imitation of Herodotus was a literary trope that identified Tarquinius as a tyrant. It does not affect the matter of Sextus' exile, which is not paralleled in the Herodotean story.

[19] A similar story is told about Zopyrus and the capture of Babylon by Darius (Hdt. 3.153–60). What makes the narrative of Sextus Tarquinius different is that it must be seen in the context of the Latin tradition of non-native exiles being named king or leader of some sort. Servius Tullius remains the most vivid example of this Latin tradition.

This practice arose many centuries before the Tarquins. The social reality was that the small Latin communities continually engaged in raids, mutual harassment, and the taking of captives. It was thus possible for men of proven military prowess, training, and intelligence to suffer *capitis deminutio*, the loss of citizenship. Men could be born as slaves but also born with ambition and unusual capabilities yet for various reasons they had a need to escape to where those abilities could have expression. Communities resolved internal conflict by exiling men whose aggression or ambition reached intolerable levels. Their numbers would never have been large, but even so they were not liable to be wasted. For the community that took them in, such men were necessarily independent of their native city, but as yet had no established loyalties or alliances within their new community. The *rex nemorensis*, the fugitive slave who became priest-king, presents a slightly different version of the same basic practices.

KINGS

Now we must turn to Servius Tullius, the penultimate king of Rome, whose kingship presents so many parallels to the ritual of the *rex nemorensis*. The accepted account of this king, as recorded by both Livy and Dionysius, was clearly influenced by the ritual; in turn, Servius' actions affected the tradition of the *rex nemorensis*. An investigation of this odd symbiosis – in which both the *rex* in the sanctuary and Servius in Rome could exist and indeed flourish – sheds light on the political and religious notions of archaic Latium.

Toward the end of Tarquinius Priscus' reign, the aging sons of Ancus Marcius sent shepherds to attack and murder him (Livy 1.40.5–7; DH *AR* 3.73). He was not killed outright, although his injuries were ultimately fatal. Through the efforts of his wife, Tanaquil, who had been a primary force in bringing him to Rome in the first place, he was succeeded by his son-in-law, Servius Tullius (DH *AR* 4.4).

Servius' history, as told by Livy (1.39, 4.1.12) and Dionysius (*AR* 4.1–4), is that his father, a nobleman, was killed in a war against Rome, and his mother, Ocrisia, was taken captive and made a slave in the palace of Tarquinius Priscus. Variant traditions report that his father was a god and his mother a slave (Ovid *Fasti* 6.624–36; Plut. *Fort. Rom.*

10 = *Mor.* 323B-D) or that his father was a Roman and his mother a slave (Plin. *NH* 36.204; Festus 182 L).

In the first century C.E., the emperor Claudius had enough information about this king to argue that he was an Etruscan named Mastarna.[20] Claudius' conclusion, reached through scholarly perusal of his sources, tells us two things: first, there was significant evidence for an alternative, nonservile origin for Servius, indicating that he, like the two Tarquinii, was an Etruscan; second, despite the alternative tradition, the story of Servius' slave origins was so well established that it had completely driven out the more "respectable" account even in the records, probably the pontifical *Annales*, that Dionysius saw. We can only conclude that, however socially disturbing Servius' slave origins may have been, at the time and in the context in which he appeared they were nevertheless regarded as acceptable, even as something to be expected.

The very openness of the story, the appearance of not only adopting the tradition of Servius' slave origin but also of actively advertising it, suggests that the details of this account were being exploited by Servius himself. Indeed, it is difficult to conceive of anyone else being behind this fabrication or its aggressive use. Had it been nothing but a canard created by his enemies, Tarquinius Superbus in particular, there would not be the solid tradition of omens, let alone the involvement of Tanaquil. A closer look at the details will tell us a great deal about the expectations and underlying traditions of the slave-become-king, a phenomenon that this account was seeking to appropriate.

Servius was marked in childhood by an omen indicating his future kingship. As a child he was allegedly found asleep in midday with flame shining forth around his head (Livy 1.38; DH *AR* 4.1–2).[21] Dionysius

---

[20] Claudius' speech at Lyons *CIL* XIII 1668 is supported, with some problems, by the paintings of the François tomb; see Thomsen 1980, 67–103. Thomsen (57–114) presents a thorough examination of all accounts and persuasively concludes that Claudius was right (103–14). That is, the historical Servius was in fact an Etruscan *condottiere* who became Tarquinius Priscus' master of the horse, and then king of Rome. The name Servius Tullius, Thomsen argues (106–8, following W. Schulze, *Zur Geschichte lateinischer Eigennamen* 1904, 231 and 246) was a Latinization of Mastarna's true Etruscan name (Mastarna being the Etruscan form of "magister," his position in Tarquinius' court).

[21] Omens were customary for the selection of kings. In one tradition the mother of Romulus and Remus was a slave, and the twins were conceived not by Mars, but

also reports an even more dramatic omen (*AR* 4.2.1–2). Once, when Ocrisia was bringing sacrificial cakes to a hearth in the palace, a phallus appeared in the fire. The queen, Tanaquil, was summoned and interpreted it as an omen that from the hearth one greater than mortals should be born. Tarquinius Priscus then decided that because the omen had appeared to Ocrisia, she must be the one for whom it was meant. He had her shut up in a room where whatever deity was represented by the phallus duly had intercourse with her, and as a result of that union she bore Servius. The factuality of either omen is not our concern. Its importance lies in its emphasis that this portent validated a future king *regardless* of his social status.

When Tarquinius Superbus – married, in a complicated story, to his sister-in-law Tullia, Servius' daughter[22] – emerged as the king's challenger, he began with a speech in the forum, positioning himself beside, or actually on, the throne in front of the Curia. The sum of his speech was an attack on Servius' origins in slavery, and the accusation that Servius had seized the kingship without either proper observance of the *interregnum* or the formal consent of the Senate or people (Livy 1.47.8–10; DH *AR* 4.31.2). When the aged Servius appeared before the Curia to protest, Tarquinius seized him and threw him down the steps. The fatally injured king[23] was at that point abandoned by

by a phallic flame (Plut. *Rom.* 2). Romulus' kingship was announced, traditionally, by twelve vultures (Livy 1.67.1–2; DH *AR* 1.86). The founder of Praeneste, Caeculus, was distinguished by fire about his head, as was Ascanius in the *Aeneid* (Verg. *Aen.* 2.680–6, cf. Ogilvie 1965, 158). According to Plutarch, Valerius Antias (fr. 12 Peter) said Servius was a grown man when the omen occurred. For Numa, the augur placed his hand on Numa's head and made a prayer for signs to indicate Jupiter's will (Livy 1.18.9–10; DH *AR* 2.60.3). Interestingly neither Tullus Hostilius nor Ancus Marcius have reigns inaugurated by omens or auguries in Livy's narrative. Dionysius mentions unspecified "favorable omens" for them (DH *AR* 3.1.3); and Tarquinius Priscus received an omen from an eagle which plucked his hat from his head and then replaced it (Livy 1.34.8–9; DH *AR* 3.47.2–3). Nor were there reported omens marking Tarquinius Superbus' accession. This in itself was taken as an omen, indicating the "criminal" nature of Tarquinius' acquisition of kingship (Livy 1.46.3).

[22] Livy 1.46.5–9.

[23] Livy's *prope exsanguis* (1.48.4) means, on the surface, that the king was pale with fear, but it also means that he was "nearly bloodless," that is, that he had lost both blood and vitality. Dionysius' Greek translates it literally: αἵματι πολλῷ ῥεόμενος καὶ κακῶς ὅλον ἑαυτὸν ἐκ τοῦ πτώματος ἔχων ([Servius went home] bleeding heavily, wholly in a dreadful condition from the fall; DH *AR* 4.38.6).

everyone and left to struggle home on his own. On Tarquinius' order, men followed Servius and killed him (Livy 1.48.3–5; DH *AR* 4.38.3–6). Tullia then arrived in the forum in a carriage and was the first to salute her husband as king (Livy 1.48.5; DH *AR* 4.39.1). She then delivered the final, vengeful, stroke to her defeated father by proceeding to a shrine of Diana where she ordered her driver to drive the carriage over Servius' dead body (Livy 1.48.7; DH *AR* 4.39.4–5).

Extraordinary though the details may have been, Servius' violent death was far from unique in the history of the Roman kings. At Rome, the king's death was almost always brought about by violence, usually that of his enemies. In some cases, the violence forms part of an alternative historical tradition. The instigators were those who aspired to be king, and their agents were often identified in some way as "the people." Romulus himself – if not taken up to heaven by Mars, a version redolent of exculpatory propaganda – was killed and cut to pieces either by the senators (DH *AR* 2.56.4) or the "new citizens" (DH *AR* 2.56.5). Titus Tatius, Romulus' colleague as king, was either murdered at an altar or stoned to death by the people of Lavinium (DH *AR* 2.52.3–4). Romulus' successor, Numa, who died in bed of old age (DH *AR* 2.76.5–6), was the exception that proved the rule. In the tradition preserved by Livy (1.31.8) the third king, Tullus Hostilius, having failed at certain secret rites of Jupiter, was struck by a thunderbolt. Dionysius, however, rejects the idea of divine involvement in Tullus' death, and elaborates on Livy's version, saying he was killed when his house caught fire, the blaze perhaps being started by a thunderbolt (DH *AR* 3.35.1). Yet according to Dionysius' own account, the majority (οἱ δὲ πλείους) held that Tullus' death was the result of deliberate arson, instigated by his successor Ancus Marcius (DH *AR* 3.35.2–3). Ancus Marcius himself, interestingly, disappears from the narrative without a mention of his death (Livy 1.40.1; DH *AR* 3.45.2). However, his successor, Tarquinius Priscus, was, as we have seen, killed by certain shepherds hired by Ancus' sons. They entered the palace on a pretext, struck the king on the head with an axe, and fled (Livy 1.40). Tanaquil, Tarquinius' wife, concealed the king's death long enough to place Servius on the throne (Livy 1.41). Servius' end we know about, and there were no longer kings in Rome when Tarquinius Superbus died.

Thus Romulus, Tatius, Tullus Hostilius, Tarquinius Priscus, and Servius are associated with a tradition of violent death, caused by either a group of citizens hostile to the reigning king or those who wanted the kingship for themselves. Only Numa (and possibly Ancus) died peacefully. Servius stands out for the ghastly pathos of his end: tossed down the stairs, stumbling alone through the streets of Rome, then dispatched by thugs and run over by his daughter's wagon. Nevertheless, what we have here is a clear and characteristic pattern of accession for the Roman kings, a sequence marked at its inception by omens and ending with the incumbent's violent death at the hands of his successor.

Although the events of Servius' reign were more dramatic, we can find precedents for them all in the accounts of earlier kings. Servius' rule, however, marked a point at which the traditional and religious account of kingship was to a great extent codified. It surely was no accident that the social and political forces in Latium were in fact moving apace in precisely the opposite direction, toward the elimination of kingship entirely. It is at such moments of crisis that traditional, inherited institutions become sharply (and often crudely) defined, allowing supporters to defend them more easily and enemies to concentrate their opposition.

It should by now be evident that the ritual of the *rex nemorensis*, with its fugitive-slave priest-king who kills his predecessor and is killed by his successor, stands well within the parameters of Roman and Latin kingship. The shared pattern must reflect a common religious basis on which such power originally rested. However, we should not assume from this – despite Servius' known interest in her – that Diana was the deity who conferred such power in every city. The pattern of exiles becoming kings existed within society at large, not merely as an extension of a single cult. There can be little doubt, however, that this sort of kingship, with its inherent grounding in the wild through the wildness of men excluded from civic boundaries, was in origin an offshoot of hunting religion. Mars no less than Diana was a hunting god; other possibilities included Quirinus, Faunus, and Picus. Any Latin city would have its own peculiar version of the practice, and the variations would have depended on the patron god or goddess as well as the city's history of internal politics and external wars.

Yet once royal power had been replaced by oligarchies, and then by Roman hegemony, of this older tradition only the *rex nemorensis* remained at Aricia, a constant, disturbing, reminder of the nature of early Latin monarchy, and of the curious relationship between marginalized men – fugitive slaves, criminals, exiles, foreigners – and the exercise of monarchical power.

DIANA ON THE AVENTINE

One other legacy of Servius' reign, preserved apart from the pontifical records, eventually magnified this king's connection with slaves. This was the Aventine festival of Diana on the Ides of August.[24]

Servorum dies festus vulgo existimatur Idus Au[gusti], quod eo die Ser[vius] Tullius, natus servus, aedem Dianae dedicaverit in Aventino, cuius tutelae sint cervi; a quo celeritate fugitivos vocent cervos.

Festus 460.33–6 L

The Ides of August is thought by the common people to be a festival day for slaves, because on that day Servius Tullius, who was born a slave, dedicated the temple of Diana on the Aventine; she is the particular guardian of deer; from whose speed fugitives slaves (servi) *are called "deer"* (cervi).

There are two points of interest to note in this passage. Festus says that the common people treated the Ides of August as a festival day for slaves. He leaves it at that, which suggests that although this development was never officially prohibited, it also was never officially approved. If true, this tells us something both about popular belief in Diana and about the Roman ruling class' attitude toward Servius' temple. The second, rather more significant, point has to do with the punning connection between *servi* and *cervi*. Diana's animal avatar was indeed the deer, which appears in many of her most popular iconographical representations. The move from "cervi" to "servi" is made easier because we know (especially from Ovid, *Fasti* 3.271) that the *rex nemorensis* was expected to be swift of foot, and that swiftness

---

[24] The Aventine cult festival was founded in imitation of the Arician. See Chapter 6 for a discussion of the political dimensions of Servius' competition with Aricia over Diana as goddess.

was associated (again through a pun both on the root *fug-*, meaning to flee, and on the cultural linking of fugitives to flight) with being a fugitive.

Originally, Diana's interest was not in slaves per se, but rather in all those who had been forced into the wild, beyond the reach of civic power. In Rome slaves worshipped at her temple because they were allowed to do so and were punningly identified both with the temple's founder and with the deer that was Diana's special animal. The exiles and fugitives who in the earliest times became kings or leaders in Latin communities had long disappeared, along with the institutions that supported them. What remained was a single day celebrated in Rome by slaves who honored Servius' life story. This ensured that Servius and his relationship to Diana would be remembered in a low-key but persistent manner. As a result, the temple on the Aventine indirectly contributed to the enduring power of the *rex nemorensis*.

ORESTES AND IPHIGENIA

Orestes embodied the myth that the Aricians chose to explain the meaning of the *rex nemorensis*. It is impossible to know just when this happened, although interest in this myth could well have arisen by the late archaic period. At the end of the sixth century, the Etruscans were importing red-figure vases with Orestean subject matter (Knoepfler 1993, pl. II–III and p. 42 = *LIMC* Aigisthos 6 = Artemis 846), and a few decades later they were producing their own (Knoepfler 1993, 84 and pl. XXII). This was a period when the Aricians had important trade and political associations with Magna Graecia.[25] In southern Italy, near Paestum, representations of Aegisthus, Clytemnestra, and probably Orestes formed part of the late archaic decoration on the metopes of a temple to Argive Hera (Knoepfler 1993, 35–9). By the fourth century, there are Etruscan bronze mirrors (Knoepfler 1993, fig. 70 = *LIMC* Erinys 28 = Klytaimestra 34) with the Orestes myth engraved on them. Praeneste, a Latin city not far from Aricia, was producing its own Orestean artifacts at the end of that century: we find

[25] See Chapter 5.

the sacrifice of Iphigenia engraved on a cistus from there (Knoepfler 1993, fig 72 = *LIMC* Agamemnon 35 = Artemis/Artumes 61 = Iphigeneia [in Etruria] 1). By the fourth century, too, the plays of Euripides were famous, and it was they that provided the core of the Arician form of the myth as we find it in the Augustan period, when, among all her other epithets, the goddess has become "Orestean Diana" (Ovid *Met.* 15.488–91).

By the third century, the myth was widespread throughout Italy. A fragment of Cato's *Origines* (Cato fr. 71 Peter) shows that at the beginning of the second century the *Italian* myth of Iphigenia and Orestes was well established.

Prob. Praef. In Verg. Bucol. Page 326 H. Item Cato originum III: Thesunti Tauriani uocantur de fluuio, qui propter fluit. Id oppidum Aurunci primo possederunt, inde Achaei Troia domum redeuntes. In eorum agro fluuii sunt sex; septimus finem Rheginum atque Taurinum dispecit: fluuii nomen est Pecoli. Eo Orestem cum Iphigenia atque Pylade dicunt maternam necem expiatum uenisse, et non longinqua memoria est, cum in arbore ensem uiderint, quem Orestes abiens reliquisse dicitur.

Cato *Origines* fr. 71 Peter

The Thesunti[26] *are called Tauriani from the river which flows nearby. At first the Aurunci controlled this town, then the Achaeans returning from Troy. In their territory, there are six rivers; the seventh acts as the boundary for Rhegium and Taurinum. The name of the river is Pecolus. To this place they say Orestes came with Iphigenia and Pylades in order to expiate the murder of his mother, and it is not a distant memory when they* [the Thesunti] *could see a sword in the tree which it is said Orestes, as he was departing, left behind.*

The Aurunci were another form of "Ausones," the generic early Greek name for Italians (Servius *ad Aen.* 7.727). On the western coast of southern Italy, just south of Taurinum (*Barrington* 46 C5), is a place called Portus Orestis, which must mark the point at which Orestes was reputed to have set foot on Italian soil. The river Taurinum and the "Taurian" Thesunti provide the connection between Iphigenia

---

[26] The names are all much in doubt. However, the scholiast on Theocritus (Cato fr. 71 Peter, n. 71) says that Orestes had to purify himself in water flowing from one spring into seven rivers and he traveled to Rhegion in southern Italy to find it.

and Orestes "among the Taurians" and this place in Italy. What is *new* in the Italic myth is the tradition that Orestes left his sword behind in a tree as he departed. This tree might well have been expected to have existed wherever Thoas was killed, but Cato's narrative shows that the Thesunti (as "Taurians") claimed it, and also asserted that Orestes was on his way elsewhere when he left it behind.[27] For the Aricians, Orestes was on his way to become the founder of the rite of the *rex nemorensis*, so it is probable that the abandonment of his sword became an etiology confirming that he had arrived in Aricia without a weapon.

Most revealing in respect of the Aricians' use of this myth, and as regards their cult in general, are the elements that diverge from the standard Euripidean account. The principal evidence for the appropriation of Orestes into the Arician cult is found in two lengthy passages of Servius (*ad Aen.* 2.116, *ad Aen.* 6.136[28]). His interpretation presents a narrative of the Orestes myth as an etiology of the cult of Diana at Aricia and is for the most part compiled from two Euripidean plays, *Iphigenia in Aulis* and *Iphigenia in Tauris*. But it is the details not found in Euripides that are most important here. The first, and most obvious, divergence is that whereas Euripides has Orestes and Iphigenia take

---

[27] Probus gives a similar account at another point in his commentary on Vergil's *Eclogues*, although this version is not ascribed to Cato and concerns various traditions associated with the origin of the bucolic genre. He provides the same details concerning the arrival of Orestes and Iphigenia with the *simulacrum* of Diana hidden in a bundle of sticks. But in this account, once Orestes has bathed in the water *ad fines Rheginorum*, he goes across to Sicily and consecrates a temple in Syracuse. The goddess is called Facelitis (C. Wendel *Scholia in Theocritum Vetera*, Leipzig 1914, 14–15). *LSJ* gives no entry for a Greek form of the adjectival formation from φάκελος, a bundle of sticks. Because Probus is reporting traditions about the origins of bucolic poetry, formalized by Theocritus, the Sicilian poet, it seems that this was the point connecting the Italian Orestes myth with Syracuse. Even in this version, Orestes lands in Italy before going on to Sicily. Cato was writing about the foundations of the Italian cities in book III of the *Origines*, and it seems unlikely that he was there concerned with Syracuse or the origins of bucolic poetry.

[28] The first passage Servius wrote to explain Sinon's report of the oracle of Apollo to the Greeks (*sanguine placastis uentos et uirgine caesa/ cum primum Iliacas, Danai, uenistis ad oras*, *Aen.* 2.116–17). The second (*ad Aen.* 6.136) comprises a central part of Servius' explication of the ritual behind the taking of the golden bough and the burial of Misenus.

Artemis' statue to Attica, the Aricians claimed that they brought it to Aricia.[29]

Second, and most crucially, the Aricians claimed that Thoas was killed by Orestes so that the *xoanon* of the goddess, hidden in a bundle of sticks (*fasce lignorum*), could be stolen.[30] (This bundle of sticks, according to Servius, was the etiology of one of Diana's epithets, Facelitis.) Now for Orestes to be the founder of the ritual of the *rex nemorensis*, his myth had to have an explanation for the killing of a king. For this purpose Thoas was preferred to Aigisthos – probably because Thoas provided the opportunity for the second essential part of the myth, the stealing of the goddess' *xoanon* in a bundle of sticks. The taking of the bough from the sacred tree is thus mythicized as the taking of the *simulacrum* from the temple, and the murder of Thoas is equated with the slaying of the reigning priest-king. In the myth, the stealing of the *xoanon* requires the murder of the king; in the ritual the stealing of the bough leads to the murder of the *rex*. Both acts transgress religious law and yet are required by divine instruction. That Thoas was a "barbarian" was also essential, for it confirmed the idea of "barbarism" in the ritual identity of the *rex nemorensis* – and yet, at the same time, the story, for all its barbaric qualities, was placed squarely in the world of Greek myth and tragedy.

This was how Orestes was adapted to become the *aition* for the *rex nemorensis*. But there was still more to the revision of the myth. Arician Orestes stole the *xoanon* and killed Thoas, we are told, because it was through these acts that he would be released from his madness (*qui [Orestes] accepto oraculo carendi furoris causa*; Servius *ad Aen.* 2.116). Bringing the *xoanon* to Aricia as an act of piety concluded the actions required of him. This supposed founding of the ritual of

---

[29] In another variant, as Pausanias reports (3.16.7) the statue was said to have been brought to Sparta to become the cult image of Artemis Orthia. This is surely the reason Lucan calls the goddess "Mycenaean Diana" (6.74), and, as Servius reports at the end of this passage, why the Arician cult was ultimately transferred to Sparta.

[30] In *IT*, Iphigenia take the statue from the temple by a ruse, telling Thoas that it had been defiled by the touch of a matricide, Orestes, and that she, as priestess, must therefore purify it in the sea (where Orestes' ship lies offshore, *IT* 1017–1088; 1152–1233). Thoas is deceived but left alive in the temple while Iphigenia and Orestes escape with the statue (*IT* 1284–1434).

the *rex nemorensis* by Orestes indicates that the Aricians believed it to be the process by which a man who was in the position of Orestes could be (and perhaps would be) released from his madness and achieve peace.[31]

THE MADNESS OF ORESTES

What was the nature of Orestes' madness? Clearly, in the first instance it was the direct consequence of the fact that Orestes had murdered a member of his family. This led to exile, the state of being a fugitive, and, probably, the condition of a period of slavery. That is how the ritual of the *rex nemorensis* was constructed in honor of Orestes, so it is fair to assume Arician Orestes' story included the period of slavery and that this was reflected in the Pacuvian *Doulorestes*.[32] His *furor*, his madness, were both the cause and the result of his fugitive state. To cure his madness he had to journey into barbaric territory and kill the king in order to steal the goddess' image. The Aricians used Orestes to present the ritual of the *rex nemorensis* as the journey through murder, exile, slavery, and barbarism to find release from the madness originating in guilt of murder and violation of the gods' laws. That is why Octavian took the bones of Orestes to Rome, to bring release to the city and the empire after the torments of the civil war.[33]

[31] *nam fugitivus illic erat sacerdos ad priscae imaginem fugae. dimicandi autem dabatur facultas quasi ad pristini sacrificii reparationem* ("for the priest there was [also] a fugitive, to symbolize the ancient flight. And indeed, this opportunity of fighting was given as though in renewal of the original sacrifice"; Servius *ad Aen.* 6.136).

[32] While the cult was, inevitably, influenced by the adoption of Orestes, Aricia in turn influenced the Orestes myth. Pacuvius' *Doulorestes* brings out an aspect of Orestes that was particularly important to Aricia. In the *Doulorestes*, Orestes, having grown up in exile, returns to Mycenae disguised as a slave to find a way into the palace to kill his mother. Hyginus, the Augustan mythographer, preserves other variants (*Fab.* 119–22), which may all derive from Latin tragedies. A fragment of Pacuvius' *Chryses* indicates that in the Latin version there was a chase and a fight between Thoas and Orestes before the murder (Pacuvius *Chryses* fr. 89 Warmington). This is not surprising. The combat between the challenger and the *rex* was just as important as the resultant death.

[33] The Orestes myth became a paradigm through which the issues of imperial violence could be reconciled. See Champlin (2004, 310–15) for a discussion of Nero's use of Orestes – he played Orestes on the stage (Suet. *Nero* 21.3) – as a means of attacking Agrippina and, of course, justifying his murder of her.

> . . . umbra perempti
> civis adest; sua quemque premit terroris imago:
> ille senum vultus, iuvenum videt ille figuras,
> hunc agitant totis fraterna cadavera somnis,
> pectore in hoc pater est, omnes in Caesare manes.
> haud alios nondum Scythica purgatus in ara
> Eumenidum vidit voltus Pelopeus Orestes,
> nec magis attonitos animi sensere tumultus,
> cum fureret, Pentheus, aut, cum desisset, Agave.
>
> Lucan *BC* 7.772–80

The shade of the slaughtered citizen is present; each man's vision of terror oppresses him; this one sees the faces of old men, that one the bodies of the young; brothers' corpses haunt another throughout his sleep, his father is in this man's breast, the ghosts of all were in Caesar. Not otherwise were the visages of the Eumenides that Pelopean Orestes saw, before he was purified on the Scythian altar, and neither Pentheus, when mad, nor Agave, on recovery, suffered worse from crazed disorders of the mind.

The madness of Orestes, according to Lucan, descended on Caesar and all the participants of the civil war, in a description that certainly reflects common and contemporary views of war and Orestes' *furor*. In World War I, this *furor* was called "shell-shock," and since the Vietnam War, more prosaically, it has been termed "post-traumatic stress disorder." It is the memories of horror that haunt sleep and torment and twist a man even during the day: "each man's vision of terror oppresses him." The experience, however, was not invented by modern men. It is reasonable, indeed, to suppose that in some fashion the sanctuary had long used the ritual of the *rex nemorensis* for resolving the disorders that arise from trauma and guilt. Orestes promoted for the cult a wider and more capacious definition of madness. Indeed, pursuit by the Erinyes became a way to describe certain medical conditions, *especially* those that were characterized by deviant or bizarre behavior (Grat. *Cyn.* 369–77; jokingly Hor. *AP* 453–60, who is pursued by teasing street urchins rather than the Erinyes). By the late Republic, the cult's concern was to resolve the madness. The measure of the cult's reputation for treating these kinds of distress can be estimated by Octavian's appropriation of Orestes, and by the fact that Orestes' remains, as we have seen, achieved equality with the Palladium and the *ancilia* of Mars as one of the seven pledges of Rome (Servius *ad Aen.* 7.188). Orestes in this context embodied a powerful myth, impressively cultivated and extended by the Arician priests and elders. As a result, the *rex nemorensis*, in combination with the legend of Orestes and Iphigenia, held a unique place in Italian culture. Through him there existed the hope of negotiating a religious escape from those great evils that seemed to breed nothing except even greater evils.

9

VIRBIUS, HIPPOLYTUS AND EGERIA

Virbius and Egeria. These two very secretive attendant figures are at once inseparable from Diana's sanctuary at Aricia and yet hard to place within it. They seem to have no relationship to each other, and yet they are almost always mentioned together in some way. There is no surviving iconography for them, and the only literary evidence we have is a curious, though revealing, mélange of apparent borrowings. They are both hidden in Diana's forest, and this above all seems to bring them together. Yet before the meaning of their relationship can be examined, each must be understood separately.

VIRBIUS

Frazer offered what seems now a fairly mundane if convoluted interpretation of Virbius, just as he had done of the *rex nemorensis*: Virbius was the archetype of the *rex*, the consort of the *regina nemorensis*, Diana, and in addition the spirit of the oak, and a sun god.[1] Wissowa, on the other hand, argued that Virbius was the goddess' helper or assistant to women in childbirth, reflecting his view of Diana as a maiden deity concerned with women's illnesses (1912, 249). Frazer,

---

[1] Virbius was Diana's consort, the "archetype" of the King of the Wood, and the mythical guardian of the sacred tree (Frazer, 1.40–1); the partner in a sacred marriage with the goddess of fertility (2.129); and the local form of Jupiter, the oak god (2.379). Specifically, he was the (guardian) spirit of the sacred oak. Because the burning of the oak tree was, mythologically speaking, one way in which the sun was "rekindled," Virbius was also identified with the sun (11.295). The association with the sun seems to be far more characteristic of late antique religious concerns.

by seemingly turning Virbius into a catch-all figure, undermined his specific analyses – which are quite illuminating – with an unpersuasive totality. Wissowa had to ignore some very specific evidence, particularly that of Servius on Virbius' relationship to Diana. Radke (1987, 166–7) made an interesting linguistic connection between "Virbius" and "Ὀρθία," seeing in both names the quality of making men "upright," that is, healthy. He also argues (1987, 171) that both Virbius and Diana/Artemis came to Italy – and to Sparta – from Illyria. It is possible, of course, that the Italic peoples, those who became the Latins among them, did reach Italy from the west coast of mainland Greece rather than from the north. As so often, though, the linguistic evidence is tenuous and difficult to use for any kind of understanding without cultural confirmation. In light of this, Pairault's comment that Virbius was a secondary divinity and quite mysterious (1969, 446) seems to sum up the matter to that point. Fortunately, Podemann Sørensen has opened up the discussion once more with the argument that Virbius was an Attis figure in whom death and wildness was ritually expressed (2000, 25–8). Since this recognizes the significance of Servius' account, it is a much more productive and inclusive view. But we must begin by examining the ancient literary evidence, which comes from Vergil, Ovid, and Servius.

VIRBIUS AND HIPPOLYTUS

As with the Orestes etiology for the *rex nemorensis*, it is evident that with Virbius a Greek myth was laid over an important part of the native cult of Diana. The overlaying was well enough established by the mid–third century B.C.E to be known and used by the Hellenistic poets, for Servius (*ad Aen.* 7.778) says that this *aition* appeared in Callimachus' *Aitia* (accepted by Pfeiffer 1949, fr. 190; Dyson 2001, 224–5). Virbius was retitled "Hippolytus," and his place in the cult was explained by the Hippolytus myth. Both Vergil and Ovid go to considerable lengths to make this clear. Virbius was not actually obscured, much less obliterated, by Hippolytus. This gives us another opportunity to see how Greek myth was employed in Latin cultic religion, and to assess the advantages, as well as the limitations, of its use. It also, I am convinced, provides an insight into Augustus' concerns both with the cult at Aricia and with the use of Greek myth as a political instrument.

Again, as with the Orestes story, it is due to Augustus' interest that we know as much as we do about Virbius. Octavian had made his claim to the remains of Orestes through his maternal connections to Aricia, and that claim was made on behalf of the Roman people at the end of the civil war. For more personal reasons, it seems, he then cultivated an interest in Virbius as a way to transform *Aricina mater* from Antony's vile insult to a courtier's compliment. This was accomplished in a most elegant and effective manner. Among the Latin heroes in *Aeneid* 7 ready to go out to fight the Trojans, Vergil includes Virbius. The first piece of information we get about him is his parentage. His father was Hippolytus.

> Ibat et Hippolyti proles pulcherrima bello,
> Virbius, insignem quem mater Aricia misit,
> eductum Egeriae lucis umentia circum
> litora, pinguis ubi et placabilis ara Dianae.
>
> *Aen.* 7.761–4

The most beautiful offspring of Hippolytus also went to war, Virbius, whom his mother, Aricia, sent, remarkable as he was in appearance; he had been raised around the moist shores of Egeria's grove, where the rich and the reconciling altar of Diana is found.

Virbius is the son of Hippolytus and Aricia. Because there is no evidence that any eponymous nymph or goddess ever existed at Aricia, not to mention the fact that Hippolytus was by definition not the marrying sort (as Servius rather crossly points out; *ad Aen.* 7.761), Aricia as the "mother" of Virbius has to have been an invention of Vergil's. As such, and given the memory of Antony's *Aricina mater*, Vergil also had to have had the approval of Augustus. It is unlikely in the extreme that Vergil would have taken liberties with Hippolytus/Virbius *and* with *mater Aricina* otherwise.

Having made Hippolytus/Virbius into two individuals, father and son, Vergil goes on (*Aen.* 7.765–82) to retell the story of Hippolytus, and he makes it clear it *was* a story (*ferunt fama*, "they say in the story"; 7.765). He spends two and a half lines gliding over the substance of the Euripidean play (7.765–7). There is no mention of Phaedra's marriage to Theseus, her love for her stepson, or Hippolytus' rejection of her. Vergil's readers would have supplied this information for themselves, but the poet was not going to encourage them to dwell on it in this context.

"By the craft of his stepmother" (7.765), in Vergil's account, Hippolytus dies, torn apart by his terrified horses, in blood satisfaction of the penalties inflicted by his father. The core of Vergil's account (7.767–82), however, concerns Hippolytus' return from death, and his fate, decreed by Jupiter, to be hidden in Diana's forest and to have his name changed to "Virbius." There, in his honor, horses were forbidden.[2] His son, however – the original Virbius – is shown by Vergil practicing chariot maneuvers (on the plain, not in the sanctuary or the crater), just like any heroic youth. He is the quintessential Latin hero-warrior. Servius in turn emphasizes that Virbius' rather complex history was presented in this way as a compliment to Augustus' Arician heritage: "he says 'mother' on account of Augustus, who had been born from an Arician mother: as if he were saying 'a city that is the origin of so great a race'."[3] The context of the catalogue of Latin heroes allows Virbius to represent, by allusion, Augustus' Latin heritage as well as his "Trojan" descent from Aeneas.

Ovid, characteristically, presents a more melodramatic and less heroic Hippolytus in the Roman book of the *Metamorphoses*. He includes (although briefly) the Euripidean material of Phaedra's love and the deceit by which she persuaded Theseus his son was guilty (*Met.* 15.497–504). The core of his narrative is a long and almost Lucanian description of Hippolytus' horrific death (*Met.* 15.505–29). This is followed by a briefer account of his rescue from the underworld by Asclepius' medicines (*Met.* 15.530–5) and Diana's determination to protect him from *inuidia* (personal hostility, of Jupiter in this case) by aging him so as to change his appearance (*Met.* 15.536–9). She also decides to put him somewhere remote – Aricia is her choice

---

[2] This special exclusion of horses was an important part of the literary tradition. Servius (*ad Aen.* 7.778) indicates that Callimachus referred it in his *Aitia*.

[3] QUEM MATER ARICIA MISIT civitas iuxta Albam. 'mater' autem propter Augustum dicit, qui fuerat ex Aricina matre progenitus: ac si diceret, quae tanti auctor est generis (*ad Aen.* 7.762).

after considering Delos and Crete – and to change his name, from Hippolytus to Virbius (*Met.* 15.540–4). "From that time," Ovid's Hippolytus says, "I have been an inhabitant of this forest, and as one of the lesser deities I am concealed under the *numen* of my mistress and I am her attendant" (*hoc nemus inde colo de disque minoribus unus/ numine sub dominae lateo atque accenseor illi; Met.* 15.545–6).

The setting of Ovid's narrative of the Virbius/Hippolytus story is just as significant as Vergil's. Whereas Vergil makes Virbius one of the Latin heroes, Ovid puts Hippolytus/Virbius' narrative after his account of Numa and Pythagoras (*Met.* 15.60–478) and the exposition of a Pythagorean universe of eternal change. "To be born," Ovid's Pythagoras says, "is to begin to be something other than what was before; and to die is to cease to be a former state" (*Met.* 15.255–7). Hippolytus/Virbius is one illustration of that truth: he ceases to be Hippolytus and becomes Virbius. In Ovid's rendering, the context, although Greek-derived, is emphatically Latin.[4]

It is clear that the Aricians had originally attached Hippolytus to Virbius because the two shared certain essential factors. Both were young men devoted to Diana/Artemis. Virbius died, and it is a fair assumption that his death had a similar cause to that of Hippolytus. As Servius says (*ad Aen.* 7.761) that Virbius was to Diana as Attis was to Cybele, it is virtually certain that he somehow violated the love Diana had given him, and it was a sexual violation. His death (quite possibly involving horses – Ovid's description of the hero being torn in two by horses is reminiscent of the death of the Alban leader Mettius Fufetius; Livy 1.28.9–11) would have been as horrible as, if not more so than, that of Hippolytus. Virbius was restored to life, as (in some versions[5]) was Hippolytus. The agent of that restoration was Asclepius, but Artemis/Diana was the one who motivated Apollo's son to accomplish the resurrection.

---

[4] Numa, in Ovid's version, is not just a Roman king, he is a Latin ruler (*Met.* 15.481), mourned by the women, the people, and the *patres* of Latium (*Met.* 15.486).

[5] According to some accounts, but not to Euripides, he was brought back to life by Asclepius, who was then struck by Zeus' thunderbolt as punishment for his temerity in raising the dead. This version goes back at least as far as the sixth century *Naupactia* (Philedemos *Piet.* (2).52; Apollodorus 3.10.3.9–10). However, Hippolytus is only one of many about whom this story is told (Edelstein 1998, 70–86).

Virbius and Augustus shared certain essential characteristics. Virbius' mother (in Vergil's account) was Aricia, and the princeps had a mother *from* Aricia; Virbius had died to be brought back to life. Similarly, the princeps, because of his adoption by Caesar, and because of his reinvention of himself as Augustus, had had one identity annulled and returned with another. Asclepius, moreover, Hippolytus/Virbius' rescuer, who had been taken from his mother's womb by Caesarian section, had certain interesting parallels (including the Caesarian birth) with Julius Caesar, the one who saved Octavian from the relative obscurity of provincial parentage.[6]

χωρὶς δὲ ἀπὸ τῶν ἄλλων ἐστὶν ἀρχαία στήλη· ἵππους δὲ Ἱππόλυτον ἀναθεῖ-
ναι τῷ θεῷ φησιν εἴκοσι. Ταύτης τῆς στήλης τῷ ἐπιγράμματι ὁμολογοῦντα
λέγουσιν Ἀρικιεῖς, ὡς τεθνεῶτα Ἱππόλυτον ἐκ τῶν Θησέως ἀρῶν ἀνέστησεν
Ἀσκληπιός· ὁ δὲ ὡς αὖθις ἐβίω, οὐκ ἠξίου νέμειν τῷ πατρὶ συγγνώμην, ἀλλὰ
ὑπεριδὼν τὰς δεήσεις ἐς Ἰταλίαν ἔρχεται παρὰ τοὺς Ἀρικιεῖς, καὶ ἐβασίλευσέ
τε αὐτόθι καὶ ἀνῆκε τῇ Ἀρτέμιδι τέμενος, ἔνθα ἄχρι ἐμοῦ μονομαχίας ἆθλα ἦν
καὶ ἱερᾶσθαι τῇ θεῷ τὸν νικῶντα· ὁ δὲ ἀγὼν ἐλευθέρων μὲν προέκειτο οὐδενί,
οἰκέταις δὲ ἀποδρᾶσι τοὺς δεσπότας.

Paus. 2.27.4

Apart from the other monuments there is an old stele; and it says that Hippolytus sacrificed twenty horses to the god. What the Aricians say agrees with the inscription of this stele, that Hippolytus died because of Theseus' curses and Asclepius brought him back to life; and when he was alive again, he did not see fit to bestow forgiveness on his father, but disdaining his entreaties, went to Italy to the Aricians, and ruled there and dedicated a precinct to Artemis, where down to my time the single combat took place and the victor was consecrated to the goddess; and the combat was not open to any freeborn person, but only to slaves who had run away from their masters.

SERVIUS' ACCOUNT

What appealed to Augustus in the figure of Virbius/Hippolytus, quite clearly, was the image of the young hunter-warrior hero who was

---

[6] Asclepius and Hippolytus were so closely connected that in Troezen there was a statue identified by some as Asclepius, by others as Hippolytus (Paus. 2.32.3–4). In this part of the Greek Hippolytus myth, Asclepius may have been the more prominent cult figure. Ovid implies as much when he recounts the death and revival of Hippolytus in the *Fasti* (6.737–62). Here it is really an account of Asclepius' power, and it belongs, equally clearly, to some celebration of Asclepius that is not in our other calendars.

devoted to Diana, and she to him. Ovid's account reinforces the understood importance of Virbius as a Latin hero, both through his association with Numa and Egeria, and by the placement of his story in the "Latin" book of the *Metamorphoses*. Virbius must be a Latin hero who was the hunter-devotee of the goddess. He committed a sexual crime, and was killed as a result. Then, because the goddess loved him, he was brought back to life.

This places Virbius squarely in a widespread and readily identifiable system of hunter myths. Fontenrose (1981, 142–59, especially 152–3) described the typical paradigm of these myths as follows. The hunting deity (whether male or female) has a human votary (again, whether male or female) who becomes a hunter and companion to the divinity. This extraordinary youth has remarkable powers but lacks control. He offends the deity through his sexuality. His death and transformation permanently locate him in the wild, and after his death he receives divine or heroic honors. In this category we find Hippolytus (Fontenrose 1981, 160–7), Adonis, Callisto, Actaeon, Meleager, and Orion.[7] Virbius in fact embodies an *older* version of such myths, because the sexuality of the hunter-hero and the consequent danger of his relationship to the goddess have not been entirely suppressed (Fontenrose 1981, 164–5). These stories have Near-Eastern and Indian parallels (Fontenrose 1981, 208–50), although this does not necessarily mean that they are all derived from Near-Eastern (or even Indo-European) originals.[8] Its significance is rather that the dangers of wildness matter deeply to all early societies. Fertility has great importance for the maintenance of culture, and fertility can *never* be separated entirely from the innate wildness of sexuality – that is, from the animal

---

[7] Fontenrose 1981, 167–74; see 171–2 and Servius Auctus ad *Ecl.* 10.18 for a version of the Adonis story that curiously mimics that of Virbius. Adonis was wrapped in a cloud by Aphrodite to accomplish his violation of Erinoma – a Cyprian maiden loved by Artemis – and then was killed by Zeus' thunderbolt. Aphrodite's laments for his death moved Hermes to bring the *imago* of Adonis back to "his people" (*ad suos*) so that he was thought to be alive. Zeus thereafter allowed this Adonis to live in the groves of his people, and Artemis brought Erinoma to him as his wife, and she bore him a son, "Taleus."

[8] For example, Luckert, "The Version of Curly Toaxedlini," (1981, 70–9), in which the hunters are accompanied by their sister, who mates with the gods in the shape of deer; she is transformed into a doe.

side of human existence. This animal-like sexuality is expressed in myth as fierce, uncivilized, antisocial, and destructive behavior – rape, incest, the violation of a goddess. These myths of the young hunter (or huntress, as Fontenrose makes clear) are really about sexuality outside the restraints of civilization.

It should not come as a surprise, then, that Servius is quite definite that there was an erotic relationship between Virbius and Diana.

cuius [i.e., Virbius] nunc filium cognominem dicit in bellum venire: adeo omnia ista fabulosa sunt. nam cum castus ubique inductus sit et qui semper solus habitaverit, habuisse tamen fingitur filium. re vera autem, ut et supra <7.84> diximus, Virbius est numen coniunctum Dianae, ut matri deum Attis, Minervae Erichthonius, Veneri Adonis.

ad Aen. 7.761

He (Vergil) says that now his son, who has the same name (Virbius) is going to war: to that extent, all these things are pure myth-making. For although he (i.e. Virbius/Hippolytus) is in all circumstances introduced as a chaste man, and one who has always lived alone, he is nevertheless presented as having had a son. However, in truth, as I said above <7.84> Virbius is a divinity linked to Diana, as Attis is to the mother of the gods, Erichthonius to Minerva, and Adonis to Venus.

Frazer argued on the basis of this passage that Virbius was Diana's consort (1.40), but otherwise, until recently,[9] Servius' clear statement has been passed over without comment by modern scholarship. The original Hippolytus myth must have turned on Hippolytus' violation of that vow (Fontenrose 1981, 164–5), and in all probability Euripides' first play on the subject, the *Hippolytus Veiled*, did not conceal this from the audience.[10] His vow of chastity was in fact characteristic, since any human who wished to spend time in sacred territory had to abstain from sex.

VIRBIUS' DEATH

According to Euripides, Hippolytus was killed by falling on the rocks from his chariot when a monster sent by Poseidon scared his horses (Eur. *Hipp.* 1198–1242). Ovid gives another, more lurid account (*Met.* 15.505–29). It is improbable, however, that in the cult itself the narrative

[9] Podemann Sørensen (2000) is the distinguished exception.
[10] Not accepted by Barrett (1964, 37–9, and n. 3), who regards the veiling of Hippolytus as an act of piety and horror at Phaedra's proposal.

of Virbius' death would have formed part of the ritual, however that ritual was constructed, though it must have affected the particular relationship recognized as existing between Diana and young men, young hunters, and how her rescue of these young men from death was envisioned within the cult. We have some interesting, although tangential, evidence that suggests that Virbius was in fact traditionally thought to have drowned in the lake. The first part of the evidence comes from a fragment of a Republican *fabula togata* by Afranius, *Exceptus*, a *togata* dating from the early first century B.C.E., in which the context of Diana's protection is vividly brought out. The main character of the *Exceptus* is, it would seem, a man who has been lost in the water and rescued by a person who happens to be out celebrating the "holy day of Diana."

I

Proficisco: res, tempus, locus, simul otium hortabatur
Vt operat<u>m illum degerem sanctum diem Dianae.

II

Consimili grassantur uia, quibus hic est omnis cultus.

III

Tum conscendo cumbam interibi l<o>ci piscatoriam,
Venio, iacitur ancora, inhibent le<n>iter.

IV

Iubeo hominem tolli et conlocari et confoueri: soluo
Operam Dianae.

Afranius[11] Exceptus frs. 1–4

I

I set out: circumstance, time, place, leisure, all at once were urging me to spend this holy day of Diana carrying out my sacred obligation.[12]

---

[11] The text of Afranius is that of Daviault (1981). On the basis of another fragment of this play (fr. X) which mentions a Neapolitan meretrix, Daviault regards Tifata as the most likely cult site of Diana appropriate for this play. Certainly this is *possible*, although Tifata is five miles from the sea, whereas Aricia has a lake. Romans attending the play, however, were clearly familiar with the *cultic* aspects of Diana the huntress and with the obligations that were indicated by the phrase "to carry out her sacred rites."

[12] " . . . aussi m'engageaient/ à employer le saint jour de Diane pour accomplir mes devoirs religieux" is Daviault's translation.

II

On a similar path they advance, to whom this entire cult belongs.

III

Then meanwhile I now board the fishermen's skiff, I arrive, the anchor is cast, they moor gently[13] . . .

IV

I order the man to be fished up and put safely aboard and cared for: I fulfill my duty to Diana.

The *fabula togata*, as Daviault says, was a comedy of *Roman* manners, in contrast to the *fabula palliata* which was more directly inspired by Greek New Comedy.[14] The nature of the *togata* was to focus on what was familiar to the Romans and of interest to them as a setting for plots of romance lost and won and happiness regained (Daviault 1981, 20–1).

Daviault identifies this "holy day of Diana" as the Ides of August (1981, 176, n. 2). This is reasonable, because 13 August was the festival day for both Roman and Arician cults of Diana. More doubtfully, he argues that the setting for *Exceptus* was the cult of Diana at Tifata, near Capua.[15] Whether at this time Diana's August festival was also celebrated in Campania is questionable.[16] In any case, an audience in Rome would have had its own experience of the Roman and Arician Ides of August foremost in mind.

Daviault describes the Tifata precinct as *ce sanctuaire de Diane, qui se trouve dans une région maritime* ("this sanctuary of Diana located in a maritime region"; 176, n. 2). However, Diana's sanctuary at Aricia is on a lake where there was (and still is) fishing, and Afranius' lifetime

---

[13] The idea, apparently, is that the rowers keep the skiff in one place as much as possible by rowing gently against the pull of the anchor.

[14] Daviault 1981, 9–10.

[15] A courtesan from Naples is mentioned (fr. X), but it would seem she was a foreigner where the action was understood to take place (fr. XI).

[16] Daviault (176, n. 2) cites Statius *Silv.* 3.1.159–60 as evidence that Tifata also celebrated Diana on the Ides of August. As we have seen, Statius makes it definitive that the festival he is describing, with Hippolytus and the lake, belongs to the Arician cult. Certainly there cannot have been an ancient pan-Italic festival of Diana on this day. However, Tifata might well have taken up this festival also during the Augustan period. It is less certain that a Campanian cult would have seen the need to adapt to the Latin calendar before this.

coincides with the great building projects in the Arician sanctuary which certainly made it the principal cult of Diana in central Italy. So however we reconstruct the ostensible place of the action (and it would be curious if a *togata* was set in a Greek city), it is Arician Diana with whom a Roman audience would have been most familiar. They would have interpreted the religious context of the actions (particularly matters like *operatum*, "the sacred obligation") in terms of the cults in Latium. This was, after all, a *togata*.

Daviault (1981, 175, n. 1) reconstructs the plot. The *exceptus* ("one picked up out of the water"; *OLD s.v. excipio* 1b) is a young man who has thrown himself into the sea following a disappointment in love. He has been rescued by an individual who cannot be easily identified but who is someone fulfilling an obligation – in his case the rescue of a drowning man – to Diana. Those whom Diana loved might meet with misfortune in places outside the city and could be in danger from water. Just as she protected them and rescued them from death, so the rescue of those in need was a service, an obligation, to Diana on the part of her devotees. This episode in Afranius recalls Virbius/Hippolytus, who died in or near water (Statius *Silv.* 3.1.157; Verg. *Aen.* 7.761–77; Serv. *ad Aen. ad loc*; Ovid *Met.* 15.492–544) and who was brought back to life because of Diana's love for him.

That Afranius' young man who nearly drowned was patterned on Virbius/Hippolytus is suggested by an epigram of Martial addressed to a young man *castior Hippolyto* ("more chaste than Hippolytus" 8.46.1–3). He is so lovely, Martial says, that *te secum Diana velit doceatque natare* ("Diana would want you to be with her, and she would teach you to swim"). Yet there is no account of Hippolytus in which he drowns. Afranius' young man was drowning and was rescued by acolytes of Diana, and by Martial's time Hippolytus had become another name for Virbius. Virbius may well have died by drowning.[17] Eventually, the cynical observer, like Martial, would begin to think that maybe, if Diana had *really* loved Virbius, she would have taught him to swim, so that he did not need rescuing in the first place.

---

[17] Dyson (2001, 50–73) discusses death by water, particularly the tradition preserved by Servius (*ad Aen.* 4.620) that Aeneas was drowned in the Numicus River, with the suggestion that he was a sacrifice.

VIRBIUS AS CONSORT TO DIANA

Virbius' violation of Diana's laws must have been sexual in nature. Podemann Sørensen (2000, 25–8) takes it as a given that the underlying mythic concern is Virbius' sexuality. Virbius, like Attis, he argues, represents the wildness that is in opposition to civilization, as the hunting life is in opposition to marriage. Yet sexual violation is only one aspect of the loss of self-control: the expression of other kinds of wildness must not be excluded. He makes a particular comparison with the myth of Erichthonius. After Hephaestus' attempt to rape Athena and her escape, his semen falls to the ground and engenders Erichthonius, whom Athena raises. She keeps him hidden in a chest, which she gives to the daughters of Cecrops. They are forbidden to open this chest, but of course curiosity gets the better of them. When they open the chest and see Erichthonius, they are either killed by a snake or driven into madness.[18]

Podemann Sørensen argues that the necessary hiddenness closely links Erichthonius and Virbius. The Erichthonian snake is phallic, and the madness of the daughters is loss of self and self-control, unmediated eroticism, the pure animal sexuality of the wild.[19] This sort of madness, Podemann Sørensen argues, occurs on the border, the margins, between civilized and wild territory. He goes on to suggest that Virbius, as a religious figure, was linked to this kind of madness in the cult (2000, 27). Although no evidence survives indicating that Virbius was himself mad, it is certainly true, as we have seen, that madness was a cultic concern, for Orestes quite clearly represents madness in Diana's cult, and strange and deviant behavior was indeed treated there (Chapter 11).

YOUTH, AGE, AND CONCEALMENT

Virbius was a human being who died, was brought back from death, and lived again. Vergil claims that he lived for an *aevum*, an "age," an eternity (*Aen.* 7.776–7). Ovid (*Met.* 15.538–9) tells us that there was both an old and a young Virbius. According to Servius (*ad Aen.*

---

[18] The myth is retold by Pausanius (1.2.6) and Apollodorus (3.14.6).
[19] Fontenrose does not treat this kind of wildness, but he recognizes that "seeing" is one of the sexual violations in hunting myths (1981, 152.5a).

7.763), Virbius was a *numen*. One interpretation of this made him a kind of living *simulacrum*: he *seemed* to do everything but in fact did not (Servius *ad Aen.* 7.776). He only *appeared* to live. Servius Auctus (in the same citation) goes further. An *aevum*, he says, has no known beginning or end: according to the ancients, the life of the gods was an *aevum*. Virbius was, therefore, worshipped among the gods. Yet it is clear in fact that the real problem was that Virbius shared the terrible burden of Tithonus and the Sibyl: eternal life without eternal youth.

cum illi pueri dicerent 'Σίβυλλα, τί θέλεις;' respondebat illa 'ἀποθανεῖν θέλω' . . .

Petronius, Sat. 48.8

When the boys would say: "Sibyl, what do you want?" she would answer: "I want to die" . . .

He thus ritually appeared in two separate forms. He was both the consort who dies young[20] and the man who is brought back to life *on earth* and cannot die again.[21] Vergil resolved this problem by making the old Virbius, as Hippolytus, the young Virbius' father.

Ovid, despite his love for decorative detail, is much more sensitive than Vergil to danger. He captures the frisson of terror, the implication of violence, the inexorable cruelty of time, all lurking behind the pleasant façade of the story, when his Virbius says that Diana "added age and left me with an unrecognizable face" (*Met.* 15.539–40). For Ovid, the aged man's appearance was yet another form of concealment – and, perhaps, another form of punishment.[22] This concealment of

---

[20] Silius Italicus (*Pun.* 4.366–95) records a different, although equally violent, death for Virbius, as one of three young men on the Roman side against Hannibal. Virbius, Albanus, and Capys (the two latter are from Alba Longa and Capua, respectively) face off against three Carthaginian/Greek warriors. Albanus and Capys are killed by their opponents. Virbius is victorious over two of the three opponents, but "by pretending to run away," he tricks the third (Xanthippus), and they then slay each other. Interestingly, Capys and Virbius are both "Egeria's sons" (*Egeriae pubes*, 4.380), and Albanus is their comrade. Statius does not mention Virbius' return to the sanctuary once he was rescued from death.

[21] When Erictho revives her corpse, she promises him he will be able to die again (*BC* 6.822–4). The second death seems to have been thought to be exceptionally difficult to manage, and perhaps impossible.

[22] The aging Augustus (in his late sixties when the last book of the *Metamorphoses* was being written) may or may not have taken this as a compliment.

Virbius, once he had been brought back to life, is agreed on by all our sources (Vergil *Aen.* 7.776–7; Ovid *Met.* 15.536–46; Servius *ad Aen.* 7.761, 775, and 776). Virbius resurrected was a hidden figure, perhaps so hidden as to be unapproachable. Servius Auctus adds the interesting detail that his statue was not to be touched: *noli me tangere* in a very literal sense. He was equated with the sun because the sun also could not be touched (*ad Aen.* 7.776). The untouchableness of Virbius' *simulacrum* may simply have been an extension of its concealment, its *intangibility.*

In sum, the Hippolytus legend indicates that Virbius was a hunter, a votary of the goddess, and her beloved consort. For some offense against the goddess or her laws – probably a violation of his vows of chastity that aroused Diana's jealousy – he was punished with death. He was then brought back from death by Asclepius, with the aid of certain herbs, at the instigation of Diana, who returned him to the forest. There he remained a hidden figure, one who could not be touched, which may reflect the ritual containment of a kind of madness, of sexuality gone wild. In cult rituals he may have represented the sun to Diana's moon. Certainly he was *sacer,* with all the ritual prohibitions that implies.

Virbius' story accords well with everything else we have learned about Diana's sanctuary. His violation (whatever it might have been) of the goddess' laws is parallel to the violation of the tree committed by the *rex nemorensis,* while his death and resurrection mirror the *rex nemorensis'* ritual descent to the underworld and return in the initiation ritual. This is what led Frazer to conclude that Virbius was the archetype of the *rex nemorensis* (1.40). Yet the Aricians clearly believed that the *rex* and Virbius were distinct figures. When mythic equivalents were sought, they assigned Orestes to one and Hippolytus to the other. Within the ritual world of the cult, the *rex nemorensis* was the fugitive, the exile, while Virbius was the beloved who died and was brought back to life. The association with Adonis and Attis suggests that his death was an annual event,[23] in which his dying was mourned and his return to life celebrated, to demonstrate the power

---

[23] As Frazer observed (1.21), it difficult to avoid the conclusion that Virbius/Hippolytus enjoyed yet another "rebirth" as a Christian saint, represented by St. Hippolytus, whose

and benevolence of the goddess. As a young man, he represented the eternal excellence of the youthful hunter; with his death it may be that he lost his youth, so that, except on the day celebrating his death and rescue from the underworld, he was the exiled male, immortal yet forever aging, hidden in the woods and untouchable.[24]

EGERIA

Egeria is rather better attested than Virbius. She was most well known for her relationship with Numa, the second king of Rome, and she had a spring in Rome and at Aricia.[25] According to Ovid, Egeria's moaning and lamentations in Diana's grove for her lost husband, Numa, impeded the rites of "Orestean Diana" (*sacraque Oresteae gemitu questuque Dianae/ inpedit*; *Met.* 15.489–90). Her weeping was unrelenting (*Met.* 15.491–4) – at which point in Ovid's narrative Hippolytus joins her, and, being an Ovidian hero, tries to cheer her by telling her about his own death, and his second life in Diana's sanctuary as Virbius (*Met.* 15.495–546). He fails: she continues to weep for her own losses (*non tamen Egeriae luctus aliena levare/ damna valent*; *Met.* 15.547–8), until Diana (appropriately, one feels) turns her into a spring at the base of the mountain, and her limbs become streams (*Met.* 15.550–1).

feast day falls on the 13 August, the day of Diana's great celebration at Aricia (Stat. *Silv.* 3.1.52–60).

[24] Mention should be made here of the curious two-headed Janus-type herm (number N 611 in the Nottingham collection), found at Nemi during the Savile excavations. One head was that of an older, the other of a younger man, both rather "wild" in expression and character. Blagg (1983, 41) describes it thus: "Plaster cast of a marble original which was already apparently missing from the collection at the time of Wallis' catalogue. It represents a double bust of aquatic monsters, one bearded, one beardless, placed back to back. An identical double bust in Copenhagen (Ny Carlsberg 245; Poulsen 1941, 29–30) was acquired from Cardinal Despuig's collection. . . . The two heads have fins sprouting from their hair and round the mouths, finny eyebrows, and collars of leaves round their necks. The hair is crisply carved and deeply drilled, giving a strong chiaroscuro effect, a technique typical of late 2nd century AD sculpture. Sockets at the sides below the shoulders suggest that the bust was mounted on a herm." What Blagg saw as fins sprouting from their hair do not look like fins, or animal ears, or horns, to me, although they are placed on the head where wolf-ears or goat-horns would go. Blagg is right that the young man seems to have fins at the corners of his mouth, but they could be leaves. Both old and young man have a leaf necklace.

[25] Livy 1.19.5; Ovid *Met.* 15.487; *Fasti* 3.261; DH *AR* 2.60.5; Plut. *Mor.* 321 B = *de Fort. Rom.* 9.

There was a spring in the crater – there are several even now (Guldager Bilde 1997a, 166) – but this one, according to Ovid, made enough noise to cover up the words and music of the rituals. Savile reported to the *Journal of the British and American Archaeological Society of Rome* on 11 May 1885, that "Egeria's spring" had once sprung "from the rocky amphitheatre which overhung the site of the temple" (73), although the spring was gone, in his time, the water having been diverted to Albano. This was the site of Le Mole ("The Millstones," where the medieval village of Nemi had its mills; Frazer, 1.17; Rosa 1856, 7). Le Mole is not far from the terrace, just around the lake to the east, at a point where the cliff beneath the village of Nemi is almost sheer, and juts outward sharply toward the lake (map 2). Ovid says he had often drunk the spring's water (*Fasti* 3.273–5). It had a powerful presence. Ovid may have been indulging in hyperbole when he said that the noise of the spring obscured the ritual, but either the spring was so powerful that it could be heard from the terrace, perhaps a quarter of a mile away, or rites were performed near to the spring, and the terrace did not necessarily define the limits of ritual space for the sanctuary. I suspect that the terrace was the anteroom for organizing visitors, and rituals that took place at Egeria's spring, in caves, and elsewhere around the northern end of the lake.

According to Vergil, when Virbius/Hippolytus was brought back to life and Diana wanted to hide him in the forest, she banished him to the grove (*nemus*) of the nymph Egeria (*et nymphae Egeriae nemorique relegat*; *Aen.* 7.775). Virbius' son, Virbius, again according to Vergil, was raised "around the moist shores of Egeria's woods (*eductum Egeriae lucis umentia circum / litora*; *Aen.* 7.763–4).[26] That a nymph should both possess the woods we would expect to be Diana's, and also be associated with Diana's beloved young hunter returned from the dead, presents an interesting and unexpected problem.

Who was Egeria, and what was her function in the sanctuary? Wissowa regarded her as a lesser deity concerned with childbirth (1912,

---

[26] In his use of *eductum* Vergil must also be playing on the multiple meanings of *educere*: to lead out, to rescue, to take out, to be born, and to be raised, or nurtured. *OLD s.v. educo* 1, 3, 4 (as in taking a fish out of water), 6, and 10, respectively. *Educo* and *egero* (with which Egeria is in all likelihood etymologically connected) have very similar meanings.

248). Frazer (1.17–19) identified her as an oak nymph (2.172; Plut. *Mor.* 321 B = *de Fort. Rom.* 9) who, along with Diana, assisted women in childbirth. He also suggested that the spring waters were used in healing and as an aid to conception (2.171). None of the explanations takes account of Egeria's tearful mourning for Numa or in any way explains her association with Virbius.

EGERIA IN LATIUM

Egeria's most famous role (because it was a native Roman tradition) was as the consort and advisor of King Numa (Livy 1.19.5, 21.3; DH *AR* 2.61–2).[27] She was established at a spring which Numa eventually dedicated to the Camenae, and it was from this spring of the Camenae that the Vestals drew their water (Plut. *Numa* 13.2). Numa consulted her – this, as Livy would have it, was a ruse to impress his impressionable subjects – on the establishment of rites and priesthoods in Rome. Livy, Dionysius, Ovid, and Plutarch are our principal sources,[28] and Egeria is mentioned by them chiefly because of her association with some other, more significant, figure. She is connected to Numa or Virbius/Hippolytus; she shares sacred space – a grove and a spring near the Porta Capena[29] – with Camena or the Camenae, or a grove and a spring with Diana.

Thus Egeria's most consistent characteristic is that she is a companion and consort, and her presence seems to be conditional on that of her companion(s). Through Numa she is associated with prophecy, or rather divine guidance and inspiration, particularly in matters concerning ritual and religion (Livy 1.19.5; Plut. *Numa* 4.2). Divine inspiration, again, and the shared spring at the Porta Capena connect her to the Camenae, female divinities understood by the earliest Roman writers to be the Latin equivalent of the

---

[27] Altheim (1930, 127) argued that Egeria was native to Rome, and only later came to Aricia. This view has not found wide acceptance.

[28] Egeria and Numa: Enn. *Ann.* 119 (Skutsch 113); Cic. *De Leg.* 1.1.4.; Martial 10.35.12–14; Ovid *Fasti* 3.154; 289–93. Strabo (5.3.12) and Ovid (*Fasti* 3.259–93) identify her firmly with a spring in Diana's grove.

[29] Vitr. 8.3.1; Front. *Aq.* 1.4); Richardson 1992, 63–4; *LTUR* 1.216.

Muses.[30] Egeria may have been considered one of the Camenae, for Livy reports Numa as dedicating a grove to the Camenae because there they, together with his wife Egeria, offered him counsel (Livy 1.21.3). Livius Andronicus begins his rendering of Homer's *Odyssey* with an invocation to Camena, and Pliny the Elder likewise invokes Camena as he begins his great encyclopaedia (*NH* 1.1). Egeria, and the Camenae in association with her, are thus associated with knowledge, particularly if divinely acquired.

Beyond all this, Egeria is also a figure of secrecy, remoteness, and darkness. When Numa consults her at her spring just outside Rome, he does so at night (*cum dea Egeria congressus nocturnos*; Livy 1.19.5), or at a dark cave in a grove (*ex opaco specu*; Livy 1.21.3), and in secrecy (συνουσία... ἀπόρρητος; Plut. *Numa* 8.6). Such remoteness, and darkness, form part of the conventional setting for a wise man's consultation with divinity, much intensified in ancient tradition by the (false) connection between Numa and the Pythagorean tradition. When Plutarch was writing – about the same time that Juvenal was at work on his satires – the Porta Capena and the grove of the Muses had become something between a bazaar and a beggars' camp (Juv. 3.15–16).[31] At Aricia, on the other hand, Egeria and her grove were still remote (Ovid *Met.* 15.487–8), at least as a protected enclave within the sanctuary. It may well be that during the historical period this enclave – the woods and the spring, and probably the cave, where she and Virbius traditionally dwelt – was used to reconstruct the imagined appearance of Egeria's grove in Rome in Numa's day.

The secrecy surrounding Egeria is important as a setting for her communication of knowledge. Those who are conduits for the words

---

[30] Liv. Andron. *Odyss.* 1.1; Naevius fr. 64.2 (Aul. Gell. *NA* 24.2); Lucilius 1064 Warmington; also Vergil, *Ecl.* 3.59 and Servius *Ecl.* 3.59; Horace C.S. 62; Prop. 3.10.1; Ovid *Met.* 15.482 (there connected specifically with Egeria as the source of ritual and the means of making a bellicose people peaceful); Juv. 7.2. Varro, *LL* 6.75 derives *Camena* from *canere*.

[31] It is worth noting that the Jews in Egeria's grove are exiles – driven from their homeland by the two great Jewish wars the Romans had waged – and that Juvenal is offended that they should have to pay rent to stay there. Egeria's grove in Rome was still a place for the rejected exile. Juvenal's complaint is not (as sometimes thought) that they were there – that was where they were supposed to be – but rather that the state had abandoned the old principle of sanctuary and was renting the space out.

of the gods must convey a remoteness to define their separation from the profane world and their intimacy with the sacred. Thus the Pythia in her temple, and the Sibyl in her cave. Yet the character of Egeria's advice, like the mode of its transmission, bears no resemblance to an oracle, and as far as we know, she never had a priestess or a medium through whom to speak. Egeria never seems to have given oracular "messages," although she did communicate, perhaps by inspiration. She, or perhaps another of the Camenae, was named Tacita, the "Silent One," by Numa (Plut. *Numa* 8.6). Ennius speaks of her melodious *sound* (*suavis sonus, Ann.* Skutsch 113), which may refer to her voice but more probably is an allusion to her spring's falling water. On the evidence, it is most likely that what connected Latin Egeria and the Camenae to the Greek Muses was that they communicated through inspiration, a vague but (to the Greeks and Romans) undoubtedly divine process.

THE TEARS OF EGERIA

Tears and the falling waters of a spring are easily equated. What is significant in Egeria's case is the *force* of her weeping, to the point that its noise affected the rites of the goddess. This detail, the hindering of *Orestean* Diana's rites, is quite extraneous even to the narrative Ovid has constructed and must be specific to conditions prevailing at the Arician sanctuary. What, precisely, is Ovid suggesting? The sounds are, unequivocally, those of *lamentation*. These, being by nature ill omened, present a problem. Ill-omened sounds would always be a reason to interrupt a ritual and begin again. Ritual lamentations must have been expected from Egeria at some point, and particularly lamentations for her losses (*damna*). Were these subsequently incorporated into the cult?

In the context of the story as Ovid tells it, Egeria's loss is her "husband," Numa. We know from Vergil that Virbius was handed over (*relegat, Aen.* 7.775) to Egeria and her woods, and in Ovid her story embraces the narrative of Hippolytus/Virbius (Egeria 15.487–92; Hippolytus 15.492–546; Egeria 15.547–51). Did she "embrace" Virbius in a myth we do not have? Was Egeria in fact another form of Diana, who saved Virbius "for love"? Possibly, but not necessarily. As Fontenrose's analysis of the structure of the Greek hunter and huntress myths (1981, 142–59) has shown, there is often an intermediary figure, male or female as appropriate, who becomes the erotic partner in place of the hunting deity. The power and attachment that is violated is still between the hunter/huntress and the deity. Ovid suggests only that Virbius and Egeria were united in their grief over their separate losses; Vergil links them only in terms of their shared space in the sanctuary. Nevertheless, linked they are. Egeria's lamentations indicate that one of her functions in the cult was to perform the essential responses to death and return to life. It is therefore likely that she mourned the death of the young hunter, surely an annual ritual event in the sanctuary. He was also placed in her care when he was brought back from the dead (*Met.* 15.548–9). Diana, as a goddess, could not perform those rites. Egeria, on the other hand, as a *numen* who belonged permanently to the earthly plane, and perhaps in part to the underworld, was an ideal candidate for both roles.

Egeria was defined as a mourner because she actually had a partner (and putative husband) whose death she lamented. This mourning may also have been a ritual event, and it must have been separate from her mourning for Virbius. For the Romans, Egeria's husband had a name, Numa. There is no reason to suppose his name was "Numa" at Aricia, but a husband must have existed as part of the ritual. We might also expect that, like Numa, he was a human, an early ruler of the city, one who was known for his concern with the establishment of religion and whose knowledge in this regard was gained from Egeria, his consort.[32] He would be a figure to whom later religious forms and practices were attributed as a mark of their antiquity.

EGERIA AND THE EXILES

Two fragments of early Latin history are relevant here. One comes from a passage in Festus (128 L) in which the grammarian records that a certain Manius Egerius consecrated the woodland grove to Diana. He had many distinguished offspring, and they became proverbial for their number. There is no telling where Festus found this information.

---

[32] Frazer, 2.172–3, 193, in a rather more expansive interpretation.

He goes on to discuss another interpretation of the proverb,[33] which he found in the work of Sinnius Capito, a grammarian of the first century B.C.E., so it may have come from a similar source. The sense of the passage is clear. The trouble about this statement is that there are no historically confirmed Manii from Aricia.

In the famous Cato fragment (fr. 58 Peter) another Egerius, who is also dictator Latinus, similarly dedicates a grove to Diana, in the Arician forest. Yet they have substantially different names. In fact, as we have seen, Egerius was not taken as a personal or a family name among the Romans. It was an epithet, or character name given to a certain kind of man – *puero post aui mortem in nullam sortem bonorum nato ab inopia Egerio inditum nomen* ("To the child [Arruns] born after the death of his grandfather [and father], and having no portion of the inheritance, the name "Egerius" was given, on account of his lack of resources"; Livy 1.34.3).

Thus "Egerius" was understood to mean a man without inheritance, one who was, in the Victorian sense, "portionless" both as an heir and as a citizen.[34] The Jews in Egeria's grove in Juvenal's time take up their residence there because they are without resources. As the narratives of the Tarquins makes clear, Egerius (Arruns), being portionless, could seek out a position of leadership in another Latin city. It would be likely, then, that an "Egerius" occurred among the mythic founders and exile-kings of Latin cities often enough to make Egerius Arruns part of a recognized pattern. Among these Egerii, it is highly plausible that the *mythic* founders, at least, would have had a consort, an Egeria, who was consulted at her (mythically remote) spring outside the boundaries of the city. The matching names indicate husband and wife, as is suggested by the Roman ritual phrase, spoken by the bride at marriage, *Ubi tu Gaius, ego Gaia* ("where you are Gaius, I am Gaia"[35]). Could Numa have been an Egerius? That is, could he have been an exile without

---

[33] Cf. the discussion in Chapter 10.

[34] Very probably Egerius is etymologically related to *egero*. See *OLD s.v. egero* 3a, to allow to escape, send out; 3b, to spit out or vomit; 4, to bring forth or yield; 6a, to use up or expend one's money. An "Egerius" would be one who had been expelled from the city (or allowed to escape from it) having used up (or never having received) his possessions.

[35] For the description of the ceremony with the citations, see S. Treggiari, *Roman Marriage*, Oxford, 1991, 168.

resources? Although according to the best accounts the mythohistoric Numa was not disinherited, he certainly was an outsider to Rome, who spent much time wandering in remote and lonely territory where he found his Egeria. There were many Egerias, just as there were many Athenas or Heras or Zeuses. There was an Egeria at Rome and another at Aricia. There is every likelihood that most Latin cities once boasted a spring belonging to an Egeria.

As we have seen, in Latium exile-kings were religious figures, and a version of the ritual surrounding them survived at Aricia in the case of the *rex nemorensis*. The death of the exile-king, like his selection, was dominated by ritual. It is possible that when one of the kings who (we presume) once ruled Aricia died, he would have been mourned by his consort, just as Egeria mourned her husband. The mythical Egeria would have served as the divine model for the real queen's part in the ritual mourning of the dead king. Given our evidence, it seems likely that such a pattern was once found generally among those Latin communities that had exile-kings. Once the exile-king disappeared, the need for the mourning would have disappeared, too. Clearly at Aricia, Egeria the mourner survived, along with the *rex nemorensis* and Virbius. The *rex* died after several decades; Virbius died (probably) every year. The ritual mourning associated with the *numen* of the spring may have been used for both.

Frazer thought there was a sacred marriage in the cult, between the priest and priestess (2.129) in which the male partner represented Virbius, and the female Egeria or Diana. It is a very tempting suggestion. The cult concerns with sexuality – the relationship between Diana and Virbius particularly – have been thoroughly obscured in our sources. That makes it particularly possible that in fact a ritual marriage, if it did take place, was between brother and sister. Claudius had his incestuous marriage to Agrippina purified by an antique ritual in Diana's grove (Tac. *Ann.* 12.8; cf. Green 1998, 777–91) and the city of Ephesus, the home of the great temple to Artemis/Diana, minted a commemorative cistophoric tetradrachm celebrating them on the obverse as a divine couple, with the legend *theogamia* ("marriage of the gods") below, while the reverse displayed Diana's cult statue (*BMC* 208). The pattern would be reflected further in the convolutions forced on Livy (1.46–8) and Dionysius (*AR* 4.28–39) to make

Servius' daughter Tullia both the sister(-in-law) *and* wife of Tarquinius Superbus, so that as a couple they can effect the sacrificial killing of the king/father and thus appropriate the throne for themselves.

EGERIA AND BIRTH

Every aspect of the stories, figures, and rituals associated with Aricia reminds us that death alone was not the only, or even the most important, concern of Diana's cult. Egeria as mourner is only one aspect of the nymph, for Egeria was also a divinity invoked regarding birth. Death was followed by (re)birth, the eternal cycle of renewal in nature. "Egeria" should in some way indicate "to lead out" (*OLD s.v. egero*), and Festus in fact says as much:

Egeriae nymphae sacrificabant praegnantes, quod eam putabant facile conceptum alvo egerere.

Festus 67L

Pregnant women were accustomed to sacrifice to the nymph Egeria, because they thought she easily led out (egerere) *the fetus from the womb.*

Women, that is, prayed to Egeria for an easy birth. Because the birthing process involves a gush of "water," the breaking of the amniotic sac, there is an inevitable connection between birth and the goddess of a spring, which also gushes water. This is certainly true for Egeria. The closeness of death at the moment of birth was part of every mother's experience. As any woman who gave birth in the ancient world would have realized, she faced the very real possibility of dying herself to give life to another. She would have prayed for a safe approach to the event, and the triumphant, easy return "out of the woods." Her prayers would have been addressed to Egeria, as to Diana and Juno Lucina. She would have wanted a companion, a guide for her journey, a divine woman who knew the wilds of childbirth well.

This double responsibility of Egeria – mourning and childbirth – made her the figure to whom Virbius, the mythical young hunter, could rightly be entrusted. Her mourning marked his death and journey to the underworld, and no doubt she functioned as a benevolent protectress in his resurrection or rebirth.

230

Egeria clearly belonged to the liminal world, to the interstices between earth and the underworld, to the cave and the water, to the spring and to Diana. Her power and knowledge came from that liminality. Those who occupy liminal space between this world and the underworld are closer to death and to the knowledge that comes from the underworld. This is no doubt how Egeria became the advisor to kings.

There is no festival or celebration of Egeria's that is known in either Aricia or Rome. There is, however, a day that might possibly have been her festival date. The celebration of Diana began on 13 August, the Ides of August. As we have seen, the Christian calendar placed St. Hippolytus' celebration on 13 August. This was also the festival day of the Camenae, the nymphs of the spring where Egeria and Numa met (Degrassi, 494–6). The Ides of August would seem to gather the Muses, Egeria, and Virbius all together.

VIRBIUS AND EGERIA

Virbius/Hippolytus and Egeria are connected because they both inhabit the sacred territory of the wood around Diana's sanctuary. In their quite different ways, their cult presence has similar characteristics. Virbius dies and is brought back to life, he is reborn; Egeria, as a spring, has a natural connection to the underworld, to death, and to inspiration; and she helps women in childbirth. Virbius' resurrected existence in the wood, after his return from the underworld, marks a separation from his old life, his youth; Egeria, similarly, is separated from her husband. They are concerned with both life and death, and with the passage from one condition to the other. They may have been part of a sacred marriage. Last of all, they are both hidden and remote from Diana's human worshippers. We know of no rituals associated with either of them, although the Ides of August has a strong claim to be a celebration in which they both had a part.

PART III

HEALING AND RITUAL

DIANA THE HEALER

Ancient Latin religion was not in the control of theologians. The élite at each city would have held the priesthoods and decided on the building programs at the sanctuaries of their deities, and of course they would be in charge of the principal city festivals and sacrifices. But large, Hellenistic-style complexes such as the Aricians built for Diana served a much wider public on a day-to-day basis. The inscriptions give an idea of how many different kinds of people came to the sanctuary and found – as their dedications attest – the help that they sought. The practice of religion at the sanctuary was shaped by Diana's worshippers. The city elders and the priests might organize the goddess' suppliants, provide guidance and instruct in rituals and their meaning, but ultimately the success of the cult was the result of the religious experiences of the people who came to the sanctuary for the goddess. Most of these experiences are far beyond our reach, but there is evidence in our literary sources for one kind of ritual experience available to Diana's petitioners. The evidence for Diana the healer will allow us precious glimpses of what actually happened in the sanctuary and will also allow us to inquire just a little into what people wanted from the goddess, what they received, and how they understood and valued it.

DIANA AND HEALING

Diana was a goddess frequently sought out by the sick. There are votives of body parts typical of healing cults in central Italy excavated from her sanctuary: representations of heads, feet, eyes, noses, wombs (figure 7), and a statue of a woman with her intestines exposed (Morpurgo 1903, 324; Blagg 1983, 52–3; Lesk 1999, 80–5, figure 8). Votive physician's instruments have also been found (Morpurgo 1931, 247; Guldager Bilde 1997d, 192). She was, of course, invoked by women in childbirth as Lucina, and she was associated with Asclepius, perhaps through Virbius/Hippolytus, to the degree that the Greek healing god seems to have been honored with a cult statue in Diana's sanctuary (Guldager Bilde and Moltesen 2002, 19).

Cynthia, Propertius' beloved, had to fulfill a vow to Diana for her escape from a mortal illness (Propert. 2.28.59–60). Horace connects Diana's anger to a range of diseases from jaundice to *error mentis*, wandering in the wits (*Ars* 453–6), and by that, implies that she will be the source of relief from those inflictions. Orestes comes to Aricia seeking release from madness, *furor* (Servius *ad Aen.* 2.116): the "pursuit of the Erinyes" became a way to describe one group of medical conditions – predominantly mental – treated by Diana, especially those causing deviant behavior (Grat. *Cyn.* 369–77).

She did not treat only humans. Grattius devotes almost a quarter of his hymn to Diana (*Cyn.* 344–482) to the care of hunting hounds, preparation for the birth of puppies, the care of their nursing mother, and how to treat wounds, mange, coughs, or rabies.

The goddess would seem, on the face of it, to have combined the various skills of family practitioner, psychiatrist, and veterinarian. This is entirely consistent with her identity as a goddess of the moon – who governs the growth of plants and animals and the physical changes that either heal or harm the body – and as a hunting deity. Hunting cults were always repositories of knowledge about plants and animals, the care of the young, and both the giving and healing of wounds. The question is, what, exactly, did Diana do for those who were ill?

RELIGIOUS HEALING AND HIPPOCRATIC MEDICINE

Religious healing has been greatly misunderstood. One hindrance to our proper understanding of the healing practices employed in a sanctuary like Diana's is due to the widespread misreading of a crucial text composed about the fourth century B.C.E.: the Hippocratic treatise

De Morbo Sacro. This treatise is rightly regarded as a basic cornerstone both of Western scientific thought and of modern medicine.

They make use of purifications and spells, and their action, it seems to me, is both most impious and utterly irreligious; for they purify those in the grip of the disease with blood and other such things as though they were afflicted with some pollution, or [pursued by] avenging furies, or were poisoned by human agency, or had done something impious. These are people who should be treated quite differently, with sacrifice and prayer, and by bringing them to the sanctuaries to supplicate the gods.[1]

De Morbo Sacro 4

I do not personally think it reasonable that a man's body could be polluted by a god – the wholly mortal by the most completely holy.[2]

De Morbo Sacro 4

But this disease seems to me in no way more sacred than the rest; rather it has the same nature that other diseases have, and the kind of cause from which each of them arises.[3]

De Morbo Sacro 5

In attacking religious healers who exploit vulnerable and guilt-ridden patients by means of gross ritual purifications, the Hippocratic author draws the line: anyone who makes the god the source of disease not only demeans godhead but also necessarily prevents proper inquiry into causes. His subject is the problematical and most traditionally "divine" of all illnesses, epilepsy, which much resembled the symptoms of divine inspiration associated with figures such as the Pythia at Delphi or the Sibyl. By diagnosing and prescribing for this allegedly "sacred" disease, the author asserts the power of reason and warns that those who practice purifications and incantations stand in the way of real knowledge by assigning the cause of a disease to the god. Rather, he argues, those who offer purifications (especially blood

---

[1] καθαρμοῖσί τε χρέονται καὶ ἐπαοιδῇσι, καὶ ἀνοσιώτατόν τε καὶ ἀθεώτατον πρῆγμα ποιέουσιν, ὡς ἔμοιγε δοκεῖ· καθαίρουσι γὰρ τοὺς ἐχομένους τῇ νούσῳ αἵματί τε καὶ ἄλλοισι τοιούτοις ὥσπερ μίασμά τι ἔχοντας, ἢ ἀλάστορας, ἢ πεφαρμακευμένους ὑπὸ ἀνθρώπων, ἤ τι ἔργον ἀνόσιον εἰργασμένους, οὓς ἐχρῆν τἀναντία τούτων ποιεῖν, θύειν τε καὶ εὔχεσθαι καὶ ἐς τὰ ἱερὰ φέροντας ἱκετεύειν τοὺς θεούς· Text is that of W. H. S. Jones.

[2] ... οὐ μέντοι ἔγωγε ἀξιῶ ὑπὸ θεοῦ ἀνθρώπου σῶμα μιαίνεσθαι, τὸ ἐπικηρότατον ὑπὸ τοῦ ἁγνοτάτου.

[3] τὸ δὲ νόσημα τοῦτο οὐδέν τί μοι δοκεῖ θειότερον εἶναι τῶν λοιπῶν, ἀλλὰ φύσιν ἔχει ἣν καὶ τὰ ἄλλα νοσήματα, καὶ πρόφασιν ὅθεν ἕκαστα γίνεται.

purifications) or use incantations and sorcery as treatment for pollution or guilt, are *not*, as they claim, acting in a pious manner. The gods are holy, and supposing them to be the source of bodily defilement by disease is, in fact, an impious notion. Such purifications and incantations, *because they are charlatanry*, are therefore an obstacle to both religious piety and to medical knowledge. *De Morbo Sacro* is undoubtedly a landmark in scientific and intellectual history.

Although there can be no question of the importance of this work, modern scholars have nevertheless vastly – and selectively – overapplied the views it expressed, reaching the conclusion that Hippocratic medicine and religious healing were virtually defined by opposition one to the other in both theory and practice. Till very recently (and in many areas still), conventional wisdom has maintained that Hippocratic medicine was rational in the modern sense, rejecting all religious explanations and actions; whereas Asclepiadean and other sanctuary medicine was fundamentally irrational, indeed prerational, rooted in *mythos* rather than *logos*.[4] Furthermore, there has been general acceptance of the idea that all sanctuary healing was based on assigning religious guilt or unholiness (mainly due to pollution, *miasma*) as a cause of disease and that the diseases themselves were invariably treated with purifications, absolutions, incantations, visits of the god during *incubatio* (the result of the patient's willing imagination, perhaps preyed on by cynical practitioners), and other kinds of hocus-pocus.

As should be evident even from the first passage cited here, this is a wholly unjustifiable conclusion. The author (in what is admittedly a polemical text) does not in any way object to religious healing as a whole, although he condemns practices that interfere with learning about disease, indeed, he seems to think that sanctuaries are the place where certain types of healing should be sought, and his argument is based on a clear view that what he is condemning is the precise opposite: deceptive charlatanry, practiced by those who exploit the gullible for profit. He quite clearly believes in the gods, and in their power. What he does *not* believe is that the gods are the specific cause of disease. Disease is a *sign*, not a punishment, and the gods

4 For example, Jouanna, 19; Longrigg, 22–5.

communicate in signs (cf. Heraclitus: ὁ ἄναξ οὗ τὸ μαντεῖόν ἐστι τὸ ἐν Δελφοῖς οὔτε λέγει οὔτε κρύπτει ἀλλὰ σημαίνει, "The king whose oracle is at Delphi neither speaks nor conceals, but he gives signs", *KRS*[2] 244).

In the last few years a great change has taken place in the scholarly view of the role of rationalist (i.e., Hippocratic) medicine and its relationship to religious healing, especially in sanctuaries. Here, as so often, Geoffrey Lloyd has led the way, especially in his most recent book, *In the Grip of Disease: Studies in the Greek Imagination*. As Lloyd[5] says, Hippocratic medicine[6] not only traditionally had its origins in sanctuary medicine, but also continued to maintain an integral role in sanctuary healing throughout antiquity. Whether it was a historical fact that Hippocrates learned his medicine at the sanctuary on Cos, as ancient tradition held[7] (Strabo 14.2.19; Pliny *NH* 29.1–2), there was no feeling among Hippocratics that such an origin was in violation of their rationalist position. In other words, it was acceptable within the Hippocratic tradition that the founder of rationalist medicine should have acquired his professional skills from the sanctuary. Not surprisingly, Hippocrates was known as an Asclepiad (Plato *Prt.* 311b6; *Phdr.* 270c). On the other hand, Asclepius, as mythical founder of the most famous of the religious healing systems, was said to have practiced

---

[5] I had reached these conclusions, and written the first draft of this chapter, before the publication of Lloyd's chapter on the *De Morbo Sacro* (2003, 40–83). Lloyd, whose earlier work had pointed me in this direction, emphasizes that the author of this treatise was not, in fact, attacking the healers of the sanctuaries but rather the practitioners who "resemble those whom we hear of from Plato who went from door to door selling charms and incantations to whoever they could persuade to buy them (*Republic* 364bc [T3.3], cf. *Laws* 909a–d)" – in other words, the snake-oil merchants, medical quacks, and Elmer Gantrys of antiquity.

[6] For brevity and clarity of distinction, I use "Hippocratic" medicine to refer to the complex system of rationalist medicine founded by, but not limited to, the writers of the Hippocratic Corpus, and the term "sanctuary" medicine for the systems of healing at temple sanctuaries such as those of Asclepius and Diana.

[7] The ancient tradition was that Hippocrates learned his medicine at the Asclepian sanctuary of Cos and was regarded as an Asclepiad (*Hippocratis Vita Bruxellensis* 2–8, Edelstein, T 156; Plato, *Phaedrus* 270 C; Edelstein T 217; *Protagoras* 311B, Edelstein T 217 note; Aristotle *Met.* E 2, 1027 a 19; Edelstein T 218; Strabo 14.2.19; Pliny *NH* 29.1–2; cf. Jouanna 10–19, who accepts that Hippocrates was an Asclepiad from Cos but not that this denotation had anything to do with the healing at the Asclepieion at Cos, 19).

surgery,[8] and thus it was acceptable to the sanctuary systems to have the god do so. Other evidence from Greece and Italy[9] confirms that there were physicians in the great healing sanctuaries who practiced conventional rationalistic medicine, including surgery.[10]

Lloyd also observes, correctly, that there is no consistent rejection of the gods throughout the Hippocratic Corpus, and indeed, that the terms of the Oath recognize the authority of the gods over physicians (Lloyd 2003, 51–2), while a passage from the Law "uses the language of religious initiation when talking about the induction of doctors into the art" (Lloyd 2003, 52). The image of the doctor and the understanding of his role owe much to the tradition founded by the "sons of Asclepius." The vocabulary of ancient medicine is imbued with religious concepts – particularly those relating to the word catharsis, purification. Some Hippocratic and Asclepieian procedures show strong similarity: both schools use dreams as diagnostic tools, practice prognosis, and conduct treatment by means of drugs and dietary regimens.[11]

The Asclepieians were themselves by no means impervious to Hippocratic theory and practice.[12] There is an inscription from their sanctuary at Ephesus recording the winners of a competition for prizes

---

[8] Pindar, *Pyth.* 3, 53; Edelstein 1998, T 1; Apollodorus 3.10.3.5–4.1; vol. 1, T 97; Asclepius' son Machaon was the surgeon, and Podalirius was the internist; Edelstein T 135–216.

[9] Pindar, *Pyth.* 3.46–55; Hart 79–90 and 135–64 (see especially the instruments on the bas-relief from the tombstone of a physician at the Athenian Asclepieion, fig. 38); Ioannes Lydus, *de Mensibus* 4.142; confirmed (in personal communication) by Dr. Stefanos Geroulanos.

[10] Cf. Hart, 79–90. Compare the very outdated but still influential Withington (152), who uses the existence of physicians in the sanctuaries as evidence for the "degeneration" of medicine after the fourth century. As a good corrective, see Hart (53–90).

[11] On Asclepiadean regimens of food: Pliny *NH* 25.2.13; Aristides *Orat.* 42 7–8 (Edelstein 1998, T 317); Suda, *Lexicon*, s.v. Δομνῖνος (Edelstein T. 427). Asclepius and drugs: Epidauran inscriptions (Edelstein T 423.4, 9, 40, 41; Diod. 5.74.6; Aristides *Orat.* 49, 28; Edelstein T 411).

[12] "The god often acts very much in the way that many of the Hippocratic doctors would ... only with this difference, that the god is infallible" (Lloyd 2003, 55). There is, I would argue, no claim to infallibility per se in cures reported by the stelae. One of these makes clear that it was quite possible, sometimes even expected, that a patient might go away from the sanctuary without being healed (Edelstein T 423.33). Obviously the stelae recorded successes. They are not equivalent to case histories and should not be read as such.

in medical essay writing, surgery, theory, and the use of instruments.[13] There is no evidence that religious healers assigned the cause of illnesses in general to the god or that they rejected scientific inquiry into the etiology of disease, pragmatic diagnoses, or the use of empirical *or* theoretical treatments of illness. The Ephesus sanctuary also had a famous library. Although Ephesus may have been exceptional in its institutionalization of this process, we should expect that in healing sanctuaries no less than in Hippocratic centers, medical knowledge was continually being gathered and codified, with new findings modifying current practice.[14] This paradigm is also congruent with what we know of two sixth-century medical schools in Italy, those at Croton and Elea,[15] which not only preceded Hippocratic theory, but were indeed largely responsible for its intellectual emergence. Both schools were closely allied with the local sanctuaries of Apollo.

What the evidence indicates is that healing sanctuaries, far from being indifferent to medical theory and practice, were in fact at the forefront of medical developments. The gods imparted knowledge. Piety would require that that knowledge be used. There is no prima facie reason why religious healers would automatically reject any practice that was known or thought to heal. The Hippocratic physicians did not reject the authority of the god: they called themselves *Asclepiadae*, sons of Asclepius. There is no more reason to suppose that the priests of Asclepius – or of Diana for that matter – rejected

---

[13] Edelstein T 573: In the inscription, second or third century C.E., the winners were P. Vedius Rufinus in σύνταγμα (composition); P. Aelius Menander, ἀρχιατρός (city physician) in χειρουργία (surgery – this word is restored); (name lost) in πρόβλημα (thesis, or theory), and in instruments, ὄργανα, P. Aelius. The competition appears to be modeled on the Olympic games.

[14] The Epidauran *Iamata* must be used carefully as evidence for sanctuary practice. These have been read as though they were the testimony of the practitioners of the sanctuary, and therefore parallel to the Hippocratic treatises. They are, in fact, the dedications of patients successfully (in their minds) healed. Patients will present a narrative of the healing experience that will differ, sometimes astonishingly, from that of their healers, relating what was important to them in the process of treatment and ignoring matters that would be significant for a medical analysis (cf. A. Frank, *The Wounded Storyteller*, Chicago, 1995, 4–13). The contemporary study of patients' narratives should be used as a guide to a better interpretation of the genre of the *Iamata*. Horstmanshoff's analysis (2004) of Aelius Aristides' account is a good beginning.

[15] Croton: Hdt. 3.125; Jouanna 1999, 43; Longrigg 1993, 47–63; Elea: Jouanna 1999, 246; Longrigg 1993, 63–4.

the knowledge physicians gained in their practice or regarded that knowledge as antithetical to religion.

Furthermore, until the advent of gladiatorial schools, healing sanctuaries were the only teaching hospitals available to those who wished to research at a practical and experimental level.[16] Sanctuaries were international: they attracted not only the sick but also those interested in healing, and formed a common center where religious and rationalist medical systems met, and their practices could be exchanged and tested. Only sanctuaries would see patients in enough numbers, with sufficiently similar ailments, to be able to practice any kind of systematic, empirically based healing on a scale large enough to form the basis for theory.

This does not mean that religious healing through purification did not occur in sanctuaries, as well as other kinds of religious healing that no Hippocratic physician ever practiced. The point is that the charge leveled against religious healers by the author of *De Morbo Sacro* – that they identified the god as the cause of disease and purification as its cure – cannot be sustained against sanctuary healing. When the evidence for healing at Diana's sanctuary is considered, we must be prepared to find rationalist, empiricist medicine as one kind of treatment quite naturally employed by religious healers. Both they and their rationalist colleagues would unite against the quacks and fakes who formed the main targets of attack in the *De Morbo Sacro*.

RATIONALIST TREATMENTS: WOUNDS

Diana was, naturally, concerned with *Mauortia bello/ uolnera* ("martial wounds received in war"; Grattius, *Cyn.* 352–3) – that is, wounds from weapons, whether used for hunting or fighting. Here is Grattius' advice for treating a gaping wound:

> Nec longe auxilium, licet alti uolneris orae
> abstiterint atroque cadant cum sanguine fibrae:

---

[16] The military would have provided a different set of medical problems, most of which would have been concerned with wounds. The same would also have been true, to a great extent, of the gladiatorial schools. The ordinary diseases and afflictions a physician met with would only have been seen consistently and repeatedly in the sanctuaries.

inde rape ex ipso qui uolnus fecerit hoste
uirosam eluuiem lacerique per ulceris ora
sparge manu, uenas dum sucus comprimat acer:
mortis enim patuere uiae. Tum pura monebo
circum labra sequi tenuique includere filo.

Cyn. 354–8

Nor is help distant, though the mouth of the deep wound has spread open and the fibers drip with black blood: then steal from the very enemy who made the wound [17] *some of his rank urine* [18] *and sprinkle it with your hand over the mouth of the torn wound, until the astringent fluid compresses the veins: for the ways of death have been opened. Then my advice will be to go round the lips and to close them with a fine thread.*

This treatment is as good as anything available until the twentieth century and the advent of modern pharmaceuticals. Although we might cringe at the idea of sprinkling urine on an open wound, for someone in the field (whether a battlefield or out hunting) the immediate need is for a way to stop or diminish the bleeding. "Urine is usually acidic in pH and that low pH could possibly help 'cauterize' small vessels. Urine in healthy animals and people is usually sterile and would make a good lavage solution. There are natural bacteriostatic/[bacteri]cidal properties to healthy urine as well." [19] When there are no antibiotics or antiseptics available, it is an effective way to treat open, bleeding wounds. Once the bleeding is stopped, Grattius recommends that the wound be sutured, but there are no incantations over the wound, of the sort found in the *Odyssey* (19.455–8).

Then he turns to smaller wounds, ones where the skin closes over the injury. The worst are puncture wounds. Animals that fight with

---

[17] A commonplace of ancient thought, and central to magical thinking, cf. Ovid *Rem. Am.* 47–50, where Ovid is proposing to undo the harm he has done in the *Ars Amatoria*, and then refers to Telephus, who was wounded by Achilles and was told he could only be cured by the spear that wounded him (Gantz 1993, 578–9, *LIMC* 7.1 856–7).

[18] *OLD eluuies* 1b (excreted matter) implies this must be feces; however, all the translators have taken it as urine: Duff: "fetid urine"; Formicola: "la fetida urina"; Verdière: l'urine fétide. Both the verb *sparge*, and the general sense of flowing liquid attested to the other uses of *eluuies* and its cousin *eluuio, -onis*, support the accepted translation as "urine."

[19] Personal letter from Dr. Paul Graettinger, DVM.

teeth and claws are particularly prone to puncture wounds, but of course humans are afflicted with them as well.

> At si pernicies angusto pascitur ore,
> contra pande uiam fallentisque argue causas
> morborum: in uitio facilis medicina <reperto>.
> Sed tacta impositis mulcent p<ecuaria palmis>
> – id satis – aut nigrae circum picis unguine signant;
> quod si destricto leuis est in uolnere noxa,
> ipse habet auxilium ualidae natale saliuae.

Cyn. 359–65

But if the injury feeds on a narrow opening, on the contrary, open it up and reveal the deceitful causes of disease: when the trouble is revealed, the remedy is easy.[20] But they ease the beasts thus afflicted with strokes of the palm[21] – that is enough – or seal the sore around with an ointment of black pitch. However, if the damage to the scraped wound is trivial, the animal itself possesses the in-born remedy of his efficacious saliva.[22]

Even minus the two emendations, the advice is once again as good as any that was available to any physician for two millennia, until the

---

[20] The end of the line is missing. Duff takes the reading of Logus' *editio princeps* – *recenti* – that is, a recent wound; Formicola accepts Kenney's *retecto* – a wound opened up. Each emendation is possible. I follow Verdière in accepting Baehrens' *reperto*, because the point seems to be that narrow wounds (among which would be puncture wounds, to which dogs would be very prone and which will become abscessed if they are not cleaned out immediately) can be treated *if they are found*. Puncture wounds can be hard to find on an animal with fur. Grattius has already said that such wounds should be treated by being opened up. The fact that they are "recent" is irrelevant to the treatment – the older the wound, the more abscessed it would be and the greater the need to open it up.

[21] Again the end of the line is missing. Verdière and Formicola (following Enk) read *praecordia olivis*, "relieve the sufferings covered with rubbings of olive oil," where *praecordia* = the feelings (*OLD* 3). Olive oil was then and is now a common way of soothing inflammations. Nevertheless, I follow Duff's reading (that of the *editio princeps*) of *pecuaria palmis* and translate "they ease the beasts thus afflicted by strokes of the palm." The "or" indicates an alternative treatment. I suggest that Grattius is recommending that once a puncture wound is opened, it should be "soothed" by having any foreign substance pressed out, which treatment should be enough.

[22] "If the intention is to keep the wound's edges apart, the pitch would cauterize chemically and not allow the edges to seal. This would allow drainage of the wound, and the wound would eventually heal by filling in with scar tissue. There are naturally occurring enzymes in saliva that have antibacterial properties (tears have similar enzymes also). Saliva also has many bacteria that could cause wound infection. The actual mechanical debridement by the tongue could possibly help" (personal letter from Dr. Paul Graettinger).

advent of modern antibiotics. And of course, what would work for a hunting hound would also work for a human being.

RABIES

Rabies is an appalling disease: its cure, and even more important, its preventative vaccine, are among the greatest achievements of twentieth-century medicine. Even so, the appearance of rabies in any animal today is still a terrible sign. Grattius knows the signs and does not promise miracles. He acknowledges the goddess' power (*Cyn.* 350–1), and he recommends what must be a ritual flight from disease as the prelude to his discussion of rabies. Leading the dogs across a broad river is "the first escape from death" (377–9).[23] The linked religious and hunting implications of paths, pursuit, and escape find (as we have seen) multiple realization in the sanctuary.

That done, however, Grattius has a practical suggestion: a small cut under the tongue which he understood would reveal the "worm" that was the cause of rabies (*Cyn.* 383–98). The cause (the worm) is physical, and the treatment is directed to it in a logical manner.[24] This is comparable to the author of *De Morbo Sacro* proposing that the cause of epilepsy is excessive moisture in the head (6–10), and the treatment is the proper adjustment of that moisture (21). Neither cutting the tongue nor drying the head would, of course, have affected the targeted illness in the least, which does not alter the fact that both treatments are rationalist, that is, a physical cause is understood to be the problem, and a remedy addressing that cause is used. The god is not involved.

---

[23] "The power of a stream to neutralize or wash away the magical powers of those who cross it has important consequences in Roman ritual" (Holland 1961, 11). Crossing running water was always an action with complex religious meaning. For instance, the various, sometimes seasonal, creeks that divided the Roman forum or the Campus Martius had long created barriers that could only be crossed with the proper religious preparation (cf. Holland 1961, 11–20). Grattius, then, is suggesting that to take one's animals across a broad stream would weaken or destroy the power of the pursuing "greedy death" (*avidissimus Orcus, Cyn.* 347), and this constitutes a first prophylactic.

[24] It is also interesting because it indicates a rationalist medical tradition independent of the theory of humors.

What is particularly useful, though, is that Grattius' discussion of rabies allows us to observe his response to magical treatments. In nine interesting lines (*Cyn.* 399–407) he accepts the use of apotropaics (collars made of various materials like cocks' combs or sacred shells, supplemented by herbs and magical incantations[25]), for their ability not to cure rabies, but rather to ease the owner's fears. These are ancient techniques, he says, belonging to a simpler age (*priscas artes inventaque simplicis aevi*, 399). He refers to them as the solace for what he calls *metus . . . falsi* (false fears; *Cyn.* 400). One of the characteristics of sanctuary healing is that it understands that *emotions* often need treatment quite as much as any physical disorder. In the face of this lethal and contagious disease, Grattius is prepared to help the owners turn away their own false fears, but he does not actually enumerate either the herbs or the incantations he knows could be used, and he offers no tales of pollution to explain the disease's onset.

SKIN DISEASES

Grattius offers a treatment for scabies or mange, a chronic disease in dogs. He spends sixty-eight lines (*Cyn.* 408–76) on it, indicating its importance. He describes the dog's body lacerated by the "deformed pleasure" (*deformi dulcedine*),[26] that is, of scratching (408), which is "the hardest road of a slow death" (*longi via pessima leti*, 409). Indeed it is, for the animal, by its uncontrollable scratching, will slowly rip apart its own flesh and die of the consequent infection. The first remedy Grattius recommends is the most drastic and consistent with the law of the wild: one must die that others may live. The first animal to show signs of the disease (which is understood to be contagious) must be destroyed.

> In primo accessu tristis medicina, sed una
> pernicies redimenda anima, quae prima sequaci
> sparsa malo est, ne dira trahant contagia vulgus.
> *Cyn.* 410–12

[25] He defines the songs specifically as "magical": *et magicis adiutas cantibus herbas* (*Cyn.* 405).
[26] Reading *deformi* with the mss. For the theory behind the medicine at the sanctuary, for which terms such as *deformis* are significant, see Chapter 11.

At the first onset, the remedy is a melancholy one, but the destruction must be bought off by the one life [of the dog] which has first been contaminated with the infectious disease, to prevent the whole pack from contracting the dread contagion.

If the scabies is mild, it can be treated.

> Quodsi dat spatium clemens et promonet ortu
> morbus, disce vias et qua sinit artibus exi.
>
> *Cyn.* 413–14

If, however, the ailment is slight, giving time and forewarnings at the start, learn the methods of cure and by skilled devices escape wherever feasible.

Once again the religious idea contained in paths, pursuit, and escape is a way to contextualize the treatment. The "escape" Grattius recommends, however, although remaining a religious concept, embodies a practical prescription: a mixture of bitumen, wine, pitch from the town of Hipponium, and the dregs of olive oil, which should be heated and used to bathe the afflicted dog (415–18). Then, Grattius says, the anger, *ira*, of the ailment can be curbed (418). Here we can see the development of the old idea that disease is a sign of divine displeasure. The metaphor of the "anger" of Diana, illness as a sign, is now used as a description of inflammation. The inflammation itself is treated not by means of petitions, penance, or prayers, but with an ointment – and that is no less religious than any other treatment.

Ointments and all kinds of oils, soothing lotions, and tonics would have been part of the understanding of natural history stored in the hunting cult rituals and prayers,[27] and that in itself makes the use of these medicaments religious. But such knowledge was not exclusive, and the herbalists, the root gatherers, the wise women and men, who were the ones who gathered the ingredients of these medications, would have contributed to the knowledge of the cult as well. The sanctuaries and the Hippocratic healers both depended on them. As

---

[27] Cf. Luckert 1981, 54–9, on Claus Chee Sonny and the gathering of "deer-plant medicine." "Deer-plants possess medicinal power because in primeval times, when the Deer-people planted them in the earth, some of their own divine deer essence was left in the plants to survive and to grow. Even the very dust which the divine Deer-people had whipped up can be used as medicine" (54). Luckert's study is entirely devoted to the hunting rituals that have become healing rituals among the Navajo.

Scarborough says about the herbalists, their actions, although governed by an understanding of the practice and theory of healing with plants, were also religious in motivation (1991, 157–8).

Bitumen is the most important active ingredient of Grattius' mixture, and, in the form of coal tar, it can still be found in over-the-counter shampoos designed to kill the skin tick that causes mange, although veterinarians will only use it now in extreme cases.[28] Bathing with the bituminous mixture was the pragmatic treatment, which Grattius then says must be supported by certain actions. These might have been taken straight out of the Hippocratic treatise *Airs Waters Places*, and probably were. The afflicted dogs must be protected from rain and chill winds (418–20) or, when it is hot, removed from exposed lowlands and placed in a sunny, protected spot so that they can sweat out the contagion (421–4) and the medicine can take effect (424–5). The advice, however, was very specific to the sanctuary. Grattius uses *nudae valles*, "exposed lowlands," to describe the hollow of the crater and the level land beside the lake where the sanctuary was laid out,[29] and where, what with sun, wind, the reflection from the lake, and the ambient humidity, the heat would have been unhealthful. But the protected space further up and away from the flatlands was where the animal could benefit from sunshine and sweat out the contagion.

Grattius closes this portion with an invocation of Apollo, citing in the process an additional remedy recommended by that god: a dip in seawater at the shore (424–6). The salt in a seawater bath would have helped a mild infection and may have prevented infestation of the tick in puppies, which Grattius specifically mentions here. Seawater baths were not, of course, feasible at the sanctuary of Diana, and Apollo had no presence at the sanctuary. It is probably significant for this contrast in healing practice that Apollo, the sun god, was fed moisture from the sea, just as Diana, the moon goddess, was fed moisture from lakes and streams (Pliny *NH* 2.223).

---

[28] Dr. Paul Graettinger again advised me on the treatment of scabies in animals. Tar is also found in older brands of over-the-counter dandruff shampoos for humans.

[29] As does Ovid: *vallis Aricinae silva praecinctus opaca/ est lacus, antiqua religione sacer* (*Fasti* 3. 263–4).

If there are any lingering doubts about the practice of rationalist medicine at the sanctuary of Diana, Grattius' invocation of the
personified and deified abstraction "Skilled Experience" (*o Prudens
Experientia*, 427) should remove them. *Prudens Experientia* might be
the very definition of empirical medicine. There is no difficulty in
using empirical methods while using a religious vocabulary, as when
infection and inflammation are described as "anger," and treatment
is spoken of as an "escape." This vocabulary had rather been able to
provide, as Grattius makes clear, a vivid and descriptive metaphor for
discussion of what was seen by the healers. We speak of an "angry
wound," one that is red and inflamed, in much the same spirit. Such
religiously grounded metaphors did not prevent the healers in the
sanctuary from seeking out, and using, the most pragmatic, scientific
methods that were available to them in treating disease.

KNOWLEDGE THROUGH RITUAL

Pragmatic, empirical medicine was thus practiced in the religious context of the sanctuary. How were such practical treatments presented
to the petitioners? Were they separate from the religious experience?
And, if not, how did the rationalism of medicine mix with religious
conduct? Grattius indicates the pattern – ritual presentation of practical treatment – in lines 430–64, immediately after his recipe for the
medicinal bath to treat scabies. The context of healing he transfers to
some springs, sacred to Vulcan, in Sicily. This displacement is not as
arbitrary as it might at first sight appear. There is a logical connection
between Diana's cult in the extinct crater, and that of Vulcan in Sicily,
and Grattius has left traces of the connection. He has already mentioned Hipponian pitch as the essential element in treating scabies,
and Vulcan's sacred springs also have bituminous oil for the treatment
of dogs (*Cyn.* 433–6). On the journey by ship from Rome to Sicily,
Hipponium (Vibo Valentia) was a major port of call,[30] famous both
for its timber and for its claim (one among several) to be the place

---

[30] Originally a Locrian Greek settlement on the western Italian coast (Strabo 6.1.5). It was
famous for its timber, which supplied the naval yards there, and a major naval station for
Octavian as he fought Sextus Pompeius (Appian *B.C.* 5.91, 99, 103, 105, 112).

from which Proserpina was carried off (Strabo 6.30).[31] The next stop sailing south from Hipponium toward Sicily would be Elea/Velia, the site of a famous Apollonian medical sanctuary[32] and the most likely source for Apollo's remedy of the seawater baths (Cyn. 424–6).

Aricia, Hipponium, Elea, Sicily: These were all well-known stops on the journey south. So Grattius' shift to Sicily (Trinacria, 430), to a grotto with bituminous springs, sacred to Vulcan (431–4)[33] would not come as a surprise to an educated and traveled Roman audience. Those who come there to have their dogs healed, he reports, make a prayer to Vulcan, asking for peace, assistance, and admission to the fountains (of bituminous oil), provided they are not guilty of something that should be punished with exclusion from sacred space and the presence of the god (437–41). The prayer is to be repeated three times and accompanied by sacrifices involving incense and branches (441–6). This is a clear reference to guilt not as the cause of the illness,[34] but as a reason one might be prevented from entering sacred space and participating in sacred rituals.

From the cave comes the priest, in the midst of flames,[35] thus confirming the presence of the god (444–7), and carrying his olive bough.

---

[31] It is also the place where gold Orphic tablets were discovered (cf. G. Pugliese Carratelli, Le lamine d'oro 'orfiche'; Milan 1993).

[32] Cf. Nutton 1970 on the medical school at Velia; Burkert Lore 280, n. 13; Cicero ad Fam. 7.20 (S-B 333). In Velia Cicero claims to have acquired a medical text on overeating. The head of the guild of physicians was the φώλαρχος, "Lair-Leader," (S. Musitelli, PP 35 (1980) 241–55; SEG 30.1225, Kingsley 1995, 225–7) which indicates the hunting origins of the medical guild. Cicero says he prefers the grotto of the Lupercal to the lair of Velia. Cicero regularly stopped at Hipponium after a night spent at Elea (Cicero in Verr. 2.40; ad Att. 16.6).

[33] It seems possible that the Lacus Palici could be the place, but from the description (esp. Diod. 11.89) the Lacus is a plain, and no cave is probable (I have not been able to do the topographical autopsy). However, there can be no doubt that bituminous springs are highly probable near or on volcanoes like Aetna, and certainly such caves did exist. However, I think it more likely that Grattius has given us a geographical veil, deliberately obscuring the place, so that he may describe the ritual he knows very well at Aricia. It is notable that he does not name the site sacred to Vulcan.

[34] The plague descended on the Achaeans from Agamemnon's insult to Apollo's priest. If "guilt" were to be a cause of illness, the dogs presumably would stand in relation to their "guilty" master as the Achaeans stood in relation to Agamemnon. This is not the case here.

[35] Setting bituminous pitch alight would be easy to do, if difficult to control.

He proclaims a prayer like that of the Sybil's *procul, O procul este, profani . . . totoque absistite luco* (Verg. *Aen.* 6.258).

> . . . "Procul hinc extorribus ire
> edico praesente deo, praesentibus aris,
> quis scelus aut manibus sumptum aut in pectore motum est."
>
> *Cyn.* 447–9

"In the presence of the god, in the presence of the altars, I ordain that all go out of the land far from here, who have put their hands to crime or contemplated it in their heart."

Then Grattius vigorously proclaims the rejection of those who have committed a crime – whoever has broken the law concerning a suppliant, murdered for gain, or violated the ancestral gods – together with the promise of the god's vengeance. But from those *cui bona pectore mens est* ("who have a mind good at heart"), the god accepts the offering, and when the fire reaches the sacrifice, his flame-encircled priest returns to his cave (456–9).

He then commands the suppliant to begin the treatment for his animal (461–3) who will recover with the treatment, and the help, of the god:

> Nec mora, si medias exedit noxia fibras,
> his laue praesidiis affectaque corpora mulce:
> regnantem excuties morbum. Deus auctor, et ipsa
> artem aluit natura suam.
>
> *Cyn.* 461–4

Let there be no delay: if the malady has gnawed right into the fibres, bathe with the remedies specified and soothe the suffering bodies: so will you expel the tyrannous disease. The God lends support, and nature herself has fostered her own skilful remedy.

Even practical, pragmatic medicine was applied in a carefully orchestrated religious context. The knowledge so dispensed was acquired through long experiments (*Prudens Experientia*), performed, recorded, and codified by mortals; but the god remained the ultimate source of knowledge. The priests and priestesses gave good advice and practiced the best medicine available, but the petitioners were never to forget that the priests and healers were the agents of the god and that the god was present in the process of healing. An initial priestly command ordered the unworthy to remove themselves: threats of vengeance were made to those with impure hearts, and promises of divine aid for the virtuous. When the altar fire began licking at the offerings, the priest retreated, and the bathing of the animals was begun.

THE DISTINCTION BETWEEN RATIONALIST MEDICINE AND SANCTUARY MEDICINE

Rationalist medicine is not distinguished from sanctuary healing because its rationality was opposed to belief in the gods. It is the context of the treatment, especially the space in which treatment was conducted, that chiefly distinguishes the two types of healing. Beginning with the Hippocratics, the great virtue of rationalist medicine – and its enduring problem – was that it was conducted by a single physician in secular space, where medical treatments were experienced as secular, rationalist actions. Rationalism, of course, carries its own authority, which also must be established through action, performed, as it were, complete with costume if necessary, as many a quack or imposter has known only too well.[36] To establish confidence in himself, each physician had to fulfill his patients' expectations,[37] as well as taking into account a wide variety of their individual experiences and demands.[38]

Sanctuary healing, on the other hand, was conducted in sacred space and was wholly and elaborately performative, as all religious ritual is.

---

[36] For modern physicians, performance is often the essential matter of wearing the white lab coat and stethoscope. There is a University of Iowa radio program on National Public Radio, called *Ask Dr. Science*, which is always introduced by "he knows more than you do," and concluded by Dr. Science himself, intoning, "I have a master's degree. In *Science*." The point of the parody is that the title, Doctor (of *Science*), is one part of the performance identifying someone who "knows more" than other people.

[37] For example, *Prog.* 1; *Acut.* 6; *VM* 1. There are many examples.

[38] Cf. Lloyd (1978, 12–21) on the precariousness of the practice of medicine before the secular rules by which a physician could be judged and his performance contextualized were established.

Confidence in the efficacy of the treatment was not based solely on belief in the god. As the *Iamata* from Epidaurus indicate, not everyone actually arrived as a believer. Ritual in itself conveys a sense of authority and a divine understanding of the cosmos and its workings. Besides, sanctuaries had the advantage of popularity. Crowds of people would always be seeking aid there; their numbers – and the visible successes – were in themselves reassuring.

Thus sanctuary medicine was a sacred performance, whether in the application of rationalist practices or in its use of ritual. The importance of this cannot be overestimated. If we are to understand how sanctuary medicine was practiced, we must recognize that the experience of healing was understood, in the first instance, as "from the god," because the practitioners were identified, by their position in the sanctuary, as priests, attendants, "sons of the god," or some other ritual designation;[39] then by the space in which healing was experienced, the sanctuary itself; and lastly by the particular manner in which it was experienced. Not every illness required an epiphany of the god, and absolute belief or confidence in the god's powers was not prerequisite,[40] although reverent conduct was.[41]

Sanctuary medicine, in addition, had the advantage of a wide range of performative transactions, from the minimalist – but still formal – prescription of herbal remedies to the full ritual panoply of lengthy *incubatio* (sometimes, it would seem, involving surgery), divine epiphanies, or dream interpretation. Sacrifice formed an integral part of the process. Dramatic and musical performances would also have had their place. Sacred space, and sacred performance, were to be seen as the god's way of authorizing, organizing, and practicing medicine.

[39] Cf. Edelstein T 423.23, where Aristagora is operated on by the sons of the god.
[40] Cf. Edelstein T423.3, 4, and 36. No doubt, especially at Epidaurus, an epiphany was a mark of the specialness of one's illness. There must have been considerable expectation, sometimes tantamount to a demand, for such epiphanies. We must not expect patients to be passive in these matters. Consider the degree of trouble Aristagora makes for the people at the Troezen sanctuary (Edelstein 1998, 423.23) when she forces them to send for the god from Epidaurus.
[41] The *Iamata* indicate that irreverent behavior was not uncommon – hence the number of healings that begin with scoffing or expressions of contempt for the god (Edelstein 1998, T. 423.3, 4, 11, 22, 36).

GRATTIUS' *CYNEGETICA* AND DIANA'S SANCTUARY

There is nothing in the surviving Greek literature about hunting that prepares us for Grattius' poem. Although little of his *Cynegetica* concerns preparation for the hunt, and there is nothing at all about the hunt itself, even so the choice of title was not inappropriate. *Cynegetica*, technically speaking, is the Greek term for all things pertaining to hunting, and of this fact Grattius takes full advantage. Treatment of diseases and wounds formed part of hunting cult practice (352–8), as did careful breeding practices (263–5), care of pregnant mothers and their offspring (278–311), and the training of young hounds (326–36). The principles, and many of the specific practices, used on hunting dogs could be transferred to the care and raising of humans. There can be little doubt that these subjects interested Grattius a great deal more than the pursuit of game. This may well have reflected the evolution of cultic concerns from the archaic period to that of Augustus. What had begun as a cult center for the protection and training of the hunter-warrior had become a sacred complex with interests covering the entire span of life and death of both humans and animals.

In genre, Grattius' *Cynegetica* is a hymn, written in hexameters, praising Diana throughout directly (1–23, 493–6), as well as implicitly, as the font of wisdom and knowledge, with Apollo (424–6) and Vulcan (430–64) also receiving honorable mention. It is in addition a didactic poem, not unlike Lucretius' *De Rerum Natura* in that it sets out to teach the reader a good deal about causes, outcomes, conduct and action, all of which form religious aspects of the hunting cult.

Grattius, in short, used the hymnic form to establish a sacred literary boundary for his teaching. He thus transmitted knowledge gained in the sanctuary in a manner acceptable to Diana, so that his readers, wherever they were, could participate in the transmission of ritual knowledge. He surely would not have been unique in this, and there may well have been other such minor works by moderately skilled Greek and Roman poets. Grattius' work alone survived, partly perhaps because medieval copyists knew about him from Ovid and perhaps also because the *Cynegetica* was a useful practical handbook.

Whatever the reason for its survival, its admittedly moderate poetic merits should not be allowed to obscure the fact that it provides a wealth information about the knowledge and practice of an important Latin cult, besides telling us a good deal about the attitudes of the educated élite toward the realities of contemporary religion and contemporary religious healing.

II

RITUAL HEALING AND THE *MANIAE*

Healing involves a very personal, individual interaction between the sufferer and the divinity (and the divinity's representatives). Illness is unlovely and difficult to clothe in Greek-style myths; healing will require action, and even more, it will often demand change on the part of the sufferer. Galen complained that Asclepius could get his patients to refrain from drinking (Edelstein T. 401) more easily than a human physician could, because of course the instructions of a god were that much more compelling. In this, Galen reveals a great deal about the frustrations confronting physicians (then as now, no doubt), and the power of divine authority – at least as it appeared to one who lacked that authority. Galen tells us, as well, that religious healers were known to make recommendations on dietary regimens. We have seen that at Diana's sanctuary they had a very rational, empirical system for the treatment of skin diseases, providing accurate, therapeutic remedies to petitioners through ritual. In a religious context, asking for help, receiving advice or recommendations, and carrying them out are all ways for an individual to express his or her confidence in the god, and form part of the process of religious healing. How that confidence is created and maintained, and the ways in which worshippers evaluate it as religion and as healing, forms an important aspect of the practice of religion in the sanctuary. Healing illnesses is – or at least many people today think it is – a test of divine power. So now we must ask: beyond skin diseases, what did Diana treat, how did she do so, and can we gain any insight into what people thought about it as a result?

SANCTUARY MEDICINE

A sensible and long-needed reconstruction of the basic elements in the success of sanctuary medicine has been undertaken by Gerald D. Hart, MD, for the Royal Society of Medicine. Hart identifies the primary Asclepian treatment as "conservative or expectant therapy" (2000, 84–5).

> Conservative therapy uses the techniques of adequate rest and relaxation, controlled diet, effective elimination, and exercise combined with reassurance and tincture of time. Many common conditions continue to respond to this routine which completely avoids the complications of medications, invasive procedures and surgery.
>
> Hart 2000, 85.

Hart's thesis can be correlated with the attitude Grattius indicates concerning the care of dogs. After treatment, dogs should be protected from rain and chills, while being kept from hot humid conditions. They should be taken somewhere out of the wind but exposed to the sun when it is gentle (*Cyn.* 419–24). The object is to let the body recover in optimal conditions without interference.

Professor Stephanos Geroulanos has pointed out that good water, enough food, rest, and exercise[1] would by themselves have brought remarkable benefits to many patients at the sanctuary. Hart adds that a simple diet high in fiber would have relieved a variety of gastrointestinal symptoms (2000, 85). The ritual drinking of water leading to a high fluid intake would alleviate digestive disorders and help flush the system of environmental poisons like lead, ingested from food and drinks kept in lead-lined or lead-glazed vessels (2000, 86). Baths and springs would aid the recovery of injuries to muscles, tendons, soft tissues, and joints (2000, 87). The hope given by the combination of abundant votive testimonials, and the reassurance of the healers, supported by the ritual connection to the god, provided "strong doses of hope and optimism" (2000, 87): another significant contribution to the patient's recovery.

---

[1] Stephanos Geroulanos, Ασκληπιός και Ασκληπιεία, published as a supplement to Ελευθεροτηπία, Athens, 2002 (no other date given), and in personal communication.

THE "ACCURSED ITCH"

All these conditions will have been common to every healing sanctuary, whether of Asclepius, Diana, or any other deity. At Aricia, as
elsewhere, there were springs for good water, pools for therapeutic
bathing, and votive testimonials in abundance testifying to Diana's
effective assistance to those in need. There were also certain illnesses
with which Diana was especially associated, sometimes in an ambiguous manner. Perhaps because she cured dogs of scabies, prominent
among such complaints were those that had itching, or other strange,
self-abusive behavior, as a symptom:

> ut mala quem scabies aut morbus regius urget
> aut fanaticus error et iracunda Diana,
> vesanum tetigisse timent fugiuntque poetam
> qui sapiunt; agitant pueri incautique sequuntur.
>
> Horace *Ars Poetica* 453–6

*as when a filthy itch goads a man, or the "royal disease," or the crazed error and
enraged Diana, those who know fear to touch a lunatic poet and run away from him,
small boys tease and rashly pursue him.*

There are three or four related illnesses brought together here, linked
by one particular symptom, a peculiar behavior that involves itching
or twitching. First, we have the *mala scabies*. *Scabies*, the same word
that Grattius uses for the mange (409), but in this case it clearly refers
to something that afflicts a human being.[2] Then there is the "royal"
disease, jaundice.[3] Jaundice causes yellowing of the skin, and itching
is one symptom of it when the bile ducts are blocked. The yellowing of the skin and the slow destruction of the liver are caused by an
accumulation of acids and cholesterol that would normally be elimi-
nated into the intestine.[4] Thus both scabies and jaundice produce the

---

[2] It would have been difficult to distinguish between the various causes of an itch, apart
from obvious causes such as lice, which the healers at the Asclepieia understood perfectly
well (Edelstein T. 423.28).

[3] Cf. Brink, ad loc.; Pliny *NH* 22.114; and Celsus 3.23.

[4] See "jaundice," in *Fitzpatrick's Dermatology in General Medicine*, 6th ed., vol. 2, I. M.
Freedberg et al., eds. New York, 2003, 1614–15, on itching and skin discoloration as
diagnostic symptoms for jaundice (cirrhosis) when the bile ducts are blocked.

behavioral contortions and lacerated, scabby skin (in the case of those with jaundice discolored as well) of people who are constantly scratching themselves, something that would indeed make the sufferers look "odd," especially to children.

Third, there is *fanaticus error et iracunda Diana*. What kind of *error* is this, and why is Diana angry? Clearly Horace is describing an affliction that makes individuals look scary and crazy by their behavior. Brink interprets *fanaticus error* as "religious mania," that is, an obsessive madness arising from religious beliefs or practices. It is also an error in the sense of "wandering in one's wits." It was especially the fugitive wandering of someone pursued by the Furies. Orestes' flight to Aricia was the paradigm of *fanaticus error*. That is the element connecting it to the goddess' anger, for the mania and Diana's displeasure were equivalent.

It is important to recognize that here Diana's "anger" is both a description of the cause and a metaphor for something (or someone) heated and inflamed. Grattius' vivid description of the inflammation of scabies as *ira . . . morbi* ("the anger of the disease"; *Cyn.* 418) shows *ira* referring to the real physical condition, inflammation from infection, but, as Horace indicates, it could equally well be also applied to a condition that we would call mental illness, an "inflammation" of the mind. It is in this sense that, according to Brink, it functions as a kind of introduction to the fourth illness, the madness of the poets. "H[orace] interprets Democritus' and Plato's notion of divine possession: inspiration is like an infectious or frightening disease."[5] Although Democritus and Plato were not the only sources of the notion, Horace *is* talking about divine possession, and this passage begins the conclusion of his poetic essay on writing poetry. In that conclusion the poet is compared to Empedocles, who threw himself into Aetna's cauldron (*AP* 465–6; came out alive, and at some point became a god, by his own account *KRS²* 399), and was a madman (*certe furit, AP* 472).

Madness is an affliction of the moon, a kind of "lunacy," and, as Brink reminds us (1971, 422), Diana, as the moon, was held particularly

---

[5] Brink, 1971 ad loc.

responsible for it. Lunacy, or rather, lunatic *behavior*, then, is the connection between these afflictions and the *fanaticus error et iracunda Diana*. As part of Horace's joke, the children pursue the sufferer like cut-price Furies. Orestes and his Furies were part of Diana's cult, and *error* – deviation from a normal path (whether real or metaphysical), but also obsessive behavior, unsteady movement, derangement of the mind[6] – was a matter of great concern to Diana Trivia. *Fanaticus* was particularly applied to votaries who behaved in crazy or strange ways (*OLD s.v. fanaticus*) – even though the reason for their strangeness could be epilepsy or other physical defects that perhaps brought on mania.

Strangeness of behavior was certainly characteristic of the *rex nemorensis*, the priest whose ritual commemorated Orestes' crazed killing of Thoas, which was itself inspired by Apollo. *Furor*, madness, was the illness that was the manifestation of the Furies' relentless pursuit of Orestes, and started him on the wanderings that led him to Aricia in search of a release from that *furor*. It is the madness of guilt; of the sense of having violated the most basic laws of gods and mortals. His murder of Thoas – a direct result of Apollo's oracle having sent him to steal the *xoanon* (Servius *ad Aen.* 2.116) – was an act that proved the madness. The inspiration of the gods had always manifested itself in bizarre, even lunatic, behavior. So *fanaticus error* in turn is readily connected to the poet's peculiar conduct. Street urchins mock the poet, and "those who know" (*qui sapiunt*) take off in the opposite direction. "Those who know" are afraid of contagion, as Brink points out. Horace's humor embraces all forms of contagion, whether due to "catching" a nasty itch, uncouth behavior, or poetic inspiration.[7]

---

[6] Obsessive behavior, or "unsteady movement of the head or eyes," is an *error* (*OLD s.v. error* 1b), as is "a derangement of the mind" (*OLD s.v. error* 4), and these are aspects of "a deviation from one's path" (*OLD s.v. error* 3) or "a departure from right principles" (*OLD s.v. error* 6).

[7] The context of the "crazy inspired poet" is ironic for Horace. Nevertheless, beneath the irony Horace places poetic inspiration alongside *fanaticus error* and *iracunda Diana* as an affliction avoided by right-thinking people. Inspiration of some kind was associated with the cult (Ovid *Ex Pont.* 1.1.41–2).

SANCTUARY MEDICINE AND THE HUMORAL
THEORY OF DISEASE

It is a generally accepted view that sanctuary healers would never have used the humoral theory of disease for diagnosis. Jacques Jouanna, in his study of Hippocratic medicine, presents the most comprehensive exposition (1999, 181–209) of the view that the rationalism of Hippocratic medicine and the practice of religious healing were antithetical. He relies entirely on the assumption that sanctuary healers *necessarily*, and in all cases, assigned cause of disease to the god and insisted on divine intervention as the only cure. Yet as we have seen, rationalist treatments were used for dogs with scabies, and Horace speaks of scabies as one of those diseases that cause crazy behavior in humans. Scabies could refer to any number of eczemas, eruptions, rashes, scabs, poxes, or ulcers on the skin, their causes ranging from infection, inheritance, and allergies to viruses or diseases of certain organs,[8] as with jaundice. Obviously, humans could be treated with ointments and baths, just as dogs were, and there is no reason to suppose that at Diana's sanctuary humans did not receive the same sort of informed, intelligent care as was given to animals.

We can assume, then, that if empirical remedies (medications, baths, diet, etc.) were available for the treatment of other ailments than skin problems, they would have been employed. Moreover, Hippocratic insights – most famously set forth in *Airs Waters Places* – into the environmental conditions that could encourage or discourage disease were also known and applied at the sanctuary. As we have seen, part of the treatment for a dog's scabies involved careful monitoring of ambient temperature, exposure to wind and humidity, and the use, as well as the regulation, of the sun to support the process of healing (*Cyn.* 418–20).

---

[8] The list of causes of eczemas is long: allergies (external and internal), cutaneous infection, funguses, viruses, inherited conditions, et al., cf. S. R. Stevens, K. D. Cooper, K. Kang, "Eczematous Disorders, Atopic Dermatitis, and Ichthyoses," in *ACP Medicine, 2004–2005 Edition*, a publication of the American College of Physicians, D. C. Dale and D. D. Federman, eds., New York, 2004, 446–64.

In fact, we have no reason to suppose that sanctuary healing was in any way hostile to the findings of rationalist medicine, the theory of humors included. Or rather, the theory of humors especially. The source of this theory was a religious cosmology, propounded by Empedocles,[9] a physician and philosopher[10] and a kind of self-proclaimed shaman or magician (KRS^2 345). Like Alcmaeon of Croton, who advanced a similar medical theory of balancing elements, Empedocles formed part of the extraordinary efflorescence of philosophical and religious thought in southern Italy during the late sixth and early fifth centuries. His theory that the universe is made up of four elements (earth, air, fire, water), combined by Love or broken asunder by Strife (KRS^2 346–82), was the main foundation on which Hippocratic medicine was built.[11] Sometimes Empedocles uses κότος, ill will, vengeance (*LSJ s.v.* κότος) for the force that causes all things to separate, the opposite of φιλότης, love (KRS^2 355.7–8). The Latin for κότος would be *ira*, which is often translated "anger" but can be ill will (*OLD s.v. ira* 2). *Ira* may then have been an accepted Latin translation of Empedocles' κότος, especially in medical contexts, as Grattius' description of a contagious infection that kills the entire pack shows:

> Quod siue a Stygia letum Proserpina nocte
> extulit et Furiis commissam ulciscitur iram . . .
>
> *Cyn.* 373–4

[9] "[Empedocles'] views on physiology and anatomy may to some extent have been conclusions based on observation, and a place was found for them in his physical theory. This theory aimed to be all-inclusive, extending from the structure of the cosmos to the simplest forms of life, but Empedocles also had an interest in some of the details for their own sake. . . . Although Empedocles ranked healing as one of the four highest careers, promised remedies, and was expected to provide them, it need not be assumed that he practiced medicine as a *techne*. The place he was later given in the history of medicine as a doctor of repute is probably due to the direct influence his physical theories had on medical science" (Wright 1981, 14). See 9–14 generally for the analysis of the ancient evidence concerning Empedocles as both physician and magician. Jouanna (1999, 262–4) takes his claim to be a physician seriously.

[10] Galen cites him as one of the great physicians from Sicily (*On the Therapeutic Method*, 1.1).

[11] For a clear discussion of the intellectual development of the theory of humors, see Longrigg 1993, 47–81. Jouanna attributes the entire theory to a "leap of the imagination" (1999, 315) by some anonymous physician after observing the flow of liquids from the body.

Whether Proserpina has brought death from the Stygian night and, having entrusted her vengeance (ira) *to the Furies, she exacts retribution . . .*

Empedocles' almost epic vision of strife, vengeance, love as the forces of the universe, working on and with four elements – air, fire, earth, and water – or humors[12] made his cosmology both vivid and persuasive. As a medical theory, the correspondence between its cosmological dimension and its practical application seemed to be in itself a proof of its validity. The body was the microcosm to the macrocosm of the universe. By studying the body, one studied the cosmos and the divine.[13] Simplicius records a fragment of Empedocles' poetry which described this theory using the metaphor of painting:

ὡς δ' ὁπόταν γραφέες ἀναθήματα ποικίλλωσιν
ἀνέρες ἀμφὶ τέχνης ὑπὸ μήτιος εὖ δεδαῶτε,
οἵτ' ἐπεὶ οὖν μάρψωσι πολύχροα φάρμακα χερσίν,
ἁρμονίῃ μείξαντε τὰ μὲν πλέω, ἄλλα δ' ἐλάσσω,
ἐκ τῶν εἴδεα πᾶσιν ἀλίγκια πορσύνουσι,
δένδρεά τε κτίζοντε καὶ ἀνέρας ἠδὲ γυναῖκας
θῆράς τ' οἰωνούς τε καὶ ὑδατοθρέμμονας ἰχθῦς
καί τε θεοὺς δολιχαίωνας τιμῇσι φερίστους·
οὕτω μή σ' ἀπάτη φρένα καινύτω ἄλλοθεν εἶναι
θνητῶν, ὅσσα γε δῆλα γεγάκασιν ἄσπετα, πηγήν,
ἀλλὰ τορῶς ταῦτ' ἴσθι, θεοῦ πάρα μῦθον ἀκούσας.
Simplicius *in Phys.* 159.27 = KRS[2] 356[14]

As when painters are decorating offerings [i.e., votive tablets], men through cunning well skilled in their craft – when they actually seize pigments of many colours in their hands, mixing in harmony more of some and less of others, they produce from

---

[12] Cf. the Hippocratic work *The Nature of Man*, 11. The number of humors varies according to authors. Alcmaeon assumed an indefinite number, whereas the various authors of the Hippocratic corpus often recognized only three: blood, phlegm, and bile (Phillips 1973, 48).

[13] "Empedocles' theory of cyclic succession for the first time provides a place for this otherworldliness within a fully philosophical system" (O'Brien 1969, 250). O'Brien, however, acknowledges (250, n. 1) that he is ignoring the religious philosophy of Pythagoras, because "Pythagorean 'philosophy' does not seem to me directly comparable with the philosophy of Empedocles and other major Presocratic thinkers." See Burkert's magisterial study of Pythagoreanism (1972) for a much wider view of religious philosophy.

[14] The text and translation are those of Kirk, Raven, and Schofield.

them forms resembling all things, creating trees and men and women, beasts and birds and water-bred fish, and long-lived gods, too, highest in honour: so let not deception overcome your mind and make you think there is any other source of all the countless mortal things that are plain to see, but know this clearly, for the tale you hear comes from a god.

Empedocles' metaphor illustrates the workings of the universe: the four elements are mixed together like paint, in a multitude of ways to produce the cosmos. Mixing is the process through which the universe functions. This is the origin of the humors, the elements whose mixture, when balanced, produces health, and when unbalanced, disease. The cosmos is divine; disease is part of the working of the cosmos. Empedocles removed the gods as direct causes of disease but not from the explanation of disease as a whole. And particularly, as part of the divine cosmos, the gods are still the source for that deductive or philosophical knowledge that allows humans to understand the mixing.

The fact that man had to use his rational faculties to learn it, and practice it, did not make it any less divine in origin. Such knowledge was not per se antithetical to the practice of healing in the sanctuary; indeed, as it was divinely derived knowledge, it would be particularly valued. There is, therefore, no reason why Hippocratic medicine, in all its complexity, including humoral theory, could not be practiced in a sanctuary by sanctuary healers. Nor is there any reason to suppose that treatment according to humoral theory had to be separated from ritual. As we have seen in Grattius' description of suppliants approaching Vulcan, rational treatment could quite naturally be offered within a ritual context.

DIAGNOSIS BY METAPHOR AND ANALOGY

The humors were the most useful, and expansively adaptive, metaphor bequeathed by Empedocles to his successors. Metaphor and analogy were the means by which Hippocratic physicians deciphered processes hidden from the naked eye. Anything visible was potentially a useful analogy. Central to the theory of the humors, and therefore to the ancient rationalist approach to disease, however, is the analogy of cooking.[15] A healthy state is one in which the humors have been properly blended (*krasis*) and cooked (*pepsis*), and the result is a visible product, the healthy body. When there was imbalance, manifesting itself in an ill body, Hippocratic medicine tried to heal by reinstating the correct balance on the Empedoclean model.

Once metaphor and, especially, analogy are accepted as a means of reading and interpreting the invisible processes of nature at work in the body, then the range of analogies is limited only by the imagination and conviction of the practitioners.[16] Grattius used the image of "deformed pleasure" to describe scabies in dogs. It is a diagnostic description as well as an elegant figure of speech. The animal's body is deformed by the injury of the scratching, and its sensibility – that is, its understanding of what is pleasurable and implicitly beneficial – is deformed, too. Furthermore, its behavior is deformed, because this scratching leads not to relief, but to death. The image of deformed pleasure crystallized knowledge about this disease, and it was the result of the same kind of observation as was used for Hippocratic diagnosis.[17]

Deformity, not in its crude modern sense, but in Grattius' sense of a deviance from what is normal, offers a definition of the presence of disease.

... πρῶτον μὲν τὸ πρόσωπον τοῦ νοσέοντος, εἰ ὅμοιόν ἐστι τοῖσι τῶν ὑγιαινόντων, μάλιστα δέ, εἰ αὐτὸ ἑωυτῷ· οὕτω γὰρ ἂν εἴη ἄριστον, τὸ δὲ ἐναντιώτατον τοῦ ὁμοίου δεινότατον.

Hipp. Prog. 2

First [the physician must examine] the face of the patient, to see if it is like the faces of healthy people, and especially if it is like its normal self; for this would be the best sign, and the most unlike its normal self the worst.

---

[15] "The fields from which Greek physicians drew visible evidence in order to deduce by analogy the internal functioning of the human body were quite varied, among them plants, animals, and arts; but cooking in the broad sense of the term remained the preferred field of reference" (Jouanna 1999, 319; cf. the entire section on analogy, Jouanna, 317–22).

[16] Sontag (1990), in a justly famous argument, attacks metaphorical thinking about illness (first cancer, then AIDS). She is certainly right about the power of metaphors to distort thinking as well as to illuminate it.

[17] Cf. Jouanna (1999, 293–303), who provides an excellent account of the very complex observations made by the physician.

Fanaticus error was another descriptive metaphor for illness as deviance from the norm, one which is also associated with Diana. *Error* was deviance. Related to these is a third, *iracunda Diana*, the enraged goddess. Grattius' vivid description of the inflammation of scabies as *ira . . . morbi* ("the anger of the disease"; *Cyn.* 418) is echoed by Horace's *iracunda Diana*. The anger of the goddess is not in either case *necessarily* a sign of pollution even if, as in the case of Orestes, it could be. The anger should be seen rather as something more like the Empedoclean κότος, an ill will that is tearing the person apart. The Furies are another externalization of the same idea. *Iracunda Diana* was a very old idea, that the goddess in her rage at some violation was vengeful toward the individual. It was also a metaphor for the condition that causes an inflamed mind, and encompasses the Hippocratic notion of excessive heat as a sign of imbalance, and therefore, of illness. It is a mistake to suppose that sanctuary healers were *compelled* by the metaphor to shift the blame for the illness onto the goddess. Grattius, when he speaks of the anger of the disease or the vengeance of Proserpina, in a context in which rationalist treatments were sought and provided, makes clear that the old metaphors could enable healers to think about disease in quite modern ways.

We must not assume, either, that sanctuary healers were confined only to the metaphors and analogies used by rationalist physicians. It is a plausible supposition that in their efforts to understand and describe disease, the healers in Diana's sanctuary made use of deformity and deviance as one set of *working* metaphors (but not the only one). They were a means of identification, and a category indicating the need for a certain kind of treatment. Because the *ira* of infection needed to be soothed, so the *furor* and other crazy behaviors also needed treatment. At the same time it is important to reiterate the fact that, although metaphors were a useful instrument for describing and interpreting symptoms, they did not stand in the way of, much less replace, physical remedies or healing practices when these were available. For sanctuary practitioners, metaphors and analogies made sense of visible symptoms that were the result of invisible processes of disease in the body. The application of such metaphors to a specific range of symptoms led, often by analogy, to treatment.

MAKING AND METAPHORS

There are two passages from Republican grammarians concerning Aricia that appear to contain references to a type of healing ritual directed toward "deformity."

MANIAS Aelius Stilo dicit ficta quaedam ex farina in hominum figuras, qua turpes fiant, quas alii maniolas appellent. Manias autem, quas nutrices minitentur parvulis pueris, esse larvas, id est manes deos deasque, quod aut ab inferis ad superos emanant, aut Mania est eorum avia materve. Sunt enim utriusque opinionis auctores.

Festus L 114 (P129)

Aelius Stilo says that "maniae" are certain figures made from pastry into the shapes of human beings, to produce those deformed objects which others call "maniolae." He says, however, that the "maniae" that nurses use to threaten small children are evil spirits, that is the male and female gods, the manes, either because they emanate from the underworld to the upper world, or because Mania is their grandmother or mother. For there are authorities for each view.

MANIUS Egeri\<us lucum\> Nemorensem Dianae consecravit, a quo multi et clari viri orti sunt, et permultos annos fuerunt; unde [et] proverbium: "multi Mani Ariciae." Sinnius Capito longe aliter sentit. Ait enim turpes et deformes significari, qua Maniae dicuntur deformes personae. et Arici[n]ae genus panni {? panis}[manici] fieri; quod †manici† appelletur.

Festus L 128 (P124)

Manius Egerius, from whom many distinguished men were descended, and continued to be for many years, consecrated the forest Grove to Diana; whence the proverb: "many Mani are at Aricia." Sinnius Capito has a quite different opinion. For he says that the ugly and deformed are indicated, in as much as "maniae" are said to be deformed individuals. And at Aricia, he says, a kind of ?bread [tattered cloth] is made; which is called †manici†.

Aelius Stilo (late second century B.C.E.) was one of the earliest grammarians at Rome, the teacher of Varro (who quotes him often) and of Cicero. Sinnius Capito (first century B.C.E.), likewise a grammarian, was a younger contemporary of Varro. They agree that *maniae* were deformed or ugly individuals and were also pastry figures, like ill-made gingerbread men. These pastry *maniae* were

closely associated with Aricia.[18] They appear to be the result of com-
bining the metaphors of deformity with a more homely variant of
Empedocles' metaphor of the painter and the Hippocratic analogy of
cooking. Instead of badly mixed paints, the *maniae* were badly mixed
flour and water, baked badly with fire and air (equivalent to the four
cosmological elements: earth, water, fire, air). Thus an "ugly" pastry
figure could very well illustrate the Empedoclean/Hippocratic theory of disease in the particular metaphor of the sanctuary, that of
deformity.

There is supporting evidence for the extensive use of such pastry
figures from Aricia itself. An inscription locates certain *horrea Sempronia*, Sempronian granaries, in the sanctuary (*CIL* XIV 4190). These
have always been something of a puzzle, even when it was supposed
that the granaries provided food for the suppliants and patients.[19] If
grain was constantly required to supply the sanctuary bakery, which
produced innumerable *maniae* for ritual purposes, then the presence
of these granaries would make sense.

It would also go a long way to explain why the attacks on Octavian
harped on the grandfather who first owned an *unguentarium*, then
latterly a bakery, and who was also a money changer. All three would
have been closely associated with the working of the sanctuary. A
bakery in the sanctuary that turned out *maniae* would have been very
profitable indeed, and no doubt bakeries in the city of Aricia were
delighted to provide their own imitations of the *maniae* to anyone
who wanted to buy them. More important, the sacred use of such a
bakery, to produce figures meant to represent deformed or diseased
individuals, illuminates the meaning of Cassius of Parma's insult to
Octavian's Arician grandfather:

[18] The connection between the children's bogeymen and the *manes* would be due to the
accretion of common usage. The fact that the *maniae* were deformed – that that was their
function in the ritual – means that a sense of awfulness, of evil, of that which must be
avoided, was part of their nature. It is not surprising, then, that, having been associated
with the *manes*, the spirits of the dead, they were then identified with the *larvae*, the
evil spirits of the dead, the bogeymen of Latin religion, or that nurses would threaten
children with them.

[19] Cf. Scheid 1980. Marius captured grain from Aricia when he was trying to starve out
Rome (Appian *BC* 1.69).

Materna tibi farina est ex crudissimo Ariciae pistrino; hanc finxit manibus collybo decoloratis Nerulonensis mensarius.

Suet. *Div. Aug.* 4.2

Your mother's farina *came out of the most primitive bakery in Aricia; the Nerulonean money-changer kneaded her into shape with hands filthy from coin-handling.*

Farina (meal or flour) is used as we would use "clay" to describe the substance of the body (*OLD s.v. farina* 1b). This is, of course, what the *maniae* did: they represented the substance of the body in pastry. *Crudus* means, fundamentally, uncooked, raw, and it is applied in that meaning to both food (the *farina*) and bricks (the bakery). It is possible that the bakery, by ritual requirement, had to be very primitive, but, because primitivism was part of the image of barbarism cultivated by the sanctuary, anything in the sanctuary could be mocked as "primitive" if need be. So Atia was supposed to be deformed by coming from a mud-brick bakery and, by association, with being "uncooked," deformed by a process of bad mixing and inadequate baking. *Finxit* is slyly coarse, suggesting sexual congress in the kneading or shaping of pastry. And of course, her father "made" her with hands filthy from coin-handling, which implies that wealth he accumulated in banking allowed him to marry the patrician Julia. Cassius was both vicious and very clever.

THE THEORY OF THE *MANIAE* IN ITS THERAPEUTIC APPLICATION

If the illness was diagnosed as the result of the imbalance of humors and the *mania* represented the patient in that condition, then the intuitive cure is to undo the mixture and remix. We can speculate that a ritual involving the *maniae* could then enact the Hippocratic rebalancing of the humors in terms of baked goods. Such speculation has good contemporary cultural justification: if the deformed pastry *maniae* were dissolved, broken down, crushed, or in some way reduced to apparent elements in the process of a ritual, the patient could then participate in a ritual remixing that would lead to the rebalancing of the elements. The ritual remixing might involve the making of a new, improved pastry.

The process could also be internalized, so that once the "deformed" self had been destroyed, the new self could be made through prayer and ritual – which perhaps included bathing, dancing (in ritual dances such as Cynthia was asked to vow, Propert. 2.28.59–60), or watching dramatic performances in the small theater. The making of the new self became what the suppliant must do to be healed. The possibility that such a ritual existed at Aricia becomes more probable because rituals having a similar basis are attested in religious healing both for premodern and modern cultures and religion, and by treatments used in modern biomedicine.

The rhetoric of transformation achieves its therapeutic purpose by creating a disposition to be healed, evoking experience of the sacred, elaborating previously unrecognized alternatives, and actualizing change in incremental steps.

Csordas 1996, 94.

Illnesses that were treated with dietary prescriptions would be especially suited to the imagery of the *maniae*. The pastries could have helped patients to understand the theory behind their illness and better come to understand what to do about it, to cooperate in their own recovery, engaging mind with the body in the process of reconstructing a healthy self. In modern biomedicine this process is called "imaging" and is used in sports medicine, cancer therapy, and a multitude of other healing situations.[20] The ritual dissolution and reformation would have led patients who could be treated by diet toward the "disposition to be healed," after which they would have been psychologically ready for the life changes involved in the treatment prescribed in terms of rebalancing the humors. No one would have

---

[20] Imagery in ritual healing: for example, Navajo healing with sand painting for the construction and reconstruction of the world (Luckert, 157–8); Catholic charismatic healing with images of the chalice or the Virgin Mary (Csordas 1994, 128–9); with the planting of a tree for long life and the construction of fences to contain evil spirits in Papua, New Guinea (A. Strathern and P. J. Stewart, *Curing and Healing*, Durham, NC, 1999, 82–3; Lademan and Roseman, passim). Imagery in modern nursing, pain management, physical therapy, dermatology, surgery: E. R. Korn and K. Johnson, *Visualization: The Uses of Imagery in the Health Professions*, Homewood, IL, 1983. The use of imagery in psychotherapy: H. Leuner, *Guided Affective Imagery: Mental Imagery in Short-Term Psychotherapy*, Stuttgart and New York, 1984.

been in any degree worse off than under the care of a Hippocratic physician.

AT THE GATES OF THE UNDERWORLD

The *maniae*, as Aelius Stilo's explanation makes clear, were associated with the *manes* and the underworld, an association no doubt validated by the folk etymology connecting *maniae* and *manes*. The *maniae* would potentially have been most vividly and intensely part of a religious experience in the treatment of mental illnesses: *fanaticus error et iracunda Diana*. This was a condition like that of being pursued by the Furies, if one took the metaphor in a literal, religious sense. In the new, Empedoclean view, however, it was a tearing apart of the fabric of the mind. Both ideas existed without displacing each other. Orestes is the paradigm. The use of his bones by Octavian confirms Servius' account that, at the sanctuary, Orestes' function was to embody the guilt, and *furor*, induced by terrible crimes against the family or the gods. At the sanctuary, he was released from his madness. His release must be associated with the rite of the *rex nemorensis*. The death of the old flawed *rex* (flawed because, even when he was victorious, he was fleeing his own past slavery, and flawed at the end when, through his own weakness, he lost the combat) and the renewal or rebirth embodied by the new, vigorous, priest-king between them form the central feature in the ritual. As founded by Orestes, the ritual releases the challenger from the guilt occasioned by the acts that made him a fugitive, in imitation of the release Orestes had found after the murder of his mother and King Thoas and the desecration of the *xoanon*. The priest was reborn, or perhaps reincarnated, as the challenger was transformed into the new *rex nemorensis*.

If the dissolution of the *maniae* represented the death of the body required by the ritual of the *rex nemorensis*, then that ritual could be adapted to be used by many others. Who would those others be? Certainly, if we take Orestes' story seriously, and I think we must, the illnesses that could thus have been treated would be those described by *furor*, by madness, lunacy, and craziness in all its forms. That people suffering in this way were treated at the sanctuary is suggested by a passage from the *Aeneid*. We have already seen that Vergil was deeply aware of the cult of Diana and that he opened book 6 of the *Aeneid* with an explicit reference to the Arician sanctuary's golden roof (*Aen.* 6.13). As Aeneas, the exile, tries to learn his way, Vergil gives us an idea of what the metaphor of deformity could mean in the sanctuary and how the *maniae* and the underworld were connected. With the Sibyl's aid, Aeneas begins his own journey to the underworld.

> uestibulum ante ipsum primisque in faucibus Orci
> Luctus et ultrices posuere cubilia Curae,
> pallentesque habitant Morbi tristisque Senectus,
> et Metus et malesuada Fames ac turpis Egestas,
> terribiles uisu formae, Letumque Labosque;
> tum consanguineus Leti Sopor et mala mentis
> Gaudia, mortiferumque aduerso in limine Bellum,
> ferreique Eumenidum thalami et Discordia demens
> uipereum crinem uittis innexa cruentis.
> in medio ramos annosaque bracchia pandit
> ulmus opaca, ingens, quam sedem Somnia uulgo
> uana tenere ferunt, foliisque sub omnibus haerent.
> multaque praeterea uariarum monstra ferarum,
> Centauri in foribus stabulant Scyllaeque biformes
> et centumgeminus Briareus ac belua Lernae
> horrendum stridens, flammisque armata Chimaera,
> Gorgones Harpyiaeque et forma tricorporis umbrae.
>
> *Aen.* 6.273–89

At the very entrance and in the first narrow forecourt of the underworld, Grief and avenging Cares have placed their beds: And pale Diseases dwell here, and morose Old Age, and Fear, and ill-counselling Hunger, and shameful Need, shapes terrible to look at, Death and Hardship; then Sleep, Death's own brother; and the Evil Rejoicings of the mind, and on the threshold opposite, death-bringing War, the iron cells of the Furies, and maddened Strife, her snakish hair bound with bloody ribands. In the middle a huge dark elm spreads out its branches and ancient arms, where what the common people call empty Dreams have their resting place and cling beneath every leaf. And besides there are many monstrous kinds of various wild beasts that have their stables at the doors: centaurs and biform Scyllas, hundred-handed Briareus, the Beast of Lerna, hideously hissing, the Chimaera armed with fire, Gorgons and Harpies, and the form of three-bodied Geryon's shade.

Here are words and ideas that echo the ritual metaphors at the sanctuary. All are deformities, and agents of deformity; they are the cause of affliction, and the afflictions themselves. Like the *maniae, terribiles uisu formae* are deformed beings. *Mala mentis Gaudia* points to *fanaticus error* and *deformis dulcedo*. Diseases – of course – are there at the gate of Orcus, and death; fear and old age; war and the caged Furies – the allusion is to Orestes – and mindless Strife. Then there are the monsters with freakish bodies, too many heads, bodies weirdly assembled from different animals, imperfect, deformed, defective. Strife must always, at one level, bring to mind Empedocles' vision of the universe torn apart by Strife and reunited by Love; monsters must likewise remind us of Empedocles' monsters, still working through their creation to a better form. Thus the extraordinary range of meaning implicit in Empedocles' cosmological theories[21] is here worked out in the familiar metaphors and landscape of Diana's Arician sanctuary. Vergil has these deformed figures, these monsters, spread their pallets at the gate of the underworld, like patients in an anteroom waiting to be treated.

Once we recognize the allusion to the Arician sanctuary and the ritual metaphors with their Empedoclean ancestry, we can understand two further details of this passage. Vergil speaks of *vana Somnia*, empty Dreams (6.283). If the healers in Diana's sanctuary also practiced incubation as was regularly done at the Asclepian centers, there were many indeed whose dreams were empty or vain, as the stelae at Epidaurus tell us.[22] This tree is where those hopeless dreams lodged. Another important point is Aeneas' fear (*trepidus formidine*; 6.290). *Formido* is both the

---

[21] Cf. *KRS²* 402, where Empedocles speaks of "the unfamiliar place where Murder and Anger and tribes of other Deaths... [they] wander in darkness over the meadow of doom." And *KRS²* 405; or 406, "There were Earth and far-seeing Sun, bloody discord and serene Harmonia, Beauty and Ugliness, Haste and Tarrying, lovely Truth and blind Obscurity." 407: "clothing [sc. the *daimon*] in an alien garment of flesh." In the commentary on these passages, *KRS²* observes, "These disconnected fragments constitute most of the surviving scraps of a passage in which Empedocles seems to have told first of his descent to a place of misery where other fallen *daimones* were assembled, and then of being led to a cave where *daimones* were clothed in alien flesh and made subject to the contrary forces which rule mortal existence.... Probably Empedocles was using eschatological myth (of which we have seen evidence in Pythagoreanism) both to give intense expression to his conviction of the alien and pitiful condition of mortal existence, and to bring home as vividly as possible the idea that life is set in more than merely human dimensions of space and time."

[22] Edelstein T. 423.25; and 33. Both patients were eventually healed elsewhere, away from the sanctuary, but it is clear that *not* having a dream in the Abaton was one possibility a patient must anticipate.

condition of fear and the hunter's line strung with red feathers, as a means of scaring animals into a trap. Grattius calls such lines the *metus falsi*, the "false fears" (*Cyn.* 89), but *metus falsi* are also the charms and amulets that make people feel safe against rabies, and the good they do is the comfort they give (*Cyn.* 400–7). Thus Aeneas, scared by this waiting room of afflictions, draws his sword, but the Sibyl assures him they have no substance (6.293–4). Aeneas instinctively responds to fear with a useless, although comforting, action.

So this is a brilliant evocation of the troubles assailing the weary occupants of a physician's waiting room, of all the things that terrify ordinary human beings and cause mental derangement. Aeneas must pass them by, for the real defense against these ills is knowledge. It is through knowledge that the self is "remade" and "rebalanced," put on the right path.[23]

Cities, too, can go mad under the pressures of pestilence or war. There is no reason ritual would not have functioned also as a means of dealing with disasters for the city of Aricia. As Homer knew (e.g., *Il.* 1.1–100) any widespread disease that caused death was just such a disaster. For instance, when Grattius describes an infected wound (*Cyn.* 359–61), he uses the word *pernicies*, a source of destruction or ruin (*OLD s.v. pernicies* 1, 2) to describe it. But when he speaks of contagious diseases such as rabies (*Cyn.* 373–7) or the mange (*Cyn.* 418–19) he uses the vocabulary of divine anger and divine revenge. Contagion thus formed a special category of disease that could be particularly marked by the archaic imagery of anger from the gods.[24] Diana's vengeance was particularly associated with the widespread destruction of a community and particularly associated with the *rex nemorensis*, as Ovid makes clear in the quatrain in the *Ars Amatoria* (1.259–62) on the Arician sanctuary that begins with the *rex nemorensis* and ends chillingly with this line

---

[23] Perhaps particularly relevant to the *Aeneid* is Empedocles fr. 410 *KRS*², "Those from whom Persephone receives requital for ancient grief, in the ninth year she restores again their souls to the sun above. From them arise noble kings, and those men swift in strength, and greatest in wisdom; and for the rest of time they are called heroes and sanctified by mankind." This could apply to Aeneas, but it could also apply to Augustus himself, the son of *Mater Aricia*.

[24] It is important to keep in mind that such imagery did not *exclude* rationalist determination of the cause or treatment. Grattius lists three potential sources of the contagion of rabies: Proserpina's vengeful anger (*Cyn.* 373–4); the air (*Cyn.* 375); and the earth itself (*Cyn.* 376–7).

on Diana the Maiden (Virgo) herself: *multa dedit populo uulnera, multa dabit* ("she has given many wounds to the people, and she will give many again"; Ovid, *AA* 1.262[25]).

So the ritual involving the dissolution of the deformed self, when the deformity is seen as a suppurating wound, could have been used for plagues, and, of course, for other disasters of similar dimension, like civil war, for which Vergil uses the plague as the appropriate metaphor and one of the Furies, rising from Stygian darkness, as the force driving the disease (*Georg.* 3.551–2), just as the Furies pursued Orestes the fugitive. The entire passage (*Geor.* 3.478–566) is deeply indebted to Lucretius' account of the plague (*DRN* 6.1090–1286), which in turn relies on Thucydides' description of the plague at Athens (2. 47–52). The resemblance between the plague and civil war lies not only in the indiscriminate destruction both inflict, but also in the way they abolish individual identity as well as all social and moral restraints. Civil war must necessarily bring helplessness, lawlessness, futility, and death (Verg. *Geo.* 1.498–514).

Thus, because Octavian returned to Rome with the (alleged) bones of Orestes and then encouraged the connection between Orestes and himself, we can be reasonably sure that a ritual existed, connected to the *rex nemorensis*, that was thought capable of dealing with the "deformation" of the city caused by civic disaster such as internal war.

FUROR, THE *MANIAE,* AND THE COMMON MAN

However, a ritual that reflected the same pattern at a more cosmologically modest level would be needed to treat the mental disorders that follow individual trauma. I would suggest that the *maniae* offered just that: a ritual that was an imitation of, and participation in, a sacred

---

[25] Ovid carefully delineates Diana's hatred of Cupid's arrows (1.261), which forms the bridge between the *rex* and her vengeance inflicted on communities, "the people." It is useful for his purpose in writing about the hunting of the beloved, but it also suggests that the *rex* could be associated not only with Orestes but also with Virbius/Hippolytus, the beloved, whose crime was sexual, leading to his death, thus justifying Diana's hatred of Cupid's love wounds. Theological clarity and distinction are not to be expected in ritual stories. Orestes and Virbius/Hippolytus were connected, clearly, by the fact that each had done something terrible, thus arousing divine wrath. Either one could be chosen as the paradigm according to its appropriateness case by case.

event, but able to be conducted at any time and at a very personal level. In the same way, Christians use the stations of the Cross, sometimes enacting them fully, sometimes employing them as exercises of the mind and spirit without physical enactment. Orestes, deformed by the *furor* that resulted from his crimes, and the *rex* by his violation of the goddess' laws, would have supplied the mythic model for the rite, while the *maniae* provided the scientific, cosmogonic, model. A parallel treatment, also a development of hunting cult ritual, is found in Navajo healing, particularly in rituals like the Flintway, where the healer draws a complete human figure on a buckskin and the holy Ant-people use the pattern to reassemble the injured person (Luckert 1981, 158). Or again, in the even more prevalent healing rituals that are conducted in a sweat lodge and use sand paintings to transport the patient to the mythical time of human origins, so that he can resurface through the "hole of emergence" in a new form (Luckert 1981, 158). Ritual birth of a new, well-formed self is the goal of all these rituals.[26]

That the destruction of the *maniae* was indeed part of the Arician ritual and the equivalent of dying is suggested by the fact that they were connected (whether rightly or wrongly in linguistic terms) with the *manes*, with the dead of the underworld, as the Festus quotations make clear. A ritual involving the breaking down of the whole into constituent elements would represent the death of the deformed self, a paradigm of a journey to the underworld. The remaking of the pastry would symbolize the process of remaking of the self in a better fashion.[27] Such ritual transformations are consistent with the

---

[26] For a detailed discussion of the history and the science of healing with imagery, see Achterberg 1985, 113–42, for the physiological and biochemical basis for this kind of healing, and 143–60 for the use of imaging in psychotherapy.

[27] Cf. Burkert 1977, 89–114, on the "extraordinary experience" of the mystery cults of Demeter, Dionysus, Isis, and the transformation of the self, frequently represented as a "birth," althrough the experience of the ritual. Plutarch takes the similarity of the verbs τελευτᾶν (to die) and τελεῖσθαι (to be initiated) to signify the similarity of experience (Plut. fr. 178 Sandbach). Plutarch also describes the state of the initiate at the beginning of the mysteries as straying and wandering (πλάναι τὰ πρῶτα καὶ περιδρομαὶ κοπώδεις· "in the beginning there is wandering [πλάναι is the same term used for the planets and the moon, as "wanderers"] and wearisome running around"), which indicates the degree to which Diana's *error*, straying from the path, was simply part of a general definition. Problems that could be addressed by initiation could be understood as "wandering,"

nature of Diana herself as moon goddess – who monthly descends to the underworld but then reappears and grows to her full and proper form.

Such a ritual could assist those who had committed acts of violence in revenge (for whatever reason, political as well as personal), and would particularly include those who had fled a psychologically destructive but legally sanctioned condition such as slavery. A ritual of transformation, involving the birth of a new and better formed self, would help the former slave to come to terms with his or her past, and enter as fully as possible into a new life as freedman or freedwoman.

Praetors, pro-consuls, kings, and Caesars might need it as well when they had to confront the guilt their violence had engendered. The similarity of treatment for the traumas of enslavement or violence would illuminate the connections that brought both senior legates and commanders such as the praetor Livius, Gaius Voconius C.f., and Lucius Licinius L.f. (see Chapter 1) and freedmen such as M. Servilius Quartus (see Chapter 2), all to make their dedications to the same goddess.

THE THEORY OF HUMORS, MYSTICISM, AND THE DEVELOPMENT OF ITALIC CULTS

All this may seem a long way from Hippocratic medicine and the humoral theory, but in fact they remain perfectly compatible. Although what we have here is a ritual supposedly founded by the fugitive Orestes and enacted by an escaped slave, the *rex nemorensis*, nevertheless its cosmology and theology were validated by a philosopher, Empedocles, who called himself an exile, a wanderer, who trusted in "raving Strife" and made that identity part of his philosophical argument.[28] Transformation of the sort implied in this ritual is quite consistent with Empedoclean/Pythagorean mysticism and theories of reincarnation,

---

being in error. For modern instances of ritual healing using hunting cult rituals and involving symbolic death and rebirth, see Luckert on the Navajo Lifeway chants (157–60).

[28] τῶν καὶ ἐγὼ νῦν εἰμι, φυγὰς θεόθεν καὶ ἀλήτης/ Νείκεϊ μαινομένῳ πίσυνος (Of these I too am now one, an exile from the gods and a wanderer, having put my trust in raving Strife; *KRS²* 401).

which are another aspect of the theory of humors: birth and death are merely points in the eternal mingling and interchange of the four elements (*KRS²* 350). It is entirely possible that the development of the ritual in historical times occurred under the influence of Empedoclean and Pythagorean mysticism. Central Italy in the late sixth century, as we have seen, had close connections with the intellectual ferment stirred up by the south Italian philosophers and the medical centers at Croton and Elea. That is not to suggest that Diana's sanctuary borrowed its essential rituals directly from the southern Italian cults or philosophical schools. It is merely to point out that these practices formed part of a wider Italic culture that inevitably were reflected in the sanctuary, in the shape of shared concerns and, particularly, common metaphors and symbols.

RELIGIOUS HEALING IN THE SANCTUARY

The sanctuary of Diana was an ideal place for such healing techniques to develop within the context of established rituals.[29] That the goddess' domain was so perfectly separated from the profane world, and that to approach it required at the least a symbolic journey from the ridge of the crater to the sanctuary by the lake, were both factors that would have contributed to the power of the healing experience. The concealment of the *rex nemorensis* in the woods, and Virbius' untouchability, reinforced the hidden power of the sanctuary's priests and priestesses. Ritual assigned an authoritative name to whatever affliction a patient endured; it also gave that affliction a well-defined place in the events described by religious cosmology. This made the suppliant an active, rather than a passive, participant in a divine process. All those who took part in rituals of this sort, if modern parallels have any force at all, gained a sense of divinely inspired mastery over the conditions that afflicted them.

Diana's concern for women in childbirth – a condition of great danger and vulnerability – was a constant symbol testifying to her gentle care for the most vulnerable and helpless. Yet her cult also

[29] I follow here Achterberg 1985, 154–9.

accepted danger, barbarism, and wildness as part of the world which she watched over. When people came to her at their most vulnerable, often in the throes of suffering long endured, the sanctuary would testify – through its rituals, its iconography, and its mythology – that Diana understood violation, cruelty, and death, and that her rituals were therefore capable of addressing those conditions.

12

CONCLUSION: DIANA AND HER WORSHIPPERS

THE WORSHIPPERS

Diana's sanctuary in the crater was an extraordinary place before man ever came to it. Yet in the end, it is the thousands of men and women who worshipped there who made it a sanctuary, and it must ultimately be seen as an expression of their religious or spiritual needs and beliefs. A scattering only of their names are known to us, mostly through dedicatory inscriptions found in the sanctuary. There were the distinguished men: the praetor Livius, and Lucullus' legates Gaius Voconius and Lucius Licinius; the aristocrats C. Aurelius Cotta, Quintus Hostius Capito, C. Lutatius Pinthia; and the distinguished women Volusia Cornelia, and Prima, the wife of L. Aninius Rufus, an Arician magistrate. Above and beyond these were the emperors and their families, Tiberius, Claudius, Hadrian, and Trajan.

Then there were the less distinguished, although still wealthy men, some possibly *liberti*, like the actor C. Norbanus Sorex, M. Servilius Quartus, M. Acilius Priscus Egrilius Planarius, and a couple, P. Cornelius Trophimus and Lania Thionoe. There were the women: Licinia Chrysarion, whose herm was dedicated by A. Marcus Bolanus; Staia Quinta, a freedwoman; and Fundilia Rufa. One, the nurse Papiria, who dedicated a bronze spearhead, was almost certainly a slave.

Whole cities were involved as well. C. Manlios Acidinos made a dedication on behalf of the people of Ariminum in the third century B.C.E., and in the first century B.C.E. the Abbaitae and the Epictetes, people of Mysia made a dedication for C. Salluvius Naso.

These names and identities, which stretch from the third century B.C.E. to the second century C.E., are important because they must stand in for so many others whom we cannot know. The Arician sanctuary served real people – as individuals, as couples and families, and in larger groups – and was the living creation of thousands of visitors, day after day, whose hopes and needs and expectations centered, however briefly, on this place. Behind each of the names that we can read, we must see the shadows of thousands whom we will never know but whose presence must be acknowledged as part of the reality of Diana's sanctuary.

They must in particular stand in for the many others who did not have the resources to set up a dedication or whose dedications have been lost. Of all those who came to the sanctuary to ask Diana for help or to thank her, many would not have had the resources to dedicate more than a terra-cotta votive. Even that small a token would have been beyond some. Yet Diana would have accepted even the poorest as a suppliant, without requiring pay. Ovid says as much (and implies that this was unusual, and specific to Diana's sanctuary).

> ante deum Matrem cornu tibicen adunco
> cum canit, exiguae quis stipis aera negat?
> scimus ab inperio fieri nil tale Dianae:
> unde tamen vivat, vaticinator habet.
> Ovid *Pont.* 1.1.39–42[1]

When the piper plays on his curved horn before the Mother of the gods, who denies him the coins of a small fee? We know nothing of the sort happens by the authority of Diana; yet her prophet has what he needs to live.

The road leading to the sanctuary was famous for its beggars (Juvenal 4.116–19), and the pastry figures, the *maniae*, suggest that those who could not afford ordinary terra-cotta votives may well have been admitted for treatment notwithstanding. At sanctuaries of Asclepius, our other model for religious centers of healing, the god appears to have accepted whatever payment the patient could afford and was willing to be indulgently amused by the gift, as when a boy suffering from

---

[1] The text of the *Ex Ponto* is that of Owen.

the stone promised him ten dice.[2] Ovid's dry comment implies, however, that Diana's command not to accept fees did not prevent Diana's
sanctuary and the priests and attendants there from doing quite well
from petitioners' gifts.[3] Concerning these gifts, dedications, and offerings, we must not be more cynical than the circumstances warrant.
The exchange of gifts between the goddess and her petitioners was
traditional and part of the inherited system of sacrifice for honoring a deity. In any day and age, no doubt, there were just as many
petitioners who thought they could pay their way to Diana's care as
sanctuary attendants who were willing to accept presents for their
services.

APPROACHING THE SANCTUARY

Leaving the Via Appia just outside of Aricia, a traveler heading for the
sanctuary would turned off to a sturdy paved road that led over the
ridge and sloped gently down the western side of the crater. The road
led directly to the sanctuary, bending slightly around the curve of the
lake to meet the terrace. Above the terrace, visible through the trees,

---

[2] Edelstein T.423.8. It is significant that the Asclepian stelae only incidentally record
ex-voto offerings. Thank-offerings were of course expected in every petition to the
gods, especially when the petitions were favorably received. Yet only seven of the forty-
three separate inscriptions in Edelstein report a dedication of any kind. In three the
payment demanded is part of the treatment (a woman is ordered to offer a silver pig
because she had mocked the healing in the sanctuary, 423.4; the attendant demands the
offering – within a year – as a way of getting a mute child to speak, 423.5; a man who is
paralyzed is told to bring a large stone into the sanctuary, 423.15). In two, the offerings
are demanded when the patients, having left the sanctuary without being healed, were
later healed. The demand for the offering is clearly both a request for payment and a
means of validating the treatment as that of Asclepius (423.25 and 423.33). In a sixth, the
stele records the inscription that was put on an unspecified offering (423.2), and in the
seventh case, a broken goblet was "healed" by the god and then dedicated as a thank-
offering. The inscription for the boy who was inspired to speak by the attendant making
a demand for the thank-offering within the year (423.5) suggests that the demand was
unexpected and that a year was a short amount of time for the sanctuary to set as a
deadline for receipt of payment.

[3] Cf. Parke (1977, 83) on the price of the cake a petitioner had to sacrifice before entering
the temple at Delphi. In the classical period the cake cost approximately one Attic
drachma, or two days' wages for an Athenian juryman. However, Delphi had an interest
in maintaining a certain exclusiveness among those who sought oracles. Diana and
Asclepius had a very different relationship to their worshippers.

the gold roof of the temple would have glimmered in the sun, and its exact image would have been reflected on the lake.

What religious experiences were the worshippers expecting to be able to find there when they came to seek Diana's protection for a safe birth, to ask for help in healing wounds, or to seek assistance in caring for children or animals?

First and always there was the crater itself. This was a sacred landscape, and the evidence of Diana's presence was everywhere, in the woods all around, in the lake below, in the springs that flowed toward the lake and caves that led away from it into the roots of the mountain, and in the sky that crowned it all. The peak of the Alban Mount pointing to the heavens, where Jupiter Latiaris was worshipped in the communal sanctuary of the Latin cities, was visible above the crater's edge. The place was full of meaning for the worshipper long before there were any buildings or sanctuary attendants. Those who came here before the fourth century would have known that this was where the alliances of the Latin cities opposed to Rome had met in a grove where the goddess welcomed warriors who put down their arms, just as she accepted the sacrifices and the ceremonies performed by the young initiates each year.

The *rex nemorensis* had been here from a very early time serving Diana, and perhaps even in historical times he mediated according to his understanding of the goddess' wishes between Diana and the Aricians. It is possible that he advised individuals as well. Slaves would have come to the sanctuary because of him, some to escape slavery by living wild, others because the *rex* guaranteed they could find divine help from Diana even in their lowly state.

Then, at the end of the fourth century, the temple with the gold roof was built, followed by another temple, and then the terrace with its portico and the rooms and niches, the theater, the baths. So by the first century, when C. Aurelius Cotta came to make his dedication, worshippers approaching the sanctuary were confronted by a magnificent Hellenistic complex. This complex redefined space, carefully and deliberately assigning meaning to it both within and without the architectural complex. We cannot tell what meaning came to be attached to each specific area nor how important any specific element was to the religious experience of visitors; but we do know that when someone like Staia Quinta came to the sanctuary, she entered a precinct with layers of complex religious significance expressed through the buildings, their relationship, and their decoration. And there was always the setting.

By the first century B.C.E., it is the wealth of religious meaning in Diana's sanctuary rather than the wealth of its resources that should make the greatest impression on us. Diana herself, as a moon goddess, had an extraordinary range of functions that could be sought in need. Her reputation had been established long ago, in the days when she had been powerful as a patron deity of the Latins; yet Papiria, a slave, could still ask the goddess for help on behalf of the child she cared for – or perhaps for herself – knowing that the goddess had always shown concern for slaves and for infants of all kinds, whether human or animal.

There were ritual purifications of terrible psychological traumas, rituals in which one could destroy the old self and bring together a new being, rituals in which one could learn treatment for skin diseases or wounds; there were prayers for the safety of the beloved and rituals for the pursuit of one's desire; and there were rituals as well that led one to a point of decision, and sacralized the crucial moments in one's life. The Pythagoreans (or those philosophically inclined) could find a Latin expression of their ideas in the ritual of the bough (although how they participated in it we again do not know). There were rituals of thanksgiving, of penance, and of supplication in all forms. Worshippers might participate in ritual baths, processions, a choral dance; they might see a theater performance, listen to the prayers of the priests, or watch the acceptance of sacrifices. Music, especially from flutes and horns, would have accompanied many of these ritual activities, not quite overcoming the racket of barking dogs and noises from other animals who were brought to the goddess. The bakery would bake the *maniae* and perhaps other kinds of baked goods; and at the *unguentaria* ointments and remedies would be prepared. Those who consulted the *vaticinator* would no doubt have a lengthy period of trial and examination before they were granted their prediction or prognosis. Others would be seen by the attendants, learn what they had to do (prayers, ointments, changes of diet, sacrifice), would do it quickly enough, and depart. Many more would simply wait.

CONSULTING THE GODDESS

An individual who had come in need of the goddess' aid would have myriad religious possibilities before her and numerous places within the sacred space defined by the sanctuary to which she might go, depending on her need: the temple, the spring of Egeria, the *nemus*, the baths, the theater, the lake. On arrival, this woman – let us call her Gaia – would have spent time talking with the attendants, possibly with priests or priestesses. The knowledge the attendants gained about her would have influenced the ritual chosen, any prophecies or revelations given during the ritual, and the interpretation of all of these to her afterward. This does not mean that the priests believed any less in the divine source of their revelation or that Gaia was necessarily credulous. The proper application and explication of the rituals in the sanctuary was a part of the sacred duty of a priest or a priestess in such a cult, as was the proper application of knowledge about human beings – another aspect of Grattius' *Prudens Experientia* (*Cyn.* 427). Sacred knowledge was sacred because it had been gained under the auspices of the goddess. Its logic, its practicality, and the fact that it required the practitioners to make human judgments in its application did not render such knowledge any the less divine in origin.

Gaia came in the first place because she had some interest in what the sanctuary had to offer.[4] If she had a vow to make or fulfill, she would undertake one kind of ritual. If she were, like Sulpicia, in pursuit of her Cerinthus, that would be another kind of ritual, surely determined by the priest or attendant's estimation of the likelihood of her success and the nature of her need in the first place. If Gaia was ill, this was a teaching hospital, or the closest the ancient world ever came to such a thing. Here the healers saw the same illnesses in many people (and animals) over long periods of time and could test and apply remedies in sufficient numbers to develop some understanding of the outcome. If Gaia had certain skin ailments, or if she had an abscess or some other condition treatable through surgery, she stood a good chance of having her condition significantly improved. The same could not be said with

---

[4] Confidence she may not have had, to judge from the inscriptions at Epidaurus, where skeptics were common (Edelstein 1998, T423.3; 423.4; 423.11; 423.36).

so much certainty for those around her who were tubercular or who had cancer, bacterial infections, or malaria. Yet some of these, too, may well have at least improved, if only because their bodies, helped by rest, a peaceful environment, good food and water, kindly attention, and religious belief, were better enabled to fight off the illness.

Then there were those among Gaia's companions whose affliction would not improve, and others whose "deformity" was fundamental, whether the result of crippling birth defects, incurable disease, or an irreparable injury.[5] There were epileptics (who, despite the Hippocratic author on *The Sacred Disease*, could not be treated effectively by any method then known); there were also the seriously demented, those fatally ill with infection or virus, and dying – whether old or young. There were those whose desires, whatever they might be, were beyond their capacities, beyond any hopes of fulfillment. Neither rationalist medicine nor religious ritual could change those facts. The ritual of dissolving the *maniae*, however persuasive or hopeful, could not straighten a deformed spine, cure epilepsy, make a slave anything but a slave, or rejuvenate the aged. These patients would emerge in much the same physical and social condition as they arrived, no matter what was done for them.

WHAT DID RITUAL HEALING ACCOMPLISH?

It might well seem, then, that in many cases – perhaps the majority – Diana was likely to offer no more than disappointment in an envelope of religious comfort. It might seem to us that the failure of her medicine would be proof of her inadequacy in general. In this supposition we

---

[5] M. L. Rose's *The Staff of Oedipus: Transforming Disability in Ancient Greece*, Ann Arbor, 2003, on Greek attitudes to disability, raises important questions on how and when conditions are defined as "disabilities" requiring treatment. Her discussion is preliminary, and the subject deserves continued attention. She reminds us, however, that we cannot assume that what for us is clearly a disability (blindness, lameness) would necessarily bring a person to a healer. Asclepius treated one man who had endured a spear tip in his jaw for six years (Edelstein T. 423.12) and another who had had an arrow in the chest, creating a suppurating wound, for a year and a half (Edelstein T. 423.30). We would expect such injuries to be so severely debilitating that treatment would be sought much sooner, if not immediately. Clearly we would be wrong.

would be mistaken. It is where our inherited tradition is so misleading, based as it is on powerful accounts of Jesus healing the blind man, casting out the Gaderene swine, and raising Lazarus from the dead. The Gospels are clear: Jesus cured, and did so with miracles. That does not mean that Asclepius, Diana, or any of the other healing gods before Christianity either proposed to, or were expected to, produce miracles on demand. Ritual healing was not about miracles – although no doubt the occasional miracle did happen, and was widely touted as such afterwards. In cultures where ritual and shamanistic healing are common today and can be studied, it has been shown that the participants do *not* expect miracles and do not abandon their critical judgment as they undergo healing rituals.

Schieffelin, in his most revealing and stimulating study of the performance of a séance among the Kaluli of New Guinea, has shown that the Kaluli were "experienced and critical séance-goers" (1996, 67), and the healer's performance was carefully judged. "At a basic minimum, the songs had to be well composed, poetically well constructed (with proper framing of place-names within a range of poetic devices), well sung, and capable of occasionally moving audience members to tears" (67) if their singers were to be judged competent as healers. The Kaluli were well aware that séances could be simulated, and they were alert for any signs of trickery (67). In the séance Schieffelin observed, it happened that two shamans were invited to perform for a child who was sick with a stomach ailment. Some of the audience were there out of concern for the child, others simply to see the performance (69). The competitive performances went on throughout the night, and gradually the difference between the shamans grew more distinct, one being challenged and harassed by the audience, the other interacting with great awareness and sensitivity to the audience and thereby gaining authority with them (70–2). The first shaman was gradually excluded from the séance, and the second, whose name was Walia, took over. What is most significant, for our purposes, however, is that the first shaman was the one promising that the child would live. Walia, however, over the long hours, listened to what the audience had to say, offering a less than encouraging diagnosis of the child's illness (caused by witches), and finally allowed the senior man in the audience to state the conclusion which in fact they had already reached but had been unable to accept – that the child was going to die (73–7). The child did indeed die. The shaman's work was, in part, to help the community come to its own interpretation of the condition of the child and to integrate the grievous event in their understanding of life and their relationship to the gods. He was not there to work miracles on behalf of the divine world.

It is a commonplace that Hippocratic medicine, unlike modern medicine, was biased toward prognosis, rather than diagnosis. "This definition, which strikes the modern mind as utterly peculiar, is to be understood in terms of the traditional prophecy of soothsayers."[6] That is, a prime function of the rationalist physician was not to identify the disease, but to *know what had happened, what was happening, and what would happen.* This is what their patients expected, and what physicians tried to provide. The healing sanctuary was attuned, first and foremost, to prophecy.[7] The question posed to the sanctuary healers and the god was this: what is happening to me, and what, if anything, can be done to change the course of this disease? Sometimes – more often than not, perhaps – the answer to that question, whether we call it prognosis or prophesy, was a blank negative: no change was possible.

But for the sanctuary healers that was not the end of the matter. There was still very much something the god *could* do for the suppliant. It was an essential part of the theory of the four humors, or of the *maniae*, that the body, in microcosm, is like the macrocosm of the universe. Religion was able to take the imbalance that was leading, so often inexorably, to death, and use the process to bring the patient to an understanding of his or her position in the context of the whole of divine creation. Death has as much a place in the universe as life. The means were creative and interactive, requiring prayer, participation in ritual, exercise of judgment, and attention to the sanctuary surroundings, to what was said and done by both priests and worshippers.

---

[6] Jouanna 1999, 101, and the discussion 100–11; cf. Hipp. *Prog.* 1.
[7] At Delphi, for instance, the prophecies were sought for advice on how to proceed. What consultants wanted – and got – was not revelation but guidance. See Fontenrose 1978, 244–416, for a catalogue of responses.

JUDGING DIANA

There may have been what we would call séances at the sanctuary of Diana. We cannot know. Nevertheless, we do know the sanctuary was heavily ornamented with dedications and large votive offerings, with gifts and honors of all sorts. These were not just donations acknowledging the goddess' power; they were the silent, yet emphatic, testimonies of those who had gone before. Worshippers like Gaia would have looked on them critically, evaluating the significance of their presence, their numbers, their appearance, and, if she could read, what they recorded. The temple and the sanctuary would have been judged as well. Rituals, prayers, conversations with the priests, attendants, and fellow worshippers, the processions, dances, theater performances: all these would have engaged Gaia and drawn her in. She would have participated in some, observed others, and determined for herself whether what happened to her was real or simulated religious experience. In some fashion her own needs would have become part of any ceremony in which she participated, whether or not her needs were consciously and overtly stated. In the end, if her need was for something more than to make a simple vow, if she wanted reassurance, advice, or help, then that was offered not as a miracle or a revelation, but as outcome and result of her engagement with the practices of the cult.

In particular, Gaia's engagement was made more vivid by the cult stories of the *rex nemorensis*, of Egeria, Virbius, Orestes, and Iphigenia. Her question was: what is happening to me? What *will* happen? This was as true, collectively, for cities that came to ask for relief from epidemics or internal dissension as for the terminally ill woman, or the man dying from his war wounds, or anyone overwhelmed by guilt for crimes whether real or imaginary. Octavian used Orestes to express the fear, the guilt, the sense of being exiled from the self which he felt – or at least knew he had to represent his country as feeling. In the same way an ordinary woman like Gaia could use those stories – no doubt with the help of the priests and of paintings and statues and frescoes and of performances of all kinds – to give sense to her understanding of her own condition. Orestes and Iphigenia would readily shape any experience of what we would now call a dysfunctional family, or of violence, enslavement, poverty, or exile from one's home for any reason. Those who betrayed or had been betrayed, and all those who had transgressed and enraged the goddess, had Virbius. Those who lived on, after others had died, and those who had lost whatever mattered most to them, had Egeria.

These narratives of Orestes, Virbius, and Egeria, however they were conveyed to the religious audience, were neither merely pretty tales of the gods, nor nothing more than helpful etiologies. They were a way of thinking, of religious thinking, about those many conditions that Diana was asked to aid. Release from the Furies might be achieved. But understanding, the knowledge of what was and was to be, remained the unique gift of the goddess.

THE GODDESS, DIANA

And then there was Diana herself, eternally multiform. The huntress was everyone's favorite, a perfect companion in the pursuit of life, gay, energetic, free, young, the vibrant divine avenger of wrongs, swift as the breeze over the grass. One could turn to her when in need, and sense that courageous drive over all obstacles toward life itself. The hero's part, plunging into battle and even killing to survive, were all part of what Diana the huntress celebrated. She was also the net maker who helped capture the thing desired, the trainer of the young – hounds, boys, and girls – till they could course along beside her in the tracks of the forest. She was the goddess of all the animals in the wild and all who lived and died there.

Diana as Trivia was a more ominous figure who exemplified the danger of transition, the crisis of choices made in the dark or without understanding. Young initiates and young men faced with making decisions in their lives, trying to learn the wisdom they needed, turned to Diana Trivia at these moments. She could be associated with Diana/Juno Lucina, for women in childbirth knew such crises intimately and lived – or died – well aware how quickly, with one misstep, an unknown act, or simply the working of fate, great promise could change to dire outcome. Anyone trying to discern their path in the obscurity of the future that lay ahead of them could turn to Diana Trivia.

Diana's triple form, most often called up when her underworld aspect was of primary concern, represented the multiplicity of her sacred existence. There was not one Diana. She belonged to the underworld, to the earth, and to the sky. That triple nature would also be exemplified by the sanctuary itself, the lake and the caves and the springs leading to the underworld, and the crater as the circle of the earth, all ruled by the moon moving slowly across the sky. Her triple nature seems particularly to have arisen from the need to affirm that when the underworld identity had to be worshipped, it remained only *part* of her identity. It affirmed that death was only part of existence. Triple Diana symbolized the idea of many states as aspects of one whole condition.

Diana was also one who loved. She was a virgin, but when her beloved, Virbius, died, she brought him back to live forever in the sanctuary. It is possible (despite her virginity) that she had a child, the Cupid who was identified with her. This aspect of Diana was both ominous and hopeful. Death could be swift and cruel, but love was powerful too. If the goddess so wished, death need not be permanent. The beloved young man could come back to life again.

And always there was the moon. No one who has experienced true dark before electrification and has seen the moon rise in that darkness could ever doubt the emotional power of her sanctuary at night. As daylight left the sky, as the music, prayers, clatter, and chatter died away, and as the night creatures came out, that dense, impenetrable darkness fell, "and the night's blackness bled the world of colour" (*rebus nox abstulit atra colorem*; Verg. *Aen.* 6.272). The gold-roofed temple would begin to pick up the gleam of the moonlight, a small gold jewel set in the depths of the forest, until the temple and the moon, each reflected with silky precision in the lake, bathed the crater in a colorless light shimmering among the trees. Or the temple would grow dark and stay dark in the dark of the moon, and the lake would become a bottomless watery blackness. There were processions, torches would be lit and carried along the road and the shore, with sparkling reflections in the lake. Light and dark, life and death, the illumination of knowledge, the impenetrability of the universe. In worshipping Diana the moon goddess, her suppliants worshipped the majesty and mystery of the sacred cosmos, of time, of the waxing and waning of all things, of the great workings of the universe which humankind can only barely comprehend.

BETWEEN ARICIA AND ROME

The cult of Diana at Aricia offers us an unusual body of evidence for the study of Roman religion. The historical and archaeological testimony has demonstrated that this sanctuary was a center of vital, practiced Latin religion from the early Iron Age on through the second century C.E. That fact has been known for a hundred years or so, and yet it has never yet been properly integrated into our understanding of religion in Rome and Latium.

Varro voiced an important concern about religion at Rome in the last century of the Republic: commitment to the state religion was seriously diminished among men of education, power, and authority.

. . . se timere ne pereant [sc. dei], non incursu hostili, sed civium neglegentia, de qua illos velut ruina liberari a se (dicit) et in memoria bonorum per eius modi libros recondi atque servari utiliore cura, quam Metellus de incendio sacra Vestalia et Aeneas de Troiano excidio penates liberasse praedicatur.

Varro *ARD* Cardauns 2a = Aug. *CD* 6.2

. . . he claims to fear the gods may perish, not from enemy attack, but through the neglect of the citizens, from which destruction (as he sees it), the gods are freed by him and through books of that sort, reestablished and maintained in the memory of good men, by a more profitable kind of attention than that by which Metellus gets credit for rescuing the sacred emblems of the Vestals from the fire or Aeneas his penates from the destruction of Troy.

At Aricia, however, by every standard we have for judging the strength of the Aricians' religious commitment to their principal city cult, both collectively and as individuals – whether wealthy equestrians, freedmen, slaves; or Republican praetors, consuls and legates – there was no danger of Diana perishing for lack of attention, no negligence, no falling off in interest, devotion, or commitment. Indeed, the period with the greatest importance for Varro's perception of decline at Rome, the late Republic, is the same period which saw the most ambitious building and expansion of the Arician sanctuary in its history. The cult of Diana, the practiced, regular worship of the

292

goddess, continued without interruption from the middle Republic to the period of the Antonines.

Another way of looking at this is to consider the sanctuary's architecture, the highly purposeful organization of sacred space. The Aricians who controlled the sanctuary had a continuing ability to relate the cult to changing religious needs, as they demonstrated by constructing a gold-roofed temple around 300 B.C.E. and following that by having all subsequent sanctuary buildings designed in accordance with Hellenistic canons of religious architecture. This was a substantial and wealthy institution, aware of international developments in religion and more than ready to embrace innovations in the organization of religious experience.

Contrast the Romans and their religion at the same time. They were, as North rightly points out, in terms of religion still "the relatively small-town Rome" (2002, 578). Politically, of course, in 300 B.C.E., they were masters of a land empire that was equal in size to any of the three preceding expansionist powers in Italy, the Crotoniates, the Oscan/Samnites, and the Etruscans, and were poised to conquer the remaining portions of Italy and half of Sicily. While Republican-imperial Rome protected its religious identity as that of a small (and poor) town, within a day's journey from the city the defeated Aricians were gilding their goddess' temple, and the people of Tibur, Praeneste, Gabii, and Lanuvium were not far behind (if at all) in planning impressive Hellenistic-style sanctuaries.

There is a difference as well in the ways in which Greek myth was appropriated. At Aricia, Hippolytus and Orestes were integrated into the cult fabric as a way of elaborating the meaning of ancient rituals and lesser deities. Virbius was not forgotten when Hippolytus was adopted, nor was the *rex nemorensis* renamed or his original ritual refashioned when Orestes was assimilated as the founder of the rite; yet both Hippolytus and Orestes became synonymous with the cult. At Rome, certainly in the cult of Diana, no similar adoption of Greek myth into the cult occurred, and in general, even though the Romans adopted the Greek iconography for many of their gods, the integration of Greek myth as an explication of cult ritual was not useful to them.

Sanctuary design, temple dedication, and ritual explication were all the expressions of the changing views of the ruling class, and the ruling class at Aricia differed considerably from their counterparts at Rome. Working within a common inheritance of Latin religion, the élite at Aricia and Rome each developed and maintained a different religious sensibility over the centuries of the Republic, making along the way their own very particular choices in responding to and adopting the religious ideas and styles and practices of the wider Mediterranean world. At the élite level, Rome was committed to a visible austerity for the city itself and resistance to the massive, popular (in the sense of crowd drawing), Hellenistic sanctuary organization, whereas the élite of the Latin cities embraced it. That did not prevent individual aristocrats from taking part in the complex religious life offered at Diana's sanctuary at Aricia, and clearly they were joined by many ordinary Romans among the multitudes who sought religious solace there.

When Varro wrote about the danger that the Roman gods might perish, he was thinking specifically of the religion of the gods at Rome, as his *exempla* of Aeneas and Metellus indicate. What study of Diana of Aricia makes so clear is that this danger – however it manifested itself to Varro and his contemporaries – cannot be taken to apply generally to the condition of traditional Latin cult religion. Diana of Aricia flourished, was seen to flourish, and went on flourishing. Here was a vital religion that had met each new challenge, adapting, appropriating, expanding at every step. The iconography and some specific mythology, followed by the sanctuary architecture, were taken from Greece, and Diana's grove blossomed into a Latin Hellenistic-style sanctuary. Philosophy – perhaps generally seen as the most serious challenge to religious belief – was also incorporated, so that the Pythagoreans and their descendants in the Republican and early empire found a natural home where their precepts were exemplified in ritual, further illuminating the goddess' power.

Southern Italian cosmologies and mysticism, Asclepian and Hippocratic medical theories and practices, were adopted and adapted, so that the figures known as the *maniae* could be used to connect the Hippocratic humoral theory with Diana's rituals, and thus extend the range of treatment for worshippers. Medical knowledge, in fact, seems to have been expanded by the healers at Diana's sanctuary, particularly in regard to skin diseases or other illnesses which had the symptoms of itching. *Unguentaria*, businesses that dispensed ointments, potions, and remedies of all sorts, appeared around the sanctuary.

At the end of the Civil War, the Aricians helped the young Octavian find the necessary religious purification for Rome and the Romans to release them from the horrors they had inflicted on themselves. The Aricians had to let the bones of Orestes go, whether voluntarily or not, but they still provided the story, the ritual, and the explanation that validated it. Somehow they must have also arranged to demonstrate that the goddess accepted this removal of the remains of her first priest. They chose to validate an act that could just as easily have been narrated as yet another violation of the goddess, another crime to be atoned. They let the sacred relics go, the Augustan imperial religious system embraced the cult, and still Diana's sanctuary expanded.

But innovation, expansion, and adaptation came to an end after the Augustan period. Diana and her cult at Aricia continued to flourish for two centuries more, but the removal of the *rex* to Sparta, probably sometime at the end of the second century, must have presaged the end of the cult, if it did not mark that end itself. There was a natural disaster, probably an earthquake, that produced a landslide, irreparably damaging the Hellenistic sanctuary. The signs were unmistakable. Diana's time as a cult goddess celebrated in ritual worship was past. Another religious culture was taking over. The Christians sanctified Hippolytus, a second-century c.e. bishop, and honored him on the Ides of August; two days later, on 15 August, they introduced a major festival to celebrate the assumption of the Christian Virgin into heaven.

The Latins worshipped Diana faithfully for centuries, from the earliest days when they came to Latium and first saw this strangely beautiful, eminently sacred, forest and lake in the crater. There is much more we have to learn about their religion, about the place they chose for the sanctuary, and about Diana of Aricia. This study is, I hope, a first step in that direction.

APPENDIX

SERVIUS *AD AEN.* 6.136

Frazer has been attacked (e.g., by J. Z. Smith 1978, West 1990) for his interpretation of the *rex nemorensis* on the grounds that he mistranslated Servius' Latin. Smith has directed particular criticism toward Frazer's understanding of *ad Aen.* 6.136, and presented a new version of the passage, a translation which itself had flaws (Green 2000, 30–6). I offer here my own version, addressing particularly troublesome points in the footnotes.

LATET ARBORE OPACA AUREUS licet de hoc ramo hi qui de sacris Proserpinae scripsisse dicuntur, quiddam esse mysticum adfirment, publica tamen opinio hoc habet. Orestes post occisum regem Thoantem in regione Taurica cum sorore Iphigenia, ut supra (2.116) diximus, fugit et Dianae simulacrum inde sublatum haud longe ab Aricia collocavit. in huius templo post mutatum ritum sacrificiorum fuit arbor quaedam, de qua infringi ramum non licebat. dabatur autem fugitivis potestas, ut si quis exinde ramum potuisset auferre, monomachia cum fugitivo templi sacerdote dimicaret: nam fugitivus illic erat sacerdos ad priscae imaginem fugae. dimicandi autem dabatur facultas quasi ad pristini sacrificii reparationem. nunc ergo istum inde sumpsit colorem. ramus enim necesse erat ut et unius causa esset interitus: unde et statim mortem subiungit Miseni: et ad sacra Proserpinae accedere nisi sublato ramo non poterat. inferos autem subire hoc dicit, sacra celebrare Proserpinae. de reditu autem animae hoc est: novimus Pythagoram Samium vitam humanam divisisse in modum Y litterae, scilicet quod prima aetas incerta sit, quippe quae adhuc se nec vitiis nec virtutibus dedit:

bivium autem Y litterae a iuventute incipere, quo tempore homines aut vitia, id est partem sinistram, aut virtutes, id est dexteram partem sequuntur: unde ait Persius <V 35> *traducit trepidas ramosa in compita mentes*.[1] Ergo per ramum virtutes dicit esse sectandas, qui est Y litterae imitatio: quem ideo in silvis dicit latere, quia re vera in huius vitae confusione et maiore parte vitiorum virtus et integritas latet. alii dicunt ideo ramo aureo inferos peti, quod divitiis facile mortales intereunt. Tiberianus *aurum, quo pretio reserantur limina Ditis.*

A golden [bough] lies hidden in a shady tree. Although, in the matter of this branch,[2] those who are said to have written about the rites of Proserpine assert that it is something used in the mysteries, nevertheless the general[3] view is as follows: Orestes, after the killing of King Thoas in the Tauric land, fled with his sister (as we stated above [2.116]), and the image of Diana that he brought from there he set up not far from Aricia. In her precinct, after the sacrificial ritual was changed,[4] there was a certain tree, from which it was not permitted

---

[1] Persius 5. 34–6:

> ... cumque iter ambiguum est et vitae nescius error
> *diducit* trepidas ramosa in compita mentes
> me tibi supposui.

[2] Servius writes a classic contrastive construction: although these (*hi*) people say *x*, nevertheless the general view (*publica opinio*) is *y*. Both concern *this* branch, that is, the golden bough, which is why *de hoc ramo* precedes both groups.

[3] *publica opinio*: Servius uses *publicus* (apart from instances of *respublica*) most commonly to mean "of or concerning the people or state" (thirty-three times in his commentary on the *Aeneid*); twice he uses it in contrast to *privatus*. *Publica* as a modifier for *opinio* appears in only two other instances in this commentary, at 5.527 and at 8.601. The first is a very neutral use, but the second, in describing the deity worshipped in a specific ceremony, most probably represents the official view of the pontifical college (*publicus* carries strong implications, especially in a religious context, of "state" or "official"; *OLD s.v. publicus* 1, 2, 3, especially 2b), because what follows is a Hellenizing reinterpretation. At 6.136, *publica* may well be in deliberate contrast to the traditionally secret explanations given for the mysteries of Proserpina. R. S. Conway's translation (*The Vergilian Age*, Cambridge, MA, 1928, 42) of *publica opinio* as "a common notion" and J. Z. Smith's "common view" both suggest that they want us to understand "common" in its negative English sense of "merely ordinary" (*OED s.v. common* 14), Shakespeare's "base, common and popular," and Smith's assertion (216, n. 27) that *publicus* "carries the same nuances as *volgaris/volgatus*" is simply wrong (compare *OLD s.v. publicus* and *volgaris*). *Publicus* does *not* have that negative quality.

[4] From the human sacrifice practiced in Diana/Artemis' name in Taurica.

to break off a branch. Moreover, the right was given to any fugitive who contrived to remove a branch thence[5] to contend in single combat with the fugitive priest of the temple, for the priest there was [also] a fugitive, to symbolize the original flight. And indeed, this opportunity of fighting was given as though in renewal of the original sacrifice: it follows that, at this point in his narrative,[6] he [i.e., Vergil] has taken his rhetorical effects[7] from here. For it was essential[8] that the bough should

[5] *in huius templo post mutatum ritum sacrificiorum fuit arbor quaedam, de qua infringi ramum non licebat. dabatur autem fugitivis potestas, ut si quis exinde ramum potuisset auferre, monomachia cum fugitivo templi sacerdote dimicaret.* infringere has a consistent meaning not only of breaking, as applied to sticks, weapons, and the like, but of depriving of vigor, injuring, doing harm, breaking the power of, or diminishing (*OLD s.v. infringo*). A verb far more regularly applied to living wood when referring to the action of cutting or breaking off limbs is *scindo* – Vergil in fact uses it in 6.182 to describe the felling of trees for Misenus' pyre – which does not have *infringo*'s strong implications of destroyed power, or diminished vigor (*OLD s.v. scindo*). Frazer was perfectly justified in taking the full implications of Servius' choice of words into account when characterizing the act that is forbidden with regard to the tree. Likewise, *potuisset auferre*. Servius' *auferre* can indeed mean "to cut off," as with hair, but again it is not *scindo*; rather it has the sense of taking what has belonged to another, of winning something, of gaining what one might indeed be prevented from taking (*OLD s.v. aufero* 2b and passim). Frazer's interpretations, whether one agrees with them or not, were solidly grounded in the text.

[6] A purely temporal interpretation of *nunc* does not make sense here. In context it clearly implies "at the present moment of one's narrative" (*OLD s.v. nunc* 1.e).

[7] *Color* was originally what its descendant in English implies, that is, pigment in painting. When applied to rhetoric and poetics, however, it is being used figuratively as "the materials of a writer or orator" (*OLD s.v. color* 2c. Cf. Cic. *ad Att.* 2.1.1–2; Seneca the Elder *Contr.* 9.2.20–1, 7.2.10–13). Wiseman (1979, 3–8) points out that the modern interpretation, that *color* as a "slant" or an "angle" is inadequate to describe ancient usage. Rather, *color* involved an elaborate system of rhetorical devices through which the speaker characterized a person or an act. Take, for instance, the *colores* Seneca (*Contr.* 9.2.20–1) noted in a speech concerning Lucius' Flamininus' execution of a criminal at a dinner party on the request of a courtesan. These *colores* were what we would regard as justifications or explanations: that Flamininus was drunk; that he had to show his severity after the conversation had turned to leniency; that he granted the request to forestall the woman asking for the death of a free man (Wiseman 7). *Color* should be understood, not as merely a tint or beautification (serving to heighten innate qualities) but rather as an actor's make-up scheme, complete with costume, which tells the audience what to expect from this individual and how to think about it. So, just as in drama the elderly skinflint or the tyrant would each, as characters, provide *color* for certain situations, so the ritual of the *rex nemorensis* and the taking of the bough – acts both necessary and inevitable – provide the color for Aeneas' conduct – equally necessary, equally inevitable – in this part of the epic.

[8] *dimicandi autem dabatur facultas quasi ad pristini sacrificii reparationem. nunc ergo istum inde sumpsit colorem. ramus enim necesse erat ut et unius causa esset interitus: unde et statim mortem*

also be the cause of one death: this is the reason why he [Vergil] also immediately appends the death of Misenus; and it was not possible to gain access to the rites of Proserpina except through the removal of the branch. And indeed to go to the underworld means to celebrate the rites of Proserpina. However, concerning the return of the soul, this is the case: we know that Pythagoras of Samos divided human life in the manner of the letter Y, meaning that the first period of life is undetermined, in that it has not yet given itself either to vices or to virtues; however, the bifurcation of the letter Y [he says] begins from youth, at which time men either pursue vices, that is, the left branch, or virtues, that is, the right branch. This is why Persius says "[ignorant error] leads fearful minds to the branching crossroads."[9] Therefore he [Pythagoras][10] says virtues must be pursued by means of the branch,

---

subiungit Miseni. ergo introduces a resultant state of affairs, or their logical consequence (*OLD s.v. ergo* 1). *inde*, when not either temporal or topographical, expresses source or consequence (*OLD s.v. inde* 9, 10, 11). "It follows that, at this point in his narrative, he has taken that particular aspect from here." What *inde* must be referring to is, at the very least, the original sacrifice, or, preferably, the entire preceding explanation. *enim* is a particle that introduces a ground or reason for something previously said (*OLD s.v. enim*, 3). *enim*, therefore, tells us that this sentence explains the *color* Vergil has adopted. As far as *necesse est* is concerned, the meanings of *necesse* do not vary greatly, but using the English derivative is not an option (cf. West 226). The *OLD* (*s.v. necesse*) gives us 1. indispensable, essential; 2. determined by natural law, inevitable; 3. necessarily consequent, or true; 4. forced or compulsory. In context, "essential" or "compulsory" probably comes closest to Servius' intention. Thus the sentence about the bough is specifically tied, first by *ergo* and *inde*, then by *enim*, to the information about the combat between the priest and the challenger – all of which then compels Vergil to include the death of Misenus at this point in his narrative. The connection is the two boughs.

9 The Persius quotation is significant. Persius' subject is not himself, but *vitae nescius error*, "the ignorant straying of (that time of) life." *Error* has a double meaning, of "departure from right principles" (*OLD s.v. error* 6) and "going astray" (*OLD s.v. error* 3). *Nescius* is "ignorant" both in the ordinary sense of not knowing, and in the specific sense of not knowing philosophy, which is why the conclusion of the sentence has Persius putting himself under the tutelage of a Socratic philosopher-teacher, Cornutus. Persius' MSS read *diducit* rather than Servius' *traducit*. I have translated what Servius has written. Persius' point, which is why Servius quotes him here, is that the immature and uncertain wanderings of youth are what bring a young man to the crossroads, where he will have to choose to turn either right or left.

10 It is just possible that it is not Pythagoras, but some other commentator, unnamed, who is the subject; but Servius' *novimus*, "we know," suggests strongly not only that he is working from memory but that he expects his readers to be as familiar with this part of the exposition as he is. It is more probable, therefore, that it comes from well-known writings attributed to Pythagoras.

which is an imitation of the letter Y, and which he[11] therefore says lies hidden in the forest, because, in the confusion of this life and its preponderance of vices, virtue and integrity truly lie hidden. This is why others say that the underworld is approached by means of a golden bough because mortals easily die as a result of their wealth. Tiberianus speaks of "gold, the price by which the doorways of Dis [the underworld] are opened."

---

[11] It is possible that Servius has once again changed subject, and the dependent clause *quem ideo in silvis dicit latere* should be translated as "which therefore he [i.e., Vergil] says lies hidden in the forest," and the *quia* clause ("because, in the confusion . . .") returns once again to Pythagoras' views. This may seem tortuous even for Servius but luckily does not affect the meaning of the passage either way.

SELECT BIBLIOGRAPHY

Achterberg, J., *Imagery in Healing: Shamanism and Modern Medicine*, Boston, 1985.

Ackerman, R., *J. G. Frazer: His Life and Work*, Cambridge, 1987.

Aland, K., Black, M., Martini, C., Metzger, B., and Wikgren, A., eds., *The Greek New Testament*, 3rd ed., New York, 1975.

Alföldi, A., "Diana Nemorensis," *American Journal of Archaeology* 64 (1960): 137–44.

Alföldi, A., "Il santuario federale latino di Diana sull' Aventino e il tempio di Ceres," *Studi e Materiali di Storia delle Religioni* 32 (1961): 21–39.

Alföldi, A., *Early Rome and the Latins*, Ann Arbor, 1965.

Altheim, F., *Griechische Götter im alten Rom*, Giessen, 1930.

Alton, E. H., Wormell, D. E. W., and Courtney, E., *P. Ovidi Nasonis Fastorum Libri Sex*, Stuttgart, 1997.

Amirante, L., *Captivitas e Postliminium*, Naples, 1950.

Ampolo, C., "L'Artemide di Marsiglia," *Parola del Passato* 25 (1970): 200–10.

Ampolo, C., "Ricerche sulla lega Latina: caput aquae Ferentinae e lacus Turni," *Parola del Passato* 36 (1981): 219–33.

Ampolo, C., "Un supplizio arcaico: l'uccisione di Turnus Herdonius," in *Du châtiment dans la cité, supplices corporels et peine de mort dans le monde antique*, Rome, 1984, 91–6.

Anderson, R., *Magic, Science, and Health: The Aims and Achievements of Medical Anthropology*, Fort Worth, 1996.

Andreau, J., *Banking and Business in the Roman World*, Cambridge, 1999.

Andrén, A., *Architectural Terracottas from Etrusco-Italic Temples*, Leipzig, 1940.

Ascani, K., "An Eye-witness Account," in *I Dianas*, 1997, 177–9.

Astbury, R., *M. Terentii Varronis Saturarum Menippearum Fragmenta*, Leipzig, 1985.

Austin, R. G., *P. Vergili Maronis Aeneidos Liber Sextus*, Oxford, 1986.

Ax, W., *M. Tulli Ciceronis Scripta Quae Manserunt Omnia, Fasc. 45, De Natura Deorum*, Stuttgart, 1980.

Barnes, J., *The Presocratic Philosophers*, London, 1982 (rev. ed.).

Barrett, W. S., *Euripides: Hippolytos*, Oxford, 1964.

Barringer, J. M., *The Hunt in Ancient Greece*, Baltimore, 2001.

Bayet, J., *Histoire politique et psychologique de la religion romaine*, Paris, 1957.

Beard, M., "A Complex of Times: No More Sheep on Romulus' Birthday," *Proceedings of the Cambridge Philological Society*, 213, n.s. 33 (1987): 1–15.

Beard, M., "The Function of the Written Word in Roman Religion," in *Literacy in the Roman World, Journal of Roman Archaeology, Supplementary Series*, no. 3, Ann Arbor, 1991, 35–58.

Beard, M., and North, J., *Pagan Priests: Religion and Power in the Ancient World*, London, 1990.

Beard, M., North, J., and Price, S., *Religions of Rome*, vol. 1, *A History*; vol. 2, *A Sourcebook*, Cambridge, 1998.

Bernardi, A., "L'interesse di Caligola per la successione de rex Nemorensis e l'arcaica regalità nel Lazio," *Athenaeum* 31 (1953): 273–87.

Birt, T., "Diana," in *Ausführliches Lexicon der Griechischen und Römischen Mythologie*, Ed. W. H. Roscher, vol. 1, pt. 1, 1884–90, col. 1002–11.

Blagg, T. F. C., et al., *Mysteries of Diana: The Antiquities from Nemi in Nottingham Museums*, Castle Museum Nottingham, 1983.

Blagg, T. F. C., "The Finds of the Sanctuary of Diana: Nottingham and Other Museum Collections," in Blagg (1983a): 21–4.

Blagg, T. F. C., "The Architecture of the Sanctuary," in Blagg (1983b): 25–30.

Blagg, T. F. C., "Architectural Terracottas," in Blagg (1983c): 31–7.

Blagg, T. F. C., "Architectural Marble Decoration," in Blagg (1983d): 38–45.

Blagg, T. F. C., "Votive Terracottas," in Blagg (1983e): 46–53.

Blagg, T. F. C., "Bronzes," in Blagg (1983f): 54–8.

Blagg, T. F. C., "Cult Practice and Its Social Context in the Religious Sanctuaries of Latium and Southern Etruria," in *Papers in Italian Archaeology IV. Part iv: Classical and Medieval Archaeology*, Caroline Malone and Simon Stoddart, eds., BAR International Series 246 Oxford, 1985, 33–50.

Blagg, T. F. C., "The Cult and Sanctuary of Diana Nemorensis," in *Pagan Gods and Shrines of the Roman Empire*, Ed. Martin Henig and Anthony King, Oxford University Committee for Archaeology, Monograph no. 8, 1986, 211–20.

Blagg, T. F. C., "Le mobilier archéologique du sanctuaire de Diane *Nemorensis*," in *Les bois sacrés*, 1993, 103–9.

Blagg, T. F. C., "The votive model. Etrusco-Italic temples from Nemi," in Brandt et al., 2000, 83–92.

Block, R., "Parenté entre religion de Rome et religion d'Ombria. Thèmes de recherches," *Revue des Études Latines* 41 (1963): 115–22.

Bodei Giglioni, G., "Pecunia fanatica: l'incidenza economica dei templi laziali," *Rivista Storica Italiana* 89 (1977): 33–76.

Bombardi, S., "Il Santuario di Diana nemorense: riesame di alcune problematiche relative al culto ed alla storia del complesso," *Documenta Albana*, ser. 2, no. 16–17 (1994–5): 37–52.

Bombardi, S., "La funzione degli attori nell' ambito del santuario di Diana Nemorense," in Brandt et al., 2000, 121–30.

Borzsák, S., Q. *Horati Flacci Opera*, Leipzig, 1984.

Bosselaar, D. E., and Van Proosdij, B. A., P. *Ovidii Nasonis Metamorphoseon, Libri I–XV, textus et commentarius*, Leiden, 1982.

Boyancé, P., *Études sur la religion romaine*, Rome, 1972.

Brand, C. E., *Roman Military Law*, Austin, 1968.

Brandt, J. R., Touati, A.-M. L., Zahle, J., *Nemi – Status Quo: Recent Research at Nemi and the Sanctuary of Diana*, Occasional Papers of the Nordic Institutes in Rome I, Rome, 2000.

Braund, S. H. *Lucan: Civil War*, Oxford, 1992.

Braund, D., and Gill, C., *Myth, History and Culture in Republican Rome*, Exeter, 2003.

Bremmer, J. N., and Horsfall, N. M., *Roman Myth and Mythography*, University of London Institute of Classical Studies, Bulletin Supplement 52, 1987.

Brink, C. O., *Horace on Poetry: The "Ars Poetica,"* Cambridge, 1971.

Brunt, P. A., *Italian Manpower 225 B.C.–A.D. 14*, Oxford, reissue with postscript, 1987.

Burkert, W., *Lore and Science in Ancient Pythagoreanism*, Trs. Edwin L. Minar, Jr., Cambridge, MA, 1972.

Burkert, W., *Orphism and Bacchic Mysteries: New Evidence and Old Problems of Interpretation*, Protocol of the Twenty-eighth Colloquy of the Center for Hermeneutical Studies in Hellenistic and Modern Culture, Berkeley, 1977.

Burkert, W., *Greek Religion*, Trs. John Raffan, Cambridge, MA, 1985.

Burkert, Walter, *Creation of the Sacred: Tracks of Biology in Early Religions*, Cambridge, MA, 1996.

Butler, H. E., *The Sixth Book of the Aeneid*, Oxford, 1920.

Capdeville, G., "Substitution de victimes dans les sacrifices d'animaux à Rome," *Mélanges d'Archéologie et d'Histoire de l'École Française de Rome* 83 (1971): 283–323.

Capdeville, G., "Les institutions religieuses de Rome selon Denys l'Halicarnasse," *Pallas* 39 (1993): 153–72.

Capdeville, G., "De la forêt initiatique au bois sacré," in *Les bois sacrés*, 127–43.

Cardauns, B., *M. Terentius Varro: Antiquitates Rerum Divinarum*, 2 vols., Wiesbaden, 1976.

Cary, E., Dionysius of Halicarnassus, *Antiquitates Romanae*, 7 vols., London and Cambridge, 1937.

Cassatella, A., and Venditelli, L., "Santuario di Diana sull'Aventino: il problema della localizzazione," in *Roma: Archeologia nel Centro*, vol. 2: *La Città Murata*, Rome, 1985, 442–51.

Castagnoli, F., "Sul tempio 'italico'," *Mitteilungen des Deutschen Archaeologischen Instituts, Roemische Abteilung* 73/74 (1966–7).

Champlin, E., "Agamemnon at Rome: Roman Dynasts and Greek Heroes," in Braund and Gill, 295–319.

Chiarucci, P. "Rassegna delle principali ville di età romana nell'area albana con particolare riferimento alle recenti scoperte," in Brandt et al., 2000, 179–92.

Civiltà del Lazio Primitivo, catalogue, by the Istituto di Studi Etruschi ed Italici e del Comitato per l'Archeologia Laziale, Rome, 1976.

Coarelli, F., *I Santuari del Lazio in Età Repubblicana*, Rome, 1987.

Conte, G-B., *The Rhetoric of Imitation: Genre and Poetic Memory in Virgil and Other Latin Poets*, Ithaca, 1986.

Conte, G-B., *Latin Literature: A History*, Baltimore, 1994.

Conticello de' Spagnolis, M., "Una dedica attestante un' aedes Dianae ad Irti," *Archeologia Classica* 38–40 (1986–8): 88–93.

Cook, A. B., "The Golden Bough and the Rex Nemorensis," *Classical Review* 16 (1902): 365–81.

Cornell, T. J., "Rome and Latium to 390 B.C." and "The recovery of Rome," in F. W. Walbank, A. E. Astin, M. W. Frederiksen, and R. M. Ogilvie, eds. *CAH* VII², part 2: 243–350.

Cornell, T. J., "The tyranny of the evidence: a discussion of the possible uses of literacy in Etruria and Latium in the archaic age," in *Literacy in the Roman World, Journal of Roman Archaeology*, Supplementary Series No. 3, Ann Arbor, 1991, 7–34.

Cornell, T. J., *The Beginnings of Rome: Italy and Rome from the Bronze Age to the Punic Wars (c. 1000–264 B.C.)*, London, 1995.

Cornford, F. M., *Principium Sapientiae: The Origins of Greek Philosophical Thought*, Cambridge 1952, rep. Gloucester, MA, 1971.

Courtney, E., *The Fragmentary Latin Poets*, Oxford, 1993.

Csordas, T. J., *The Sacred Self: A Cultural Phenomenology of Charismatic Healing*, Berkeley, 1994.

Csordas, T. J., "Imaginal Performance and Memory in Ritual Healing," in Lademan and Roseman, 91–114.

Daviault, A., *Comoedia togata: fragments*, Paris, 1981.

Day Lewis, C., *The* Aeneid *of Vergil*, New York, 1952.

De Grossi Mazzorin, J., "Testimonianze di allevamento e caccia nel Lazio antico tra l'VIII et il VII secolo a.C.," *Dialoghi di Archeologia*, 3rd ser., 7 no. 1 (1989): 125–42.

de Grummond, W. W., "The 'Diana Experience': A Study of the Victims of Diana in Virgil's Aeneid," *Studies in Latin Literature and Roman History* 8 (1998): 158–94.

Delbrück, H., *History of the Art of War within the Framework of Political History*. Vol. 1. Trs. Walter J. Renfroe, Jr., Westport, CT, 1975.

Della Seta, A., *Museo Villa Giulia*, Roma, 1918.

Dench, E., "Beyond Greeks and Barbarians: Italy and Sicily in the Hellenistic Age," in *A Companion to the Hellenistic World*, A. Erskine, ed., Oxford, 2003, 294–310.

Dewar, M., "Octavian and Orestes in the Finale of the First Georgic," *Classical Quarterly*, n.s. 38.2 (1988): 563–5.

Dewar, M., "Octavian and Orestes Again," *The Classical Quarterly*, N. W. 40.2 (1990): 580–2.

Downey, S. B., *Architectural Terracottas from the Regia*, Ann Arbor, 1995.

Drummond, A., "Rome in the Fifth Century, I: The Social and Economic Framework," in F. W. Walbank, A. E. Astin, M. W. Frederiksen, and R. M. Ogilvie, eds. *CAH* VII2, part 2, 1989, 113–71.

Duff, J. W., and A. M. Duff, *Minor Latin Poets*, vol. 1, Cambridge, MA, 1935 (rev. ed.), repr. 1982.

Duff, J. D., *Lucan: The Civil War (Pharsalia)*, Cambridge, MA, 1928; repr. 1988.

Dumézil, G., *Archaic Roman Religion*, vols. 1 and 2, Chicago, 1970, repr. Baltimore, 1996.

Dunbabin, T. J., *The Western Greeks*, Oxford, 1948.

Dyson, J., *King of the Wood: The Sacrificial Victor in Virgil's Aeneid*, Norman, OK, 2001.

Edelstein, E. J., and Edelstein, L., *Asclepius: Collection and Interpretation of the Testimonies*, vols. I and II, Baltimore, 1945, repr. 1998.

Edlund, I. E. M., *The Gods and the Place: Location and Function of Sanctuaries in the Countryside of Etruria and Magna Graecia (700–400 B.C.)*, Stockholm, 1987.

Eliade, M., *The Sacred and the Profane: The Nature of Religion*, Trs. Willard R. Trask, New York, 1959 and 1987.

Eliade, M., *Shamanism: Archaic Techniques of Ecstasy*, Trs. W. R. Trask, Princeton, 1964.

Faraone, C., and Obbink, D., eds., *Magika Hiera: Ancient Greek Magic and Religion*, New York, 1991.

Fenelli, M., "I votivi anatomici in Italia: valore e limite della testimonianze archeologiche," in *From Epidaurus to Salerno*, Krug, A., ed., PACT, Belgium, 1992, 127–37.

Fontenrose, J., *The Delphic Oracle: Its Responses and Operations, with a Catalogue of Responses*, Berkeley, 1978.

Fontenrose, J., *Orion: The Myth of the Hunter and the Huntress*, Berkeley, 1981.

Formicola, C., *Il cynegeticon di Grattio: Introduzione, testo critico, traduzione e commento*, Bologna, 1988.

Formicola, C., *Studi sull'esametro de cynegeticon di Grattio*, Naples, 1995.

Foster, B. O., *Livy I, Books I and II*, Cambridge, MA, 1919, repr. 1988.

Frank, A., *The Wounded Storyteller: Body, Illness, and Ethics*, Chicago, 1995.

Frank, T., *An Economic History of Rome*, Baltimore, 1927.

Frazer, J. G., *The Golden Bough*, vols. 1–12, London, 1911–15.

Frazer, J. G., *Publii Ovidii Nasonis, Fastorum Libri Sex*, vols. 1–5, London, 1929.

Frier, B., *Libri Annales Pontificum Maximorum: The Origins of the Annalistic Tradition*, 2nd ed., Ann Arbor, 1999.

Fullerton, M., *The Archaistic Style in Roman Statuary*, Leiden, 1990.

Gantz, T., *Early Greek Myth: A Guide to Literary and Artistic Sources*, Baltimore, 1993.

Ghedini, F., "Il dolore per la morte di Druso Maggiore nel vaso d'onice de Saint Marice de'Agaume," *Rivista di Archeologia* 2 (1987): 68–74.

Ghedini, F., "Augusto e la propaganda Apollinea nell'amphoriskos de Leningrado," *Archeologia Classica* 38–40 (1986–8): 128–35.

Ghini, G., *Museo Navi Romane, Santuario di Diana, Nemi*, Rome, 1992.

Ghini, G., "Modern Times: New Excavations in the Sanctuary of Diana," in *I Dianas*, 1997, 179–82.

Ghini, G., "Ricerche al santuario di Diana: risultati e progetti," in Brandt et al., 2000, 53–64.

Giardino, C., "Il ripostiglio di Nemi," *Documenta albana*, Albano Laziale, Museo civico Albano (1985) 4, 1985, 7–16.

Gierow, P. G., *The Iron Age Culture of Latium*, vol. II.1, *Excavations and Finds*, Lund, 1964.

Gierow, P. G., *The Iron Age Culture of Latium*, vol. I. *Classification and Analysis*, Lund, 1966.

Gizzi, S., "Il restauro del santuario di Diana a Nemi: problemi e prospettive," in Brandt et al., 2000, 65–82.

Glucklich, A., *Sacred Pain: Hurting the Body for the Sake of the Soul*, Oxford, 2001.

Goold, G. P., *Propertius: Elegies*, Cambridge, MA, 1990.

Gordon, A. E., "On the Origin of Diana, *Transactions and Proceedings of the American Philological Association* 63 (1932): 177–92.

Gordon, A. E., "The Cults of Aricia," *University of California Publications in Classical Archaeology* II (1934): 1–20.

Gordon, R., "From Republic to Principate: Priesthood, Religion and Ideology," in Beard and North, 177–98.

Gradel, I., "Old Money: Diana on Coinage," in *I Dianas*, 1997, 200–3.

Graf, F., *Eleusis und die orphische Dichtung Athens in vorhellenistischer Zeit*, Berlin, 1974.

Graf, F., *Der Lauf des rollenden Jahres: Zeit und Kalender in Rom*, Stuttgart and Leipzig, 1997.

Grandazzi, A., *The Foundation of Rome: Myth and History*, Trs. Jane Marie Todd, Ithaca, 1997; English translation of *La fondation de Rome: Réflexion sur l'histoire*, Paris, 1991.

Granino Cecere, M. G., "Contributo dell'epigrafia per la storia del santuario nemorense," in Brandt et al., 2000, 35–44.

Gras, M., "Le Temple de Diane sur l'Aventin," *Revue des Études Anciennes* 89 (1987): 47–61.

Green, C. M. C., "The Necessary Murder: Myth Ritual and Civil War in Lucan Book 3," *Classical Antiquity* 13.2 (1994): 203–33.

Green, C. M. C., "Did the Romans Hunt?," *Classical Antiquity* (1996a): 222–60.

Green, C. M. C., "Terms of Venery: *Ars Amatoria I*," *Transactions of the American Philological Association* 126 (1996b): 221–63.

Green, C. M. C., "Free as a Bird (Varro *De Re Rustica* 3)," *American Journal of Philology* 118 (1997): 427–48.

Green, C. M. C., "Claudius, Kingship, and Incest (*Annales* 12.8)," *Latomus* 57.4 (1998): 766–91.

Green, C. M. C., "The Slayer and the King: Rex Nemorensis and the Sanctuary of Diana," *Arion*, 3rd ser., 7.3 (winter 2000): 24–63.

Green, C. M. C., "Varro's Three Theologies and Their Influence on the *Fasti*," in *Ovid's* Fasti: *Historical Readings at Its Bimillennium*, Geraldine Herbert-Brown, ed., Oxford, 2002, 71–100.

Green, P., *Alexander to Actium: The Historical Evolution of the Hellenistic Age*, Berkeley, 1990.

Green, P., "Delivering the Go(o)ds: Demetrius Poliorcetes and Hellenistic Divine Kingship," in *Gestures: Essays in Ancient History, Literature, and Philosophy Presented to Alan L. Boegehold*, G. W. Bakewell and J. P. Sickinger, eds., Oxford, 2003, 258–77.

Griffin, J., "Chopping Off the Golden Bough," *New York Review of Books*, 8 October 1998, 44–7.

Gruen, E., *The Last Generation of the Roman Republic*, Berkeley, 1974, with new introduction, 1994.

Guenther, M., "From Totemism to Shamanism: Hunter-Gatherer Contributions to World Mythology and Spirituality," in *The Cambridge Encyclopedia of Hunters and Gatherers*, Eds. Richard B. Lee and Richard Daly, Cambridge, 1999, 426–33.

Guldager Bilde, P., "The Sanctuary of Diana Nemorensis: The Late Republican Acrolithic Cult Statues," *Acta Archaeologica* 66 (1995): 191–217.

Guldager Bilde, P., "Diana's Mirror: Introduction," in *I Dianas*, 1997a, 166–9.

Guldager Bilde, P., "For Worship and Honor: The Cult-statues of the Sanctuary," in *I Dianas*, 1997b, 197–200.

Guldager Bilde, P., "East and West: Hellenistic Architecture in Italy and Greece," in *I Dianas*, 1997c, 182–4.

Guldager Bilde., P., "By Torch-light: The Cult in the Sanctuary," in *I Dianas*, 1997d, 190–2.

Guldager Bilde, P., "*Chio d(onum) d(dedit)*: Eight Marble Vases from the Sanctuary of Diana Nemorensis," *Analecta Romana* 24 (1997e): 53–75.

Guldager Bilde, P., "The Sculptures from the Sanctuary of Diana Nemorensis, Types and Contextualisation: An Overview," in Brandt et al., 2000, 93–110.

Guldager Bilde, P., and Moltesen, M., "Great and Small: The Sculptural Decoration of the Sanctuary," in *Hellige Lund*, 1997, 207–9.

Guldager Bilde, P., and Moltesen, M., *A Catalogue of Sculptures from the Sanctuary of Diana Nemorensis in the University of Pennsylvania Museum, Philadelphia, Analecta Romana Instituti Danici*, Supplementum 29, 2002.

Guthrie, W. K. C., *A History of Greek Philosophy*, vol. 2, Cambridge, 1965.

Haffner, G., "Das Relief vom Nemisee in Kopenhagen," *Jahrbuch des Deutschen Archäologischen Instituts* 82 (1967): 246–74.

Hänninen, M.-L., "Traces of Women's Devotion in the Sanctuary of Diana at Nemi," in Brandt et al., 2000, 45–50.

Hart, G. D., *Asclepius: The God of Medicine*, London, 2000.

Hasius, B., Creuzerus, F., and Roether, G., *Ioannis Laurentii Philadelpheni Lydi De Mensibus*, Leipzig, 1827.

Heurgon, J., *Trois études sur le 'ver sacrum'* (Coll. Latomus 26), Brussels, 1957.

Holland, L. A. *Janus and the Bridge*, Rome, 1961.

Holland, L. L., *Epigraphical Evidence for the Cult of Diana in Italy*, Ph.D. Diss., University of North Carolina, 2003.

Holloway, R. R., *The Archaeology of Early Rome and Latium*, London and New York, 1994.

Hölscher, T., "Augustus and Orestes," *Travaux du Centre d'Archéologie Méditerranéenne de l'Académie Polonaise des Sciences, 30, Études et Travaux* 15 (1991): 164–8.

Hölscher, T., *The Language of Images in Roman Art* (English translation of *Römische Bildsprache als semantisches System*, Heidelberg, 1987), Trs. A. Snodgrass and A. Künzl-Snodgrass, Cambridge, 2004.

Horsfall, N. M., "Myth and Mythography at Rome," in Bremmer and Horsfall, 1–11.

Horstmanshoff, H. F. J., "Asclepius and Temple Medicine in Aelius Aristides' *Sacred Tales*," in *Magic and Rationality in Ancient Near Eastern and Greco-Roman Medicine*, H. F. J Horstmanshoff, and M. Stol, eds., Leiden, 2004.

Hübner, E., *Die Antiken Bildwerke in Madrid*, Berlin, 1862.

Hull, D. B., *Hounds and Hunting in Ancient Greece*, Chicago, 1964.

Hunink, V., *M. Annaeus Lucanus: Bellum Civile, Book III: A Commentary*, Amsterdam, 1992.

I Dianas Hellige Lund: Fund Fra En Helligdom I Nemi (In the Sacred Grove of Diana: Finds from a Sanctuary at Nemi), Ny Carlsberg Glyptotek, Copenhagen, 1997.

Jenkinson, J. R., *Persius: The Satires*, Warminster, 1980.

Jentoft-Nilsen, M., *Diana on Roman Coins*, Ph.D. Diss., University of Southern California, 1985.

Johannes, R., *De Studio Venandi Apud Graecos et Romanos*, Ph.D. Diss., Gottingen, 1907.

Jones, H. L., *The Geography of Strabo*, vol. 2, repr. 1988, Cambridge, MA, 1923.

Jones, W. H. S., *Hippocrates*, vol. 2, Cambridge, MA, 1967.

Jouanna, J., *Hippocrates*, Trs. M. B. DeBevoise, Baltimore, 1999.

Känel, R., "Das Dianaheiligtum in Nemi: Die Baudekoration aus Terrakotta," in Brandt et al., 2000, 131–44.

Karras-Klapproth, M., *Prosopographische Studien zur Geschichte des Partherreiches auf der Grundlage Antiker Literarischer Überlieferung*, Bonn, 1988.

Keijwegt, M., "Textile Manufacturing for a Religious Market. Artemis and Diana as Tycoons of Industry," in Jongman, W., and Kleijwegt, M., eds., *After the Past: Essays in Ancient History in Honor of H. W. Pleket*, Leiden, 2002, 81–133.

Kenney, E. J., *P. Ovidi Nasonis: Amores, Medicamina Faciei Femineae, Ars Amatoria, Remedia Amoris*, Oxford, 1989.

Kingsley, P., *Ancient Philosophy, Mystery, and Magic*, Oxford, 1995.

Kirk, G. S., Raven, J. E., and Schofield, M., *The Presocratic Philosophers*, 2nd ed., Cambridge, 1983.

Knoepfler, D., *Les Imagiers de Orestie: mille ans d'art antique autour d'un mythe grec*, Zurich, 1993.

Kretschmer, P., "'Dyaus, Zeus,' und die Abstrakta im Indogermanischen," *Glotta* 13 (1924): 101–14.

La Rocca, E., "Juno Sospita," in *Lexicon Iconigraphicum Mythologiae Classicae*, vol. 5.1, 1981–1999, 814–56.

Laderman, C., and Roseman, M. *The Performance of Healing*, New York, 1996.

Latte, K., *Römische Religionsgeschichte*, München, 1960.

Lattimore, R., *Themes in Greek and Latin Epitaphs, Illinois Studies in Language and Literature* 28, no. 1–2, 1942.

Lauchert, F., *Das Weidwerk der Römer: eine archäologische Abhandlung nach den Quellen*, Rottweil, 1848.

Laurence, R., *The Roads of Roman Italy: Mobility and Cultural Change*, London, New York, 1999.

Leclant, J., "Diana Nemorensis, Isis et Bubastis," in *Studies in Pharaonic Religion and Society; in Honour of J. Gwyn Griffiths*, Ed. A. B. Lloyd, London, 1992.

Lee, Richard B., and Daly, Richard, eds. *The Cambridge Encyclopedia of Hunters and Gatherers*, Cambridge, 1999.

Lehmann, Y., *Varron théologien et philosophe romain*, Brussels, 1997.

Lenzi, G., "Il territorio nemorense dalla preistoria al medioevo," in Brandt et al., 2000, 155–78.

Leone, A., "Darius Rex a Nemi," in Brandt et al., 2000, 29–34.

Les bois sacrés, Actes du Colloque International organisé par le Centre Jean Bérard et l'Ecole Pratique des Hautes Etudes (Vᵉ section), Naples, 23–25 Novembre 1989, Naples, 1993.

Lesk, A. L., "The Anatomical Votive Terracotta Phenomenon: Healing Sanctuaries in the Etrusco-Latial-Campanian Region during the Fourth through First Centuries B.C.," M.A. thesis, University of Cincinnati, 1999.

Levi, M. A., "Appunti su Roma Arcaica," *Parola del Passato* 256 (1991): 122–34.

LiDonnici, L. R., *The Epidaurian Miracle Inscriptions: Text Translation and Commentary*, Atlanta, 1995.

Lilli, M., *Ariccia: carta archeologica*, Rome, 2002.

Linderski, J., "Libri Reconditi," *Harvard Studies in Classical Philology* 89 (1985): 207–34.

Linderski, J., "The Augural Law" *ANRW* II No. 16.3, 1986: 2146–2312.

Lindsay, W. M., *Sexti Pompei Festi: de Verborum Significatu Quae Supersunt cum Pauli Epitome*, Stuttgart, 1947.

Liou-Gille, B., "Les rois de Rome et la ligue latine," *Latomus* 56.4(1997): 765–83.

Liou-Gille, B., *Une lecture "religieuse" de Tite Live 1: Cultes, rites, croyances de la Rome archaïque*, Paris, 1998.

Lloyd, G. E. R., *Magic, Reason and Experience: Studies in the Origins and Development of Greek Science*, Cambridge, 1979.

Lloyd, G. E. R., *Methods and Problems in Greek Science*, Cambridge, 1991.

Lloyd, G. E. R., *In the Grip of Disease: Studies in the Greek Imagination*, Oxford, 2003.

Longrigg, J., *Greek Rational Medicine: Philosophy and Medicine from Alcmaeon to the Alexandrians*, London, 1993.

Lucidi, E., *Memorie Storiche dell' Antichissimo municipio ora terra dell'Ariccia*, 1797, reprinted with an introduction and appendix by Renato Lefevre, Rome, 1976.

Luckert, K., *The Navajo Hunter Tradition*, Tucson, 1981.

Lunais, S., *Recherches sur la lune*, Leiden, 1979.

Majno, G., *The Healing Hand*, Cambridge, MA, 1975.

Malaspina, E., "Diana Nemorensis vs. Diana Aventinensis: priorità cronologica e paradigmi storiografici," *Documenta albana*, Albano Laziale: Museo civico Albano, ser. 2, no. 16–17 (1994–5): 15–35.

Malaspina, E., "*Nemus* come toponimo dei Colli Albani e le *differentiae verborum* tardoantiche," in Brandt et al., 2000, 145–54.

Meiggs, R., *Roman Ostia*, Oxford, 1973.

Michels, A. K., *The Calendar of the Roman Republic*, Princeton, 1967.

Mikalson, J. D., *Athenian Popular Religion*, Chapel Hill, 1983.

Mikalson, J. D., *Religion in Hellenistic Athens*, Berkeley, 1998.

Mikocki, T., *Sub specie Deae*, Rome, 1995.

Moltesen, M., "*Ale and Antiquities*," in *I Dianas*, 1997, 172–6.

Moltesen, M., "The Marbles from Nemi in Exile: Sculpture in Copenhagen, Nottingham, and Philadelphia," in Brandt et al., 2000, 111–20.

Momigliano, A., "Sul *dies natalis* del santuario federale di Diana sull'Aventino," *Atti della accademia nazionale dei lincei, Roma, Classe di Scienze morali, storiche e filologiche, Rendiconti* 17 (1962): 387–92.

Montanri, E., *Identitá culturale e conflitti religiosi nella Roma repubblicana*, Rome, 1988.

Montanri, E., *Mito e storia nell'annalistica Romana delle origini*, Rome, 1990.

Morpurgo, L., "Nemus Aricinum," *Monumenti Antichi* XIII Reale Accademia (Nazionale) dei Lincei (1903): 297–368.

Morpurgo, L., "Nemi – *Teatro ed altri edifici romani in contrada 'La Valle'*," *Notizie degli Scavi di Antichità*, Reale Accademia Nazionale de Lincei (1931): 237–305.

Mozley, J. H., *Statius*, vol. 1, Cambridge, MA, 1928, repr. 1967.

Mynors, R. A. B., *P. Vergili Maronis Opera*, Oxford, 1969.

Nielsen, I., "For Pleasure and Leisure: The Baths and the Theatre," in *I Dianas*, 1997, 187–90.

North, J., "Religion in Republican Rome," in F. W. Walbank, A. E. Astin, M. W. Frederiksen, and R. M. Ogilvie, eds., *CAH* VII², part 2, 1989, repr. 2002, 573–624.

Nutton, V., "The Medical School at Velia," *Parola del Passato: Rivista di Studi Antichi*, 130–3 (1970): 211–25.

Nutton, V., *Ancient Medicine*, London, 2004.

O'Brien, D. O., *Empedocles' Cosmic Cycle: A Reconstruction from the Fragments and Secondary Sources*, Cambridge, 1969.

Ogden, D., *Greek and Roman Necromancy*, Princeton, 2001.

Ogilvie, R. M. "'Lustrum Condere'," *Journal of Roman Studies* (1961): 31–9.

Ogilvie, R. M., *A Commentary on Livy, Books 1–5*, Oxford, 1965.

Orth, F., "Jagd," *RE* 9 (1916): 558–604.

Owen, S. G., *P. Ovidi Nasonis, Tristium Libri quinque, Ibis, Ex Ponto Libri Quattuor, Halieutica Fragmenta*, Oxford, 1985.

Pairault, F. H., "Diana Nemorensis, déesse latin, déesse hellénisée," *Mélanges d'Archéologie et d'Histoire de l'École Française de Rome* 81 (1969): 425–71.

Pallottino, M., *A History of Earliest Italy*, Trs. M. Ryle and K. Soper, Ann Arbor, 1991.

Palmer, R. E. A., *Roman Religion and Roman Empire: Five Essays*, University of Pennsylvania Press, Philadelphia, 1974.

Parke, H. W., *Festivals of the Athenians*, London, 1977.

Pascal, C. B., "Rex Nemorensis," *Numen* 23 (1976): 23–39.

Pasqualini, A., "L'incesto di Silano e il bosco di Diana (Tac. Ann 12.8.2)," *Analecta Romana Instituti Danici* 27 (2001) 141–9.

Pease, A. S., Cicero, *De Natura Deorum* Cambridge, MA, 1958.

Peiffer, R., *Callimachus: Works*, 2 vols., Oxford, 1949 and 1953.

Peter, H., *Historicorum Romanorum Reliquiae*, vol. 1, Leipzig, 1914.

Phillips, E. D., *Greek Medicine*, London, 1973.

Podemann Sørensen, J., "Diana and Virbius: An Essay on the Mythology of Nemi," in Brandt et al., 2000, 25–8.

Poulsen, F., *Catalogue of Ancient Sculpture in the Ny Carlsberg Glyptotek*, Copenhagen, 1951.

Préaux, J.-G., "Virgile et le rameau d'or," in *Hommages à Georges Dumézil*, Collection Latomus 45, Brussels, 1960, 151–67.

The Protohistory of the Latin Peoples, Museo Nazionale Romano, Terme di Diocleziano, Rome, 2000.

Purcell, N., "Becoming Historical: The Roman Case," in Braund and Gill, 12–40.

Raaflaub, K. A., ed., *Social Struggles in Archaic Rome: New Perspectives on the Conflict of the Orders*, Berkeley, 1986.

Raaflaub, K. A., "Stages in the Conflict of the Orders," in Raaflaub, 198–243.

Rabinowitz, J., "Underneath the Moon: Hekate and Luna," *Latomus* 56.3 (1997): 534–43.

Radke, G., *Zur Entwicklung der Gottessvorstellung und der Gottesverehrung in Rom*, Darmstadt, 1987.

Rathje, A., "A Banquet Service from the Latin City of Ficana," *Analecta Romana* 12 (1983): 7–29.

Rawson, E., *Intellectual Life in the Late Roman Republic*, Baltimore, 1985.

Richardson, L., Jr., *A New Topographical Dictionary of Ancient Rome*, Baltimore, 1992.

Riddle, J. M., "Folk Tradition and Folk Medicine: Recognition of Drugs in Classical Antiquity," in Scarborough, *Folklore and Folk Medicines*, 33–61.

Riis, P. J., "The Cult Image of Diana Nemorensis," *Acta Archaeologica* 37 (1966): 67–75.

Rosa, P., "Relazione dei ruderi esistenti in prossimità del Lago di Nemi come i più corrispondenti al tempio di Diana Nemorense," *Monumenti ed Annali pubblici dall' Instituto di Corrispondenza Archeologica*, 1856, 5–8.

Rose, H. J., *Ancient Roman Religion*, London, 1948.

Rüpke, J., *Kalender und Öffentlichkeit: Die Geschichte der Repräsentation und religiösen Qualifikation von Zeit in Rom*, Berlin, 1995.

Rüpke, J., *Die Religion der Römer: eine Einführung*, München, 2001.

Savage, S., "Remotum a Notitia Vulgari," *Transactions of the American Philological Association* 74 (1945): 157–65.

Scarborough, J., ed., *Folklore and Folk Medicines*, Madison, 1987.

Scarborough, J., "Adaptation of Folk Medicines in the Formal Materia Medica of Classical Antiquity," in *Folklore and Folk Medicines*, 21–32.

Scarborough, J., "The Pharmacology of Sacred Plants, Herbs and Roots," in Faraone and Obbink, 138–74.

Scheid, J., "Lex horrea Sempronia du nemus Aricinum," *Académie des Inscriptions: Comptes rendus* (1980): 287–92.

Scheid, J., "Diana," in *Oxford Classical Dictionary*, 3rd ed., Oxford, 1996.

Scheid, J., "Diana," in *Der Neue Pauly*, vol. 3, col. 522–5, Stuttgart, 1997.

Scheid, J., *La Religion des romains*, Paris, 1998.

Schieffelin, E., "On Failure and Performance: Throwing the Medium out of the Séance," in Laderman and Roseman, 59–90.

Schilling, R., Ovide, *Les Fastes*, vols. 1–2, Paris, 1993.

Schnapp, A., "Eros the Hunter," in *City of Images*, Princeton, 1989, 71–88.

Scullard, H. H., *Festivals and Ceremonies of the Roman Republic*, Ithaca, 1981.

Shackleton Bailey, D. R., ed. *Cicero's Letters to Atticus*, vols. 1–6, Cambridge, 1965–7.

Shackleton Bailey, D. R., *M. Annaei Lucani: De Bello Civili, Libri X*, Stuttgart, 1997.

Simon, E., "Ianus" in *Lexicon Iconigraphicum Mythologiae Classicae* 5 (1990): 618–23.

Simon, E., and Bauchhenss, G., "Diana" in *Lexicon Iconigraphicum Mythologiae Classicae* 1 (1984): 792–855.

Smith, C. J., *Early Rome and Latium: Economy and Society c. 1000 to 500 B.C.*, Oxford, 1996.

Smith, C. J., "Servius Tullius, Cleisthenes and the Emergence of the Polis in Central Italy," in *The Development of the Polis in Archaic Greece*, Eds. L. G. Mitchell and P. J. Rhodes, London, 1997, 208–16.

Smith, J. Z., "When the Bough Breaks," in *Map Is Not Territory*, Leiden, 1978, 208–39.

Sokolowski, F., "On the Episode of Onchestus in the Homeric Hymn to Apollo," *Transactions and Proceedings of the American Philological Association* 91 (1960): 376–80.

Sontag, S., *Illness as Metaphor*, New York, 1978.

Sourvinou-Inwood, C., *Studies in Girls' Transitions: Aspects of the Arkteia and Age Representation in Attic Iconography*, Athens, 1988.

Spineto, N., "The King of the Wood oggi: una rilettura di James George Frazer alla luce dell'attuale problematica storico-religiosa," in Brandt et al., 2000, 17–24.

Stamper, J. W., *The Architecture of Roman Temples: The Republic to the Middle Empire*, Cambridge, 2005.

Steinby, E. M., ed., *Lexicon Topographicum Urbis Romae*, 5 vols., 1993–2000.

Stewart, R., *Public Office in Early Rome: Ritual Procedure and Political Practice*, Ann Arbor, 1998.

Tatton-Brown, V., "Glass," in Blagg 1983, 68–9.

Tavenner, E., "The Roman Farmer and the Moon," *Transactions and Proceedings of the American Philological Association* 49 (1918): 67–82.

Thilo, G., Hagen, H., *Servii Grammatici Qui Feruntur In Vergilii Carmina Commentarii*, vols. 1–3, Leipzig, 1881, repr. 1986.

Thomas, R., *Literacy and Orality in Ancient Greece*, Cambridge, 1992.

Thomsen, R., *King Servius Tullius: A Historical Synthesis*, Copenhagen, 1980.

Treggiari, S., *Roman Freedmen during the Late Republic*, Oxford, 1969.

Turcan, R., *The Gods of Ancient Rome: Religion in Everyday Life from Archaic to Imperial Times*, Trs. Antonia Nevill, New York, 2001.

van Proosdij, B. A., *P. Ovidii Nasonis, Metmorphoseon Libri I–XV*, Leiden, 1982.

Venditelli, L., "Diana Aventina, Aedes," in *Lexicon Topographicum Urbis Romae*, vol. 1, Ed. E. M. Steinby, Rome, 1992, 11–13.

Verdière, R., *Gratti Cynegeticon Libri Quae Supersunt*, vols. 1 and 2, Wettern (Belgique), 1968.

Versnel, H. S., *Inconsistencies in Roman Religion I, Ter Unus: Isis, Dionysios, Hermes, Three Studies in Henotheism*, Leiden, 1990.

Versnel, H. S., *Inconsistencies in Greek and Roman Religion II: Transition and Reversal in Myth and Ritual*, Leiden, 1993.

Vidal-Naquet, P., *The Black Hunter: Forms of Thought and Forms of Society in the Greek World*, Trs. A. Szegedy-Maszak, Baltimore, 1986.

von Fritz, K., *Pythagorean Politics in Southern Italy: An Analysis of the Sources*, New York, 1977.

von Staden, H., *Herophilus: The Art of Medicine in Early Alexandria*, Cambridge, 1989.

von Ungern-Sternberg, J., "The Formation of the "Annalistic Tradition," in Raaflaub, 77–104.

Warde Fowler, W., *The Roman Festivals of the Period of the Republic, London*, 1899.

Warmington, E. H., *Remains of Old Latin*, 4 vols., Cambridge, MA, 1979.

Watson, A., *Roman Slave Law*, Baltimore, 1987.

Webster, J., "Creolizing the Roman Provinces," *American Journal of Archaeology* 105.2 (2001): 209–26.

Webster, J., "Art as Resistance and Negotiation," in *Roman Imperialism and Provincial Art*, S. Scott and J. Webster, eds., Cambridge, 2003, 24–51.

Weise, F. O., *Die Griechischen Wörter im Latein*, Leipzig, 1882, rpr. Leipzig, 1964.

West, D. A., "The Bough and the Gate," *17th Jackson Knight Memorial Lecture*, Exeter 1987, repr. in *Oxford Readings in Vergil's* Aeneid, Oxford, 1990, 224–38.

Wiedemann, T., *Emperors and Gladiators*, London and New York, 1992.

Williams, G., *Tradition and Originality in Roman Poetry*, Oxford, 1968.

Wilson Jones, M., *Principles of Roman Architecture*, New Haven, 2000.

Wiseman, T. P., "The Mother of Livia Augusta," *Historia* 14 (1965): 333–4.

Wiseman, T. P., *Clio's Cosmetics: Three Studies in Greco-Roman Literature*, Leicester, 1979.

Wiseman, T. P., *Historiography and Imagination: Eight Essays on Roman Culture*, Exeter, 1994.

Wissowa, G., "Diana," *RE*, vol. 5., 1905, 325–42.

Wissowa, G., *Religion und Kultus der Römer*, München, 1912, repr. 1971.

Withington, E. T., "History of Greek Therapeutics and Malaria Theory," an appendix to *Malaria and Greek History*, by W. H. S Jones, Manchester, 1909, 137–56.

Witt, R. E., *Isis in the Greco-Roman World*, Ithaca, 1971.

Wright, M. R., *Empedocles: The Extant Fragments*, New Haven, 1981.

Zahle, J., "Floating Palaces: The Ships and the Emissary," in *I Dianas*, 1997, 169–70.

Zanker, P., *The Power of Images in the Age of Augustus*, Ann Arbor, 1988.

Zevi, F., "I santuari 'federale' del Lazio," *Eutopia* 4.2 (1995): 123–42.

INDEX LOCORUM

CICERO (*Cont.*)
Tusc. (1.44), 43n20
in Verr. (2.40), 250n32
CINCIUS
ap. Festus (s.v. praetor, 276 L), 94
COLUMELLA
(2.10.12), 134

DIONYSIUS OF HALICARNASSUS
AR: (1.16), 52n33;
(1.66.2), 190n10;
(1.86), 197n21;
(2.33), 189;
(2.50.3), 73, 101n32;
(2.52.3–4), 198;
(2.56.4), 198;
(2.56.5), 198;
(2.60.3), 197n21;
(2.60.5), 222n25;
(2.61–2), 224;
(2.67), 91;
(2.76.5–6), 198;
(3.31.4), 92n11;
(3.34.3), 89;
(3.35.1), 198;
(3.35.2–3), 198;
(3.43), 190n10;
(3.45.2), 198;
(3.46.2), 191;
(3.46.4–5), 192n15;
(3.46–49), 192;
(3.47), 191;
(3.47.2–3), 197n21;
(3.50.1–3), 192;
(3.50.3), 192;
(3.73), 195;
(4.1–2), 196;
(4.1–4), 182, 195;
(4.2.1–2), 197;
(4.4), 195;
(4.25.3–4), 13;
(4.25.3–6), 98n26;
(4.25.3–4.26.5), 98;
(4.26), 89n6;
(4.26.3–4), 100;
(4.26.4), 98n25;
(4.26.4–5), 100n30;
(4.26.5), 13;
(4.27.7), 99n27;

(4.28–39), 229–30;
(4.31.2), 197;
(4.38.3–6), 198;
(4.38.6), 197n23;
(4.38–9), 104;
(4.39.1), 198;
(4.39.4–5), 198;
(4.39.5), 104;
(4.45), 103;
(4.45.3), 89;
(4.45.3–46.1), 91;
(4.45–8), 90, 92;
(4.47.2), 91;
(4.48.1), 92n10;
(4.48.2), 91;
(4.53–4), 193;
(4.53–8), 193;
(4.55.1–2), 193;
(4.55.3), 193n16;
(4.55.4), 193;
(4.56–8), 194;
(4.59–61), 101n34, 102n34, 103n37;
(5.36), 14, 16n26, 77;
(5.36 and 7.6), 14, 16n26
(6.95), 13;
(7.4–8), 181;
(7.6), 14, 16n26, 181;
(12.9.1), 102n35;
DIODORUS SICULUS
(5.74.6), 240n11;
(11.89), 250n33

EMPEDOCLES
KRS², fragments: (345), 262;
(346–82), 262;
(350), 277–8;
(355.7–8), 262;
(356), 263–4;
(399), 259;
(401), 277n28;
(402), 273n21;
(405–7), 273n21;
(410), 274n23
ENNIUS
Ann.: (119 (Scutsch 113)), 224n28, 226;
(240 Skutsch), (fr. 40 Courtney),
131
Tragedies, Andromeda (fr. 127
Warmington), 128, 130n20

(1.39.1–3), 193;
(1.39.5), 193n17;
(1.39.6–10), 194;
(1.40), 198;
(1.40.1), 198;
(1.40.5–7), 195;
(1.41), 198;
(1.45), 13, 41, 89n6, 98;
(1.45.1–3), 99;
(1.45.2), 98n25;
(1.46.3), 197n21;
(1.45.3–7), 100;
(1.46.5–9), 197n22;
(1.46–8), 229–30;
(1.47.8–10), 197;
(1.48), 104;
(1.48.3–5), 198;
(1.48.4), 197n23;
(1.48.5), 198;
(1.48.6), 104;
(1.48.7), 198;
(1.50), 89, 103;
(1.50.2), 91;
(1.50–1), 90;
(1.51.2), 91;
(1.51.7–9), 90n8, 91;
(1.53.4–5), 193;
(1.53.5), 193;
(1.53–4), 193;
(1.54.3), 193;
(1.55.1), 101n33;
(1.55.6), 101;
(1.67.1–2), 197n21;
(2.8.6–8), 102n36;
(2.14.5–6), 77;
(2.14.5–7), 14, 16n26;
(2.18.3), 92n11;
(2.33.9), 13;
(4.1.12), 195;
(5.13), 77;
(5.13.4–6), 102n35;
(7.3.8), 102n36;
(22.3–6), 43;
(22.10, 33.44.1, 34.44), 52n33;
(27.4.12), 89n5;
(29.11), 43;
(30.26.11; 27.9), 21
LUCAN
(1.136–43), 163;

(1.137–8), 163;
(1.203, 225), 157;
(1.446), 31;
(3.86), 31;
(3.305), 157;
(3.312–20), 157–8;
(3.358–74), 159;
(3.399), 161;
(3.404–5), 161;
(3.407–8), 161;
(3.426–31), 161;
(3.433–4), 161;
(3.434), 161, 163;
(3.436–7), 161;
(5.403), 107n40;
(6.74), 204n29;
(6.619–23), 134;
(6.822–4), 220n21;
(7.772–80), 206;
(7.776), 31
LUCILIUS
(143–5 Warmington), 72;
(1064 Warmington), 225n30
LUCRETIUS
(6.1090–286), 275

MACROBIUS
Sat.: (1.7), 47;
(1.8.6–10), 47;
(1.15.14), 74;
(1.18.16), 74n7;
(7.3), 37–8
MARTIAL
Epig.: (2.19), 3;
(7.28.1), 89n5;
(8.46.1–3), 218;
(10.35.12–14), 224n28;
(10.70.7), 121n7, 122;
(12.32.10), 66
Spect. (12.1, 13.5–7), 135n29

NAEVIUS
(fr. 64.2), 225n30

OVID
AA: (1.259), 26, 31;
(1.259–60), 28–9, 123;
(1.259–62), 154n13, 274–5;
(1.260), 150, 154;

SERVIUS
ad Aen.: (1.219), 122n9;
(1.653), 43n20;
(2.116), 7, 40, 41, 45n23, 67–8, 78, 203,
    204, 236, 260;
(4.511), 121n7;
(4.620), 218n17;
(6.118), 133;
(6.136), 11, 45–6, 78, 130, 139, 149,
    150n5, 150n7, 153, 155n14, 159, 162,
    170, 203, 205n31;
(6.177), 171–2;
(6.221), 170n42;
(6.282), 174n51, 180–1;
(7.151), 75;
(7.188), 41, 43, 207;
(7.515), 6n11;
(7.727), 202;
(7.761), 143, 210, 212, 215, 221;
(7.761–77), 218;
(7.762), 150, 211;
(7.763), 219–20;
(7.775), 221;
(7.776), 220, 221;
(7.778), 209, 211n2;
(11.226), 40
ad Ecl.: (3.26), 128, 133;
(3.59), 225n30;
(4.10), 40
in Georg. (1.5), 133
SERVIUS AUCTUS
ad Aen.: (1.310), 25;
(7.776), 221
ad Ecl. (10.18), 214n7
SILIUS ITALICUS
Pun. (4.366–95), 220n20
SIMPLICIUS
in Phys. (159.27), 263–4
SOPHOCLES
(F. 370), 165n33
STATIUS
Silv.: (3.1.52–6), 60–1;
(3.1.52–60), 106, 154n13, 222n23;
(3.1.60), 62;
(3.1.61–75), 61n14;
(3.1.68), 61n14;
(3.1.80–5), 62n17;
(3.1.157), 218;
(3.1.159–60), 217n16;

(5.3.60), 133
Theb. (10.365–6), 130n20
STRABO
(4.1.4), 77, 78n17;
(4.1.5), 78n17;
(5.3.12), 3, 31, 40, 78, 147, 150, 153–4,
    161, 224n28;
(6.1.5), 249n30;
(6.30), 250;
(14.2.19), 239, 239n7
SUETONIUS
Cal.: (14, 19), 58n8;
(24), 59n10;
(35), 154n13;
(35.3), 58, 68n25, 154;
(36.1), 59n10
Div. Aug.: (2.3), 37n6;
(4), 20n36, 21;
(4.1), 35n3;
(4.2), 21n37, 36–7, 268–9;
(7.1), 37n6;
(29.5), 44n21
Div. Jul.: (46), 27n49;
(59.2), 29
Nero (21.3), 205n33
SUIDAS
(s.v. Δομνῖνος), 240n11

TACITUS
Ann.: (12.8), 229;
(12.8.2), 59
Hist. (3.72), 101n33, 102n36
TERENCE
Adelphoe (581–4), 131n21
THUCYDIDES
(2.47–52), 275;
(7.50.3–4), 132
TIBULLUS
(3.9.19–22), 122n9, 124

VALERIUS ANTIAS
(fr. 12 (Peter)), 197n21
VALERIUS FLACCUS
Arg. (5.235–44), 133
(305), 154n13
VARRO
ARD: (2a Cardauns), 292;
(276 Cardauns), 128, 160n21;
(279 Cardauns), 160n21

INDEX

NOTE: References to 'sanctuary' are generally to that of Diana at Aricia. Footnotes receive specific reference only when their content would not be found through a reference to the main text.